LEEDS UNITED,
When The Stars Almost Aligned

**Following Leeds United through the
2016/2017 season**

By the same author:

All books available from Amazon.co.uk

LEEDS UNITED,
IN PURSUIT OF
THE PREMIERSHIP
The 2010/2011 season

LEEDS UNITED,
LIGHT AT THE END OF
THE TUNNEL
The 2011/2012 season

LEEDS UNITED,
Déjà vu
The 2012/2013 season

LEEDS UNITED,
FIASCO
The 2013/2014 season

LEEDS UNITED,
The Kids Are Alright!
The 2014/2015 season

LEEDS UNITED,
MISSION: IMPOSSIBLE
The 2015/2016 season

Click link to view books on Amazon: **www.amazon.co.uk**

LEEDS UNITED,
When The Stars Almost Aligned

Following Leeds United through the 2016/2017 season.

The author recounts his story of following Leeds United home and away.

David Watkins

ACKNOWLEDGEMENTS

My original intention was to write just one book, based on the belief I had back in 2010/2011 that it would only take Leeds one more season to return to the Premier League. Consequently, I only expected to put my proof readers, friends and family through this chore once! I'm thus indebted to all who've played a part in bringing this seventh tome to life and to all those who allowed me to selfishly devote myself to the task. In particular, I'm again indebted to my good friend Brian for his dedication to duty in proof reading yet another book about a team he doesn't even follow and similarly to my wife Karen for methodically going through it with a fine-tooth comb despite having only a passing interest in the game.

I also thank Russell Davies for coming up with the front cover picture idea and Carmel Garland, aka @SwissWhites, for permission to use her fabulous picture of Pontus performing his magic with the ball at the Barnsley home game (see page 126).
Finally, to all the fans that know me and whom I may or may not recognise on a match day (I have an appalling memory for faces), thanks for your company and for providing many of the stories without which this and the previous books would be very dull reading indeed. Many of you will be mentioned by name or alias in the following pages.

There is a special bond pulling all Leeds United fans together that I don't believe exists between the fans of other teams and I look forward to sharing the future of our great club with you all. Keep the faith and keep MOT!

David Watkins

When The Stars Almost Aligned

At Loftus Road in August when the weather was fine
I felt sure this was the season the stars would align.
Then early defeats and despite winning a shoot-out
Made it seem far more likely that we'd end up wi nowt.

But then four wins on the bounce got Monk out of the mire
And I was dreaming again of what might just transpire.
Leeds were beaten at Bristol and at Derby away
But at Elland Road our youngsters would mostly hold sway.

The next five games unbeaten and more goals for Chris Wood
Another League Cup shoot-out saw Vieira come good.
He got a goal down at Norwich, a very last gasp
And a place in the play-offs was now well within grasp.

We did lose at Anfield but with no rub of the green
It was still one of the best games that we've ever seen.
Then another solid run saw six wins and a draw
When just three goals were conceded and fourteen we'd score.

A home win against Derby brought lots of emotion
And suddenly our thoughts turned again to promotion.
The home game with Notts Forest saw our finest goal yet
As Souley Doukara's shot nearly broke through the net.

A defeat in the F A Cup our progress did halt
But was little surprise with a team not worth its salt.
The Sunday trip down to Sutton brought nothing but pain
For about 700 Leeds fans at Gander Green Lane.

Losses at the John Smith's and home to Cardiff weren't fun
But we put those behind us with another good run.
Hard fought wins over Bristol and Wednesday and the Blues,
Then winning v Brighton meant it was now ours to lose.

But we started to struggle with the pressure it seems
And our team of bright young starlets just ran out of steam.
Monk told us his novices weren't quite ready to shine
In this "nearly" season **When The Stars Almost Aligned**.

Cellino maintains habit and brings in Monk

T he whole month of May was spent playing the game; the guessing game. No, not whether the UK would vote 'in' or 'out' in the forthcoming EU referendum but rather, *"Who'll be head coach at Leeds United?"* Names flashed up on the bookies' leader boards and then disappeared again as rumours did the rounds and then died away as the managerial merry-go-round went into full swing. Former Leeds star John Sheridan was an early 1/6 favourite, with the Daily Mirror writing that Cellino was in discussions with him. But before the end of the month Sheridan was hired by Notts County.[1] Foreigners Ivan Jurić and Beppe Lachini were then said to be under consideration but they joined Genoa and Udinese respectively. Cellino was then rumoured to have offered the job to Karl Robinson, the young manager of MK Dons and then Darrell Clarke, another young gun who was masterminding the rise and rise of Bristol Rovers. Both were offered better deals to stay where they were... and they did. Folk were beginning to think Steve Evans might yet get another contract out of our maverick Italian owner as he appeared to be the only bloke willing to work in the manic environment of Leeds United and, what's more, he loved it.

---

[1] http://www.hitc.com/en-gb/2016/05/27/leeds-united-managerial-candidate-john-sheridan-takes-notts-coun/

Evans rarely spoke publicly after the season ended but when he did it was always to express the hope that he'd be given the chance to continue in post; he was convinced he was the man for the job and told the media he could deliver a top six finish if only Cellino would support him with a few new players and a contract. Evans had played himself into the hearts of many Leeds fans by this time, as the manner in which Cellino was ignoring the Scotsman was grating with them just as it had in previous close seasons when first Brian McDermott and then Neil Redfearn were similarly left in limbo until, ultimately, both were jettisoned. McDermott briefly appeared on those bookies' leader boards as a potential returnee when Reading sacked him late in May, especially since Cellino had now proclaimed he was, *"OK"*, with British coaches after all. Equally, that also suggested that maybe Evans would keep his job and be given the chance he so desperately wanted.

We'd have to wait until 2nd June to see our new coach unveiled; Garry Monk, former boss of Swansea City. By this time we'd already learned it wasn't going to be Evans; the club announced two days earlier: *"Leeds United can confirm that the Club has parted company with head coach Steve Evans"*

Cellino was reported on the official website (OS) saying:

"I would like to thank Steve Evans for his efforts as the head coach of Leeds United. Steve completed the job he was brought in to carry out – to keep the team in the Championship - and his hard work here has been greatly appreciated. I wish him and Paul Raynor the very best for the future. We have, however, decided that a different approach is required in order to achieve our targets for the new season. The Club is now looking to appoint a new head coach to build on the good work of Steve and Paul and deliver the special season which our supporters deserve".[1]

---

[1]

http://www.leedsunited.com/news/article/v5xndospy3p51p6dj2huhq0 wo/title/club-statement-steve-evans

Garry Monk came out with all the usual first day clichés at his unveiling press conference (great club, fine history, great fans etc. etc.) hosted by Eddie Gray and another new face at Leeds; recently appointed main board Director, Niccolo Pio Barattieri di San Pietro… that is only one bloke by the way. Barattieri, an Italian businessman, was chief executive of Northacre, a luxury property developer owned by Abu Dhabi Financial Group (ADFG), the largest stakeholder in former Leeds owner, and still minority shareholder, GFH. His only involvement in football to date was that he acted as an adviser to Sunderland AFC between 2013 and 2014, or so his LinkedIn profile told me. Whether the appointment of Barattieri was a sign of any future developments at the club, no one seemed to know but many speculated, or perhaps hoped, it might be a sign that Cellino was selling up. Oh, and Barattieri's other claim to fame was that at 44 years of age he was currently dating 25 year-old 'Kitty' Spencer, niece of the late Lady Di. Any bloke who can pull that off is a cool dude in my book and I just spent several minutes scouring the internet and enjoying pictures of the delectable Kitty.

There was still plenty of pressure on Cellino despite him being cleared in Italy of the charges that led to his most recent Football League (FL) ban which had now been rescinded. Another trial had recently begun in Italy concerning alleged corruption over the renovation of the IS Arenas stadium, home of Cellino's previous club, Cagliari.[1] There was media speculation that the charges facing Cellino in this case were so serious that he could well face a jail term if found guilty never mind another FL ban that would surely then be inevitable. That trial would most likely take years to come to a conclusion but the English FA was investigating another potential time bomb for Cellino that could result in much earlier damage.

It was announced that Leeds United had been charged with breaching FA agent regulations during the transfer of Ross McCormack to Fulham back in 2014 and once again Cellino

---

[1]   http://the72.co.uk/54479/is-arenas-rial-involving-leeds-united-cellino-owner-begins/

was centrally implicated. It was alleged that an unauthorised payment of £185,000 was made to McCormack's adviser, Barry Hughes, a Scottish boxing agent, with the full knowledge of the official agent Derek Day and Massimo Cellino. If proven, Leeds probably faced a hefty fine but, for his involvement, Cellino could once again find himself banned.

A long time sponsor of the Club, Crosswater Holdings, had decided it had seen enough of all the negative publicity surrounding Cellino and announced they were pulling out of their sponsorship deal. Their name appeared last season on the side of the players' tunnel at Elland Road (ER) although maybe they were pulling out as it read *"Cost"* when folded back! It reminded me of that old joke about the Welshman who appeared to have Ludo tattooed on his todger but when he got excited it could be seen to be Llandudno! Crosswater chairman, David Hance, was reported in the Yorkshire Evening Post (YEP) as saying he was embarrassed to be associated with the club under the Cellino regime. In an email Hance sent to Cellino and copied to the YEP he wrote:

"After 10 years supporting the club as a true fan, and longest-serving sponsor, I have had enough of how you run our famous club.

"For my brand to be associated with Leeds United is now an embarrassment to both me and my customers."[1]

A few weeks later though and the plumbing magnate had done a complete U-bend, I mean U-turn, having apparently had conversations with both Commercial Director Paul Bell and Massimo Cellino that made the bathrooms man pleased that:

"...the Club is now operating on a solid platform and that the Club is once again looking forward... I am therefore delighted to increase my firm's long-standing support and sponsorship of the Club into next season with sponsorship of the West

---

[1]   http://www.yorkshireeveningpost.co.uk/sport/football/leeds-united/leeds-united-long-time-whites-sponsor-withdraws-support-saying-cellino-is-an-embarrassment-1-7941135

Stand."[1] It was one of those weird overnight changes of tack we often see at Leeds that just leaves you wondering what the hell the real story was. It was such an about turn that I did wonder if there was something going on behind the scenes after all; maybe Cellino *was* selling up.

One businessman whose support was unwavering was lifelong Leeds fan, Steve Parkin, who'd increased the sponsorship activity of his Clipper Logistics outfit to become our secondary shirt sponsor. A new primary shirt sponsor, online casino outfit 32Red, had also been secured. Their logo would appear on the home shirts in blue to save any criticism of having the dreaded red on our shirts, though to some fans, the mere sight of the word 'red' was bad enough. Clipper had already agreed a deal whereby their name appeared all over the East Stand and that advertising and the Crosswater signwriting on the West Stand could now be seen clearly from the M621. Parkin's increased involvement was another intriguing development that made some fans wonder if Cellino was paving the way for an exit. Cellino himself had said he *was* now ready to sell, not that many believed him. In an interview with the Times, again also noted in the YEP, he reportedly said: *"I've had enough. It's better to walk out"[2]* although he'd said this before of course, several times and he was still there.

So, quite how Cellino had persuaded a nice young man like Garry Monk to step inside the hornets' nest of Leeds United, goodness only knows. He'd been given a 12-month rolling contract but most fans expected him to last maybe 'til October...

I'd been desperately hoping Steve Evans would be retained as I felt he was one of very few men hard-faced enough to work

---

1

http://www.leedsunited.com/news/article/v00uzj5473xn1n45fzx0ffeb9/title/crosswater-enter-west-stand-sponsorship

2   http://www.yorkshireeveningpost.co.uk/sport/football/leeds-united/leeds-united-i-m-ready-to-sell-the-club-cellino-claims-again-1-7909466

successfully under Cellino; someone who could ignore the Italian's antics and just get on with the job. But it was not to be and, although I was not initially convinced Monk was mentally tough enough to cope with Cellino, I was willing to give him his chance. The one thing I was aware of was that Monk had been a centre-back in his playing career with Swansea and a good one at that; I'd watched him and his defensive partner Alan Tate play us in the 2-1 win we had over the Swans at ER as recently as 2010. Tate also turned out for Leeds a few times on loan in 2012/13 of course when initially he also looked a great player. Then, as all our loanees tend to do, he deteriorated rapidly and became just one more in a long line of poor centre-backs we've had the misfortune to endure. If there was one skill Leeds needed to improve, it was our ability in the centre of defence; we'd been dire in there for years, frequently conceding sloppy, needless goals. Perhaps Monk could change that particular habit.

The days passed and there seemed to be nothing happening at the Club; not even any announcements as to who we'd be playing in pre-season. Even my 'other' team, non-league Worcester City had all their pre-season fixtures sorted well before we heard anything from Leeds. Recently relegated Aston Villa were the main visitors for the City.[1]

From mid-June, football fans were kept ticking over with Euro 2016 'en France' where the early games were more characterised by hooligan activity than on-field fireworks. A frequently asked question was how Russian and Croatian fans managed to smuggle flare guns into the stadiums despite the increased security following the terrorist attacks in Paris. *"Sorry Lads, I'll have to unscrew that Coke bottle top and confiscate it, don't want you throwing a full bottle of Coke on the pitch and injuring someone. What else you got in there? A flare gun; Oh that's OK, be a bit of a laugh that will; in you go lads, enjoy the game…"*

---

[1] *Villa would beat City 5 -1 but it will be remembered as the game in which Villa hero Stiliyan Petrov made his comeback. 'Stan' is fighting to restart his career after a long battle with Leukaemia.*

Ins and Outs

As May morphed into June the situation at Leeds was spookily similar to the previous two seasons; the names had changed but the song remained the same. Cellino refused to speak with his outgoing coach, even to the extent of announcing the retained list without apparent input from the manager. A fresh faced chap was unveiled in front of the LUTV cameras by a new Director (in previous seasons Cellino introduced Hockaday and then Adam Pearson was the new man in the boardroom who accompanied Uwe Rösler) and once again we were all asking why such a nice bloke would take on the poisoned chalice of Leeds United. As with Rösler, Monk was promising, *"I've not come here to do the average or mediocre"*; he may as well have said he was bringing us heavy metal football.

That retained list contained few surprises; eight out-of-contract players were offered new deals, including five young pros and three scholars. Those allowed to leave were: Goalkeeper Eric Grimes, Lewis Walters, Ross Killock, Jake Skelton, Robbie McDaid and Tom Lyman. No new contract was offered to Mirco Antenucci and predictably Scott Wootton was allowed to seek alternative employment and was by now presumably hod-carrying on a building site in Bury. Tom Adeyemi, Liam

Bridcutt and Muzzy Carayol all returned to their parent clubs following the end of their loan deals.

The surprise departures were probably Lewis Walters and Robbie McDaid, both of whom were seen as rising stars not that long ago. For me, if we could ensure the rest remained at the club through the summer transfer window, then I reckoned we needed four or five quality additions in key positions through the centre of the team to turn us into a promotion challenging outfit. We had a good young side but last season highlighted again that we had a soft centre and a crap defence.

The early days of June were marked with a couple of deaths of iconic heroes of my youth. Dave Swarbrick, an ever present in my musical taste since school days, passed away at the age of 75. 'Swarb', a virtuosic fiddle player, was the central figure in the folk-rock band, Fairport Convention, whose albums form a sizeable chunk of my music collection. The man could make a fiddle talk, sing even. Then, later the same day, news broke that Muhammad Ali had passed away at the age of 74. The crackling late night radio commentaries of his many title fights are another vivid memory I carry from my teenage years. George Foreman, who lost his world title to Ali in the famous 'Rumble in the Jungle' in Kinshasa in 1974 called him simply, *"one of the greatest human beings"* he had ever met...[1]

Back on planet Leeds, the inevitable court cases rumbled on. Lucy Ward had already won her case for unfair dismissal and sex discrimination against the club but the embarrassment for Leeds continued with more revelations at the tribunal remedy hearing. Massimo Cellino initially arrived to give evidence in person but then turned on his heels when he saw the massed ranks of the press corps in attendance and took no part in the proceedings. It was reported that Cellino, incredibly, had offered Ward her old job back but unsurprisingly Ward refused it, stating: *"It's a toxic environment in there now; I don't think anyone could seriously expect me to go back."*[2] I had to admit, it did seem a bit fanciful. When the costs were

---

[1] http://www.bbc.co.uk/news/world-us-canada-16011175
[2] http://www.bbc.co.uk/news/uk-england-leeds-36499988

adjudicated early in July, it was another big hit to the Leeds United coffers; damages of over £130,000 and both parties' costs to pay. Former assistant to Brian McDermott, Nigel Gibbs also won his case for constructive dismissal and that was rumoured to be another £330,000 down the crapper.

It seemed very much like Groundhog Day, the specific details of the court cases had changed and the names were different but there was an uncanny similarity to the events of last summer. This year it was Garry Monk; last year it was Uwe Rösler putting together his backroom staff. Leeds announced, after the usual weeks of media speculation, that Pep Clotet and Darryl Flahavan would assist him. Clotet was named as Monk's assistant but was no novice (sorry, couldn't resist that one!); the two worked together at Swansea. Flahavan was appointed goalkeeping coach. Flahavan had a brief loan spell at Leeds back in 2009 but never played and coincidentally I'd seen him keep goal for Crawley Town as recently as last season in a 4 – 2 defeat at Barnet in one of my '92' games. James Beattie would later join the coaching set-up, having also been with Monk and Clotet at Swansea. That trio could hardly be said to have been successful by the way. While they were together, from June to December 2015, the Swans won just 4 of their 17 games and when they were all given the chop, the Welsh side were only two points above the relegation zone. We could only hope they'd do better for us.

The previous season began with Cellino strengthening his management team, bringing in the likes of Adam Pearson and this summer he was doing the same. In came yet another new CEO, Ben Mansford who quit his role at newly promoted Yorkshire rivals Barnsley to supposedly help Cellino *"grow the club"*. Was this another sign Cellino was selling up then...? Away from Leeds, it was all about Europe. The Euro 2016 Championship was well underway with all four British Isles teams heading into the knockout rounds. In the group stages, England sneaked a last minute 2 - 1 win against Wales and were then handed a seemingly easy knockout game against the smallest nation in the competition, Iceland. Wales faced Northern Ireland and the Republic of Ireland would face the hosts, France.

The other European issue was the small matter of the referendum that was building up to an intriguing vote on June 23rd. A week before the vote, campaigning was brought to a shuddering halt as Jo Cox, MP for Batley and Spen and self-proclaimed *"proud Yorkshire Lass"* was brutally murdered in Birstall, West Yorkshire. The murder appeared to be politically motivated as Jo Cox was well known for her humanitarian activities, including opposing air strikes in Syria. One of the most burning issues in the referendum, once campaigning began again, was that of whether or not immigration was a problem or an opportunity for the country. It would become possibly *the* main issue as the 'leave' and 'remain' support appeared to be running neck and neck.

When the fixtures finally came out on 22nd June, Leeds were handed a first day trip to QPR, well, not quite the first day as predictably Sky TV had already picked our first game for a live TV broadcast and it was immediately switched to the Sunday rather than the Saturday. Our first round English Football League (EFL) Cup (the Capital One sponsorship having ended) game would be a trip to Fleetwood Town the following Wednesday. By the time that came round Uwe Rösler would be installed as their manager.

The fixture list was somewhat overshadowed by the breaking news that we had our first new signing of the summer; Marcus Antonsson, a Swedish striker. Antonsson joined on a three-year contract for a fee said to be in the region of £2 million. He'd averaged a goal every other game for Kalmar FF over a period of a season and a half in the Swedish Allsvenskan. Having lost the goals of Antenucci this was seen as a great replacement for the moody Italian and the Swede was well known to Pep Clotet who worked with him at Halmstads in 2011.[1]

June 23rd, 2016; incredibly, and defying all the bookies and all the financial markets' predictions, almost 52% of the UK's

---

[1]   http://www.yorkshireeveningpost.co.uk/sport/football/leeds-united/confirmed-kalmar-striker-marcus-antonsson-agrees-to-join-leeds-united-1-7975381

citizens who bothered to vote, voted to leave the EU. The nation was in shock. David Cameron resigned as PM, sparking a leadership battle in the Tory party which quickly ended as the candidates all realised there was only going to be one winner; Theresa May. A bloke called Hammond would soon become Chancellor too; with May and Hammond leading the Tories it was getting more like Top Gear by the minute. For his part in failing to get Labour voters to back the 'remain' campaign, Jeremy Corbyn was fighting for his political career. His shadow cabinet members did a passable impression of rats, falling over themselves to get out of a seemingly sinking ship. Prominent 'leave' campaigner Boris Johnson, who many expected to take over from Cameron, ruled himself out of the race to lead the Tories as protestors barracked him outside his home while Nigel Farage would later step down as UKIP leader. It seemed all the prominent 'leave' politicians were now distancing themselves from the 'victory' they'd achieved and none seemed willing to take on the difficult task of piloting the good ship UK through the turbulent post EU waters they'd whipped up. Maybe none had expected to win. The ramifications of the vote were far reaching; crikey, even Top Gear's new lead man, Chris Evans quit after just one series.

It was all as nothing though compared with the shock of England's exit from the Euros at the hands of little Iceland. In football, as in politics, the price of failure is usually resignation and 'Woy' Hodgson fell on his sword before most of us had changed channels after the game. England were dire while Wales edged out Northern Ireland in a battling encounter and the Republic fought bravely in only succumbing 2 - 1 to the French. Wales then went on to beat Belgium 3 − 1 with an amazing performance to set up a semi-final with Portugal billed as 'Bale v Ronaldo'. Germany, who beat Italy on penalties, and France who easily saw off the might of Iceland would contest the second semi. France and Portugal eventually won through to the final with Portugal winning a dour 1 − 0 game in extra-time to secure the trophy.

Leeds fans may or may not have been pleased to see former Whites' striker Sam Vokes power home a header to seal that 3

– 1 win for Wales (he only got one goal in nine outings while on loan to us from Wolves in 2009) but there was no doubting the general joy amongst most Leeds fans on Twitter earlier the same day as the OS announced: *"United defender Giuseppe Bellusci has joined Serie A side Empoli on a season-long loan...The Club would like to wish Giuseppe the very best of luck during his time in Italy."*[1] As the rumours started about his imminent departure, thousands of Twitter followers were offering their services to drive him to the airport or pay his taxi fare and there was much dancing in the streets of Beeston. Interestingly, at his first press conference at Empoli, reported on Twitter by Adam Pope, Bellusci told the press: *"I wanted to come back* [to Italy] *for so many reasons. I love working on the defence and in England this wasn't done."* Ah! Now *that* might explain why we were so crap at the back last season! Tommaso Bianchi had also left Leeds; completing a transfer to Italian Serie B side Ascoli as had Casper Sloth who'd signed for Danish club Aalborg BK for an undisclosed fee on a three-year deal. Experienced pros were thin on the ground in LS11 for a few days.

A couple of hours after we were told that Peppe was out came the news that Kyle Bartley was in. The OS told us: *"We are delighted to announce the signing of Swansea City defender Kyle Bartley on a season-long loan."*[2] Bartley, a 25 year-old centre-back, had played with and for Garry Monk at Swansea and finally I was happy that someone realised we needed to strengthen that defence of ours. Monk confirmed: *"I think defence is an area where we need to add strength to the quality that we already have. Kyle has worked with me and he knows how I work, so that helps. I think he's at a stage of his career where he wants to prove himself and try and fight for a*

1

http://www.leedsunited.com/news/article/14a0i266hehbi1py6apw4es dx4/title/bellusci-makes-loan-switch

2

http://www.leedsunited.com/news/article/1mtyao4rabv4g14d2iytgcv5 1w/title/defender-bartley-arrives-on-loan place. He's big, he's strong and he's a very good defender. He's a good leader, he talks very well; he's a good organiser and a good communicator." He sounded exactly what we needed and with those Bellusci balls-ups now banished to Italy, optimism about the new season was on the up. But, when I checked his stats I was less convinced about Bartley. In the previous six seasons he'd only played 92 senior games and most of them on loan whilst on the books of Arsenal and Swansea. I also remembered that he played the whole game in the centre of the Birmingham City defence when we played them at Elland Road in October 2013. He didn't do much of a job that day as Leeds won 4 – 0 and big Matt Smith got two. I still hoped he'd prove to be an improvement for us though and noted that he's a veritable giant at all of 6ft 4 inches tall.

Our pre-season games had finally been announced and I was relatively happy that the first two would be in Dublin where we were due to play Shelbourne and then Shamrock Rovers, both in the space of four days. I casually suggested to Mrs W that Dublin would be a superb location to celebrate our 32nd Wedding Anniversary... Further games were announced at Guiseley and Peterborough and the final pre-season shakedown would be against Serie A side Atalanta, at ER on July 30th.

When the team left for Ireland to begin their training camp over there, they had a stowaway. 24 players were named as being on the trip but eagle-eyed observers noted there was one extra involved in the first training session. Internet sleuths soon worked out it was Hadi Sacko, a 22 year-old winger-come-midfielder on the books of Sporting Lisbon. The Frenchman must have made an immediate impression as within a few hours it was reported on the OS that he'd signed a season-long loan deal with the Whites. That was three useful looking additions, albeit we were still down on numbers compared with last season having lost Antenucci, Wootton, Sloth, Bridcutt, Adeyemi, Carayol and Bellusci; all regular members of the first team squad last year. The expectation had to be that more would follow.

Leeds soon announced a fourth signing and intriguingly it was a goalkeeper; Rob Green, he who we've serenaded on many occasions with, *"You let your country down!"* Football is a funny old game! In fact it never ceases to amaze me. Hard on the heels of Rob Green, came signings number five and six within the space of 24 hours. Five was another import from Swansea, their 20 year-old midfielder Matt Grimes, signed up on another season long loan; he'd celebrate his 21st birthday during the Dublin trip. He was another player who'd been at Swansea with Monk and Clotet. But it was the sixth signing that blew me away; Kemar Roofe, on a four-year deal from Oxford United.

I saw Roofe play a few times last season whilst completing my '92' and every time he impressed me. He's a real live-wire who'll usually come up with something special, as he did in Oxford's visit to Bristol Rovers when I was there. He curled in an amazing 25-yard shot from out wide on the left hand side to win that game and pick up the Man of the Match award. I'd seen him just a couple of weeks before that too, scoring again in a 3 – 1 win over Notts County although he missed a boat-load of chances in that one. Roofe won the Sky Bet League Two Player of the Year award last season and was named in the League Two Team of the Year having scored 26 goals in 49 appearances to help Oxford win promotion. He has a bit of the Beckford look about him too, including that tendency to miss a few in-between scoring his goals and the odd sulk. The fee for Roofe was officially undisclosed but was rumoured to be in the region of £3m and it certainly looked as if Cellino was giving it one last big push. It all impressed Roofe as much as it did me as the 23 year-old told us: *"You can tell there's something exciting happening here with the signings we're making – they're all good signings. I can't wait to start getting to know the squad and playing football again."* [1]As far as I was concerned Leeds were building something decent and, as everyone knows, to build anything that's going to last the first thing you need is a good Roofe…

---

[1]

http://www.leedsunited.com/news/article/19e2f16xtwobx1h2zp33jcg6 b9/title/united-complete-roofe-signing

Dublin

The lead-up to the trip to Dublin was all about Lewis Cook. Once again it was a bit Groundhog Day-like as we contemplated reports that Bournemouth had made an offer, just as we were told during the last winter transfer window. This time the reports seemed to hold more water and were being reported by both Phil Hay at the YEP and the BBC's Adam Pope. Twitter was split as usual between those appalled that Cellino could contemplate selling our crown jewel and those who realised that an offer of £30,000 a week was going to be hard to refuse by young Cookie. Cellino was saying an offer had been accepted so it was now up to Cook and his agent whether he left or not. The offer was said to be anything from £6m to £15m depending on who you believed. There was also said to be interest for Charlie Taylor but in his case Cellino was being openly hostile, saying that since Taylor and his agent were refusing to discuss a new contract there was no way he'd be allowed to walk away even if that meant him walking for free at the end of his current contract in a year's time. It was a shame that all the positive news of the six new signings was now being overshadowed by this uncertainty and especially since the squad was now presumably being trained in formations and tactics at the training camp in Dublin. If Cook left now we'd need a new recipe pretty damn quick.

Actually I was sanguine about losing Cook; I still felt he'd one day be a really important player for some team somewhere but as yet, useful as he was, he was not the crucial component in getting Leeds promoted. In fact, looking at it dispassionately, we'd probably be better served at this time with a much more experienced mid-fielder in that position. Cook was still showing last season his lack of experience when his little dashes through the opposition would more often than not result in him losing possession without making an incisive pass. Despite his incredible goal against Fulham, he'd not thus far added enough goals to his game either. Whether another year's development would mean he'd be a much more important cog in our wheel this coming season we could only guess. As it was, we'd not get the chance to see, as on Friday 8th July the OS announced Cook had decided to get out of Hell's Kitchen to seek out the warmth of the South Coast.

The changes were coming thick and fast now and the next to be announced was that Lee Erwin (remember him?) had left; he'd gone out on a season long loan to financially troubled Oldham Athletic. We'd also heard the surprising news that Marco Silvestri had been sent back to Leeds and was no longer with the rest of the lads in Dublin. Even more surprising was that he'd apparently been banished to train with the under 21s at Thorp Arch (TA). That could only mean that Rob Green was in pole position for the goalkeeper's jersey. Most assumed Silvestri would soon be another one on the bus out of Leeds although others thought he'd probably miss it…

Something else Marco missed was a team-bonding session in Ireland. It was a clay pigeon shoot at Dublin's Courtlough Shooting Grounds from where several tweets emanated. Encouragingly, LUTV man Thom Kirwin tweeted: *"Great day, good fun and I can assure everyone that*

@AntonssonMarcus is indeed a sharp shooter…" Mmmn, we were told that about Chris Wood twelve months ago too.

We nearly got new face number seven just before the Ireland games; Joel Ekstrand, a Swedish centre-back recently released by Watford, was at TA for a medical. He had a history of injuries that had limited his career appearances and so I guess it was no real surprise that he failed the test. Leeds apparently then tried to get him on a pay per play basis but that didn't come off.

"Hello Karen!" I was just coming out of the toilets at Liverpool airport when I heard the unmistakeable tones of Kentley greeting Mrs W. My Stokie Leeds buddy Kentley and his dad Chris were on the same flight to Dublin. Surprisingly, I only spotted two other Leeds fans on the flight but I was sure they were the couple I saw racing out of the station at Salzburg during last pre-season. This Leeds United planet is very small! It was early Wednesday morning and I guessed many fans would be on later flights as our first game was a 7pm kick-off that evening. Others would come out for the second match on Saturday afternoon once work was finished for the week. Mrs W and I were there for the four days to take in both games while Kentley and Chris were going home on Thursday morning. Kentley was then coming back for the day on Saturday to hook up with us again. The flights were actually far cheaper than a night in a Dublin hotel.

An uneventful flight saw us arrive in Dublin around 10am and after a short bus ride into the city, Mrs W and I made our first sightseeing venture into town. We visited the excellent 'Little Museum of Dublin' (well, entrance was free with our 'hop-on hop-off' bus passes saving us 10 euros each!) that boasts it can go through the history of this great City in 29 minutes. It did a good job too and I was surprised by how little I knew about the various attempts by the Irish to secure their independence from us Brits. A quick change into our Leeds tops back at the hotel and we set off for Tolka Park, home of 'The Shels', Shelbourne FC.

We'd arranged to meet up with Kentley and Chris at Fagan's, a famous old bar and restaurant in Drumcondra, just around the corner from the magnificent 83,200-seater Croke Park

Stadium that rises into the sky like a huge stainless steel drum, all shiny and new... ...and the slightly less magnificent 6,000 capacity Tolka Park Stadium that lurks in the shadows between rows of terraced houses and could do with a lick of paint. There were only a handful of Leeds fans in Fagan's when the four of us sat down with our first pints of Guinness but within an hour or so the place was rammed and it soon felt like any Leeds pre-match drinking session anywhere in the world; Leeds shirts everywhere and accents from all corners of Britain including many clearly from the Emerald Isle.

Mrs W and I had walked down to the ground as soon as we arrived in Drumcondra expecting to pick up our pre-ordered match tickets to avoid the inevitable long queues that would form nearer kick-off. Sadly, a scrap of paper pinned to the ticket office door told us: *"Ticket collection from 5:15pm"*. So, around 5:20pm Kentley and I jogged back to the stadium to collect all the tickets – including one for Nigel who'd by this time arrived and who'd entrusted his credit card to Kentley as proof of purchase. There was no queue and we were soon back in Fagan's supping more Guinness.

As kick-off time approached, the pub began to empty and we started to gather up our coats. It was at that point that Nigel decided to look for the credit card we'd handed back to him on our return. *"Did you give me back that card?"* he asked as he flicked through his wallet. *"Dave gave it you when we got back"*, Kentley assured him. And then we all had one of those moments when you doubt what you were once absolutely certain of. We all start to search through our own wallets and then we're scrambling about under the tables checking it's not dropped on the floor. It's amazing what you see under the tables in a pub in mid-summer and I'm soon apologising profusely to young ladies around one particular table trying to explain that I wasn't really looking up their skirts like some sort of pervert. Soon half the punters in the pub have joined the search and I'm even retracing my steps back towards the door thinking I may have dropped the card on the way in, forcing my way through the phalanx of Leeds fans now leaving the pub; everyone's having a panic attack. We ought to have known better, this was Nigel we were dealing with here.

Eventually Kentley grabbed the wallet from him and commenced his own forensic examination and within seconds found the card. Everyone's heart was beating a little harder as we thanked everyone for their help and then hastily made for the exit.

Tolka Park was opened in 1953; I was born in 1957 and I can proudly report I've weathered much better than this stadium. It's hidden away between two rows of terraced houses and the River Tolka and as mentioned already, it's a tad dilapidated. To be fair to the current occupants, Shelbourne FC, they only moved here in 1989 and they have built the one new stand in the ground, a smart but small modern unit that fills one half of the Drumcondra End. We sat in the Riverside Stand, built over one bank of the Tolka and it was comfortable enough with a decent view of the pitch, but over to our right the Ballybough End was strictly out of bounds apart from the most rustic of toilet blocks that resembled the Black Hole of Calcutta. What was once no doubt an impressive place to watch football (as long as it wasn't raining as that end has no roof) was now a sea of colourful seat backs.., no seats, just the plastic backs. All the seat bottoms had been broken off, presumably at the request of health and safety officers to ensure no one could sit there anymore. The H & S folk must have run out of time though and couldn't have visited those despicable bogs as they were still open, despite most definitely being unfit for purpose. They were quite possibly the origin of the expression "sh** hole".

Shelbourne FC are a mid-table second tier outfit in the Irish League these days and, like all Irish sides, were in the middle of their season; a season that runs from March to October. Somehow, they were cramming in three friendlies against English sides between their league games on the 8th and 16th July. They lost at home 1 - 2 to Ipswich Town on Saturday and then lost 0 – 1 to Swindon Town on Tuesday night, 24 hours before our game. As far as I could make out, having studied some team sheets from recent games before we flew out, they had about half of their regular first team players in the starting XI to face Leeds. The reason Shelbourne agreed to our fixture in this hectic schedule is probably only due to their Chairman being a lifelong Leeds fan and season ticket holder. In his programme notes, Joseph Casey wrote: *"I am not unique in Ireland to support Leeds United, as I would comfortably say that they are the 4th best supported from these shores behind Celtic, Liverpool and a certain team from Lancashire. You only have to be at Dublin airport on a Saturday morning to see the numerous white scarves waiting at the Ryanair gate for the 8:30am to Leeds."*

Garry Monk opted to play two completely different XIs in this game. For the first hour it was:

Turnbull

Coyle Bartley Diagouraga Denton

Sacko Phillips Murphy (C) Mowatt

Roofe Doukara

Leeds had 25 players in Ireland but Gaetano Berardi and Liam Cooper were carrying knocks and Rob Green didn't feature at all in this game leaving a nice round 22 to make up the two teams. The obvious problem we had was a distinct lack of centre-backs and hence the reason we saw 'Dave' lining up alongside the giant figure of Kyle Bartley. Luke Murphy wore the captain's armband.

A crowd of 3,096 was squeezed into three sides of the little stadium and the late evening sun had finally broken through the clouds as the game got underway. Judging by the colours worn I'd estimate that 3,000 of the crowd were Leeds fans.

It was no surprise Leeds dominated the early exchanges as several of the Shelbourne lads were no doubt trying to shake off the fatigue from playing the previous night and after just nine minutes Leeds grabbed the lead. From a throw-in, deep in their own half, Shelbourne worked the ball back to their keeper who knocked it out towards the right back. Kemar Roofe blocked the full-back's poor clearance and the ball fell nicely for Doukara who now had half the goal to aim at with the keeper stranded at the far post. The Douk didn't let us down, smacking the ball home through a defender's legs, just inside the near post. Cheers rang all around the ground.

Four minutes later it was 2 – 0 as Alex Mowatt split the home defence and Hadi Sacko ran onto the ball to side-foot it home from a tight angle. The final pass came after a long spell of

Leeds possession and involved almost every player having a touch; it was an Arsenal type goal. There was the initial fear that this was going to be all too easy; I remembered the hoo-ha that came after our 16 – 0 win against FC Gherdeina in Dave Hockaday's first pre-season game as manager. Many Leeds fans believed the opposition that day were so poor as to be no test at all and moaned it was all Cellino's fault for skimping on pre-season. Shelbourne would prove to be made of sterner stuff though and the score remained 0 – 2 through to half-time, although we did see a glimpse of last season's defensive frailties as we allowed a Shelbourne player to get free at the back post from a corner. Ross Turnbull also made a bit of a Horlicks of a clearance. I shuddered.

I shuddered again as I queued outside those horrendous bogs at half-time. I'd left my coat in the stand and now it was raining and the queue was moving at a snail's pace. The darkened sky and lack of any form of light inside the toilet block meant it was now almost impossible to see what you were doing in there or, more to the point, where you were doing it!

Five minutes into the second half, the home side raised some noise from the smart little stand at the Drumcondra End when they pulled a goal back. I know this was only the first game of a new season, and I know we had a few new faces in there, and I know these things take time, I do honestly, I know... but the goal we conceded looked like so many scruffy, needless goals we conceded last season and I rolled my eyes and shook my head as we lined up for the restart. Kalvin Phillips let the ball get away from him and had to dive in to rescue the situation, giving away a needless free kick in midfield. There was some quick thinking by Cian Kavanagh as he played the kick from about 35 yards out to an unmarked Lorcan Shannon on the right wing. The Shels' man slipped the ball across the face of goal, behind the Leeds back four and Adam Evans bundled it across the line. Sloppy!

Leeds continued to dominate possession and created a few half chances before the 11 subs took to the field just on the hour mark. It was a chance to see how youngsters Alex Purver and Paul McKay measured up.

Peacock-Farrell
Purver P. McKay, Bamba (C), Taylor
Vieira Grimes Botaka
Stokes Wood Antonsson

To be honest, the rest of the game was not a great spectacle, with only Jordan Botaka showing a few neat touches and a couple of attempts on goal while we could easily have given away an equaliser had it not been for a sharp save by Bailey Peacock-Farrell. It was becoming a tad tedious to be frank and I think we were all happy to hear the final whistle. I know! It was only the first game! McKay did OK without being stretched while Alex Purver was busy if not always accurate, the academy midfielder playing in an unaccustomed full-back role.

As a consequence of all the pre-match Guinness, I decided I couldn't make it back to the city centre without one last trip to the bogs. By this time of course it was dark and inside the Black Hole of Calcutta it was, well, completely black. I could see nothing at all in there now so my only reference point was a pair of fluorescent trainers the bloke in front of me was wearing. As the trainers shuffled forward and then stopped I heard the unmistakeable sound of a zipper and I manoeuvred to the right assuming I'd then be at the urinal wall. *"Steady tiger!"* a gruff Yorkshire voice called out as I bumped into a bloke already in that slot. I paddled back out in what I hoped was the rainwater flooding the floor and not second-hand Guinness. We thought our experience was bad enough but Mrs W had ventured into the ladies next door and she point blank refuses to talk about her adventure and now wakes in the middle of the night screaming about rats in toilets.

As Kentley, Chris, Mrs W and I sat on the 41C bus back to the city; I pondered what I'd learned. On the plus side, Kyle Bartley is a giant; Shelbourne were not good enough to give us any clue as to whether he's any good, but he is undeniably huge. Jordan Botaka has lost none of his magic over the summer break while Roofe and Sacko showed at least some glimpses to suggest they may come good in time although they both looked 'leggy' tonight. The biggest negatives for me were the half dozen or so glaring defensive errors we made, one of which resulted in giving a goal away. But, as I kept telling myself, it was early days.

The four of us made our way to the Temple Bar district and had a final Guinness or two before heading for our hotels. The following day, July 14th, was our wedding anniversary; Bastille Day. We will not forget our 32nd anniversary.

We had a day sightseeing using the 'hop-on hop-off' bus again, trying to ensure we got full value for those three day tickets. Then we had a fabulous evening at the Gaiety Theatre in South King Street, watching the 21st anniversary show of Riverdance. We've seen several previous Riverdance performances over the years around the world but I have to say I never tire of it and seeing it in Dublin was undeniably special. We finished the night with the obligatory Guinness in the hotel bar and then retired to our room and switched on the TV.

Sky News was reporting on yet another terrorist atrocity, this time in Nice, South of France. In the name of the so-called ISIS terrorist group, a 19 tonne truck drove intentionally into a crowd of men, women and children who'd spent the evening on the beach watching a fireworks display celebrating Bastille Day. 84 were initially declared dead with countless others critically injured. It brought back the memory of a similar night Mrs W and I spent in Gran Canaria the previous November when I opened the Kindle to check how Leeds got on in a friendly game at Wycombe only to see the breaking news of the Paris terrorist attacks. This world of ours is a sick place and getting sicker by the day.

Friday was another sightseeing day, visiting Kilmainham Gaol and learning more about the Irish struggle for independence in the early twentieth century. A few more pints of Guinness and a two hour walking tour around the city and I was ready for some more football!

Kentley met us at our hotel bang on time at 10:15am on the Saturday morning and informed us that at least half of the passengers on his flight were Leeds fans; the army was mobilised. We breakfasted at Ann's Bakery in town and then Kentley and I caught the tram to Tallaght while Mrs W went off to sample the city centre shops.

As the tram made its way out towards the Tallaght Stadium, home of Shamrock Rovers, more and more Leeds shirts began to appear. In the ticket office, the staff reckoned there could well be around 4,000 in the ground today and most would be wearing the white, blue and gold of Leeds.

Shamrock Rovers are still in the top tier of Irish football and have a long history of prestige games against top European opposition as more often than not they're in the qualifying rounds of the major European competitions. In the glass display cabinets that line the ticket office there are lots of mementoes of those games. In 1957 they played the Busby Babes of Manchester United in the preliminary round of the European Cup and since then they've had memorable ties against the likes of Juventus, Bayern Munich and, as recently as 2011, faced Spurs in the group stages of the Europa League, having knocked out Partisan Belgrade to qualify. The great Johnny Giles was player manager at Shamrock in the late 70s and he visited the Leeds training camp on the eve of the Rovers game.

This season, Rovers sat fourth in the Irish Premier League behind Dundalk, Cork and Derry City and they'd been involved in a huge local derby against bitter rivals Bohemians the night before our game which they won 3 – 1. We knew therefore that few if any of their first team regulars would be available for our game. In the event it was pretty much their U21s. Former Leeds player Stephen McPhail, now a 36 year-old veteran, was on Rovers' books but wouldn't feature.

The pre-match drinks venue today was the bar of the Maldron Hotel opposite the ground and I have to say it is quite possibly the smartest venue Leeds fans have ever had the pleasure to frequent! They even laid-on a piano player who sang a few songs although he frequently had to wait for a break in the singing of the Leeds fans to fulfil his contract for the day. I would say the prices matched the venue at 5 euros a pint but to be fair that was pretty much the price of a Guinness all over Dublin. Kentley and I had a couple of pints and sat in one corner of the bar that was decorated in Rovers memorabilia whilst watching the antics of the throngs of our fans who eventually filled the bar. Even at 5 euros the Maldron ran out of Guinness long before kick-off.

Everything in this corner of Dublin appears to be relatively new. Served by the shiny new Dublin Luas Red Line commuter trams from the city centre some six miles North West of here, the town of Tallaght is a sort of Irish Milton Keynes with around 72,000 inhabitants these days; 50 years ago it was a small village. The Tallaght Stadium was only opened some seven years ago but as a new build it is surprisingly pleasing on the eye.[1] Many of the plastic seats are in the club colours of green or white but with a sprinkling of red and yellow as well the two main stands do have a bit of a Lego look to them. Both ends are currently open, with a big blue scoreboard at the South End being the only structure. By the time we arrived, a vast array of Leeds flags tied to the railings along the South End added to the colourful scene on a bright sunny day. We'd met up with Nigel in the Maldron but as usual we'd lost him by the time we found seats at the south end of the West Stand.

Once again Garry Monk opted to play two different teams for this one although he'd mixed things up from the line-ups we saw at Tolka Park.

Green
Purver Bartley Bamba (C) Taylor
Vieira Grimes Botaka
Antonsson Wood Roofe

The starting line-up gave us our first view of Rob Green in goal while most of the rest were the players who played the final half-hour against Shels. With the exception of Alex Purver, who was presumably vying with Lewie Coyle to deputise for the injured Berardi at right back, I thought this line-up was actually worthy of a start once the competitive season got underway. Rovers had none of the side who started against Bohemians in their starting XI but six of their subs from that game did start; the rest were from their U21 squad.

---

[1] *http://www.footballgroundguide.com/leagues/republic-of-ireland-premier-league-clubs/shamrock-rovers.html*

This game began very much like the previous one – with Leeds in the lead as early as the 7th minute. Ronaldo Vieira won the ball in a strong challenge on half-way, down in front of us on the right wing. He drove forward to the edge of the penalty area before slipping the ball inside to Antonsson and the Swede swept the ball home inside the near post. This lad Vieira was starting to look like the obvious Cook replacement and, whisper it quietly, I think he may be better than Cookie!

Leeds were pretty much dominant from that point on, although we had to wait until the half-hour mark for a second. Matt Grimes touched the ball to Jordan Botaka who jinked and weaved his way to a shooting chance about 25 yards out. The shot was half-blocked and ballooned over the defence to Kemar Roofe but as Roofe attempted to bring it down, a high boot from a Rovers defender sent Roofe to the turf instead and the referee immediately gave the penalty. Chris Wood picked up the ball with no one else showing any obvious interest and placed it on the spot. That disastrous miss up at Donny last season was still in everyone's minds as big Woody strode up to the ball but this time he sent the keeper the wrong way and the ball nestled in the bottom left corner.

For the final few minutes of the half we began to see what Kemar Roofe will bring us; time and time again he got free on the left hand side to put in telling crosses. The only disappointment was that both Wood and Antonsson spurned the chances he was making. Wood hit the angle with one such chance and did his Donny thing with another sending the ball into orbit somewhere over Dublin and Antonsson did the same. Obviously getting fed up of this, Roofe decided to have a go himself and this time, after cutting in from the left, he curled a delightful right foot shot around the diving keeper only to see it cannon back to him off the inside of the far post. Once again no-one was alert enough as he fired the rebound back across goal.

That was his final work for the day, as at half-time he and Bartley went off and Hadi Sacko and Paul McKay took their places. It was more of the same though in the second half as Rovers offered little resistance and first Matty Grimes strode forward to hammer a shot against the bar and then Leeds grabbed a third. A nice move down the Leeds left culminated with Charlie Taylor sending the ball over. The merest touch from a Shamrock head just lifted the ball over Chris Wood at the near post but Marcus Antonsson was free at the back to nod it home. On the hour mark, the rest of the subs took to the field and Leeds then lined up:

Turnbull
Coyle Diagouraga P. McKay Denton
Phillips Murphy (C) Mowatt
Stokes Doukara Sacko

Still Leeds dominated but a combination of inspired goalkeeping and poor Leeds finishing kept the score at three and that's how it finished. Against a very young Shamrock side Leeds had bossed the game and played some neat and tidy football to create many chances but let themselves down by not converting enough of them. It was one of last season's failings of course and we needed to rid ourselves of it. The other failing, our porous defence, really hadn't been tested in either game and with Diagouraga, McKay, and even Luke Murphy having spells at the back it was clearly an area of work-in-progress for Garry Monk.

For the second half, Kentley and I wandered down to the other end of the stand where we found a couple of seats near the press box. Thom Kirwin and Phil Hay were doing their stuff. As we looked around we then spotted Gaetano Berardi and Stuart Dallas sat just a couple of seats away looking very anonymous and getting little attention from the locals who clearly hadn't recognised them. Berardi sat stony faced for much of the half while Stuart D's attention often drifted towards the beautiful hills away to our right behind the goal at that end. Dallas had only linked up with his team mates this weekend having been given extra time-off for his Euro exploits with Northern Ireland.

After the game, Kentley and I got the tram back to The Spencer Hotel where Mrs W was waiting with our bags and then we all got on the 747 bus back to the airport. There was just time for one last glass of the black stuff. It had been a good trip.

"We're gonna win four three!"

The news ahead of our back to back friendlies at non-league Guiseley and League One Peterborough United was that Garry Monk was going to divide up his players into two teams that would each be given their first 90 minute outings. I couldn't conceive that we would do anything other than play our strongest side against Posh since they were clearly going to be more formidable opponents than the little non-league Yorkshire outfit.

With Kentley's BMW undergoing minor surgery, I was going to be on driving duty for both trips; a total of around 450 miles in 29 hours. Picking Kentley up just after 3pm on Friday afternoon, we were straight into motorway jam avoidance mode but he picked out a route that got us into the free car park over the railway behind Nethermoor just after 5:30pm.

It was hot; the UK had finally seen the arrival of summer and it was an evening more suited to the junior cricket match that was getting underway on the ground just next to Nethermoor. We were meandering our way through the Guiseley AFC car park en route to The Station, a pub on Otley Road, just down the road from the ground. We chuckled at the sight of the A4 paper notices Sellotaped to traffic cones denoting various VIP parking spaces. There was one marked, "MANSFORD ONLY", for Leeds' new CEO and another that read "LORIMER ONLY". Guiseley director and Leeds fan and sponsor Steve Parkin also had one; sort of 'Parking for Parkin'. Anyone parking here clearly wasn't short of a few bob to pay for repairs as any shot missing the target at this end would surely smash into the vehicles. Did they not know Chris Wood was playing here tonight and not at Peterborough tomorrow?

In The Station pub it was also bloody hot; they had a pizza oven doing good business just behind the bar and the place was full of Leeds fans as you'd expect. On the TV screens Yorkshire's Joe Root was doing his stuff for England as they piled up a big first innings score in the Second Test against Pakistan. Root was on 140 and would go on to score 254 as England posted a total of 589 and eventually won the game to square the series 1 - 1. We found a table with a good view of the TV and tucked into our pizzas and pints. Studying the menu we noticed we could have 'gone large'. A note on the pizza section informing us: "Add four inches for £2". I commented with a schoolboy smirk to Kentley how that seemed a decent offer!

We were joined eventually by Sean, aka @DoctorT1992 who was looking for a ticket and, luckily, Martin aka @mucky_fat who just happened to have a spare. It had been announced that no tickets would be sold on the night for this one.

Silvestri
Coyle P. McKay Diagouraga Denton
Phillips, Vieira, Botaka
Stokes, Wood, Doukara (C)

Subs: Turnbull, M Taylor, Shackleton, J McKay

The teams emerged just as we found a spot behind the barrier at the one end where we bumped into Nigel. Former Leeds player Aidy White was standing just along from us as was Will Hatfield's brother, there to watch Will playing for Guiseley. Will was on Leeds' books for a time too. I once bumped into his mum who was working in a branch of Lloyds in Leeds city centre! I tell you, it's a small world!

The main surprise to us all was the sight of Marco Silvestri in the green goalkeeper's jersey, trotting out with the team. Having been sent to the naughty step and forced to train with the U21s recently, he'd suddenly been given a reprieve by Garry Monk who said he was now, *"back in the fold"*. That was a disappointment to many Leeds fans who thought they'd seen the last of Marco McFlappyhands in a Leeds shirt. Other than that, the rest of the side looked like our second XI, although the inclusion of Chris Wood did confuse us. Was he in there as he was now no longer our number one striker or was he just boosting an otherwise understrength side? The continued absence of Liam Cooper through injury meant young Paul McKay got another chance at centre-back while his twin brother, Jack, a striker, got a spot on the bench. Mike Taylor, 16 year-old Jamie Shackleton and Ross Turnbull completed the subs. Gaetano Berardi was still struggling with ankle ligament issues but it was interesting to see that Lewie Coyle filled in for him tonight and Alex Purver would be at Peterborough. The inevitable suggestion was that Alex had overtaken Lewie to get that deputy right back spot.

So, everyone knew this was largely a second string side but there was absolutely no excuse for them as a group of Championship squad players to go 3 goals down after only 24 minutes. That was about as surprising as seeing a massive dog dressed up with a lion's mane being led around the ground. Guiseley are known as the Lions of course but it was the young Leeds lions being tamed out there on the pitch.

All three goals were the result of poor Leeds defending and even given that Diagouraga was only filling in at centre-back and the rest of this defence were unlikely to regularly feature in the Championship, it was at the very least disappointing that Monk, a former centre-back himself let's remember, didn't have this group looking more solid. The first came as early as the 7th minute and came after a sustained spell of Guiseley pressure where we just could not clear the ball away; several crosses coming in from both flanks. One back-post header from an unmarked striker had already tested Silvestri and now another right wing cross found Palmer free at the back post. He nodded the ball efficiently past Marco into the bottom corner. The second came 5 minutes later. A long ball over the back of the Leeds defence resulted in another right wing Guiseley corner that was quickly taken short. A first-time cross found a Guiseley head in the centre of our box and although the header appeared to be going wide, Silvestri dived and got a hand to it, merely pushing it onto the boot of Jake Lawlor who stabbed it in. And to complete the misery, Palmer got his second and the home side's third on 24 minutes. This time a floated free kick from the right was actually headed down in the box by an unchallenged Diagouraga onto a Guiseley boot and although the initial shot was going wide it was touched in by Ash Palmer at the back post. OK, I know Dave was only filling in... but Jesus Christ!

So, after less than half an hour we thought this game was over and those of us going were already turning our thoughts to the trip to Peterborough the following afternoon. Surely the 'First XI' would put up a better show than this! By this time we'd been joined by Mike and Lynn who both sit behind us at ER and to be honest we spent more time chatting and catching up with their news than watching the game. Martin did mention a few famous 4 – 3 comebacks we'd achieved in our long history though, including that one at Southampton in 2005 when 3,500 Leeds fans sang, *"we're gonna win 4 – 3"*, as we trailed 3 – 0, twenty minutes from time. That day, goals from skipper Paul Butler, Robbie Blake and a David Healy penalty got us level before Liam Miller's mishit shot gave Leeds an unlikely victory. No one thought this bunch of youngsters would replicate that.

Like a boxer getting up off the canvas, Leeds slowly started to clear their heads and began to show some spirit. A couple of shots flew over the crossbar to our right and into the car park; one Chris Wood effort bouncing over into the hedge and disappearing. Then, on the stroke of half-time another Chris Wood shot was blocked and when it ricocheted back to Eoghan Stokes he fair blasted it into the left corner of the net; half-time, 3 – 1 to Guiseley.

Leeds completed that unlikely comeback in the second half with a really decent display. It seemed that as long as we could pin Guiseley back in their own half and prevent them getting at our defence then we had a chance. For the record, the goals came from Botaka, Phillips and Doukara and they were all fine efforts. Botaka scored from close range after cleverly rounding a defender; Phillips hammered in a dipping shot from 25 yards out; and Souleymane Doukara cut in from the left to steer a right-foot shot low into the far corner as we've seen him do a few times before. Had you only watched the second half you'd have been impressed with Botaka, Doukara and Kalvin Phillips and would have felt they were all in with a chance of making that first starting XI at QPR in a fortnight's time. One man who'd be sweating a bit between now and then was Chris Wood; it was hard to come up with anything positive to say about his contribution at Guiseley and I did wonder if Garry Monk might decide to go without a big man up front or even consider playing Doukara and not Woody. Time would tell.

Kentley and I said our farewells and then made our way out into the car park where Kentley disappeared behind a row of cars in front of the hedge. He was looking for the ball Chris Wood launched over the bar. Unlike the one that went into orbit over Doncaster last season never to be seen again, there is now a match-used ball on a shelf in a house just outside Stoke on Trent. He may have shunned that extra four inches in the pub… but he did leave Guiseley with an extra ball…

Guiseley 3 **Leeds United 4** (Palmer (7, 24), Lawlor (12), **Stokes (45), Botaka (63), Phillips (71), Doukara (73))** 2,412, **(Leeds, most of them!)**

Posh too smart for us

Leeds United's U21 squad was involved in the Steel Park Cup tournament at the home of Corby Town. They were playing two games, one at noon on Saturday against PSV Eindhoven and one on Sunday against Corby. Benitez's Newcastle United U21s were in the same tournament under the watchful eye of their mentor Peter Beardsley. Driving home after Guiseley, Kentley decided he wanted to do our game v PSV and then rush over to London Road for the senior game with Posh. I considered it for all of a nanosecond and then told him: *"No fookin way mate!"* I knew perfectly well Kentley wouldn't even be ready when I arrived on Saturday at 9:30am, let alone the 8am start that we'd need to be in Corby for a game kicking off at noon. As he stepped out of the car, half asleep, just after midnight on the Friday night he murmured: *"Well, think about it on way home Dave and if you change mind text me"*…

Saturday morning arrived and I was outside Kentley's home; he wasn't ready! *"Just give me 2 mins"* he texted. Ten minutes later we set off. He was still muttering about Corby as we hurtled down the M6 but in reality even he knew it was a game too far. The lads we'd been talking with at Guiseley, Will Hatfield's brother and his mate, thought we were bonkers doing a two hundred mile round trip to watch Leeds play a friendly at Guiseley, let alone trying to fit in two games the day after. A Leeds squad containing the likes of Mike Taylor,

Jamie Shackleton and Thom Pearce lost 4 – 1 to PSV and then lost 3 – 0 to Corby. Newcastle won the tournament.

We arrived in the blistering heat of the Costa del Peterborough just as the U21s would have been kicking off down the road at Corby. Many Leeds fans were meeting up at the Wetherspoon in town, The Draper's Arms, but that was a twenty minute walk from the ground. The Cherry Tree is just a short stroll from London Road and they do food, real ale and have a beer garden. The thought of walking far in the thirty plus degree heat meant we stopped at the Cherry Tree.

There was only a handful of Leeds fans in there when we arrived but it would soon fill up and before we left for the game there were a few lagers with the sold-out signs up. Kentley and I got special treatment too. The barman whispered to us that if we got in quick whilst the kitchen wasn't too busy, the nice lady doing the food would let us order off the main menu rather than the shorter list posted up by the serving hatch. I ordered an all-day breakfast and Kentley chose the chicken burger. I was also armed with a foaming pint of Timothy Taylor's Landlord. When the meals arrived there was a gasp around the beer garden. A few of the lads were muttering that we'd do well to get through them. I had four rashers of bacon, two eggs, three hash browns, two pieces of toast, mushrooms, fried tomato, sausage, beans and a ton of chips, all crammed onto a plate the size of a four-man dinghy! Many of the regular away day folk arrived over the course of the next couple of hours including Martin and his three lads, big Cliff, Simon C, Conor and his mate, Nigel and Jack and everyone had to seek out the shade as the sun just got hotter and hotter. It was going to be a real test of the players' fitness this afternoon and a real test of my new blue away top; would it stand up to the sweat pouring down my back?

The Leeds team selection came up on Twitter just after 2pm as normal and the names were exactly as Kentley and I had discussed in the car on the way down.

Green
Purver Bartley Bamba (C) C. Taylor
Grimes Murphy Mowatt Sacko
Antonsson Roofe

Subs: Huffer, J McKay, M Taylor, Shackleton.

The four subs were all part of the U21 squad involved at Corby and would be named in the side playing there on Sunday. Remembering that Cooper and Berardi were still recovering from injury and that Dallas was still being rested after his exploits with NI, this was in my view the strongest team we could put out. Interestingly, it included all six of the summer signings. The only changes I'd have considered were maybe putting Vieira in there instead of Mowatt and possibly Coyle for Purver. There was that lingering question too as to whether Monk would prefer Chris Wood in a front three or not. I wouldn't.

As the Leeds fans took their places in the relatively new Motorpoint Stand (the away end was still terracing the last time we played here) we marvelled as the Posh mascot, Peter Burrow played with his giant carrot, seemingly immune to the oppressive heat despite a heavy furry costume. As he continued to massage his brightly coloured and ever so slightly phallic carrot, the Leeds fans gave him a quick round of, *"What the fu***** hell is that?"* before running through a few Leeds anthems as the two teams did the pre-match hand-shakes. It was positively uncomfortable and I was now mopping my brow with a very soggy handkerchief to keep the sweat out of my eyes. I could see my old buddy Phil B a couple of rows behind also looking frayed at the edges.

Despite the heat though, Leeds played a really good first half. Kemar Roofe took the eye out on the left wing and most of our moves ended up at his feet out there. Grimes and Murphy were calling the shots in midfield while Alex Mowatt appeared to be enjoying a slightly more forward role. At the back, the Bamba-Bartley combo had little to do while Rob Green looked splendid in a brand new kit the colour of his own name.

Roofe had already set up one Alex Mowatt shot which Posh's Ben Alnwick (a Leeds loanee back in 2010, albeit never played a competitive game) did well to turn away but then, in the 16th minute, he was weaving back and forth again on the left hand side of the area at the far end of the ground. The beauty of Roofe is he can go either way and use both feet and this time he went outside and hammered the ball across where

Mowatt did well to get his left leg on it. It flashed into the net. It was a well worked goal but in hindsight the chant of, *"We're gonna win the league"*, that broke out from the Leeds ranks was a tad premature!

In the course of that first half, Mowatt must have had half a dozen shots and arguably should have gone off at half-time with more than the one goal. The only slight blot on our first half performance, apart from not increasing our goal tally, was when Rob Green came to collect a right wing cross under a challenge from the lively Posh centre forward, Shaquile Coulthirst but only managed to drop it at the feet of the Posh striker. Thankfully, after a bit of a scuffle, Green did enough to take the pace off a shot and Alex Purver was able to stop the ball short of the goal-line.

At half-time, there were a lot of very hot Leeds fans going off in search of some shade in the concourse. Kentley nipped out just before the whistle to get us some bottles of water. He returned with the water and a couple of chunky Kit-Kat chocolate bars which quickly became pouches of drinking chocolate. Many fans in the rows in front of us which had no shade whatsoever decided to find places elsewhere while a few of the lads stripped off their tops. There would be some sore shoulders to go with the inevitable sore heads in the morning. Quite a few fans were still enjoying the cool of the concourse as the second half kicked-off and many will have missed the Borough equaliser... but they will have seen a few very similar goals if they've been watching Leeds in recent seasons. It was our old friend 'the long ball over the top'; Kyle Bartley rose to beat his man in the air but his header dropped only yards away to that man Coulthirst. The Posh striker had far too much space and time in which to let the ball bounce twice before arrowing a left foot shot into the bottom left corner. You can argue that Bartley had done his bit in winning the header and that a defensive midfielder should have been on hand to pick up the second ball. Or you could argue it was a weak header from Bartley. Either way, it was a soft goal that will have to be filed in that ever growing portfolio of such things. In the 65th minute we had to open that particular file again. Perhaps the Leeds players had not got the hint when they looked at the match-day programme; Coulthirst's picture was all over it; I knew this as I was using it to fan myself!

This time Coulthirst, now a known danger-man of course, was allowed to run across the edge of the area from left to right without the merest hint of a challenge. Matt Grimes was tracking him but allowing him far too much space. Eventually Coulthirst pulled the trigger with his right foot and the ball flew inside the right hand post with Green helpless again. That really took the edge off a damn good day out and with the sun continuing to burn down it all became a very unpleasant last quarter of an hour. It was somehow typical of Leeds that our most influential player, Kemar Roofe, had been withdrawn just seconds before the goal went in with young Jack McKay taking his place. It would later be reported that he was suffering from stomach cramps. You might say that when the Roofe came off we were left open to the elements…

At the end of the game there was some booing from sections of the Leeds crowd although it was quickly drowned out by the majority who broke into a supportive chant of *"We are Leeds"* and *"We all love Leeds"*. None-the-less, individual voices could be heard throwing insults at the Leeds players as they slowly walked over to show their appreciation for our support. The vast majority behaved but it was sad to see any having a go before the season proper had even begun. I was disappointed, of course I was, I still had my doubts that we'd done enough to prop up the defence that let us down so often last season and I was still hopeful we'd get that much needed additional centre-back as well as maybe concluding the deal for a Liam Bridcutt return. We probably missed having either him or Diagouraga operating in front of the defence today. As we made our way back to the car, I was trying to be optimistic by focussing on our first half display. I've always been a big fan of Kemar Roofe and the more I see of him the more I feel he can make a huge difference to our ability to break down Championship defences. To be any use though, that has to be matched by stopping teams getting through our own.

Peterborough United 2 **Leeds United 1 (Mowatt (16)**, Coulthirst (48, 65))

4,152 **(Leeds 1,750)**

Atalanta

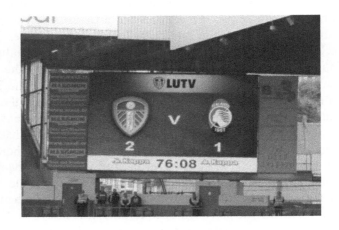

In the week between the Posh and Atalanta games, Ben Mansford, Leeds United CEO, told us that Charlie Taylor had no intention of extending his stay at Leeds once his current contract expired. There was the usual outcry on Twitter that Mansford had merely joined the clique of Cellino arse-lickers and was just protecting the Italian from the inevitable claims that he wanted Taylor gone to pocket more cash while I merely saw it as another young player realising his worth and not wanting to jeopardise the chances of a big move to a Premier League club. By the Tuesday of the following week, Taylor's agent had handed in a formal transfer request.

In a wide ranging interview on LUTV, Mansford condemned the Time To Go Massimo (TTGM) protestors as often going too far while noting that everything would be a lot quieter if the team got off to a good start. *"If we win the first six games of the season or, better still, get promoted, it doesn't matter so much if the pies are occasionally a bit cold or the beer's a bit warm."* He clearly hasn't been in the Pavilion on a match day when that's generally the case whatever the results!

The only thing that calmed the waters a little was a story doing the rounds that a Chinese consortium was looking at the possibility of taking over the club. Several posts appeared on Twitter and then the YEP posted confirmation that there was more to this story than just, err, Chinese whispers. Apparently a consortium was being put together by life-long Leeds fan and Yorkshireman Steve Tappin. Tappin was the CEO and founder of the consultancy firm, Xinfu, as well as fronting the BBC's 'CEO Guru' series on BBC World. He was saying talks had recently taken place in Beijing and had been reported as saying: *"there is definite interest in buying Leeds."*[1]

There was a comforting familiarity about Saturday 30th July, my first visit to Elland Road of the new season. As always I set off just after 10am for the 3pm kick-off and by 10:20am I was stuck in a queue on the M6. Thankfully, the Fighting Talk team on BBC Radio 5 Live did their usual sterling job in keeping me amused. It was exactly 50 years to the day since big Jack Charlton and the rest of the England side won the World Cup with that 4 – 2 extra-time win over West Germany. 5 Live was celebrating the Golden Anniversary with a whole series of special programmes and Fighting Talk had commentator Barry Davies among their contestants. It was a cracking show and filled a nice chunk of the two and a half hour trip until I pulled up in my usual spot at the top of Lowfields Road.

Walking down to the Pavilion, I was suitably impressed with the new paint job on the north end of the East Stand. A magnificent winged horse filled the huge end plate of the roof section. It's an image from the current Clipper Logistics advertising campaign. I wondered absentmindedly if they'd thought to coat it with some kind of paint that would prevent the TTGM campaigners beaming their slogans onto it as they did last season.

In the Pavilion it was all refreshingly familiar; it was still £3.60 to get in and that got you a voucher for a pint of Foster's (although I confess I handed over my extra 20p for a pint of

---

[1]   http://www.yorkshireeveningpost.co.uk/sport/football/leeds-united/could-chinese-consortium-linked-to-bbc-presenter-buy-leeds-united-1-8040325

Heineken); the lads from Co. Durham, George, Trevor and Tony were all sat at our usual table with Steve and Mick; and eventually Peter Lorimer and Terry Yorath arrived with Jed Stone to do their pre-match stint. Yorath was still complaining that we had a *"couple of comedians"* in defence although he didn't name them this time. Nothing much had changed at all seemingly, nothing that is apart from everyone being heavily laden with a generous dollop of pre-season optimism.

I sat and chatted with Phil B and Steve R before Nigel and then Alan and John appeared, all clearly keeping to their time honoured match-day rituals. As I say, it was comfortably familiar. Just after 2pm though the team was spotted on someone's phone and, compared with the side we saw at Deepdale on the final day of last season, there were of course quite a few changes:

Green
Perico Bartley Bamba (C) Taylor
Diagouraga
Dallas Vieira Mowatt
Wood Roofe

Subs: Silvestri, Turnbull, Berardi, Coyle, P McKay, Denton, Grimes, Murphy, Phillips, Botaka, Sacko, Antonsson, Doukara.

The interesting one was Gabriele Perico, a trialist who'd been training with the club for the previous few days while Garry Monk ran the rule over him. Perico was a 32 year-old right-back who'd enjoyed a low key career in Italy, most recently with Serie B side Cesena. The rest of the defence was pretty much what everyone expected to see at QPR the following weekend for our opening league game as there was still no sign of Liam Cooper and no sign of the arrival of the additional centre-back I felt we still needed. The appearance of Gaetano Berardi on the bench meant that he might just make Loftus Road if Perico didn't work out although with Lewie Coyle also on the bench it looked as though he'd won the right to be deputy in that spot over Alex Purver whose name was conspicuous by its absence. Charlie Taylor's presence next week would depend on whether he was still with us or not.

In midfield I was pleased to see Vieira given another chance and it was good to get Stuart Dallas back. Alex Mowatt seemed higher in the pecking order than the likes of Grimes, Murphy and Kalvin Phillips in the race to grab a midfield spot. Wood and Roofe filled the two front roles suggesting Wood was still most likely to play the target man role. Whether by coincidence or design the two of them featured on the front of the programme; a sort of 'Wood n Roofe' that we wouldn't mind catching fire ...

Inside the stadium there were more little cosmetic changes; the front facia of the massive East Stand was now adorned with the Clipper Logistics logo and name while the front facia of the West Stand had also been refurbed in the style of the main stand at Loftus Road. I hoped that in due course we'd have our club crest in the centre of ours as they do with theirs down in West London. The '32 Red' styled logo was also now prominent all across the West Stand and in red surprisingly although the 'Global' branding on the South Stand has been in red for a couple of seasons now. With the pitch looking magnificent the whole stadium looked ready for action. I squeezed past the usual culprits already in their seats in row GG, stopping to shake hands with several and muttering the usual, *"here we are again, gluttons for punishment"*, type greetings before finding my own seat, GG 81. I gave Jo a quick hug and then turned to take in the vista; Elland Road looked, quite frankly, magnificent and, daft as it sounds, I was quite emotional!

It would look even better when all four sides were open of course; today only the Revie Stand and the lower tier of the East Stand were being used although a crowd of over 11,000 nicely filled those up. A few flags fluttered at the back of the South Stand but it was otherwise spookily empty while about 140 Italians, I presume they were Italians, occupied the far end of the West Stand. As *"Marching on Together"* belted out for the first time this season I had goose bumps; the whole season stretched ahead of us, all nine months of it or even more if we made those play-offs in May; anything was possible at that precise moment of course.

The game itself could not be described as a classic but Atalanta showed sufficient ability and fitness to ensure it was a good work out for the lads in white. The new home strip had been positively received by the majority of fans when it was unveiled as recently as Thursday night with the usual fanfare at a do in the Pavilion. Atalanta, in a very Italian looking blue and black strip, opened strongly and tested Rob Green as early as the eighth minute, albeit from 25 yards out. Charlie Taylor and Ronaldo Vieira made vital blocks as well while Perico safely played a cross behind for a corner. At the other end Kemar Roofe did what he will always try to do; cut inside from the left and try to curl the ball inside the far post. This time he hit his shot over the bar into the empty South Stand. We were all just starting to settle in for the day with about 25 minutes gone when Alex Mowatt was cynically pulled back 'Italian style' and Leeds were given a free kick about 35 yards from goal; Stuart Dallas and Mowatt both stood over the ball. Dallas clipped it into the box and all we could see was a bit of a kerfuffle which ended up with the ball in the Atalanta net. I've watched numerous replays since and I've been unable to spot what referee Bobby Madley apparently saw; he awarded a penalty for handball. Chris Wood took the kick and smashed it cleanly to the keeper's right, just inside the post. That nightmare at Doncaster had now almost been forgotten and Wood seemed to have perfected the fragile art of penalty taking even though you wouldn't stake your house on him scoring from that distance in open play.

Sadly, the lead didn't last too long; just six minutes in fact. Once again I had to remind myself that this was only a pre-season friendly but still I was disappointed with the manner of the goal. Kentley told me that these days I say every goal we concede is a poor one; *"Well"*, I replied, *"There's a fu***** good reason for that!"*

It began with a sloppy short pass from Vieira that was intercepted just inside the centre-circle. Atalanta quickly moved the ball forward and then out towards their right wing to Franck Kessie. As Kessie slotted the ball through to Marco D'Alessandro, in the inside right channel, he had Toumani Diagouraga right with him but 'Dave' was expending more energy waving his arm in the air claiming offside than tracking the Italian. Predictably, D'Alessandro strode onto the ball and fired it, first time, across Green and into the far corner of the net. Bugger! New season; same old errors.

The goal seemed to unsettle Leeds and for the next few minutes Atalanta began to make us look a bit ragged. Our old friend 'the long ball' cropped up next, one floated diagonally into our box to find Alejandro Gomez running in unmarked. He beat Green to the ball and knocked it towards our goal-line with his outstretched right boot but this time Sol Bamba's telescopic legs rescued the day with inches to spare. The half-time whistle came at a good time for Leeds.

The second half stuttered into action with little quality on show from either side until a long range shot from Andrea Conti woke us up causing Rob Green to fly through the air. Thankfully the shot went narrowly wide. Leeds had made two half-time substitutions with Sacko and Lewie Coyle on for Dallas and Perico, both logical changes. In the 62nd minute Monk made two further changes that no doubt showed he was not yet fully decided on that starting XI to walk out at Loftus Road. Phillips replaced Mowatt and Matt Grimes came on for Diagouraga. It might of course have been that Monk already knew that Alex and 'Dave' would definitely start in London and he was merely protecting them. Who knows?

Then, in the 67th minute, Leeds came alive again and we saw the sort of play our new look side was capable of. Ronaldo Vieira stole the ball deep in his own half and set off at speed 'a la Cook'. Hadi Sacko managed to keep pace and overlapped on the right wing, easily outsmarting the full back as he got to the byline in the north-east corner and he clipped the ball across. Kemar Roofe was in there stooping to make the header but a defender just managed to knock it behind before he made contact. It was a lightening quick break that had us all dreaming of the possibilities for the season ahead.

Kalvin Phillips took the corner from the left wing and we could see big Kyle Bartley trying to meet it at the near post, just ten yards away from us. A defender had a handful of Bartley's shirt and pulled him away but the ball crashed against Roofe's knee and flew in to the net. It was a scrappy goal but worthy reward for the move that led to the corner.

Leeds had the ball in the net again but Bartley was adjudged offside as he bundled in a Matt Grimes free-kick, while Leeds continued to show their old defensive frailties at the other end. Rob Green hit a poor clearance but then atoned with a magnificent save from the resulting long range shot that he clawed away from his top corner. And then Green was on hand again to stop a close range effort resulting from a sloppy midfield pass from Bartley that gave up possession cheaply just when we ought to have been managing the game to its conclusion. This time we got away with the errors but I knew that may not prove to be the case when points were at stake. There were a few more substitutions towards the end with Antonsson replacing Wood, Botaka for Roofe and Luke Murphy for Vieira. My guess was all three of those taken off would start the following week; Wood, Roofe and Vieira. My gut feel was that we'd been given clues to three more who'd start the QPR game too; Mowatt, Dallas and Dave all being "saved" earlier in the game. In the event that no additional new faces arrived and assuming Taylor was still with us, my pick for Loftus Road was therefore:

Green
Coyle or Berardi Bartley Bamba Taylor
Diagouraga
Dallas Vieira Mowatt
Wood Roofe

After the game, Garry Monk confirmed my own summary when he told LUTV: *"I'll be honest; I don't think we were at our very best with the ball today."* Thom Kirwin then did his best to get Monk to comment on particular players but Monk refused; I'd yet to hear him comment on any specific player's performance. Asked if Vieira would be key this season, Monk merely commented that every player was key; every player would play a part at one time or another. I think Thom, like me, felt young Vieira had done enough to get the call.

Leeds United 2 Atalanta 1 (**Wood, (Pen 25**), D'Alessandro (31), **Roofe (68)**) **11,832** (Atalanta 140)

Car Crash

F licking through the BBC Sport website after the Atalanta game, the name 'Uwe Rösler' cropped up. I know I go on about how strange coincidences seem to litter football more than other walks of life but once again this was a typical example of what I mean; Rösler had been appointed manager of League One Fleetwood Town, where Leeds were heading in the first round of the EFL Cup in just over a week's time. That would come days after our first league game of the season at QPR, where Jimmy Floyd Hasselbaink was in charge and indeed throughout August we'd come up against many familiar faces who once plied their trades at Elland Road.

Signing number seven was announced this week; Spanish International midfielder Pablo Hernandez, on a six month loan from Qatari club Al-Arabi. 31 year-old Hernandez looked like another Monk inspired signing as he played with and managed Hernandez at Swansea. The Spaniard was the Swans' record signing in 2012 when they laid out £5.5m for him. It was expected Hernandez would fill the number '10' role, in behind the main striker and it looked like Monk intended him to play a major part as it was said a deal had been agreed to make the move permanent in January. Most folk, including me, were still hoping the next signings would be a centre-back and a defensive midfield general but time was running out to expect them to turn out at Loftus Road. Hernandez wouldn't make it either as Al-Arabi failed to get the paperwork through in time.

One player seemingly not leaving LS11 any time soon and who *would* feature in London was Charlie 'Fackin' Taylor. In response to the transfer request his agent had lodged, the Club put out a statement: *"Garry Monk and Club President Massimo Cellino agreed at the start of the transfer window that Charlie would not be sold and, therefore, the transfer request has been formally rejected. The Club has every confidence that Charlie will continue to conduct himself properly and play his part this season as the Club pushes towards the top of the Championship. The Club will not make any further statement on this matter."[1]*

Those who felt Taylor and his agent were the evil ones here pointed at the statement as evidence that Cellino was not after pocketing the cash from a Taylor sale at all. But the anti-Cellino brigade didn't believe a word of the statement and suggested Taylor would be sold right at the end of the transfer window when it would be too late to recruit a replacement, thus ensuring Cellino kept all the proceeds. Folk in the middle, like me, were only concerned that we might have an unhappy camper in the squad. One of the funniest tweets I saw following the Taylor transfer request was from @michaeloc who wrote: *"When Cellino said we'd be in the Premier League in 2 years I didn't realise that he meant 1 player at a time!"* Following the club statement there were also lots of funny lines about Massimo ensuring he kept hold of his Charlie…

This was a busy week for me on the football front; I was determined to get my '92' back up to date as quickly as possible and when West Ham announced that tickets for their

---

[1]

http://www.leedsunited.com/news/article/2nuz0hb14ylq1cb1bw1p01 62c/title/club-statement-charlie-taylor

Europa League qualifying game with N K Domzale would go on general sale I jumped at the chance to get the London Stadium done. I was joined on the trip by Kentley and met up with Andy the Shrimper and his lad Jim before the match. Andy had been knocked back to 91 after West Ham left the Boleyn Ground at the end of last season while I also needed Cheltenham's Whaddon Road, after they were promoted to the Football League.

The London Stadium, formerly the Queen Elizabeth Olympic Stadium, was the scene of one of the greatest nights in British Olympic history of course when, four years earlier almost to the day, Jess Ennis, Mo Farah and Greg Rutherford all won gold. Now the stadium is a fine modern football venue and it was packed with almost 54,000 for the Hammers' first ever game there. West Ham overturned a first leg deficit of 2 – 1 with a 3 – 0 win, with Sam Byram playing in defence. Kentley and I enjoyed the trip apart from our first experience of the massive Westfield Shopping Centre car parks. After the game we had to use the Centre's state of the art car location system to find the bloody car! There are actually three car parks all next to each other and we were in the wrong one. I also had a long battle with the pay station as I tried for several minutes to get the machine to accept our little green plastic token... eventually a cracking looking young lady in a tiny mini skirt pointed out I was putting it in the wrong slot. I was far too polite to say what first came into my mind...

The following day, the Championship season got underway with a Sky televised game between Fulham and pre-season favourites Newcastle United. In true Championship manner Fulham saw the Toon off with an unlikely 1 – 0 win, courtesy of a Matt Smith header. Smith probably owed his place in the side to the fact that Ross McCormack had recently left for Aston Villa in a £12 million deal.

At Leeds, the squad numbers were finally announced and Sol Bamba was confirmed as Club Captain. There were no surprises other than the fact that number '2' was still vacant; the trial for Gabriele Perico had ended with no contract offer from the club. Latest signing Pablo Hernandez would wear the number '19' shirt.

With the Leeds game pushed back to the Sunday for TV, Saturday was free for me to complete my '92' again with a trip to Cheltenham who faced Leyton Orient in the Robins' first game back in the League. It was a decent encounter; the archetypal 'game of two halves'. Orient took a 3rd minute lead and battered the home side for 45 minutes without adding to their score. Then, Cheltenham dominated the second half, eventually grabbing an equaliser in the 76th minute. It finished 1 – 1. As I sat in the car preparing to journey home after the game, I flicked through the Championship results for the day. The stand out performance came at Ewood Park where Norwich City hammered Blackburn (now with Owen Coyle as manager) 4 – 1. Unusually, there were plenty of goals around with seven scored at the City ground where Forest beat newly promoted Burton Albion 4 – 3. Ipswich beat another newly promoted side, Barnsley, 4 – 2. Blackburn therefore fell straight to the bottom of the table with a minus 3 goal difference. As long as we didn't get beat by three or more on Sunday, we'd at least end the first round of games off the bottom...

With the QPR game a noon kick-off, it was inevitably a very early start. Fortunately it was a beautiful morning at 6:15am when I set off to collect Kentley. I was astonished by the number of magpies foraging at the side of the roads at that hour and I dutifully saluted each one for good luck. I didn't see a solo bird anywhere so I was happy this trip would not end in sorrow...[1]

We'd been told the prime meeting place today was a Wetherspoon pub in Hammersmith but to make that worthwhile we'd have had to set off even earlier and so gave it a miss. Instead we drove straight to Loftus Road, found a roadside parking spot near the ground and then walked into Shepherds Bush. Kentley spotted on his iPhone that Belushi's Bar was set aside for Leeds fans but when we got there it was

---

[1] *One for sorrow, Two for joy, Three for a girl, Four for a boy, Five for silver, Six for gold, Seven for a secret never to be told, Eight's a wish, Nine's a kiss, Ten is a bird you must not miss, MAGPIE.*

already full and stewards were adopting a 'one out, one in' policy. We chatted with big Cliff for a while as we waited but then took his advice and made for the Wetherspoon in the shopping centre just along the road. Cliff told us they weren't letting Leeds fans in but since we wore no colours we gave it a try anyway. Sure enough, at the door we were stopped by two burly security guards. *"Home fans only here mate"* the one tells us as we arrive, *"Can I see your match tickets please?"* *"Err, we're not football fans"* I tell him and then, out of the corner of my eye, I spot that Kentley is wearing his Euro 2016 souvenir T-shirt! He had his arms folded over the logo on his chest. *"Can we see some ID then please mate?"* first security man asks. *"Me?"* I ask with incredulity, *"No one's asked me for ID in 40 years!"* I knew what they were checking for of course, they wanted to make sure we didn't have a Yorkshire post code. I pulled my wallet out of my pocket and prayed that my season card wasn't visible; it wasn't. I showed him my driving license and he studied it. Whether he had any idea where TF9 was I'm not sure but he let us in anyway.

It was wasted effort really, as when I ordered a pint of Doombar I was told they weren't selling alcohol until 11:00am and it was still only 10:45am. We had a pint of Coke each and waited for the team announcement on Twitter.

Green
Berardi Bartley Bamba Taylor
Diagouraga Vieira
Dallas Grimes Roofe
Wood

Subs: Turnbull, Coyle, Cooper, Phillips, Mowatt, Antonsson, Sacko.

Kentley and I reckoned that was the best side we could put out, although we both had doubts over Matt Grimes' inclusion. He'd not shown up well in pre-season at all. We were glad Vieira was given his chance and the rest picked themselves, with Cooper only just getting back to full fitness. The fact that Turnbull was on the bench and not Silvestri, seemed to be due to an injury to the Italian keeper. Five players in the starting XI were making their full debuts.

A half-hour walk back to Loftus Road and about twenty ticket checks through a phalanx of stewards left us hot and sweaty as we took our seats in the upper tier, just to the left of goal. It's a fantastic position up there; in the front row you can lean forward and almost be over the top of the net. The ground was filling up nicely and the pitch obviously looked immaculate. In the distance I counted 10 orange crane gantries behind the stand opposite while a constant stream of planes flew over the back of the main stand to our right. Welcome back to London!

Leeds had over 3,000 fans in the BT School End and from the start we were in great voice. There was a definite feeling of optimism, a feeling that this really might be *the* season. We taunted an 'R's fan over to our left who was wearing a blue and white sombrero and who was thus the spitting image of Steve Evans. *"Your kid's ashamed of you!"* we sang as his little lad appeared to cringe while dad danced around waving his hands and pointing at us. Then Leeds kicked off and we belted out a quick MOT.

Loftus Road was pretty much full, despite the game being shown live on Sky and the atmosphere was boiling in more ways than one. Thankfully we were just in the shade of the roof but it was still roasting. Kentley contemplated opening a Mars bar he'd bought at the services on the way down but by now it was a small pouch of warm liquid; he took my advice and threw it under the seats. When Nigel arrived seconds later he stood on it and a caramel and chocolate stream shot about three feet along the row causing an impromptu Mexican wave as folk leapt out of its way!

Our recent history is littered with moments where we've gone into games full of optimism, convinced things are on the up, only to have the great boot of fate stamp down on our heads from on high. Today would be another one of those. In the 3rd minute we gasped in horror as the Hoops carved through our defence and won the first corner of the day. It was way too easy and then came the car crash.

The left wing corner came winging its way into our box from over to our right and fell to a Rangers' player, unmarked beyond the back post. He scuffed it towards goal on the half volley and it was blocked near our goal line. Another Rangers' boot was first to react as Leeds defenders were spinning round looking for the ball and this time it ballooned into the air directly above the crossbar. If our fans at the front of the upper tier had been quick enough they could have reached out and caught it. But they didn't, and neither did Rob Green. As the ball descended we all expected Green to tip it over the bar and sort out the chaos ready for another corner. But no, instead he launched himself at the ball and flapped with both hands like a blind man trying to catch a balloon in a strong wind. He missed it and, as it continued its descent towards the goal line, it was bundled into the net by Nedum Onuoha. At the time we were all convinced it had to be a foul on Green, someone must surely have barged him out of the way. But replays showed he just fu***** missed the ball! We've nicknamed Silvestri "McFlappyhands" but I'm convinced he'd have made a better fist of this incident. It was a desperate moment; the whole trip spoiled, all the pre-season optimism gone in 180 seconds.

The remainder of the first half was pretty much one way traffic; all of it hurtling towards us and the net just below. There was another horrendous defensive gaff as young Vieira tried to hack the ball away from inside his own box but he only managed to smack it against a QPR boot and the ricochet fired the ball against an upright. Not long after and Sol Bamba lost possession in the centre circle and another quick-fire break had Sebastian Polter racing towards us with the ball. He weaved inside and outside and then inside again before hammering a shot that beat Green but smacked against that same upright and once again away to safety. I thought about all those magpies I'd seen first thing this morning and wondered if our luck was indeed changing for the better. Could we ride out the storm and regroup at half-time? Well, we got there without further damage but as the whistle went there were boos coming from some sections of the Leeds support. This wasn't in the script at all. Massimo Cellino was at the front of the stand to our left and would have heard the chant of *"Time To Go Massimo"*. It was as if there had been no summer break, we'd merely picked up where we left off last season; in a mess. Kentley and I slumped down in our seats and contemplated a dire first half in which Leeds failed to have a single shot on target. How many times last season did we emulate that? Former Leeds and QPR star, Tony Currie was interviewed on the pitch at half-time; how we could do with a player like him now. Asked for a score prediction he replied: *"A three-all draw... well, I have to say something like that don't I?"* I'd have taken that.

Fair play to Leeds, they came out for the second half with purpose and for a while gave it a good go. We still weren't particularly precise in any aspect of the game but we got hold of the ball and attacked with some spirit. Gaetano Berardi had been an early casualty with an injury that saw him replaced by Lewie Coyle after only 22 minutes and now the youngster was bombing down the right wing at every opportunity while Charlie Taylor finally seemed to reawaken on the other side, defying many of our fans who could be heard complaining that his heart wasn't in it. We finally had something to cheer and we roared every time we surged forward although it still looked more like 11 individuals than a team effort out there. We won a couple of free kicks in decent areas and Grimes put one just inches over the bar while Wood hammered another into the wall... the defensive wall for once, not the car park wall. Lewie Coyle fired a shot in that was blocked and Sol Bamba just failed to convert the resulting corner. We were giving it a go, no mistake, but still there was a big fat duck egg in that 'shots on target' column. At the other end, QPR still looked dangerous on the break and Green had to parry one away from the near post which he did well enough. Leeds had now sacrificed Grimes for Antonsson to bolster the attack but all the good work came to nothing in the 73rd minute when we did that other thing we did so often last season; we self-destructed.

Just when we thought we could see the glimpse of a chance to grab an equaliser, QPR suddenly broke away down the right wing. There didn't seem to be any real danger as Steven Caulker slotted the ball in behind Vieira but the next thing we see is Jordan Cousins getting in a tangle with young Ronaldo and down he went, sprawling in the box. The referee immediately pointed to the spot and we knew then that the comeback would never materialise.

Tjaronn Chery despatched the penalty and the game was up. Leeds took off a subdued Kemar Roofe and injected some much needed pace and trickery courtesy of Hadi Sacko but it was all too little too late. When Sacko did create a clear chance for Antonsson, with just the keeper to beat, the Swede shanked the ball wide. We'd end the game still without a single shot on target, not a single test of their keeper Alex Smithies who we've traditionally put plenty of goals past during his long career at Huddersfield. In the final minute we succumbed yet again to a simple diagonal ball over the back of our defence that had Lewie Coyle failing to cope with Polter's strength and the Rangers' man lashed the ball into the top corner from a tight angle to send the home fans into raptures and Leeds to the very foot of the table.

More boos rang out from the ranks of the Leeds fans all around us and I winced; my limited understanding of psychology tells me that can only make things worse. We need to support the lads at times like this, not batter them. They need their confidence boosted, not trodden underfoot like that squidgy Mars bar. As it was, Sol Bamba gathered his weary troops together and herded them over towards us; it was a brave move. About half of our fans applauded them as they applauded us but the other half were vitriolic in their abuse. Fans turned on each other at that point as some no doubt were aware, like me, of the damage the flying insults could do to this young team. As the players turned to leave the pitch I thought the worst was over but then a chant of *"What the fu***** hell was that?"* broke out and had plenty of support. I winced again and tried to think how I'd feel if I was a player getting that sort of ridicule from my own fans. Surely it can't do any good? I could imaging Charlie Taylor getting straight on the phone to his agent yelling *"Get me the f*** out of here!"*

Kentley and I made our way back to the car and carefully climbed in; it was like an oven! As we picked our way through the streets around the ground we went wrong umpteen times as we were distracted by girls in various stages of undress on the pavements of Shepherds Bush. It was only mid-afternoon of course and the sun was still beating down. Eventually we worked our way onto Western Avenue and then the motorways heading north. As we passed one of the Leeds coaches, one with a *"Jolly Leeds"* flag in the back window, Kentley regaled me with the post-match comments made by Garry Monk which were now doing the rounds on Twitter. *"In the second half we were better without being at our best. We had a bit more of a reaction but you can't make those individual mistakes and concede the goals we did"*. That was the key for me. All last season our defence was guilty of stupid, silly errors that gifted the opposition goals, goals that cost us games while at the other end we just were not clinical enough with our own finishing. We thought we'd strengthened our defence with the addition of the experienced Rob Green and big Kyle Bartley but here we were again, after the very first game of the new season, discussing exactly the same problems. It was a worry.

"Woah, what the f*** is he doing?" I braked sharply as a little Honda Jazz drifted into the middle lane in front of me. We were on the M6 near junction 5; Kentley was asleep in the passenger seat. I initially thought the Honda was pulling out to overtake something and hadn't seen me behind him but now he continued to drift into the outside lane and I had to brake further to avoid undertaking it. I could see cars in my mirror all starting to slow, wondering what the hell the Honda was doing. Still he drifted to the right and then ran off the carriageway altogether and crashed into the Armco, sliding along it throwing debris and sparks onto the carriageway as it went. We were now past it, narrowly avoiding a van coming up the inside and Kentley was now wide awake and screaming *"What the f****'s he doing?"* at the top of his voice. We could only surmise the driver had fallen asleep at the wheel and that had left him drifting slowly towards the central reservation; it was a miracle he'd not collected anyone on the way or caused any of the cars behind to pile into each other. We'd motored on a few more miles before I began to wonder if maybe those magpies had protected us from sorrow today after all…

QPR 3 **Leeds United 0** (Onuoha (4), Chery (73 pen), Polter (90+4)) 16,764 (**Leeds 3,213**)

Fleetwood Mac and the four blondes

I'd been looking forward to the trip to Fleetwood with greater anticipation than normal. When I did Highbury Stadium back in March 2015 for the Cod Army's game with Preston as part of my 'doing the 92', Mrs W came with me but we'd not really had a good look round as the weather was so awful. We decided to try again for our League Cup tie. Blow me down; we awoke on the morning of the game to another miserable, cloudy and wet outlook. I joked on my Twitter account that I'd be taking my Fleetwood Mac…

We aborted our plan to drive straight to Fleetwood and instead headed for Blackpool; we reasoned there'd be more to occupy us there on a wet day. We had lunch and the first pint of the day in the Albert and Lion, a Wetherspoon pub on the front near the Tower where I'd been on previous visits when Leeds played at Bloomfield Road; it's a sort of homing instinct we Leeds fans have. The place was rammed and we were lucky to find a free table having narrowly missed out on another when a fat bruiser of a bloke in a Burnley top muscled in front of Mrs W saying: *"Oi! That's my f****** table don't be thinking of sitting there love"*. I was on the point of debating the issue with him when I spotted a tattoo on the back of his neck. It read simply: *"Burnley suicide squad"*.

Other Leeds fans were demonstrating the homing instinct too; within minutes of sitting down, first Nigel strolled up and then Martin, Daniel and Billy. Nigel had clearly not checked the weather forecast as he had a summer short-sleeved shirt and not much else on. He was due on the 11pm train back to Dewsbury via Manchester so was hoping the game didn't go to extra-time or he'd be buggered; stranded in the North West with, unless he got lucky this afternoon, precious little to keep him warm. The other lads had already booked rooms in what must be the cheapest doss house in Blackpool at twelve quid a night! Martin clearly knew the risks of such prudence and said he'd likely as not sleep on the floor rather than risk the no-doubt well used bed linen. It wasn't just Leeds that couldn't ever get a clean sheet in Blackpool. We left the lads to it and went exploring along the sea front, leaning into the wind and trying to dodge the showers but eventually gave up the struggle and had coffee and cake in a café on the North Pier.

We'd arranged to pick up Keith and Gill from their hotel up on Queens Promenade around 4:30pm; they'd journeyed up from Southend and were stopping in Blackpool for a couple of nights. We then headed on up to Fleetwood where we'd decided to partake of the hospitality of Syd Little at his 'Little Restaurant' in The Strawberry Gardens pub. Syd is one half of the comedy duo 'Little and Large' and these days runs the restaurant with his wife Sheree. Syd is often said to be Fleetwood's most famous son even though he was actually born down the road in Blackpool. The 'Strawberry' is a fine old brick built Victorian pub on a street corner five minutes from Highbury Stadium and is well worth a visit.

Arriving before 5pm there weren't many in at first but over the course of the next two hours the usual flood of Leeds fans poured in to sample not only Syd's excellent home cooking but also a huge array of well-kept real ale. We both had our wives with us but Keith and I still worked our way through four different blondes[1] during the evening and enjoyed them all. Nigel appeared at one point, still in shirt sleeves and oblivious to the rain we could see pouring down outside. He'd arrived by tram and had avoided a soaking so far.

There'd been much speculation over what team Monk would put out for this game. On the one hand some thought he'd play the same XI we saw in London to give those players a chance of redemption. On the other hand some felt he may need to rest a few to ensure everyone was fresh for Birmingham on Saturday in what would surely be considered a more important

---

[1] That would be Lancaster Blonde (4% ABV, Lancaster Brewery); Junior (3.6% ABV, Old School Brewery, Warton Crag, North Lancs); Old Trout (4.5% ABV, Worsthorne Brewing Co, Lancs): and Corby Blonde (4.2% ABV, Cumberland Brewery).

game; after all we were never going to win the EFL Cup were we?

Green

Coyle Bartley Cooper (Capt) Taylor

Vieira Phillips

Sacko Hernandez Roofe

Wood

Subs: Bamba, Antonsson, Dallas, Grimes, Turnbull, Mowatt, Denton.

So it was pretty much the defence that finished the QPR game but with Cooper instead of Bamba to give Coops some match practise after his lay-off. Phillips was in for 'Dave' and Pablo Hernandez got his debut now his clearance had come through. In contrast to the way most Championship sides played substantially weakened sides this week, this was a strong Leeds XI. Birmingham for instance, who were our next league opposition, played Oxford the previous night and started just 2 of the players from their opening league fixture. They paid the price too; losing 1 – 0. The excitement for most fans was the first opportunity to see Pablo Hernandez; how would he cope with a wet 'n' windy Wednesday night on the Fylde coast?

Having quaffed our fourth blonde, Keith, Nigel and I said farewell to the ladies and headed out into the rain and down the road to Highbury. Keith and I had terrace tickets in the Percy Ronson Stand while Nigel had opted for the seating section to our right. We stood with Kentley, @Muckyfat, Jo and several other familiar faces; Chris and Phil M and Smithy were all in our section.

The scene was set for a classic English cup tie under the floodlights with the rain drifting across the pitch. With Leeds playing in their new blue away strip and the Cod Army in Arsenal-like red shirts with white sleeves the scene reminded me very much of a famous game played at the other 'Highbury' back in 2003. On that occasion Kewell, Harte and Viduka all scored to pull off an unlikely 3 – 2 win that kept us in the Premier League. The following season there would be no late season relegation escape though and we've been trying to get our place back ever since.

I felt sure Garry Monk would have this team of ours up and at it from the first minute; another defeat, especially to a League One side when playing our best available selection, was unthinkable and potentially fatal to Monk's tenure remembering how quickly Dave Hockaday and Uwe Rösler bit the dust following poor early results and League Cup exits. I expected a big Leeds win. The Fleetwood fans are a confident lot mind and up at the back of the stand opposite was a Fleetwood flag with the legend: "Ultras de Cod"!

Fleetwood played towards the Percy Ronson end in the first half so we got to see their attacks at very close quarters; there were plenty of them. It was like QPR all over again. Here we were full of expectation and hope and yet out on the pitch it was the home side calling the shots. The only difference was that last Sunday the game was played in brilliant sunshine and thirty degree heat while tonight it was peeing down and freezing cold. Once again our back four looked about as likely to grab a clean sheet tonight as Martin and his mates in that Blackpool boarding house. It was about as useful in keeping the Cod Army out as Nigel's flimsy shirt was against the Fleetwood rain.

The game was only minutes old when Fleetwood had their first meaningful strike at goal. A long clearance from Chris Neal in the home goal was misjudged by Cooper and the ball skidded off his head and straight into the path of Devante Cole. Fortunately this Old King Cole didn't become a merry old soul and he flashed the ball wide. But in the 13th minute we were not so lucky. A right wing corner was initially headed away by Leeds but the ball went straight back to the corner-taker. He had loads of time to weigh up his options with Kalvin Phillips adopting no more than a watching brief. When the ball came over again it skidded off the top of Wood's head and fell at the feet of Victor Nirennold, tussling with Lewie Coyle at the back post. Just as on Sunday at QPR, Coyle was muscled out of the way and the ball ran forward to Aaron Holloway who got his foot in before Coops to poke it into the net. Heads in hands time yet again and suddenly it wasn't only the weather looking bleak.

Leeds huffed and puffed their way through the rest of the first half but you'd have been hard pressed to tell me whether the Championship team was playing in red or blue had you been a visiting alien who'd dropped in to see what was going on and who just happened to speak English. The only positive aspect for Leeds was the obvious talent possessed by Pablo Hernandez, although he had a very strange, *"What the f*** am I doing here?"* look on his face throughout. He was clearly going to bring us something we have very little of; quality on the ball.

Liam Cooper was replaced at half-time, Monk obviously wanting to ease him back in gently after his long lay-off. Sol Bamba loped onto the pitch to take his place. Gradually, minute by minute, Leeds started to get a grip of the match much like they did at QPR in the second half down there. That response was eventually snuffed out with another defensive calamity but there were no further episodes of that yet tonight. Leeds' good approach work was still being regularly squandered though, usually with shots flying over the stand we were sheltering in. I couldn't remember what was behind our stand but whatever it was it was now full of balls; I could see Kentley dashing round there after the game to see if he could add to his collection. We were looking much brighter but it was getting very late; we were into the last couple of minutes.

Mowatt and Antonsson had replaced Sacko and Vieira midway through the half and it was this pairing that conjured up our late, late equaliser. Charlie Taylor had the ball on the left wing but he stopped and touched it inside to Mowatt. Alex went past one defender and then scuffed his left foot cross towards Antonsson at the near post, right on the angle of the six-yard box. In a flash, a single touch from Antonsson allowed him to swivel 180 degrees and lash the ball high into the roof of the net, beating the keeper at his near post. It was some finish. We'd all accepted defeat by this time so that was a special moment of redemption celebrated by the players right in front of us and it wasn't long before a chant of *"Wemberley! Wemberley! We're the famous Leeds United and we're off to Wemberley!"* broke out in a sort of hysterical reaction from the Leeds fans. It even looked as though Leeds could snatch an unlikely winner in the final seconds as, roared on by a now crazed 1,300 fans, Leeds tried to batter the Cods into submission. (This isn't just thrown together you know!) Mowatt fluffed a great chance when he mishit a back-post shot into the turf and the keeper was able to turn it over. The corner came to nothing and the ref blew the whistle. It would be extra-time again, just as it was at Donny last season.

The extra thirty minutes was frenetic; mostly with Leeds pressing forward as we looked the fitter of the two sides. We had the momentum now too and it only took four minutes for us to grab the lead. Kemar Roofe turned in the inside left channel before lobbing a clever little ball over the home defence. Marcus Antonsson was there and he was shaping to strike it on the first bounce but Ashley Eastham was there too, albeit on the wrong side of his man. His attempt to get his boot to the ball merely caused him to catch Antonsson on the thigh and our man went down. Penalty! Chris Wood strode up; those Doncaster demons now long banished and struck the ball firmly into the corner of the net. Cue more *"Wemberley"* chants and I'm texting Mrs W to tell her she could make her way to the pub car park to pick me up in twenty five minutes.

I guess we should have known better with our years of experience of watching Leeds give up winning positions but this is a new era, we were entitled to think things would be different weren't we? That faith was misplaced of course and with just nine minutes to go we fu**** up again.

Most of us weren't watching the game, we were discussing who we wanted in the next round; Chelsea away seemed favourite but no one seemed to know if they were one of the Premier League teams due to enter the competition in Round 2 or whether they were exempt until Round 3. I was checking my phone to see if Mrs W had responded. Fleetwood had the ball at the far end of the ground, near the corner on their right wing. Suddenly it's crossed low into our box and we can see Fleetwood's Ashley Hunter, a big white '22' on his back, all alone in acres of space. The next thing we see is all the Fleetwood players celebrating and a Mexican wave heading around the rest of the ground as the Fleetwood fans sprang to their feet. Bugger! It was one of those moments, one of those bloody Leeds United moments; 17 minutes of joyful expectation and celebration and then stunned silence and profanities all around. Triple bugger! '17' minutes did I say? That bloody number continued to haunt us.

The game went to penalties and to be honest there was no particular tension amongst the Leeds fans; we all expected to lose at that point, probably with one or more of our players ballooning the ball miles over the bar. But you know what? All five of our kicks were immaculate. Even Chris Wood, who strode up to take the first, varied his technique and smashed his into the roof of the net. Antonsson, Mowatt, Kalvin Phillips and finally, Hernandez all followed suit; not that Fleetwood weren't as clinical mind. Rob Green had no chance with the first four of their kicks. But then up stepped Eggert Jonsson and of course the pressure had now ramped up a fair bit; if he was to miss, Leeds won the game. The Leeds fans knew this as well of course and whereas for the previous kicks we'd remained fairly calm, now we were hollering at the tops of our voices in one of those ridiculous crescendos we often do when the opposition keeper is taking a goal kick. The one that ends with, *"Woaaaaaah you fat bas****!"* Jonsson struck his kick towards the right side as we looked on 100 yards away and we could see Green had guessed correctly and was sailing through the air that way. Incredibly he got both hands to the ball and pushed it away! Leeds won 5 – 4 on penalties.

There was no sign of Nigel as Kentley and I made our way back to the car park to meet Mrs W but we spoke about how ridiculous it was that he'd come out today with no jacket or coat. It was raining quite hard now and even with coats we were both soaked...

Mrs W had just parked the car on the drive at home when my mobile rang. It was Martin B... he had Nigel with him, a cold, wet Nigel who was stranded in Blackpool with no coat and no place to stop. I think Martin was telling me off for not looking after him. As it was, Martin did the decent thing and smuggled Nigel into his B & B room; I'd have loved to be a fly on that particular wall!

Fleetwood 2 **Leeds Utd 2 AET** (Holloway (13), **Antonsson (89), Wood (pen 94)**, Hunter (111)) 3,326 (**Leeds 1,325**)

"Soft"

Leeds continued to rack up new signings with number eight arriving the day after Fleetwood. Luke Ayling, a 24 year-old defender and occasional midfielder from Bristol City joined for an undisclosed fee on a three-year contract. That spare number '2' shirt was given to him and he spoke about how he was looking forward to turning out at Elland Road against Birmingham. Those were two good indicators that Ayling would be our first choice right-back. While Ayling was signing on, Jordan Botaka was signing off as he went to join Charlton on loan for the season. It seemed that Hadi Sacko had got the nod as team wizard.

I'd also joined a new team; I was travelling with the Shropshire Whites. I'd decided to try to cut down on the mileage I was putting on the car and spotted that the 'Shroppy Whites' were trying to increase their numbers to run a bigger coach. They regularly run match-day transport from Wolverhampton going via Telford, Shrewsbury and Whitchurch which is just 14 miles up the A49 from me.

More often than not the Shropshire Whites only fill a 17-seat mini-bus and I've frequently seen it trundling along the highways and byways of England when making my own way to games. Today though, for the first competitive home game of the season, they'd almost filled a 52-seater. It was very pleasant letting someone else cope with the stresses and strains of the driving as I sat flicking through my Twitter timeline. We had a trouble free run up to Leeds although we could see the M6 going South was the usual car park; miles and miles of stationary traffic caused by a couple of minor accidents.

The coach dropped me and a few others off outside Billy's Bar on Elland Road before carrying on to take the rest into Leeds where they'd have a few sherbets before coming back to the ground. I was heading for my usual session in the Pavilion or 'Fans' Village' as it had now been rebranded. On the face of it, the changes were good; the entrance fee for members had been reduced to just £3 and you could still get that back against a pint at the bar. There were four new 'themed' areas too which you would have thought would make getting food and drink easier. Strangely though, the opposite seemed to be the case; there were huge queues at all the bars long before kick-off. No one appeared to have told the bar staff the entrance vouchers had come down in price either. I handed over my three pound voucher together with three pound coins for my 'two pints for six pounds' deal and I carefully made my way back the table with my booty. Just as I put down the beers a chap tapped me on the shoulder and gave me 90p in coins; *"You forgot your change mate"* he told me. In fact it turned out that the vouchers were now worth £3.90 even though we only paid £3 for them. Things were looking up!

The other downside of the revamped Pavilion was that they'd decided we needed live music; for the avoidance of doubt Mr Cellino, *"WE DON'T NEED F****** LIVE MUSIC!"* They tried this a couple of years ago and we all complained; we go in there to have a pint or three and chat football with our mates or watch the TV game, not to be deafened by some young wannabee rock stars. The band today was 'Jela', a three man outfit from France playing a range of classics from the Stones' 'Jumping Jack Flash' to Bowie's 'Rebel, Rebel'. They were good... but, *"WE DON'T F****** NEED IT!"* and they played for a bloody hour and a half!

We had a good turnout of regulars crammed round our table; all the Durham lads were there, Kev, Nigel, Derek and Shirley, Wigan White aka Alan, Smithy, John and Alan and I think most of us thought Leeds would get off the mark today. There was nothing about the team Monk picked to change our minds.

Green
Ayling Bartley Bamba (Capt) Taylor
Sacko Vieira Hernandez Mowatt
Wood Antonsson

Subs: Turnbull, Coyle, Cooper, Grimes, Phillips, Dallas, Roofe.

I was happy with it, though I did feel Chris Wood was very definitely in the last chance saloon having offered very little to us throughout pre-season and in our first two games at QPR and Fleetwood. I'd have gone with Roofe and Antonsson.

Elland Road looked good; over 27,000 nicely filled all four sides, with only the upper tier of the East Stand and a few rows of seats around the thousand or so Blues' fans in the West Stand left empty. The West Stand was now adorned with new advertising for Crosswater and Burlington and the pitch of course looked fabulous.

In his programme notes, Garry Monk spoke of how the only thing he wanted from the fans was for them to *"bring 'THE NOISE'. Give these players everything you have and back them with everything you've got for every minute of every game, through the good and difficult moments."* We're actually OK at dealing with the good moments but we do struggle a bit with the difficult ones, despite having had far more practice with those over the years.

For 14 minutes, Leeds had us roaring them on and making plenty of noise as they tore into the Blues playing some lovely attacking football while we sang *"We are Leeds"* and MOT with a gusto befitting the first home game of the season; voice boxes had been well rested over the summer. Seven of our side started at Fleetwood of course but there was no sign of any tiredness despite the extra-time and the heavy conditions up there. In contrast, few of the Blues started in their EFL Cup defeat at home to Oxford and in any case they'd had an extra day's recovery having played on Tuesday not Wednesday.

Leeds should really have taken the lead when the ball fell to Antonsson, 15 yards from goal, but he contrived to blast the ball against the crossbar. Bartley and Mowatt also had chances. The worry, as so often, was that we were not hitting the target. It became more than a worry in the 15th minute though, as our defence once again proved to be about as watertight as a cracked colander.

It all came from a blocked Mowatt shot but then Stephen Gleeson picked the ball up deep in his own half and set off at pace into Leeds territory with three Leeds players tracking but never challenging him. At precisely the right moment he stroked the ball forward, dissecting Bamba and Bartley and finding Maghoma running onto it with Charlie Taylor caught the wrong side. Green came charging out just as Taylor slid in and all three players collided in a heap. Unluckily, the ball ricocheted off Taylor and into our net. It was that miserable feeling of being teased again. Teased that we'd got things sorted and we were finally starting to show what we can do, only to then shoot ourselves in the foot through a piece of sloppy, super-soft defending. The Leeds fans were temporarily silenced despite this being one of those 'difficult moments' Monk had mentioned. For ten minutes we found it tough, as did our lads on the pitch, but fair play, eventually we got it together again and in the 27th minute we levelled it up.

Leeds played their way from deep with a series of careful passes before Vieira purred away with the ball like a newly serviced Rolls Royce; he touched the ball to Antonsson. Marcus held the ball up well and then poked it back to Alex Mowatt. Mowatt half stumbled over an attempted tackle but still managed to come out the other side and thread the ball inside the full back and there was Hadi Sacko running onto it. To be honest, Sacko's shot from a tight angle had no right to beat a Championship keeper but the usually reliable Tomasz Kuszczak made a right Horlicks of it and it squeezed in under his body. That was another good moment and up we all went again, suddenly full of optimism that this was that long awaited turning point from which we'd go on to win the game, go on a long unbeaten run and end the season at least in the top six... Ok, Ok, I admit it; I forgot we are Leeds for a split second. Leeds continued to impress up to half-time with new boy Luke Ayling powering a shot on the half-volley that stung Kuszczak's fingers; it was still a rare shot on target for Leeds though. The home fans were reasonably satisfied with the first half despite that latest example of our chronic defensive issues. Same again second half and we ought to get some points on the board…

Quite what happened to us in the second half, no one really knows but once again we'd show our astonishing propensity to self-destruct and a complete lack of battling spirit. It could possibly have been the exertions at Highbury catching up with us and certainly Pablo Hernandez looked a very tired player as he started to get caught in possession and regularly left his passes a yard short doing a passable impression of Lewis Cook on a bad day. That defence of ours was looking fragile too; clearances were finding touch more regularly than white shirts. The nervousness apparent on the pitch spread to the stands and the first mutterings of dissent could be heard; Charlie Taylor inevitably came in for a verbal bashing as folk assumed his failings were down to him wanting away, not tiredness. That horrible tendency to pass the ball back and forth along the defensive line also returned; the one we regularly saw last season when we ran out of ideas. In short, we looked soft all over the pitch, brushed off the ball too often, too easily. The new half was ten minutes old when the inevitable happened.

A right-wing Birmingham corner came to nothing and was eventually cleared but culminated with a simple left wing cross into the Leeds area. The ball bounced back off Vieira with no one seemingly taking control of the situation. Michael Morrison was first to react and lashed the ball into the roof of the net and 26,000 dreams were broken.

Many Leeds fans suddenly forgot Monk's plea to *"bring THE NOISE"* or at least I don't think the noise we then heard was what he had in mind. Five minutes after conceding the goal Leeds made a substitution and as soon as fans saw the big red number '9' on the fourth official's board, many began to cheer the fact that Chris Wood was being substituted. Kemar Roofe trotted on perhaps thinking the roars of approval were for him and perhaps some were, but it was mostly a vote of no confidence in Wood.

Roofe injected some urgency and we were better in the last half-hour without looking likely to score. Further subs saw Phillips replace a tired Alex Mowatt and, very late on, Dallas replaced an exhausted Hernandez. Roofe should probably have got us a point but he fluffed a header from ten yards. With a defence like ours we can't be so wasteful and we'd register just three shots on target in this game from eleven attempts although admittedly those stats were identical for Birmingham too. Games are won and lost by fine margins in the Championship. There were boos ringing around Elland Road at the final whistle and once again the unpleasant sight of fans gesticulating and hurling abuse at the players as they came to applaud us. It was not a majority by any means but more than a few. After the game, Garry Monk was livid and constantly told the assembled press how we were *"soft"*. He even referred to being told the club had been *"soft for years"*.

"I'm not here to cover everything up – it was softness, and I don't like to see that. I know we've got a young group with a lot of young players, but you have to be a man when you're a professional footballer. Nobody can stop you from battling and trying to win those second and third balls. Nobody can stop you from putting a shift in. We didn't do that in the second half and, ultimately, that was what cost us".[1]

That was a good summary; Monk knew we had a problem and was determined to try to deal with it. There wasn't much time though ahead of the next game versus Fulham who had a perfect league record of two wins from two. Three other clubs shared that record; QPR, Huddersfield and Bristol City. Leeds climbed off the bottom of the table only by virtue of the fact Blackburn got walloped again; this time 3 – 0 at Wigan.

Leeds United 1 Birmingham City 2 (Maghoma (15), **Sacko (27)**, Morrison (55)) **27,392** (Birmingham 960)

---

[1] *http://www.leedsunited.com/news/article/1jcff7sv25s4013m044f1lu5 4y/title/birmingham-garry-monks-verdict*

Earo!

The eve of the Fulham game saw yet more news on the transfer front. The Liam Bridcutt saga had been going on for weeks, possibly months if Sunderland and Leeds had, as was believed, been talking since the end of last season. Earlier in the week the news broke that the clubs had agreed a deal and then it was just a matter of Bridcutt agreeing personal terms. That took a few more days but then on Monday 15th August, Phil Hay tweeted: *"Bingo - Liam Bridcutt to undergo a medical with Leeds United tonight. He's accepted a two-year contract. #lufc"* Bridcutt seemed to make a huge difference to Leeds' results when he arrived in November under Steve Evans and was actually one of five nominees for player of the season despite not doing the full term, such was his perceived impact. The feeling amongst Leeds fans I knew was one of relief; it was like getting back an important jigsaw piece that had temporarily been lost down the back of the sofa. The unknown factor though was that Leeds now had a very different jigsaw, although the issue Bridcutt seemed to fix last time was in protecting a suspect defence; thus far that issue hadn't gone away. Bridcutt was rumoured to be the highest paid player on Leeds' books.

If the Liam Bridcutt news wasn't good enough for anyone, late in the evening, still on that eve of Fulham day, rumours began to do the rounds that yet more signings were in the offing. It was said Leeds were close to signing 24-year old full-back, Bryan Verboom from Belgian side S.V. Zulte Waregemand and Swedish international centre-back Pontus Jansson from Torino. I had no idea if either was any good but I was absolutely certain we had to do something different with the defence. If these latest rumours were true, we could be close to a completely new back five compared with last season and that just had to be an improvement… didn't it?

There was a time on the day before the Fulham game that I thought I might not be there. The weather was perfect on the Monday and Mrs W and I decided to have a go at the garden. Our garden is mainly bushes and surrounded by hedges and trees so it's mostly a matter of zipping round with the hedge-trimmer. I was attacking the tallest of our hedges; a 12 foot high mixed hedge of mostly holly. Now I'm very much an amateur in the garden so have none of the right equipment and even the hedge-trimmer I have is donkeys' years old and weighs a ton; it's electric and the lead is about three yards shorter than it was originally due to the number of times I've cut through it. So there I am, perched on the top of my aluminium ladders with an old mattress wrapped around the top to prevent it falling through the hedge and I'm up there grappling with this huge, heavyweight trimmer with Mrs W hanging on to the ladder for dear life. Quite how she'd make any difference were I to topple off I'm not sure; think eight stone woman at one end trying to hold up ladder with fifteen stone bloke and hedge trimmer attached to the other end and you get the picture. Anyway, it's all going spiffily well and we're almost finished for the day when suddenly I'm aware that amongst all of the dust and debris I'm disturbing from the top of the hedge there appear to be a lot of flying things as well. Undeterred I keep going and then all of a sudden I feel this excruciating pain in my left hand between my thumb and first finger, right in that fleshy part between the two. *"Ah f***, what the f*** was that?"* I scream at the top of my voice, swinging the hedge-trimmer off to the right to check my left hand. *"Splut"* goes the trimmer in a shower of sparks as the blade slices through the cable while I vaguely hear Mrs W shouting *"David, shut up, the neighbours will hear you!"* *"F*** the f****** neighbours"* I scream, now having thrown the immobilised cutter onto the top of the hedge so I could more closely inspect my damaged hand, *"Something's just f****** stung me"*. The pain now emanating from the sting was incredible, I've never experienced anything like it; it throbbed and ached and felt like it was going to swell up like a balloon. The pain in my hand had taken my mind off the more important task of keeping my balance and now the still live cable snaked its way towards me. I swayed out of the way but the ladder wanted to go the other way and I threw out my good hand to steady myself. *"Oh f****** hell!"* I screamed again as I grabbed a handful of holly with my previously good hand to stop myself falling. Holding my throbbing left hand in my stinging right I slowly slid down the ladder still effing and blinding while Mrs W is grappling with the cable like she's got hold of a poisonous snake by the tail; she'd thought she was helping by pulling it out of the way!

We eventually discovered two bees' nests hidden away in the top of the hedge and concluded that one little bugger had been despatched to see off the alien that was disturbing their homes; he did a good job too as that was the end of gardening for the day and it would be a month before we ventured back to complete the job. As to the hand, well, weirdly it hurt like hell for twenty minutes as I held it first under the cold tap and then poured Dettol over it and then amazingly the pain disappeared as quickly as it began.

The mini heat-wave continued as Kentley picked me up from home on Tuesday afternoon. It was 4pm. It would prove to be another nightmare trip that began in weird circumstances. As we sat on the bridge over junction 15 of the M6 waiting for the traffic lights to change, I happened to look down to the slip-road joining the M6 southbound. Incredibly, there was a bloke on crutches making his way down the slip road and then, horror of horrors, he started to edge into the carriageway with the rush hour traffic flying by in all three lanes! Somehow, a van driver managed to come to a halt and sort of blocked him from manoeuvring any further into the road. Another van cottoned on to what was happening and came to a halt behind the first one to make an even longer barrier. Cars and lorries were now backed up on the slip-road as well as the three lanes of the carriageway and from somewhere under the bridge another pedestrian appeared and began talking to the bloke on the sticks. Sadly, our lights changed and we had to set off and of course we were heading north up the M6 away from the incident. I've tried in vain to find out exactly how the incident ended and what on earth the bloke thought he was doing. Kentley tried to lend some levity to the situation by winding down his window and shouting at the top of his voice: *"It's only been three games mate, don't f*****g give up on us yet, give it bloody time man!"*

It was gone 7pm when we rolled up in the car park at Elland Road after coming across numerous hold-ups on the roads. That meant there was no point going in the Pavilion as we guessed it would take 'til kick-off to get a beer. The only option was to grab a burger from the van at the top of Lowfields Road and then go straight in the ground. Kentley was obviously in good form as he joked with the woman serving in the van that *"grandad"* would pay...

There were four changes to the Leeds line up from Saturday:

Green
Ayling Bartley Cooper (Capt) Taylor
Dallas Phillips Hernandez Roofe
Wood Antonsson

Subs: Turnbull, Coyle, Bamba, Doukara, Vieira, Mowatt, Sacko.

The game had just started when I took my seat and I had to quickly scan the numbers on the backs of the shirts. It wasn't the side I wanted – it had far too much dead Wood in it for me – but it was an attack minded side with Dallas and Roofe

- 71 -

either side of just the two specialist midfielders. In the red shirts of Fulham there were several familiar faces including former Leeds striker Matt Smith, the evergreen Scott Parker and former Leeds youngster Tom Cairney. Cairney was released by Leeds at the age of 16 having been at the club since he was seven and he's been tormenting us ever since, including the game at Elland Road the previous season when he scored a fine goal in the 17th minute. Lewis Cook equalised that one with his wonder goal of course. Once again, it might have been advisable for the Leeds players to have a read of the match-day programme; particularly the "Ask Away" section in which Tom 'I'd Radebe Leeds' Bradley asked a Fulham fan for his views on the game. The comment on Tom Cairney was: "Tom has started really well and I feel will be one of our key performers. He is more than capable of striking the ball and if Leeds don't pick up this threat he will cause plenty of problems."... Fulham also included 16 year-old wonder kid Ryan Sessegnon in their side.

Fulham were these days playing without their deadly duo of last season, Ross McCormack and Moussa Dembele, who'd both left in the summer for Villa and Celtic respectively but Smith and new boy Sone Aluko had made a good start and Fulham had won all three of their games so far. Leeds were yet to win one so this was going to be another tough encounter.

A better than expected crowd of over 21,000 was inside Elland Road with just the Cheese Wedge spoiling the look around the ground even with a huge '32Red' banner spread over half the seats in that section. It would prove to be an entertaining game but most of the entertainment came from the team in red who looked a bit like Man U in their red shirts and black shorts and socks. They played a bit like them too.

Fulham passed the ball about neatly and quickly and in the early stages bossed the midfield. Thankfully though, their ability to hit the target with the chances they were carving out was hardly any better than ours. They did strike a post and Smith had a couple of towering headers go close but the best chance ironically fell to Leeds. Antonsson fought his way through a tackle to find himself one on one with Fulham keeper, David Button, but in a carbon copy of his chance down at Loftus Road he pulled his left foot shot wide of the right post in front of the South Stand. He was looking far more lively and useful than Chris Wood though who also made a complete hash of a decent chance. I did wonder if he'd be subbed at half-time for Doukara who was seemingly in favour again. Leeds hung on and went in to generous applause at half-time; the Leeds fans appreciative of the effort if not the quality on show from their heroes. Quite what Liam Bridcutt and Pontus Jansson thought about the display we could only guess but they were both sat together up in the West Stand.

The second half began as the first had ended with Fulham having the lion's share of the ball and creating the majority of the chances and Matt Smith powered yet another of his trademark headers against a post. Leeds had short spells when they wrestled the initiative from the visitors and during those spells the crowd did their bit in urging them on. Roofe and Hernandez both tested Button with fierce shots. On the hour mark Monk made his first change as Ronaldo Vieira replaced Stuart Dallas who'd taken a couple of knocks. Chris Wood spurned another chance as he was put through by Hernandez and there were more murmurs of discontent from the Kop. It was the last contribution for Pablo who was then replaced by an eager looking Alex Mowatt, spurred on no doubt by the knowledge that midfield slots were becoming few and far between with Bridcutt and Hernandez presumably guaranteed to start.

Still Fulham fizzed the ball about, with Scott Parker orchestrating them in the middle and Cairney full of inventive little runs. We were getting close though and Kentley suggested he was looking likely to see his nil-nil prediction come true. There were 13 minutes to go but it was unlucky for us.

Fulham moved the ball about in quick triangles down in the southwest corner and eventually it came to the feet of Kevin McDonald who'd worked himself about six yards of space from Charlie Taylor. Charlie looked mesmerised by the sheer speed at which Fulham were shifting the ball. It was then moved inside to that little lad Cairney, the 'too small for Leeds' Cairney who is these days six feet tall. He let the ball run across behind him thus evading any challenge from Vieira and then he turned and curled a perfect shot past the diving Rob Green into the far corner of the net. It was a lovely strike, reminiscent of something Mirco Antenucci might have come up with last season. There was an audible sigh from the Kop all around me as everyone contemplated another defeat; not that any of us had ever seen Leeds lose the first three league games of a season... that hadn't happened since 1936!

Garry Monk sensed the significance of the looming defeat too and immediately turned to Hadi Sacko to try to rescue the situation. The fact he took Kemar Roofe off baffled me mind, I would have thought we might have sacrificed someone from the back if we were chasing an unlikely equaliser but what do I know? The minutes started to tick by at a phenomenal rate now although Leeds were at last throwing the kitchen sink at the problem with Sacko attacking down the right and Charlie Taylor on the left. Just as the added time board went up, we were all celebrating as Chris Wood found space at the back post and rose majestically in the air to meet Marcus Antonsson's cross. Then we all had our heads in our hands as our lump of a £3 million striker thumped his header so hard into the turf that it bounced up and over the bar. There were more than murmurs coming from the Kop now as Wood ambled away, feet pointing in opposite directions and a bemused look etched on his face; he was fast becoming the modern day Billy Paynter.

Four minutes of added time were ebbing away as Kalvin Phillips tried his luck from distance; it was a poor effort but it took a deflection and went away for a corner. It was our ninth corner of the game and like the other eight it came to nothing. But then Leeds collected the ball wide right from a poor Fulham throw-in and Leeds worked it out to the left. For one of very few times in the game Charlie Taylor whipped the ball back into the middle first time and Kyle Bartley, moving away, managed to get his head to it to knock it back towards goal. Chris Wood had his back to goal as the ball looped towards him but in a flash he was on his back in the air performing a very decent looking overhead kick. The ball came off his boot perfectly and nestled in the corner of the net!

Elland Road exploded and Wood wheeled away in front of the Kop but rather than celebrate the goal with us he decided this was pay-back time and with teeth gritted and the veins standing out on his neck he cupped his right hand around his right ear and gestured to us as if to say... *"Can't hear you moaning about me now!"* Was that necessary Chris? Many fans near me were convinced it wasn't and immediately vented their anger at the big striker; I've never seen fans berate a goal-scorer like that before. For me it spoiled what could have been a fabulous moment; yes it was still great to have levelled the game so late on and, in all probability, to have got our first point on the board but this should have been a landmark moment, a turning point in the relationship between the fans and Wood, a moment like that one up at Preston a few years back when Billy Paynter broke his duck. On that occasion big Billy, Barn Door Billy as we'd christened him, was happy to take the adulation of the fans in a grateful, thankful manner, and he became an overnight hero. This, from Wood, was too much like modern day footballer telling the fans to *"shove it, you know nothing"*, more 'earo' than 'hero'.

The game ended a couple of minutes later with Leeds still pressing forward trying to find a winner in a game we were actually lucky not to lose. When the whistle blew the majority of fans on the Kop stopped to applaud the players but it was noticeable that Wood didn't hang around down our end of the ground long. I wondered if he was already regretting his celebration, a celebration that reminded me of a certain Ryan Giggs a few years ago when he scored in front of the Kop shortly after taking serious stick from the fans about his complicated love life. That was entirely appropriate from Giggs in the circumstances and was a great way for him to put us in our place at the time. But even he did it with a smile on his face and no doubt tongue firmly in his cheek.

Back in the car with Kentley, heading down the M62, we listened to Garry Monk's post-match interview with Adam Pope on BBC Radio Leeds.

"I was happy for the group and happy for Chris as well because he'd missed the chance just before that and he could easily have felt sorry for himself. It was exactly the message

the whole team sent out, we could have all felt sorry for ourselves but we didn't ..."

Monk was rambling on somewhat but he clearly believed his young team had grown up a bit tonight particularly in the way they fought back having gone behind so late in the game. The patient appeared to be up and running again and no longer on crutches... speaking of which, I wonder how that bloke got on down at junction 15?[1]

In this round of games we again saw the unpredictable nature of the Championship, most notably at Burton where Sheffield Wednesday lost 3 -1. Newcastle got off the mark with a 4 – 1 win over Reading while the last remaining 100% record went bump as QPR lost 3 – 2 at Barnsley. Leeds ended the 3rd round of games in 21st spot with Simon Grayson's Preston and Owen Coyle's Blackburn still without a point and Rotherham below us on goal difference. Four teams shared the lead, Brighton, Norwich, Huddersfield and Fulham. It was starting to shape up already.

Leeds United 1 Fulham 1 (Cairney (77), **Wood (90+3)**) **21,204** (Fulham 391)

---

[1] I read the following day that Staffordshire Police arrived and managed to take the man to safety. He was described as being "in a state of distress". Maybe he was a Leeds fan after all! http://www.stokesentinel.co.uk/police-help-man-found-walking-along-m6-with-crutches-in-state-of-distress/story-29629755-detail/story.html

The Winking Man

P ontus Jansson was duly announced as the tenth signing of the summer. It was another season-long loan with a reported option to buy next May. The 25 year-old had eight Swedish caps to his name and was an unused member of their Euro 2016 squad. Since his transfer to Torino in 2014 though, he'd only made 16 appearances in Serie A so he was another player, like Kyle Bartley, who hadn't had an awful lot of first team football in recent years.[1] The trail of Bryan Verboom seemed to have gone cold which was a shame with a name like that.

There was still talk doing the rounds that a Chinese consortium was buying a stake in Leeds but another report now said a separate bid was being fronted by an Italian businessman, Andrea Radrizzani. It was apparently only in the very early stages but Radrizzani was reported to be in talks

---

[1] *http://www.bbc.co.uk/sport/football/37106330*

with Cellino[1] and had been seen sitting with him at recent games. In fact it was being said that at least three separate parties were now looking at the possibility of mounting a takeover bid even though there was no particular sign that Massimo was intending to sell. For Leeds fans it was a bit like your regular Friday night dilemma; *"Now, do I fancy Italian or Chinese?"*

Mind you, for the time being Massimo was still there and reports had also surfaced this week that he was getting fed up with Garry Monk; @MirrorAnderson tweeted: *"Cellino was ready to sack Monk before Antonsson's late goal against Fleetwood saved them and is losing confidence in the ex-Swans boss."* Some Leeds fans were immediately very nervous but I had a bucket full of salt ready to sprinkle on all these rumours as we'd seen before that the papers do often make much of this stuff up and even if they were getting it direct from Massimo we all knew that what he says and what he does are often poles apart.

With ten players now having joined during the summer it was hardly surprising that a few were also going in the opposite direction. This week saw the club announce that both 'Dave' Diagouraga and Luke Murphy were surplus to requirements and free to leave if they could find a club, while youngster Alex Purver was shipped off to Guiseley for a season's loan. It was getting hard to keep up with all the comings and goings.

Our hopes for the game with the Owls were boosted by their mid-week 3 – 1 defeat at newly promoted Burton Albion. Manager Carlos Carvalhal put that down largely to the absence through injury of their regular centre-back pairing of Glen Loovens and former Leeds man Tom Lees. The Owls' website confirmed on Friday that Lees was expected to return this weekend but there was still doubt about Loovens. That had some commentators suggesting the 4/1 price for a Leeds victory was generous...

---

[1]   *http://www.thebusinessdesk.com/yorkshire/news/738597-italian-bid-on-the-cards-for-leeds-united.html*

I was driving for this one and picked Kentley up at 9am... well, it was 9:05 by the time he rushed out still munching his breakfast. The shortest route to Sheffield was all pretty much his territory so he navigated the way up past the Roaches and the Winking Man pub on the A53 between Leek and Buxton. The pub takes its name from the small outcrop of rocks going towards Leek called 'Ramshaw Rocks' where a face shape in the rocks seems to wink at you when you drive up the hill towards the pub. It's the effect of a small hole being 'filled in' by the rock face behind as you drive past.

The options for getting a pre-match pint anywhere near Hillsborough are always limited, with most of the pubs in the vicinity having a home fans only policy. We were headed for the White Horse at the top of Halifax Road, half a mile from the ground. It's where I usually park the car on the roadside outside the pub. We managed to find a parking spot but the pub was clearly a no-go; it was boarded up. We wandered down the road towards the ground, passing the Railway and the Bridge pubs which both appeared to be out of bounds for us and then settled on the café in Sainsbury's; it was no surprise to find it was almost exclusively full of Leeds fans. We passed an hour or so over a big breakfast and coffees and chatted with a few familiar faces before then studying Garry Monk's latest team selection.

Green
Ayling Bartley Cooper (Capt) Taylor
Bridcutt
Sacko Vieira Mowatt
Wood Antonsson

Subs: Silvestri, Coyle, Bamba, Hernandez, Roofe, Phillips, Doukara.

Surprisingly, Monk had changed all four of his midfield players from the line-up that faced Fulham in mid-week with Hernandez, Phillips and Roofe on the bench and Dallas missing completely from the 18. It was a brave move. There was no sign of latest signing Pontus Jansson in the squad but Liam Bridcutt was in there as we expected. Glen Loovens had not recovered and was not in the Owls' defence but Tom Lees was listed and was named as captain. Former Leeds loanee

Barry Bannan played and another one, Will Buckley, was also in the Wednesday 18.

Kentley's ticket was for the lower tier of the West Stand while mine was in the upper so we went in via our separate turnstiles and I made my way up to my seat where Nigel was already waiting. Hillsborough looked magnificent with the sun shining again; the pitch was pristine and most areas were nicely full. Leeds had sold their full allocation of almost 4,000 tickets and there were over 29,000 in the ground. The only disappointment with the view we had was that one of the four massive supporting pillars at the front of our stand was obscuring a sliver of the action. Wednesday, like Leeds, charge the best part of £40 for away tickets and I felt I was being denied at least a couple of quids' worth of view.

The noise from the Leeds fans was excellent from the start with all the usual anthems belted out but the early moments of the game were giving cause for concern as it was the Owls who were flying. The fact we now had Liam Bridcutt patrolling in front of the defence didn't seem to be making us any tighter in that department to begin with and Forestieri was looking very dangerous despite the fact he'd reportedly refused to play in Wednesday's 0 – 0 draw with Norwich the previous week. He'd been linked with a possible transfer to either Derby County or Newcastle United but had now apologised and was apparently 'back in the fold'. We still chanted *"Forestieri, he don't wanna play!"* every time he had the ball though. Twice in the space of a few minutes he should have made us pay for our bad manners as first he was clean through after the ball rebounded off Charlie Taylor's leg and then a ball over the top of our back line again saw him bear down on goal. The first time he poked the ball wide and the second time Liam Cooper headed off the line after he rounded Rob Green and clipped the ball towards goal. A free-kick crashed off the top of our crossbar and the home fans were singing *"You're fu***** sh**!"* to us as we struggled to get a foothold. There were some positives to dwell on though as we caught our breath at half-time with the scores still blank. Hadi Sacko had been on several sorties down the right wing and had he been able to deliver the ball more accurately we might have had more chances. As it happens, he seemed to think our strike force was twelve feet tall. He had a good chance himself too that he put wide, as did Marcus Antonsson with another carbon copy of his misses against QPR and Fulham, just dragging a left foot shot to the right of goal. He really needed to practice that.

At half-time, Wednesday substituted Almen Abdi with Gary Hooper; I remembered he just about single-handedly destroyed us at Hillsborough last season with two goals in the space of three minutes. Another Hooper was causing us problems this season though; referee Simon Hooper whose fussy decisions seemed largely to go against us. In that game last season of course, referee Anthony Taylor caused us pain when he messed up a Wednesday substitution and disallowed a Liam Cooper goal. This particular encounter often seems to be about Hoopers and Coopers.

The second half saw both sides hold sway at one point or another; Sacko was still looking bright on the Leeds right but still hadn't found his range with his crosses while at the other end Wednesday had one spell of pressure with a number of corners. Bartley and Cooper were just starting to look a bit more solid in dealing with them though. Then, just after the hour mark, Leeds put together their best move of the game; maybe of the season so far.

Charlie Taylor twice broke down a Wednesday attack, first with a header and then coming away down the left of the Leeds defence with the ball. He shifted it forward to Chris Wood who in turn played it out to the right wing. With the Leeds fans scenting blood and roaring him on, Sacko burst into the area down below us to our left and then cleverly back-healed it to Luke Ayling. Ayling gave it straight back to the winger and momentarily we thought the chance was gone. But this time Sacko clipped the ball first time to the back post and there, all on his own, was Marcus Antonsson to dive forward and steer his header into the net with the Owls' keeper Westwood committed at the other post. The infamous old Leppings Lane End erupted in an explosion of noise as we celebrated like only we know how while the players engulfed Antonsson down below us. I was trying to capture the moment with my camera and suddenly was aware of the stench of a flare going off somewhere nearby… somewhere *very* nearby! The tell-tale blue smoke was mushrooming out from under a seat right in front of me and suddenly there were bodies flying everywhere as folk tried to escape the choking acrid smoke. I gave up with the photos and swung a leg over the back of my seat to try to climb into the row behind but my foot got stuck on the top of the plastic seat. I was in danger of toppling over until a lad grabbed me by the arm and pulled me up. We were all now engulfed in a blue fog and our eyes were stinging but still the noise of roaring Leeds fans filled our ears; it was mayhem for a few moments. A chap had now picked up the flare and was clearly unsure where to throw it as it continued to spew its foul blue smoke into the air around us. It was comical as he circled round and round creating a chimney shaped blue funnel around himself looking for somewhere to lob it. Each time his arm went round the lads in the firing line would duck and shout *"No, not this bloody way for Christ's sake!"* and dive out of the way. For one minute I thought he was going to lob it over the edge of the upper tier into the crowded section below; perhaps thinking it was empty down there. Thankfully someone grabbed his arm and he dropped it down again at the front of our section. It was a very scary moment that could have easily gone wrong. A steward eventually took the canister away and slowly the air cleared and we could all concentrate on the celebrations again.

Back out on the pitch, the home side were trying to rise to the challenge and that man Hooper struck a fierce shot that Green did well to shovel away as we urged our heroes to see the job through. Garry Monk made his first change by withdrawing Antonsson and bringing on Souleymane Doukara and both got rapturous applause from the West Stand. The game was end to end now and both sets of supporters were raising the noise levels even more, trying to urge their respective teams to press forward. Wednesday made their final two substitutions with David Jones and Will Buckley now joining the fray while Leeds responded with Roofe and then Kalvin Phillips replacing Mowatt and Sacko. In the midst of the substitutions I was amazed to hear the Leeds fans break into a chant of, *"We are Leeds, we are vile, David Jones is a paedophile"*. At first I thought it weird for the name of former Wednesday manager Dave Jones to crop up at that precise moment until I remembered they now had a player with the same name on the pitch! It's a chant I can never condone and it was even less appropriate, if that's possible, aimed at the 31 year-old midfielder recently bought from Burnley.

The clock ticked on slowly but Leeds were looking assured now and were actually looking the more likely to score as Wednesday chased the game and opened themselves up to the counter-attack. Sacko was revelling in the space he was now finding and even orchestrated our support when Leeds won a late corner just down below us. Not wanting to disappoint him and loving his obvious passion we took the noise up another level. He then set up Doukara on the edge of the box but the Douk pulled his shot wide. There were now five minutes left plus whatever ref Hooper decided to add on...

Kemar Roofe was seeing almost as much ball out on the left wing as Sacko was seeing on the right by now and in the 85th minute Liam Bridcutt slid the ball through. Roofe teased his marker one way and then the other before whipping the ball across low with his left foot. Chris Wood was lurking at the near post in a yard of space and he touched the ball beyond Westwood with his right instep. Cue delirium again! There was no ear-cupping this time, just pure joy as Wood leapt up onto the advertising hoarding, arms aloft, taking the plaudits of the crowd. Eventually the rest of the players all joined him and we had one of those all too rare occasions when players and fans could celebrate without fear of the moment being ripped away from us. It would be the disaster of all disasters if we threw this win away in the short time left. We didn't; in fact Charlie Taylor ought to have got us a third as he curled a shot over the angle deep into stoppage time. At the final whistle the rest of the ground was almost empty. We'd been singing joyously *"Time to go"* for the last few minutes as Wednesday's fans streamed away in their thousands. The Leeds fans mostly stayed put though to savour the moment. All the Leeds players made their way over to us at the end and they too milked it for all it was worth; it was a magic moment.

The chatter amongst the fans as we slowly wandered back to the car was all about this being a turning point; *the* turning point we'd been hoping for over the last few seasons. We'd been here before of course, only for it to all fall apart within a few games. Was this going to be any different? I thought it might well be. I'd been likening us to a jigsaw recently; just a few pieces missing from the full picture. With the arrival of Bridcutt I hoped we were almost there. He was immense last season when he first arrived and we'd been crying out for his experience and punch in midfield throughout pre-season. We'd looked much better at the back today probably due to the protection he offers the defence. Bartley and Cooper looked strong and we've seldom been able to say that about our centre-back partnerships. Luke Ayling also had another great game at right-back. Up front, Wood seemed finally to be coming good and Antonsson looked sharp, albeit like Wood, not always one hundred per cent clinical in his finishing. I was convinced there was more to come from Kemar Roofe too and Sacko ran riot at times today on the right wing. We hadn't yet seen what Pontus Jansson could give us either. It all looked as positive as I could remember.

After the game Garry Monk was as down to earth as ever as he told the BBC: *"We had a game plan today and the players followed it pretty much to the letter.*

"We're still not the team we want to be, but this was a game which showed a real improvement which is important for the development of our young players."[1]

In the car, Kentley and I concluded it was not the perfect performance by any means as Wednesday were sloppy at times but still undid us, especially first half, but it was a damn good effort and a classic counter-attacking display. The Winking Man winked knowingly as we sped past on our way home just as the heavens opened once more, flooding the roads; I winked back wondering if this was *the* season.

Sheffield Weds 0 **Leeds Utd 2 (Antonsson (63), Wood (85))**
29,025 **(Leeds 3,703)**

---

[1] *http://www.bbc.co.uk/sport/football/37067320*

"Pa-blo Hernandez, he plays for United with Dallas and Mowatt"

❛❛*We really do need to rethink our strategy on some of our away trips matey!"* I was chatting with Kentley in a McDonald's in the centre of Luton as we hurriedly scoffed our Chicken Sandwich Meal Deals; it was almost 7:15pm. We'd set off from home at 3:45pm with the best intentions of meeting fellow fans in one of the pubs in town but we hadn't arrived and parked until gone 6:30pm having had a nightmare journey and then got stuck in the rush-hour Luton traffic along with the Leeds players' coach, presumably after it had dropped off the players. Nigel had already eaten in Wetherspoon's and Keith L had been and gone from at least two town centre pubs. They'd both given up on us while Conor had already texted to say he was at the ground. We'd tried in vain to get in the Wetherspoon but the Spanish Inquisition on the door refused us entry as, not surprisingly, we couldn't prove we lived in the Luton area. Quite how Nigel and Keith got in there we didn't know but the doormen were probably less fussy before the masses turned up. We were left walking the streets looking for somewhere to eat. We couldn't say there was no choice; every conceivable nationality seemed to be represented in the high street restaurants here – mostly Asian but also Eastern European and African. In fact, according to the 2011 census, Luton has become one of three white British-minority towns in the United Kingdom. It was announced in a report based on the census figures that along with Leicester and Slough, Luton was one of only three towns outside London where the white British were now a minority, making up only 45% of the local population.[1] We could believe that as we spotted McDonald's in the distance, an oasis of American English food in a positive desert of hot spicy alternatives.

With mild indigestion and with the sweat now pouring off us due to the thirty degree heat we were jogging along in, we made our way back through the cosmopolitan streets of Luton towards Kenilworth Road with an ever growing number of bright orange Luton tops for company. It will never be described as a pretty ground, set as it is midst rows of terraced housing; literally in respect of the away end, the entrance to which is built into the row of terraced homes on one side of Oak Road. It is one of the most quirky entrances to a football ground I have ever come across as once through the turnstiles you climb the steps up to the back of the away stand and can look down into the back yards of the houses, many with their washing lines full of Saris and other Asian garb. The only ground that comes to mind as being similar is Fratton Park, home of Portsmouth. There too the rear of the away stand looks down on the back gardens of the local residents and there too most of them are not English rose gardens...

---

[1]

http://www.neighbourhood.statistics.gov.uk/dissemination/LeadTabl eView.do?a=7&b=6275157&c=luton&d=13&e=62&g=6394327&i =1001x1003x1032x1004&m=0&r=1&s=1472046207002&enc=1& dsFamilyId=2477&nsjs=true&nsck=false&nssvg=false&nswid=13 66

The Hatters of Luton Town have been at Kenilworth Road since 1905 and parts of the ground appear to be pretty much as they were then but in a worse state of repair! The tiny toilet block at the top of the steps is a case in point. Three urinals, one wash basin and two cubicles is hardly satisfactory for 1,500 visiting fans, most of whom would pass that way, so to speak. Suffice to say the basin was getting plenty of use although not so much for hand-washing.

Arriving in the stand as we did only a few minutes before kick-off, it was pretty much full and the policy of unreserved seating meant we had to scout around for some spare standing room. We spotted Mike, who sits behind us on the Kop, and he gestured that there was one space next to him so Kentley and I left that one for Nigel while we continued on along to the right. Conor had texted to say there was room near him too and eventually we found him and squeezed in. By this time I was totally drenched in sweat and even Kentley had to extract himself from his Liam Gallagher style jacket in a sort of Houdini-esque manoeuvre. All around us the Leeds fans were building up the atmosphere with the first round of the new Pablo Hernandez chant:

"Pab-lo Her-nan-dez, Pab-lo Her-nan-dez, His name is Pablo Hernandez and he plays for United with Dallas and Mowatt" all sung with gusto to the dance inducing tune of Ritchie Valens' La Bamba. On and on it went for most of the game with almost all the stand eventually jigging along and clapping their hands.

We'd learned the team while we were getting that dose of indigestion in McDonald's and now we could see them making their way onto the pitch from the tunnel just to our right. This is one of those quirky grounds where the coach and subs have to walk right across the pitch to the dug-outs on the opposite side to the tunnel; no quick escape after the game if they mess this one up I thought! It was a complete surprise in light of Garry Monk's comments over the last couple of days when he'd stressed how he'd put out a side capable of winning the tie and how he felt getting the momentum of another win was going to be important going into the Forest game on Saturday. That led us all to believe there wouldn't be that many changes to the side that so efficiently disposed of Sheffield Wednesday the previous weekend. In fact there were just the eleven. *ELEVEN!*

Silvestri
Coyle Bamba (Capt) Jansson Denton
Dallas Grimes Murphy Hernandez
Doukara Roofe

Subs: Green, Ayling, Cooper, Antonsson, Phillips, Sacko, Mowatt.

As another EasyJet plane from nearby Luton Airport rose into the sky above the stand at the Kenilworth Road End, Leeds got the game underway. Within a minute of the start, Matt Grimes made his mark on the game and on Jake Gray with a badly timed tackle that earned him an entry into the referee's notebook. And that sort of typified the first twenty minutes of a helter-skelter kind of a game between two evenly matched sides that continued to be played against the backing track of *"Pa-blo Her-nan-dez. Pa-blo Her-nan-dez…"* Then, with 23 minutes gone, Leeds scored.

It was at the far end of the ground from us and we were watching from under a low roof and looking around a pillar, but even in those circumstances it looked a great goal. Doukara was out on the left wing, almost in the corner and was being marshalled by two orange shirts when Stuart Dallas dashed inside heading into the inside left channel in the Luton area. The Douk slid the ball between his two markers into Dallas's path and the Irishman immediately poked the ball back to Kemar Roofe on the edge of the box. A defender got a boot in the way but it still found its way to Roofe and he spotted Tyler Denton steaming in towards goal. Roofe sort of blocked the ball towards Denton who hit it first time with the outside of his favoured left foot and it rippled the net near the top right-hand corner! I think I'd been brainwashed by the chanting and I thought it was *"Pa-blo Her-nan-dez"* who hit the shot but it was actually Denton running across to the Leeds bench to celebrate with Monk and the substitutes; Kentley and Conor soon put me right on the scorer. It was a fine goal on the lad's full debut.

For the next ten minutes or so, Leeds piled on the pressure and looked half decent. Roofe had an acrobatic effort fly back off the angle of post and bar and Dallas hit the rebound at the keeper. But then gradually the home side began to get on top and the middle of the Leeds defence started to look decidedly shaky, particularly when Sol Bamba was involved. Every long ball seemed to catch him out whether on the floor or in the air while the giant Pontus Jansson looked far more solid on the other side. In fact I wasn't sure they shouldn't have suspended those EasyJet flights for fear of him nodding a plane out of the sky! A thunderous shot from Jack Marriot stung the fingers of Silvestri and lobbed into the air before bouncing back down on the crossbar with Marco not really knowing how he'd stopped it or where it subsequently went. Another shot from Olly Lee was then saved in the bottom right corner. The half-time whistle came at a good time for Leeds.

Kentley went off in search of water during the break and on his return I gulped down a whole bottle to try to rehydrate; I was just starting to cool down by this time having sweated buckets due to the heat and the jigging about to La Bamba!

In the second half Luton continued to dominate and really ought to have stolen the game had they been a bit more accurate and not to take anything away from a fine performance by Marco Silvestri too. It was clear to me that this most definitely was a second XI and if we ever played this line-up in the Championship we'd most likely get tonked. We looked very much like the Leeds side we saw all last season; weak in midfield, fragile in the middle of defence and wasteful of the few chances we did create. Even players who most would consider first XI contenders – Hernandez, Dallas and Roofe – were not standing out and therefore not doing their chances much good. Somehow though, Luton failed to capitalise. Leeds brought on Kalvin Phillips for Murphy on 58 minutes, Mowatt for Hernandez to the inevitable chorus of *"Pa-blo Her-nan-dez..."* ten minutes later and then Liam Cooper for Jansson 15 minutes from the end. Right at the death Leeds had a great chance to make the game safe when Doukara won the ball deep in Luton territory and then chased his own header down the inside right channel just yards away to our left. He spotted Roofe, free near the penalty spot and found him with an inch perfect ball across the area only for Roofe to smash it at the goalkeeper's legs and away to safety. The lad needs the confidence of putting one of those away and he needs it quick.

It was all smiles at the final whistle when both sets of fans forgot their tongue in cheek chants that filled the final ten minutes; Leeds fans chanted *"You only sing when you're bombing"* and various dubious songs about terrorists while the Luton fans hit back with various ditties about Jimmy Savile. The racist chanting was pretty much lost on the Luton fans as I didn't see many non-white supporters amongst their ranks.

As we left the ground and wandered back to the car, we saw the two very different sides of football policing. At one point four surly looking coppers marched past almost knocking us out of the way and then two on horseback almost cleared Kentley out with no sign of an *"excuse me"* or apology. Then within yards we came across some Yorkshire coppers who'd travelled down for the game. I spotted one of them casting admiring glances at a shapely rear packed into a pair of tight white jeans on a young female Leeds fan and we exchanged a knowing wink and then Nigel spotted one of them he'd met before who told us he was *"from the posh end of Dewsbury...Huddersfield!"* Why can't they all be like that?

After the game, Garry Monk told LUTV: *"We probably should have capitalised on a couple of opportunities to make it a little bit more comfortable, but I thought the players did really well – especially in those last 10 minutes when we had to dig in and grind it out... We had periods where we had to defend and I thought we did that well. I also thought we attacked really well – we just needed to be a bit more clinical. "All in all, we can be pleased to get into the next round and with the performance of all the players."*[1]

Luton Town 0 **Leeds United 1 (Denton (23))**
7,498 **(Leeds 1,510)**

---

[1] *http://www.leedsunited.com/news/article/157tjoat427ls1hfjzjm9urz6 r/title/luton-garry-monks-verdict*

Weekend in the Forest

I sat and watched the last knockings of the Accrington Stanley v Burnley EFL Cup tie on TV, the day after the Luton trip. It was delaying the Third Round draw which was to be shown live immediately after the game. Accrington snatched an unlikely win, albeit against a second string Burnley XI in the final minute of extra time.

Leeds were ball number '11' and there was much speculation, or rather hope, that we'd be matched up with one of the giant Premier League sides in the draw. Any of Chelsea, Man U, Liverpool or Everton was the hope. In the event, quite early in the draw, ball number '11' was drawn at home to ball number '2' and I switched the TV off...

Ball number '2' was Blackburn Rovers who we would now play on September 20th in the cup exactly one week after playing them in the league... two mouth-watering games coming up there.

I didn't do the away game at Nottingham Forest; I was instead in Belgium for the Grand Prix at Spa as I continued to tick off that particular list; Grand Prix races around the world. This was number nine of those for me. In my usual manner I'd swung it with Mrs W on the basis of taking her away for her birthday which always falls near the August Bank Holiday. The GP was over the weekend of the 27th and 28th. So, I was sat in the grandstand on the outside of Eau Rouge in the Ardennes Forest watching the first GP2 race of the weekend while Leeds were trotting out to face Nottingham Forest at the

City Ground. I wouldn't see the result until we got back to our hotel in the lovely town of Namur, about 40 miles south east of Brussels. The BBC Sport website informed me of the 3 – 1 defeat.

It would not be until I got home on the following Tuesday night that I could watch the game in full on LUTV and when it ended I sat in silence just staring at the screen of my lap-top. Everything about the game screamed out that nothing, absolutely nothing had changed from last season... apart from the names on the shirts of course. Leeds bossed the possession and in the middle third of the pitch looked half decent but three times our defence performed no better than a Sunday League side after a big night on the ale while the strikers hit the ball no better than Granny with her slippers on. It was so disappointing after the elation of that win up at Hillsborough when so many of us started to think it was all coming together.

Green
Ayling Bartley Cooper (Capt) Taylor
Bridcutt
Sacko Vieira Hernandez
Wood Antonsson

Subs: Silvestri, Coyle, Jansson, Phillips, Mowatt, Roofe, Doukara.

The starting XI was the same as we saw at Hillsborough apart from one change; Pablo Hernandez (I can't get that ruddy La Bamba tune out of my head every time I type his name) came in for Alex Mowatt who dropped to the bench. I did question why that change was necessary as I'm a firm believer in the 'don't change a winning team' philosophy and I wasn't sure Hernandez was yet acclimatised to life in the Championship. As one of our few 'older' players I also couldn't see the logic of playing him twice in one week but, hey-ho, what do I know. Leeds had a warning as early as the 12th minute when we somehow scrambled away a corner that was allowed to bounce on the edge of our six-yard box but just four minutes later we succumbed to an exact same ball. Oliver Burke got free at the front post to back-head the ball to the back post and there was Pajtim Kasami to hook the ball into the top corner of the net from six yards out with Ayling just too plain slow to get his foot in first.

There then followed another 50 minutes of huffing and puffing from Leeds throughout the rest of the first half and well into the second when we held the ball well but did absolutely bugger all with it. The few times we created openings for Wood or Antonsson to have a go at goal they fluffed them, either mishitting the ball or missing the target. It looked like a real effort for our players while Forest appeared content to sit back and defend, ready to pick Leeds off when we did let go of the ball. In the 66th minute Garry Monk made his first change, on came Kalvin Phillips and off went young Vieira who would later sign a new three year contract with the club. Another four minutes and Monk made his second change with Kemar Roofe making his now accustomed substitute appearance, this time in place of Hadi Sacko. Sacko had just joined the ranks of the seemingly inept in front of goal as he screwed a left foot shot well wide. Within a minute of that, Forest doubled their lead.

Leeds dealt well enough with a rare Forest attack as Kyle Bartley got the ball safely away for a corner, this time out on the Forest right wing, the opposite side to the one the first goal came from. A high looping in-swinging corner made its way to our back post where Liam Cooper was marking Damien Perquis. For some reason known only to Coops, at the last second he took a step away from Perquis allowing the Forest man the room to just nick a header inside the back post; shocking, shocking, shocking defending once again. If I had a pound for every goal Leeds had given away in the last few seasons then I'd have more than a few quid.

Some nine minutes from the end, Monk made his final change, throwing on Alex Mowatt for the 'La Bamba' man, presumably hoping Alex could grab a life-line with one of his trade mark free-kicks and just a couple of minutes after coming on it looked like he may have his chance; Marcus Antonsson was fouled in a tussle about 25 yards out. Up stepped... Kalvin Phillips! Not Alex, but Kalvin Phillips with his right foot. He hit it sweet and true and it fled past Forest keeper Henderson beating him at his near post. It was the signal for a final ten minute flurry from Leeds but all too often, despite getting chances we were no more than feeble in trying to convert them. By the end of the game we would have created 13 openings but only managed to get three on target and two of those were weak efforts that hardly troubled the keeper. The other one was Kalvin's free-kick.

In the 4th minute of added time Forest rubbed our noses in it with a third goal. A clever solo effort from Oliver Burke who made three Leeds defenders look total chumps as he weaved around them near the byline to the left of goal before slotting the ball through Rob Green's legs from the tightest of angles. It just added to our misery that it was former Leeds player Eric Lichaj who fed the ball through to Burke; 3 – 1, and the game well and truly over.

I couldn't argue with much of Garry Monk's summary of the game, posted on the club website, but I was starting to think that although he appeared to know what was wrong – we can't defend and we can't hit the target at the other end – he didn't seem to be able to do anything to change it.

"We had the chances to equalise – we just need to be more clinical. Our general play was good but errors cost us.

It's something we need to improve quickly. If the players can't do that, things will need to change. We gifted them two soft goals, which made it difficult.

We need to cut out the sloppiness and the individual errors. We have the squad to address this."

I worried that the bit Monk was wrong about was his last sentence; did we really have the squad to address those errors? The team he picked at Forest was clearly error prone and couldn't hit the target but it was no different really to the performance we saw at Kenilworth Road from the 'B' team when Bamba looked just as suspect as Coops and when Roofe missed a sitter at the end amongst other chances. That was all of our current squad represented in those two games and with the possible exception that Jansson looked good for the short time he was on the pitch and of course we had Gaetano Berardi to come back, where were those options for change?

Nottingham Forest 3 **Leeds United 1** (Kasami (16), Perquis (71), **Phillips (83)**, Burke (90+4)) 20,995 (**Leeds 1,925**)

Long ball? Short ball?
Or no balls at all?

The final day of the transfer window brought more strength to Leeds in that suspect defence of ours and some much needed power up front.

OK, I'm lying about that. In fact it brought in another midfielder, as if we didn't already have enough of those. Eunan O'Kane, a 26 year-old with recent Premier League experience at Bournemouth was signed on a two-year deal for an undisclosed sum. O'Kane, who was away with the Republic of Ireland preparing for the first round of games in their 2018 World Cup qualifying campaign, was our 11th signing of the Summer; effectively a full new team. By most people's reckoning we thus had nine central midfield players in the first team squad; Murphy, Grimes, Hernandez, Phillips, Vieira, Mowatt, Bridcutt, Diagouraga and now O'Kane. That was assuming we classed Stuart Dallas and Hadi Sacko as wingers rather than midfielder players too. The sad thing was, I still didn't know who the best three or four out of that list were and I was pretty sure Garry Monk didn't know either!

The final change to the squad was announced at noon on the day after the window closed; Sol Bamba was released by mutual consent due to *"personal reasons"*; that's club code for *"he was pretty crap anyway"*.

In the course of writing this chapter I studied long and hard the 2016/17 squad and compared it to the group Steve Evans finished the previous season with. I was hard pressed to see much improvement. I still felt there was so much we hadn't yet seen from the current crop but I was starting to doubt Garry Monk was the man to bring it out. Kemar Roofe had been a disappointment so far albeit he'd only been played sparingly but I was still a big fan of his remembering the devastating displays he pulled out for Oxford last season. Chris Wood was, in my opinion, not showing us anything like his best form and we had yet to even see the Bartley-Jansson partnership in the middle at the back so we really didn't know if that would be any good or not. The general belief was that Hernandez was class too but we'd thus far only seen glimpses of it and he currently seemed well down the pecking order. Gaetano Berardi was still out injured so we had him to come back of course and now we had this lad O'Kane who we hadn't yet seen in action. So, still early days and still lots of scope for a turnaround in fortunes but none the less I was worried and though we were still only in early September I felt the upcoming game with table topping Huddersfield was vital to at least show Monk was on the right track.

England scored in the final seconds of added time to beat Slovakia and get their 2018 World Cup campaign up and running under new manager Sam Allardyce and there were wins for Wales and Scotland too with the Scots winning 5 – 1 in Malta thanks largely to a Rob Snodgrass hat-trick. Northern Ireland and the Republic both drew their games on foreign territory. So far so good on all the home fronts but with me missing the Forest game, boy had this seemed a long break.

Things were going on at Leeds that started to suggest that maybe there was indeed a grain of truth in the takeover rumours. Most learned commentators subscribed to the view that there were three potential suitors either speaking with Cellino or waiting in the wings. In the days leading up to the

Huddersfield game information began to surface that GFH had converted their shareholding into debentures; effectively meaning that Cellino now owned or controlled 100% of the shares with GFH now, to all intents and purposes, just a creditor, albeit a big one with some £17 million still owed them. If true, then that could well be seen as a precursor to a sale of some or all of Cellino's interest in the club. Fridges were being stocked and parties were being arranged all over Yorkshire.

The day before the Huddersfield game we were told by the United website that Liam Bridcutt would be the new club captain following the departure of Sol Bamba. It was to be hoped the appointment of a Scottish skipper this time around would have the same impact as certain previous captains; Billy Bremner and Gordon Strachan were midfielders of similar stature of course… Bridcutt's first challenge was to tame those Terriers.

I travelled up to this one on the Shropshire Whites' mini-bus – an intimate experience with all 17 seats filled and 'Mr Humph' driving. At the first pee break, just before we got on the M56, one of the lads pointed out that the nearside front tyre was very low but no-one seemed too bothered and off we went again! They're a pretty laid back bunch these Shropshire lads.

Some of the lads carried on into Leeds for their pre-match beers but I strolled down to the Pavilion as usual and worked my way through a few pints of Foster's knowing I'd not be driving for another eight hours or so. All the usual gang were in and we soon had a dozen or so gathered around our table discussing the prospects against the Terriers whilst watching the Manchester derby on two screens, the Old Firm derby on two more and simultaneously listening to some bloke strumming his guitar and singing. There could have been a stripper performing on a nearby table and we'd not have noticed as there was so much else going on!

Green
Ayling Bartley Jansson Taylor
Bridcutt (Capt)
Sacko Phillips Mowatt
Antonsson Wood

Subs: Silvestri, Coyle, Cooper, Vieira, Hernandez, Roofe, Doukara.

With the exception that there was still too much Wood in it and the obvious question as to why new boy O'Kane was missing, I had few other problems with the team selection.

Huddersfield came into the game sitting on top of the table with four wins from five and 13 points and their quirky manager David Wagner seemed to have found a winning combination. It was obviously not going to be an easy game but I, like most fans, felt sure that after a two week break Monk would have them fired up and ready to erase the memory of that slip-up at Forest. Having said that we had a notorious reputation for losing the first game after any break...

From the outset this was a turgid, meandering game in which neither side seemed to have much spark at all. The fans of both sides started vocally enough but with precious little to feed off on the pitch even the spirit of the crowd was battered into submission. The applause in the 29th minute for a Leeds fan called Paul who'd recently passed away was genuine enough but it was a rare moment of activity during a limp first half. Chris Wood missed yet another glorious half-chance as he directed a near-post header wide from a Phillips left wing corner and Marcus Antonsson appeared to be hauled down in the box according to most in the ground apart from referee Roger East. In fact East seemed to be in a particularly generous mood all round as a reckless two-footed challenge by Aaron Mooy, the Terriers bald-headed midfielder, was punished with yellow and not the red it deserved, just before the break. Huddersfield defender Chris Schindler was putting himself about a bit too and left a mark on several Leeds players; a sort of 'Schindler's list'...

The only positive thing for Leeds was that the new centre-back pairing of Kyle Bartley and Pontus Jansson looked very solid and Pontus looked just the sort of player we need as he tried to urge the fans to sing up following a good bit of work in the north-east corner. As I struggled through the crowds heading towards the bogs at half-time there was not much discussion going on about the game, so little had we seen to comment on although most felt aggrieved by the Mooy tackle on Bridcutt.

The first ten minutes of the second half saw little change; the game continued to be a dour battle in midfield with the Terriers having the bulk of possession but seldom doing much with it. Then, in the 55th minute, Leeds fell behind and predictably it was Aaron Mooy, he who should not even have been on the pitch, who broke the deadlock.

Replays would later show the ball just about crossed the byline to the left of the Leeds goal in front of the South Stand but once again Roger East waved play on and eventually the ball went out for a throw-in, level with the edge of the box on the Terriers' left wing. Mooy received the ball from the throw and whipped it into the Leeds box but it was headed away by Alex Mowatt towards Jack Payne, about thirty yards from goal. Payne then left it for Mooy who took aim and fired the ball past Rob Green into the left corner of the net. It was a stunning strike but no Leeds player closed him down so he really could pick his spot which he did unerringly. The 2,700 Huddersfield fans went bonkers over in the West Stand while for the Leeds fans it was that familiar feeling of doom and gloom. We tried to lift the players but it was hard going and when Chris Wood found himself free on the end of an Alex Mowatt cross only to mistime his header yet again, most of us had had enough. It could have been worse for Leeds as Rajiv van La Parra spotted Green way off his line and tried his luck almost from half-way, but the back-peddling Green just got there in time to touch the ball over his own crossbar. Doukara replaced Antonsson to a few boos from the Kop and then Roofe came on for Sacko a few minutes later but it made no discernible impact on the game and it finished 0 – 1. Football is supposed to be an entertainment and I'd waited almost three weeks for this game but as I sat on a very quiet Shropshire Whites' mini-bus on the way home I actually felt cheated. Monk had two full weeks with the majority of his players and this was all they could serve up. It quite simply wasn't good enough and I began to fear for our chances this season.

In his post-match interviews Garry Monk also seemed stunned; just repeating over and over again how he felt both teams had *"cancelled each other out"* and how it was *"ironic that the goal was scored by a player who shouldn't have been on the pitch"* On BBC Radio Leeds, Adam Pope questioned Monk as to what the *"identity"* of his team was, presumably trying to establish what game plan we'd gone in with but Monk was clearly irritated and refused to answer, instead asking Pope what *he* thought it was. Then, when Pope asked what Massimo Cellino had said to him about the performance Monk snapped back, telling Popey it was *"none of your business!"* and then walked out saying *"I think this interview's done".* Pope's question about the team's "identity" was valid and later on Pontus Jansson would come out and tell the press how the game plan was to use long balls and how maybe in the next game the team needed to play more football. Someone on Twitter suggested that next time Popey should ask Monk if his team was indeed *"a long ball, a short ball or a no balls at all team!"* The key point was that we didn't seem to have *any* identity, no clear game plan; no pattern to our play and certainly no plan B when things went wrong.

In the days following the Huddersfield defeat, a defeat that left us 22nd in the table with just Preston and Blackburn below, there was the inevitable speculation as to whether Cellino would wield his well-honed axe any time soon. Most assumed that another defeat, in the home game against Blackburn on Tuesday, would definitely see the blade fall on Monk's neck, especially as he and some of his players were now telling us that nothing less than three points in that game would be acceptable. My pre-season fears that Monk didn't have the experience to deal with such pressure now resurfaced and his behaviour towards Adam Pope only reaffirmed them. Many had commented how he looked a forlorn figure on the touchline too, stood for long periods with his hands stuffed in his pockets, showing little or no emotion or passion and his decision to replace Ant with Douk had left many cold. The beauty of the Championship though, was that we wouldn't have long to wait until the next game when, by Monk's own admission, we could judge him and his players' reaction. We'd get to see then if they did indeed have the balls to turn this crisis around.

Leeds United 0 Huddersfield Town 1 (Mooy (55))
28,514 (Town 2,721)

Sacko and ashes

I must admit it's sometimes hard to keep abreast of all that goes on behind the scenes at Leeds. Take the morning of the Blackburn game for instance. I was just checking Twitter while I waited for Kentley the Stokie to arrive and up popped a tweet from Phil Hay reminding everyone that the Ross McCormack bung case was due to be ruled upon by the FA later in the week. I'd completely forgotten that one. It was the case whereby it was alleged an unauthorised payment was made to an unlicensed representative of McCormack when he was sold to Fulham back in 2014. It was alleged that the payment of £185,000 was made by McCormack's agent, Derek Hay to an advisor of McCormack's, Barry Hughes with the full knowledge of all involved including Massimo Cellino and Leeds United. Was this the moment Cellino faced another exile?

Before that was due to be decided upon in court, Leeds had the vital game with Blackburn to navigate. Everybody was convinced that this was a case of three points or bust. Hardly anyone believed Monk could survive another defeat especially at the hands of the bottom side in the division. Phil Hay was also tweeting that Francesco Marroccu, former Sporting Director with Cellino while they were at Cagliari, had been seen at training sessions for the previous couple of weeks and was widely expected to be appointed to a similar role with Leeds. That couldn't have been easy for Garry Monk, having his every move scrutinised and I did wonder if that was behind his tetchy responses to Adam Pope at the weekend. The stress was beginning to tell maybe?

I stood with my tasty Yorkshire Blonde at the bar in the Peacock pondering the Championship table being shown on Sky on the TV up in the corner of the room. With every side having played six games, Leeds were third from bottom with four points. Below us; Preston had three points and tonight's opponents Blackburn had just two. Kentley had dropped me off at the Pavilion but it wasn't yet open so, on a clammy warm afternoon I wandered up to the Peacock to grab a pint in there. It was almost deserted as yet; a few lads were chatting at the other end of the bar and when I wandered outside there were a handful sat in the beer garden outside the marquee. There were some ominous clouds forming away in the distance and I hoped they'd stay there.

Eventually I drank up and sauntered down towards the Pavilion, bumping into my old pal Bogdan on the way. We settled ourselves down with our pints and soon the place was buzzing as always. In fact it was buzzing a bit too much really as a young foursome performed a sound check on the stage at the back of the room sending a high pitched feedback squeal right through us. I ushered one of the girls who seemed to be in charge over to our table and we tried yet again to get her to relay the message through that we really didn't *need* or indeed *want* live music in there. It was obviously too late for today but hopefully the message would get through if we all continued to complain. She did pop back at one point to say the lads would finish playing at 7pm to allow us some peace at last. I actually felt sorry for the lads playing; they were all very young, with the little drummer looking no more than 11 or 12 years-old. They were good too, all turned out in their blue 'Greenpeace' Leeds tops… but they were too feckin loud.

There were three main discussion points in the Pavilion this particular evening; obviously the music issue was one. The second was the seemingly random prices still being charged for the beer. The price of entry was £3, and for this we were given a voucher that could be redeemed against food or beer. But depending on which bar you went to, and seemingly what your name was, you got a different deal. The voucher had £3.90 shown on it – even though we'd only paid £3 – and if your name was Kev and you went to the Foster's area you could get two pints in exchange for a voucher and £2.10 whereas on Saturday I got two pints at the main bar for a voucher and £3. If your name was Tony though, you got charged a voucher plus £3.90! Poor old Tony was beside himself. Later in the evening it appeared someone had twigged there was a problem and hopefully by the next home game this "discriminaTony" pricing would be sorted.

The third topic of conversation concerned Chris Wood. There seemed to be an almost unanimous call for him to be left out; the hope being that Monk would drop his recent 4 – 4 – 2 formation and revert instead to 4 – 2 – 3 – 1 but with Antonsson, not Wood up top. Either that, or play Roofe and Antonsson as the front two. As it happened, we'd later hear that Kemar Roofe had an ankle injury and wouldn't feature at all in the squad but Monk did go back to his preferred 4 – 2 – 3 – 1 and Antonsson got the nod up front.

Green

Ayling Bartley Jansson Taylor

Bridcutt (Capt) O'Kane

Sacko Hernandez Dallas

Antonsson

Subs: Silvestri, Coyle, Cooper, Phillips, Mowatt, Wood, Doukara.

Looking at the Blackburn squad, the only name that stood out was that of Marvin Emnes, the former Middlesbrough star. He was another one of those players who always relished playing us and usually came up with something special, a bit like Tom Cairney, Jordan Rhodes and Charlie Austin often do. He'd scored against us for Boro in the past and even more worryingly… he wore the number '17' shirt! Fortunately he was only on the bench.

We'd played $4 - 4 - 2$ since that ill-fated game at QPR and the penalties win at Fleetwood even though Monk was believed to favour a lone striker. Once Roofe was fit again I did wonder if Monk would revert to $4 - 4 - 2$ but with Antonsson and Roofe at the head of the formation. Or maybe this was just to give Wood a kick up the arse.

As I took up my usual place near the front of the Kop, the sky over the South Stand looked very angry; dark and foreboding, a bit like the consequences of losing this game. Only 19,000 were in Elland Road and there was plenty of space all around me; on Saturday we could hardly move. As the game kicked off, the first flashes of lightning flickered across the inky black sky and the rain soon began to fall. It fell lightly at first and then in a torrent. Mike soon had the news that the Champions League game at the Etihad between City and Borussia Monchengladbach had been called off as had the non-league game at Stockport County. We were all a bit nervous that ours would end early too as we discussed the risks of playing football in lightning and despite the "ooohs" and "ahhhs" from the crowd that accompanied each clap of thunder and each flash in the sky, we all feared for our own safety.

There was less to "oooh" and "ahhh" about in respect of the football, although we did all gasp in the 6th minute as a long ball was aimed towards the edge of our area. Rob Green came racing out but as the ball bounced up he realised it was outside his area and so launched himself into a header just as Blackburn's Sam Gallagher did the same; Gallagher got there first to head the ball towards the corner while Green arrived a split second too late and clearly took the Blackburn man out. There was a sickening clash of heads and Gallagher went down heaviest and stayed down. It didn't look a good challenge at all but referee James Adcock only showed yellow. Green shed blood from his head wound and was soon bound up a la Kisnorbo while Gallagher also eventually continued although five minutes passed before the game restarted. Blackburn's only meaningful attempt on goal came from the resulting free kick, as first Ben Marshall's shot was blocked by

Bartley's leg and then Conway volleyed his follow-up shot inches over the bar. At the other end, Stuart Dallas had a weak header and a shot over the top while Ayling had a long range effort easily saved and new boy Eunan O'Kane fizzed one over the bar. That was the extent of the first half entertainment apart from the spectacular lightshow going on in the heavens and the sight of Leeds fans with pitch-side seats all around the ground scrambling to find cover from the rain.

The second half began in better conditions with the worst of the storm seemingly having passed over. Liam Bridcutt didn't get the benefit though as he succumbed to an ankle injury picked up in a first half challenge to be replaced by Kalvin Phillips in a like for like swap. Kyle Bartley took the captain's armband. Slowly but surely, Leeds began to dominate the game, although such efforts as we created resulted only in tame attempts from Dallas and Antonsson as we finally recorded a couple of shots on target. Hadi Sacko was beginning to shine out on the right wing too and most Leeds attacks were fed in that direction. It was the success Sacko was having in getting to the byline that probably swayed Garry Monk to make his next change. Just after the hour mark, Chris Wood made his way on to replace Marcus Antonsson. More worryingly for me was that at the same time Blackburn's manager Owen Coyle made *his* first change as that man Emnes came on for Danny Graham, a big white '17' on his back. Massimo Cellino must have been squirming up there in the East Stand at that moment sat alongside Francesco Marroccu and the ever present Andrea Lore, aka "The Spy" as the former Miami furniture salesman and now club scout is apparently nicknamed inside the club. But we needn't have worried, not yet anyway, as the next thing we saw on the pitch from Leeds was a thing of beauty.

Rob Green gathered the ball and threw it out to Pontus Jansson, just left of centre and five yards outside the Leeds area. Jansson passed it right to Eunan O'Kane and he in turn touched it further right to Kyle Bartley. The big centre-back knocked it short to Luke Ayling, hugging the touchline in front of the East Stand, mid-way in the Leeds half. Ayling quickly launched the ball down the line to Sacko. Hadi had Corry

Evans in close attendance but suddenly the Leeds winger lit the afterburners and raced past his man to the byline. Four Blackburn defenders were now around Sacko but he somehow threaded the ball through a muddle of legs and Chris Wood was on hand, five yards out, to prod the ball home. From start to finish no Blackburn player touched the ball; it was a fine goal. All we had to do now was keep a clean sheet. The problem is though we hadn't kept a clean sheet at home since February; ten games had passed since we held Middlesbrough to a goalless draw at Elland Road on February 15th! Oh, and there was the curse of that number '17'.

Blackburn made their final two substitutions and inevitably the nerves started to get to the Leeds players and the fans in equal measure; we lasted just over ten minutes. The stadium had gone eerily silent as Leeds sat deeper and deeper and suddenly that man Emnes had the ball just outside our penalty area, almost in the exact same spot from where Aaron Mooy hit the Huddersfield goal from on Saturday. It was like watching an action replay as Emnes took one touch before lashing the ball past Green, just inside that left hand post as we looked on from the other end of the ground. Incredible! We learn nothing from our mistakes; the definition of stupidity is doing the same things all the time and expecting a different outcome; we are plain stupid. Once again no Leeds player managed to get to Emnes to close him down; a known danger man and hardly inconspicuous with his trademark dreadlocks flowing behind him, allowed the freedom of Leeds. I did wonder if Cellino was on the phone that second or maybe shuffling along to speak with Steve McClaren who was also seen up in the East Stand corporate section. Perhaps he was to be our next coach? At least he'd have his brolly with him; poor old Monk looked drenched over there in front of the West Stand. I thought it was now a matter of hanging on to try to at least keep the point but I was convinced we'd be driving home listening to the obituary of Garry Monk's tenure as head coach. But strange things happen with Leeds when you least expect them; in fact we should all by now have learned to expect the unexpected…

A few more minutes went by and actually Leeds still looked positive; Alex Mowatt was on for O'Kane and he was immediately involved, although our positive attitude was leaving the odd hole at the back. Suddenly Chris Wood did that infuriating thing he does by losing possession tamely and Blackburn broke away with pace to feed the ball through to Emnes again, now behind the Leeds defence. This time his fierce shot was beaten away by Green and then our oft maligned keeper acrobatically stopped the follow-up from Sam Gallagher, pushing the ball out for a corner. It was a reminder to everyone calling for Marco Silvestri to regain his place that Green is probably just as good a shot-stopper as the Italian, albeit just as prone to a calamity every now and again. The corner came to nothing and Leeds launched the ball up towards Chris Wood, out near the East touchline and this time the big man did his job and held the ball up superbly before succumbing to a foul; Alex Mowatt placed the ball and waited for the big guys to arrive in the middle.

For once, it was the opposition that got their defending all wrong and big Kyle Bartley found a yard of space to himself to guide his header inside the near post. Had it been Leeds' defence doing that, I'd be raging about another piece of dire defending.

There was still one final onslaught to defend as Blackburn tried with everything they had to grab another equaliser. Five consecutive corners were won in the final few minutes and four times the giant Pontus Jansson got his head to the ball to nod it away for the next one. Hadi Sacko was there to deal with the odd one out and then the all action winger was racing down field with a chance to put the game beyond doubt. He only had to slot the ball past Jason Steele in Rovers' goal or slip it across to Wood or Mowatt and we were sure to score but Hadi got it all wrong and lamely scuffed the ball into the side netting. It was another sign of the inexperience that often surfaces with this young side of ours. This time it was of no consequence, as seconds later the final whistle blew and we were home if not dry.

After the game, Rovers' manager, Owen Coyle told the BBC:
"We picked ourselves up, scored a wonderful goal and had two fantastic chances to get in front and win the game.

"Rob Green has made two unbelievable saves at that point. Whether he should have been on the pitch, I think that's a big debate. If that's not endangering an opponent, when I've got Sam Gallagher in my dressing room with stitches in his head, then I don't know what is."

There was a degree of irony in the fact that this time the decision had gone with us and Green had to all intents and purposes won us the game. On Saturday, against Huddersfield, the decision went against us when Aaron Mooy was only given yellow and he went on to win the game for the Terriers. They do say these things even themselves out in the long run but seldom does it happen in consecutive games! Hadi Sacko was most fans' Man of the Match, despite his late blunder in front of goal and that was another little irony. We'd all expected to be talking about Monk getting the sack tonight; instead we were all raving about Sacko. You might say it was a case of Sacko not ashes for the Monk.

Leeds would end the day in, err, 17th in the table (sorry Massimo) but after two more games the following evening we'd be down to 18th. There were some eye-catching scores in this round of games including Newcastle's 6 – 0 win at QPR where Jimmy Floyd was now under pressure and Barnsley's 4 – 0 victory at Wolves. Huddersfield still led the way with 16 points despite suffering their first defeat, a 1 – 0 reverse at Brighton. Newcastle were 2nd and Barnsley 3rd, followed by Norwich, Birmingham and Fulham. With seven points, Leeds were 5 behind Fulham.

Leeds United 2 Blackburn Rovers 1 (**Wood (65)**, Emnes (77), **Bartley (86)**)
19,009 (Rovers 327)

The Prince of Wales

Oh Pontus Jansson's magic,
He wears a magic hat,
And if you throw a brick at him,
He heads the fu***r back.
He heads them to the left of us,
He heads them to the right,
And when we win the Championship,
We'll sing this song all night!

The games were coming thick and fast now and no sooner were the celebrations of Tuesday night over than our thoughts turned to Cardiff. The Welsh were struggling even more than we were having recorded only one win so far this season, a 2 – 1 victory over Blackburn exactly as we'd achieved this week. They'd also lost three on the trot, including a humiliating 3 – 0 reverse at Preston who themselves were at the wrong end of the table. If there was ever a good time to visit the Welsh Capital, this felt like it.

I was driving for this one and picked Kentley up at 7am. It was a three hour run to Cardiff and bang on time we pulled into the away fans' car park at the ground and Kentley shelled out the eight quid to park the car. EIGHT FU***** QUID! Just another example of how football is pricing out the travelling fans these days; travelling fans in our case who bring a real atmosphere to the games. This one was live on Sky TV too but I had a funny feeling the 'atmosphere' we'd be providing later might not be to Sky TV's liking.

We walked into the city centre heading for the Prince of Wales, the Wetherspoon where we ate before our game last March; football fans are creatures of habit and superstition and defying all the odds, we won that game 2 – 0 of course.

Green
Ayling Bartley (Capt) Jansson Taylor
Vieira O'Kane
Sacko Hernandez Dallas
Wood

Subs: Silvestri, Coyle, Cooper, Mowatt, Phillips, Roofe, Antonsson.

I learned of the team as I was finishing off my Spoon's 'Large Breakfast' and my only disappointment was that Chris Wood was starting again. The general conclusion was that Antonsson didn't do a great job in the lone striker role and that when Wood came on the other night he did well. But I was frustrated by Wood's inclusion; on the one hand I accepted we had no one else suited to the role but I also recognised a poor striker when I saw one although I still understood that he was better than he was currently showing us. The other change was enforced, as Liam Bridcutt was still not 100% fit following the knock he picked up against Blackburn; Ronaldo Vieira returned to fill that defensive midfield role.

We met Nigel at Cardiff Central and the three of us got the little single-carriage train down the line one stop to Ninian Park and then made the short walk round the corner to the stadium. At the turnstiles, after a brief frisk, a steward asked *"Have you been here before sir?"* *"Yes, a few times"* I replied and then was slightly shocked when the steward responded: *"Well, welcome back then and have a great day!"* If Carlsberg did football stewards...

The Leeds fans were in our usual corner of the CCS and it was pretty well populated. We had over 2,000 in our relatively small section while the rest of the stadium looked very sparsely occupied. I'd learn later that only 16,608 were in the ground, a ground that can hold more than 33,000. I guess that was a reflection not only of the Bluebirds' poor start to the season and their ongoing dislike of their Malaysian owner, Vincent Tan but also the fact that the game was live on Sky at lunch-time. If anyone had forgotten that last fact they were soon reminded as the first full chant of the day blasted out from the ranks of the Leeds fans; *"Sky TV is fu***** sh*t, Sky TV is fu***** sh*t..."* The roof of the stadium here extends such a long way over the pitch that the sound is channelled down towards the playing area and there was a muffled microphone propped up just below us. That must have sounded great on TV! We soon worked our way through all our usual songs and added in the National Anthem and a rousing "Eng-er-land, Eng-er-land" for good measure.

The first half was another cagey example of Championship football at its tightest with little between two average sides. Chris Wood had a great chance to put Leeds ahead but yet again his hurried strike found the keeper and not the other seven yards of goal he had to aim at. At the other end a combination of the woodwork and Rob Green prevented the home side grabbing a couple of goals. At half-time most Leeds fans would have been happy to go in all-square, whilst I was still bemoaning that Wood miss. He really is more balsa than oak. Someone who most definitely was a 'heart of oak' sort of a fella was Pontus Jansson; once again he was the stand out performer in the Leeds defence as time and time again he headed crosses clear and the Cardiff danger man, Rickie Lambert was getting absolutely no change from the big Swede. Pontus was destined to be our Prince of Wales today.

Cardiff had a little flurry at the start of the second half and won a couple of corners but Jansson's head seemed to be a magnet for the ball and gradually the balance seemed to shift towards Leeds. Cardiff's supporters were now silent (not that they'd made much noise in the first half) while we seemed to sense another away win was within our grasp and we notched up the volume even more. Gradually, Pablo Hernandez was starting to dictate our every move, operating just in behind Wood or even ahead of him on occasions. The chances began to arrive as Cardiff started to fade; first Wood blazed another one over the bar, albeit under a challenge and from a tight angle and then he had another limp effort from the opposite angle that went away for a Leeds corner. Hernandez wandered over to take an in-swinger with his right foot from just down below us to a chorus of his own special *"Pab-lo Hernandez"* chant. As the ball lofted into the box we could see the huge figure of Pontus Jansson, unmistakable in his bright orange boots, toppling over like a giant redwood in a forest of saplings. Then there was a shrill blast on the referees whistle and Graham Scott was pointing to the spot.

The big issue at all levels of football at this time was that of holding and shirt pulling at set pieces in the area. The football authorities had publicly pledged to stamp it out and several penalties had been given in high profile Premier League games recently for just that offence. This ref, Graham Scott, had incensed us throughout the first half with numerous strange decisions including a booking for Luke Ayling when he appeared to cleanly take the ball albeit following through to take his man as well. Scott also appeared to change his mind a few times after initially giving decisions our way. No matter, he was now our best friend. Matt Connolly had effectively wrestled Pontus to the ground with an arm lock around the big man's neck; in fairness it was the only way they were going to stop him getting his head on the ball!

There was the usual apprehension as Chris Wood picked up the ball and placed it on the spot but Woody calmly sent the keeper the wrong way and slid the ball into the bottom right hand corner. 1 – 0 Leeds and now another win in Cardiff was looking on the cards.

The Bluebirds had another little period of pressure and we saw another example of Rob Green's penchant for coming for a lost cause as he was left stranded away from his goal line but, after another couple of corners were dealt with efficiently enough, Leeds grabbed the initiative again.

The goal seemed to give the Leeds players even more confidence and the little conductor in the middle, Pablo Hernandez, started to look a very good player indeed. Leeds flooded forward now and Cardiff looked a beaten side. Kemar Roofe got another chance to show us what he's about as he replaced Stuart Dallas in the 71st minute, although I have to admit Kemar looked way short of both pace and stamina and was frankly a disappointment. But soon that man Hernandez was breaking away again from deep within his own half; Chris Wood was free on his right but I guess Pablo was by now familiar with Wood's scoring ratio so he went on his own. It was the wrong decision in hindsight and his tame shot was easily saved by Ben Amos in the Cardiff goal. Hernandez then slid the ball through to Hadi Sacko who had his shot saved at the foot of a post. It was all Leeds now. Rob Green rolled the ball out to Charlie Taylor and he lofted a long ball down the inside left channel; it was headed back to Hernandez, mid-way in the Cardiff half. As Pablo drove on towards the box the Cardiff defenders backed off and backed off and then, jinking to his right, Pablo curled a delightful right-foot shot into the top right corner. 2 – 0 and, barring disaster, game over. Droves of Cardiff supporters thought so anyway, as they upped and left, streaming down the steps to our right to a chorus of *"time to go"* from the Leeds fans. Pablo got his own reception as he was subbed by Kalvin Phillips late on and then in added time Marcus Antonsson replaced Chris Wood. At the final whistle it was all hugs and kisses in the Leeds section and that was just us blokes. It was another magic, magic away day, just as we had down here back in March.

After the game, Garry Monk told the BBC:

"We have a new group, new manager, new ideas, and we are taking it step by step. We are right at the start of that journey and if we give this group time to show their quality they can potentially grow into something very good. This is another step in the right direction. We are getting there slowly, we've not yet had that complete performance but we are growing. It was important to get those back-to-back wins and see how these young players deal with that momentum."

It read like a thinly veiled plea to Massimo Cellino to leave him alone and give him more time and if he'd do that then the players would deliver. There were still rumours going around that Massimo had already made his mind up though so I was prepared for all eventualities.

Leeds were up to 15th in the table, just 4 points behind the top six with Huddersfield still top followed by Norwich and Newcastle. Next up was a home EFL Cup third round tie with Blackburn, on Tuesday night. The big question everyone was asking was just what team would Monk send out for that. Would he rest his key players and save them for the next league game or would he play a similar side in the hope of building even more momentum. Blackburn walloped Rotherham this weekend to pick up their first league win of the season so they would have a similar dilemma.

Cardiff City 0 Leeds United 2 (Wood (62 pen), Hernandez (82)) 16,608 **(Leeds 1,800)**

Up for the Cup

I was with the Shropshire Whites again for the EFL Cup tie with Blackburn, well, three of them anyway! As I stood at the bus stop outside Sainsbury's in Whitchurch with Woggy and Andy I was surprised when the vehicle that arrived to pick us up was a little silver sports car. Gaz was driving and as I scrambled to squeeze my 6ft 2inch frame into one of the rear seats he explained there were only four of us travelling to the game and hence the sensible thing to do was use the car. It was the usual stop go mid-week trudge up the motorways but we arrived at the ground pretty much on schedule at 6:30pm. We were nervous they wouldn't let us park in the coach park behind the Pavilion but there was just one coach and one other car in so far and the attendant told us it was his first day in the job so he'd go by whatever we said. We told him we were the Shropshire Whites and the charge for a car was £5; job done. When Gaz explained we normally had a mini-bus the bloke nodded and told us he understood: *"I think that'll be t'case with all t'branches tonight"*, he said, *"We're only expecting 7,000!"*

It was no surprise therefore that the Pavilion was only one quarter open and even that small space wasn't busy when I strolled in. The girl I spoke to about the music the other day was on the desk and she recognised me. *"No music today!"* she proudly announced with a smile and went on to explain that she'd put our case to her bosses and believed they understood. I thanked her and went in to join the lads from County Durham, George, Trevor and Tony who were all sat with Steve, as usual they'd been queuing at the door at 4:45pm.

"I'm going to pick a team that can win the game; I want to keep this momentum with us. I'll pick the strongest team possible in terms of freshness and who will be ready. But I don't particularly want to make too many changes."[1]

That was Garry Monk speaking on the eve of the game. It's always a matter of interpretation of course as to what constitutes *"too many"* but the seven changes he actually made from the starting eleven at Cardiff seemed a lot to me!

Silvestri
Coyle Bartley Cooper (Capt) Taylor
Vieira O'Kane
Phillips Mowatt Roofe
Antonsson

Subs: Green, Ayling, Denton, Dallas, Grimes, Hernandez, Wood.

On the other hand it was not as many as Owen Coyle made to his Blackburn side. He made a total of nine changes from the side that picked up its first league win of the season against Rotherham at the weekend. I was happy enough to see that Marvin Emnes, number '17' remember, was only on their bench again.

I wandered over to the stadium with Nigel at our normal time, twenty minutes before kick-off; it was very quiet. When we got to our seats there were gaps everywhere around us. Even Jo, Mike and Lynn were AWOL. Kentley did arrive, albeit some 15 minutes into the game and he'd brought his buddy "Little Isaac". Isaac is a season ticket holder with another team; one I dare not mention by name in here. The crowd was a little bigger than the 7,000 we were warned about; 8,488.

Leeds began the game with some pace and invention and inside the first few minutes Roofe had a shot blocked and Lewie Coyle blasted the rebound towards the top corner of

---

1

http://www.leedsunited.com/news/article/1l8i0es2hcoqs1k2ie06ni1zp w/title/efl-cup-monk-keen-to-maintain-momentum

David Raya's net; the Rovers' keeper just stretching to tip the ball over the angle for a corner. But then that initial urgency seemed to dissipate and the game started to look much like the league game here the previous week, despite the fact only six players on show tonight featured in that one. Gradually the noise from the Kop subsided and with the South Stand empty, the ground went very quiet; the sort of quiet where the rare moments of applause echo eerily around the stadium. At our end of the pitch, just before the break, Silvestri pulled off one acrobatic save diving away to his left, a mirror image if you like of the one Raya managed at the other end. At half-time though it was still all square at 0 – 0 just as it was seven days earlier. The biggest cheer of the first half came from the Kop when Silvestri finally managed to kick a ball straight down the middle and not away over the touchline in front of the East Stand where all the others went. There was also a welcome moment of humour when referee Darren Deadman went to collect a replacement flag for the liner on the east touchline; Deadman ran right across the pitch with the yellow flag held aloft and then swirled it around his head like a second rate matador before handing it to his bemused liner with a flourish. That drew a huge cheer and applause from the Kop. We need more characters in the game.

An hour passed and still we were marooned in a goalless sea of tranquillity but then Vieira picked up an injury and *"Pab-lo Hernandez, Pab-lo Hernandez"* made his way purposely onto the pitch and it was as if a switch had been flicked. The crowd was roused too and each time Pablo got the ball there was an audible reaction. I did have one little concern though; soon after Pablo came on, Blackburn sent on two of their subs. One of them wore '17' on his back but it was almost obscured by the dreadlocks flowing out behind him; Marvin Emnes. He was straight into the thick of the action too as a fierce left-foot shot was blocked by the legs of Silvestri. The ball flew in the air and Marco was up to punch it away and then was down to save the follow-up shot from Elliot Bennett. Leeds then looked to Chris Wood to liven up the Leeds attack; he replaced Antonsson who'd been very quiet.

It was Pablo taking the eye now though and next he floated a free kick in that beat everyone apart from Raya who had to fling himself to his left to tip the ball around the post. More noise from the Kop, more urging the team on; we sensed it was only Leeds who looked like scoring to avoid the dreaded extra-time. Matt Grimes was the final Leeds sub, replacing Alex Mowatt. Leeds were enjoying a long spell of possession that seemed to have ended as a Blackburn defender hoofed the ball away but Grimes stretched out a leg and intercepted it. He was back on his feet in an instant to knock the ball past his marker and Pablo Hernandez glided onto it like a curling Subbuteo man. He took a couple of touches and then lashed in a shot that Raya managed to push away from his left hand post to an "ooooh" from the Kop, but Kemar Roofe was running in and next he tried his luck but horribly mishit it into the ground across the face of goal. Another gasp from the Kop and much holding of heads but then we see Chris Wood is there swinging a right leg at the ball, six yards out with just the keeper in front of him. Bugger me he only hits it straight at Raya! The enormity of the miss is just entering our minds when our eyes see that the ball has bounced back off the keeper right on to Wood's head and this time it rebounds past Raya into the net! Talk about jammy! The thing about this bloke Wood is that, as poor a finisher as he is sometimes, he did now have six goals this campaign and he was well on the way, ahead of schedule actually, to his 20 goals for the season; incredible really. To be fair to Wood though, he was starting to look far fitter and sharper than he did throughout last season.

There were a couple of Blackburn forays towards the Leeds goal in front of the empty South Stand and Kemar Roofe had a couple more tame shots at goal in front of the Kop but Leeds saw the rest of the game out reasonably comfortably. Three wins on the trot, three in three for Chris Wood and a fourth clean sheet of the season were all good stats to record but I kept reminding myself that Blackburn were a poor side as were Cardiff on Saturday. Still, a win is a win as the man says and we were in the last sixteen of the EFL Cup.

Leeds United 1 Blackburn Rovers 0 (**Wood (85)**)
8,488 (Rovers 463)

The Tractor Boys

Massimo Cellino had been quiet, but not *that* quiet. Everyone was still waiting for the FA to announce its conclusions following the McCormack "bung" investigation that, as these things always seem to, was taking an age. But news then came out that Club Secretary, Stuart Hayton, a veritable gold watch long-service candidate with over a year in post, had left the club, although no one seemed to know why. Another leaver, albeit temporary, was young striker Frank Mulhern; he was off to non-league Southport on a three-month loan. That was a tad ironic as only this week the national press ran a story claiming the youngster would be included in the squad for the Blackburn cup game; although on the night he was nowhere to be seen. I did wonder if he'd spoken out of turn and this was his punishment. Another former young Leeds striker, Lewis Walters was this week snapped up by Nottingham Forest so I made a mental note to look out for him banging the goals in left, right and centre as all our former strikers tend to do once they leave us.

"Bloody typical; look we're stuck behind the Ipswich team bus!" It was the voice of one of the lads at the back of our coach. I peered through the big windscreen and there in the distance at the front of a queue of traffic was an old tractor, trundling along through the Cheshire countryside as we headed for the M6. I'd just been picked up at Whitchurch and today the Shropshire Whites had managed to almost fill a full sized coach for the trip to Elland Road where the Tractor Boys, Ipswich Town, were the visitors.

My heart sank when I walked into the Pavilion as the first thing I noticed was that the stage was set up for another band despite the promise from that nice lady on the desk the other night. It was the same group of young lads we saw the other day – a band called Trigger Happy – and they quickly ran through their set and then disappeared and we could settle down for a chat and to watch the big screens showing the Man U v Leicester City Premier League game. Man U would go on to win it 4 – 1 as the Champions continued to struggle to defend the crown they so surprisingly won last season. Miss nice lady came over to see us and once again told us that Commercial Director Paul Bell was fully aware of our gripe about the music and once again led us to believe our comments had been taken on board.

Peter Lorimer and Terry Yorath followed the band onto the stage with compere Jed Stone who was clearly beside himself with joy at the recent run of results. Jed asked Yorath if he thought big Pontus Jansson had made the difference to the defence and the Welshman replied in typical forthright manner: *"Jansson?, well he's better than those two idiots we had last season!"* Ah, Bamba and Bellusci, remember them?

Green
Ayling Bartley (Capt) Jansson Taylor
O'Kane Phillips
Sacko Hernandez Dallas
Wood

Subs: Silvestri, Coyle, Cooper, Mowatt, Grimes, Antonsson, Roofe.

As expected, Garry Monk reverted pretty much to the team that did so well down at Cardiff, with just the one change; Kalvin Phillips replaced Vieira to fill the slot left open by the continued absence of the injured Liam Bridcutt. Vieira was also rumoured to be carrying a knock. Two names that had conspicuously fallen out of the squad list in the match day programme were Luke Murphy and 'Dave' Diagouraga. I guessed we were unlikely to see either of them again this season although they'd failed to attract any interest from other clubs thus far despite being free to go.

The Ipswich game was to prove a revelation. Within the first ten minutes Hadi Sacko had fired a shot wide and Chris Wood had thundered a long range effort against a post and that really set the stall out for the rest of the afternoon. Leeds were simply dominant in all aspects of the game apart from the important one of sticking the ball in the net. Chris Wood now looked a completely different player, running from halfway where he collected Pontus Jansson's clearance up the left wing before cutting in and striking that shot that clattered the woodwork. He would prove the difference between the two sides and would have his best game in many months. At the back, Pontus was immense once again and after leaving Brett Pitman prostrate on the pitch after a thunderous tackle he once again turned to the Kop and roared at us as he urged us to crank up the noise. The man is truly a beast! The only problem was that Pontus hit Pitman so hard that he had to go off and it was age-old Leeds foe Leon Best who replaced him. I did wonder if Gaetano Berardi had mentioned to Pontus that Best once did him with an elbow and whether our big Swede would now be after him too.

The key moment of the game came shortly after the half-hour and it was another wonderful flowing move from Leeds that began in our own half. Bartley touched the ball forward to Hernandez who in turn freed up Sacko to set off at pace with the ball. He knocked it left to Chris Wood who held it up before touching it to Dallas. Dallas shaped to strike at goal but then checked and played it down the left wing into the corner where Charlie Taylor ran on to it. He stood the ball up to the centre of goal, six yards out and Wood rose above Christophe Berra to nod it down and past Bartosz Bialkowski; for once, it was a text book header from Wood. It was his fourth goal in four games and his seventh in all this season and even I, one of his biggest critics, finally accepted he was a changed man.

Leeds had several more excellent opportunities to put the game to bed but the one problem that continued to afflict us was an inability to convert chances. Chris Wood had a few and Hadi Sacko was also wasteful. In fact Sacko had an excellent game apart from his finishing and final touch. Leeds would conjure up 16 attempts on the Ipswich goal – more than twice the Ipswich tally – yet only four hit the target. It was the one area Garry Monk and his coaching team had not yet seemingly corrected. It was a shame, as the 1 – 0 score-line hardly did justice to our domination and a display that was almost perfect. I couldn't remember the last time a Leeds team so completely bossed a game.

Afterwards, Ipswich manager Mick McCarthy, a known Leeds fan and gruff Yorkshireman, told the BBC: *"I thought Chris Wood was outstanding, the focal point and the big difference in the team. When they hit it up there they stuck up there and he ran in the channels. He showed why he had good money (spent on him) and why he's a good player. Leeds have a very good player. He played well."*

As usual, Garry Monk was reluctant to single out any individual player for comment but of the performance he told BBC Radio Leeds: *"Each time the team goes onto the pitch, and you can see it when I look at the start of the season to now, that understanding of what is expected and how we are going to do it is getting better.*

"We are taking steps forward for sure. Improvements are there and when you look at that first game, it is pleasing.

"I have a plan that I work to and everyone is clear with that, they understand exactly where they need to get."

Leeds had made their worst start to a season in 40 years with just four points coming from their first six league games. Now, that Huddersfield defeat seemed light years ago and we'd recorded four successive victories for the first time since the 2009/10 season when that famous 1 – 0 FA Cup win at Old Trafford completed four on the trot. The last time we recorded five or more wins in a row came at the start of that season when we won eight consecutive games in all competitions. If we were to make it five in a row this season, then we had to next beat a flying Bristol City at Ashton Gate next Tuesday.

Leeds ended round 9 of the campaign in 12th spot with 13 points; just 3 points behind 6th placed Birmingham City and 7 points behind Norwich who now topped the table. Bristol shocked many with a 4 – 0 demolition of Fulham at Craven Cottage this weekend with teenage sensation, Chelsea loanee Tammy Abraham, getting his tenth goal of the season. Could Pontus stop him?

Leeds United 1 Ipswich Town 0 (**Wood (35)**)
22,554 (Ipswich 902)

All good things...

An uneventful drive down to Bristol brought Kentley and I to the Bedminster Cricket Club car park, just after 4:30pm. The place wasn't really open yet but a bloke told me I could *"park anywhere you like mate"* So, I did exactly that, right against the wall of the club house. *"Nah, you can't leave it there mate, that's for disabled drivers..."*
It was a warm and muggy afternoon and the cricket ground looked magnificent. The beautiful Clifton Suspension bridge could be seen glinting in the sunshine in the distance and the grand buildings of upmarket Clifton stood proudly a bit further to the right as we looked on from the clubhouse. Bedminster CC dates from at least 1847 and moved to its present ground on "The Clanage" in 1912. Prior to that it shared Ashton Gate with Bristol City and its other claim to fame is that a certain W.G. Grace once played in their colours. In fact, WG recorded just three "pairs" (a duck in both innings) in his whole career and one of them was for Bedminster in a game in 1870.[1]

---

[1] *http://bedminstercc.co.uk/clubhouse-and-events/history/*

We were joined by Kev W, Keith and Nigel in the clubhouse for a few pints as news began to filter through that big Sam Allardyce had left his multi-million pound job as England Manager *"by mutual consent"*. Sam had fallen foul of a sting operation by The Daily Telegraph in which he'd alluded to knowing how to get around FA rules on third party ownership of players and negotiated himself a £400,000 fee for various appearances on behalf of a fictitious Far East company. His position was clearly untenable and he would thus become the shortest serving England boss of all time at just 67 days. The Telegraph was promising more revelations in the days and weeks to come as they waged war on corruption in football. We all wondered if the name of Massimo Cellino would crop up in their disclosures.

When the team was announced for the clash with the Robins we were surprised there was still no Liam Bridcutt in it. We would later hear that he was in London undergoing another MRI scan on his troublesome foot and hence why he wasn't even on the bench. When we eventually learned the result of this latest scan it was clear we wouldn't be seeing Liam in a Leeds shirt for another six to eight weeks. The new scan revealed a slight fracture to a bone in his foot which had previously been thought to only be bruising. It was a blow. The team to face Bristol was therefore the same side that began the Ipswich game:

Green
Ayling Bartley (Capt) Jansson Taylor
O'Kane Phillips
Sacko Hernandez Dallas
Wood

Subs: Silvestri, Coyle, Cooper, Mowatt, Grimes, Antonsson, Roofe.

Leeds had the backing of over 2,000 fans at the newly renovated Ashton Gate, all housed to the right hand side of the Atyeo Stand at one end of the ground. The fabulous and massive Lansdown Stand that was in its early stages of construction when we were here this time last season was over to our right and was now complete and operational; it was the only area that wasn't particularly full but can hold 11,000 if needed. The atmosphere was excellent and there was a good noise as the two teams emerged from the tunnel down below us. The tall figure of Tammy Abraham, wearing number '9' for the Robins, stood out as the sides lined up in front of the Lansdown Stand; he was the teenage loanee from Chelsea who'd already bagged ten goals this season. His battle with our own giant, Pontus Jansson, would be crucial.

The first half was entertaining with both sides creating half-chances but all of them went begging largely due to poor finishing. The referee, Keith Stroud, was doing his best to spoil the game with a number of inconsistent decisions and needless bookings but when he really ought to have been alert as Bristol's Lee Tomlin lashed out at Stuart Dallas in our penalty area, he clearly didn't see what happened and both players got a yellow card; Tomlin was a lucky boy not to get red.

That incident happened just before the break but minutes before that our superman defender, Pontus Jansson, also got himself a caution, albeit in his case it was needless and daft. Pontus took issue with the match-ball and decided it was not fit for purpose but instead of tossing it to the referee, when it next went dead for a goal kick Pontus launched it *"Ave it"* style out of the open corner of the ground. It went many a mile and sadly the referee deemed that to be Pontus 'kicking the ball away' which of course is an automatic yellow. Worse still though was the fact our man was now feeling his hamstring, possibly having overstretched when putting the ball into orbit where it would now circle the earth for ever more, in tandem with Chris Wood's Doncaster penalty. Pontus was clearly in some trouble as he limped down the tunnel at half-time.

Sure enough, after the break Pontus didn't reappear and Liam Cooper took his place alongside Kyle Bartley. There were lots of apprehensive faces in the Leeds crowd. I became even more nervous in the 53rd minute when Bristol made their first substitution; Taylor Moore replaced Mark Little and on the back of Moore's shirt was the number '17'. Was it an omen? Who knows, but six minutes later Leeds were a goal down.

Pablo Hernandez was brought down by Marlon Pack in a tussle for the ball near the centre circle, Pablo left on the turf appealing to the referee. But Keith Stroud was waving play-on and now Lee Tomlin was racing towards goal and Pack was keeping pace with him to his left; there was a hole in the Leeds defence. Tomlin shifted the ball to Pack and he lifted it expertly over the diving body of Rob Green. It all happened in the blink of eye; one momentary lapse and the game was probably lost. Pablo complained long after the goal was scored and got himself a booking for his troubles and Garry Monk would get himself sent to the stand for his abusive comments to the officials. That would earn him a £2,000 fine and a touchline ban for our trip to Derby in a few weeks' time.

Leeds had more chances, better chances than the home side actually, but that same old problem of poor decision making and rotten finishing meant they came to nothing. Hadi Sacko and Chris Wood both ought to have scored but they didn't and the game was lost despite the fans holding out hope right up to the final whistle. It was here last season of course that we threw away a two goal winning margin in added time. A thoughtful looking Garry Monk trudged across the pitch with his hands thrust deep in his pockets and disappeared down the tunnel below. Later he would sum up the game perfectly as he told the BBC:

"We had the best clear-cut chances in the game. We did not always make the right decisions in the final third and we need to be more clinical." [1]

We had one more chance to put this malaise right before the next international break; Saturday, in a home Yorkshire derby against free-scoring Barnsley who were surprising all the pundits by more than holding their own in the Championship having won promotion from League One only last season. Our four match winning streak was ended; all good things eventually come to an end; ask Sam Allardyce.

Bristol City 1 **Leeds United 0** (Pack (59))
19,699 (**Leeds 2,065**)

---

[1] *http://www.bbc.co.uk/sport/football/37414319*

Distraction Derby

It's Magic! ©cgarland

It wouldn't be normal if any corruption investigation didn't include a reference to Massimo Cellino and sure enough the Telegraph sting operation soon published details of a meeting they'd had with the Italian. Video of that meeting as well as a similar one with Jimmy Floyd Hasselbaink and details of cash changing hands between the sting crew and Barnsley's assistant manager, Tommy Wright, all appeared the day after the Allardyce revelations. Within 48 hours of the videos being aired, Wright was first suspended and then sacked, the second casualty of the sting. Everyone in Football must have been feeling a tad nervous. There were rumours that Wright was well regarded by Cellino and even that the Italian once tried to recruit him. Another fellow recently connected with Leeds was also mentioned in despatches by The Telegraph; Francesco Marroccu, who'd been seen at Thorp Arch during training sessions and who once worked for Cellino at Cagliari.

The allegation against Cellino was that he, like Allardyce, was offering ways around third party ownership rules and if the FA investigated Cellino over this video, as surely they must, then it would be just one of several cases still outstanding against him; the McCormack case, elements of the Lucy Ward case and even the Adryan transfer case wasn't yet fully concluded. That IS Arenas case in Italy was still ongoing too. Blimey, the bloke had more cases than Samsonite! Around midnight on 28th September the Club issued a statement denying there was anything improper contained in the video clips they'd seen. It was a *"non-story"* they claimed.

As the nights began to draw in, the first managerial casualties of the new season began to appear. Division One Leyton Orient were the first to blink as Andy Hessenthaler and Kevin Nolan were given the big E with Orient languishing 16th in League Two. Warren Feeney of Newport County (bottom of League Two) and Tony Mowbray of Coventry City (bottom of League One) quickly followed and I guess Alan Stubbs at Rotherham was shifting uncomfortably in his leather chair with the Millers currently occupying the bottom spot in the Championship. It was that time of year; the silly season.

The TTGM group were planning a demonstration at the ground before the next game... as were a group of fans who wanted to protest against the protestors! As to the rumours of an imminent takeover of the club, those had now gone very quiet and on the eve of the Barnsley game, Phil Hay of the YEP tweeted: *"v unclear. This isn't confirmed but I was told by two people last w/e that whatever Radrizzani was planning is no longer happening"*. And if all this wasn't enough to distract us from the job in hand, watching Channel 4's 'Couples Come Dine with Me' this week I nearly fell off the sofa. One much stressed couple made the classic mistake of warming their dinner plates on the hob with the usual outcome that they all exploded from the heat. Popping next door to borrow more plates who should be there but Jordan Botaka! Bizarrely, the Wizard had a small football in his hands. I could only assume his flat was so big he had a football pitch in there! So, with all this stuff going on, The Sun came up with its own name for our all Yorkshire clash; they called it the *"Distraction Derby"*. Barnsley had turned to JC for divine help, quickly replacing the sacked Tommy Wright with former Ipswich defender Jamie Clapham. I only hoped it wasn't going to be Leeds left 'Up the Junction'.

Late on Friday afternoon we had one more distraction that took our thoughts away from the upcoming game. News began to filter through that Soccerex founder and CEO Duncan

Revie, son of the Don, had passed away. It was immediately announced there would be a minute's applause before the Barnsley game and within minutes the TTGM group announced they were postponing their planned protest as a mark of respect. It was time for the whole Leeds United family to come together and pay its respects; it's what we always do.

It was cold and drizzling with rain as Woggy and I waited at the bus stop opposite Sainsbury's; the Shropshire Whites mini-bus was twenty minutes late. Humph was at the wheel and was clearly determined to make up time as he pulled off while we were still trying to scramble into our seats. I was pitched forward onto Gary T's lap, and nearly head-butted him in the process and there was a roar of approval from the lads at the back of the bus. It was going to be that sort of a day. The journey was a bit like a Carry On movie – Carry on up to Leeds. The first problem came as we attempted to make a toilet stop for one of the girls. It was decided we might as well find a pub so the lads could have a quick top-up pint while we waited and someone eventually came up with the Stretton Fox, just off junction 10 of the M56. The battered old mini-bus screeched to a halt outside the front door and everyone piled off ... but there was a problem; the pub was closed! 11:30am on a Saturday morning and the bloody pub was shut! Undeterred, Gaz is straight on his phone to look up the telephone number and then eventually gets through. He failed in his bid to get them to open up to serve beer but he did pull off a bit of a coup in getting the girls into their loos. *"We've got a pregnant lady on board who's desperate for the loo mate"* he told the lad on the other end of the line. Well, he could hardly refuse could he? Back on the bus we'd only been going another hour or so and blow me down Claire needed to go again! It had nothing to do with her being pregnant and everything to do with the copious cans of Carlsberg she'd been supping! This time we skidded to a halt at the entrance to a service area, nearly shunting into a lady in a wheel chair and sending her wheeling off down the slip road onto the motorway! Five minutes later and we were back on the road.

The regular stops and the fact we were late setting off in the first place meant I was nervously glancing at my watch wondering if I was going to make my usual pre-match rendezvous with the lads in the Pavilion. Then Gaz dropped the bombshell that we were dropping off in the city centre first and then the ground and not the other way round. So we went hurtling past the ground on the M621 and then wound our way around the streets of Leeds before dropping most of the lads just near the station. Despite the fact it was making my Pavilion appearance later and later, it was fascinating seeing Leeds on a match-day morning. Everywhere you looked there were folk rushing round in Leeds tops, a long queue was already assembled waiting for the regular double decker buses to the ground and the pubs were all bustling with activity. I made a mental note to join the lads in Leeds one of these days.

Arriving at the Pavilion not long after 1pm, I grabbed a couple of pints (two for six quid remember) and joined the folk at our usual table; Tony broke the news that another rock band was due on stage any moment. Our regular pleas to the management appeared to be falling on deaf ears and ours were soon being deafened by the band while we struggled to concentrate on the Swansea v Liverpool game being shown on the big screens. 'Pool' would continue their good start to the season with a decent 2 – 1 win.

Garry Monk named an unchanged side for a third consecutive game, meaning the injury worry over the mighty beast going by the name of Pontus Jansson had gone away. Someone suggested Pontus probably gave his troublesome hamstring a withering stare and it instantly healed itself; the man was attaining godly status around Elland Road.

Green
Ayling Bartley (Capt) Jansson Taylor
O'Kane Phillips
Sacko Hernandez Dallas
Wood

Subs: Silvestri, Coyle, Cooper, Roofe, Antonsson, Vieira, Mowatt.

Over 27,000 were in the ground today and it was nice it was so busy as we paid tribute to Duncan Revie with that minute's applause. Midway through it the Leeds fans at both ends of the ground spontaneously broke into a chant of *"There's only one*

Don Revie". Duncan's son Aidan and other members of the Revie dynasty were present and it must have been some comfort to them to see the esteem the family is held in.

Barnsley had enjoyed a fantastic start to their Championship season, although they'd faltered in their most recent three games, failing to win any of them. They still began this game three points ahead of Leeds though and were the division's leading scorers with eleven different goal scorers in their stats book. Such was the turnaround in our fortunes during the last few weeks though that most Leeds fans were confident the Tykes could be overcome; so often in the past Barnsley had pulled off surprise and often comprehensive wins over us but we'd seldom been in good nick at the time.

For half an hour we saw a typical Championship battle ensue as both sides tried to impose their styles on the other and it looked as though it would be another very close encounter. Then, in the 36th minute, Charlie Taylor won a corner on the left. Pablo Hernandez trotted over to take it and stood with both arms in the air signalling to the big men in the middle; both Kyle Bartley and Pontus Jansson were waiting. The ball curled in towards Bartley at the near post and he reacted first to get his left knee onto it and guide it home. The celebrations were ecstatic as Bartley raced over towards the dug-out and slid down onto his backside with his team-mates racing to catch him. Following Leeds had become a very pleasurable experience in the last month or so and as the players walked off at half-time not a gripe was to be heard; no boos, no anger, just satisfied approval of a very solid first half.

At the start of the second half things looked even better. Leeds were now on top in all areas of the pitch and the drive was typically coming from Pablo again. He seemed to come into his own once we got any sort of a lead as the opposition then had to try to press forward leaving the Spaniard more space, space that his skills could exploit. Within seconds of the start of the new half he was weaving his way into the penalty area in front of the Kop and probably ought to have done better than just shave the left hand post with his curling shot. But soon after he was at it again and this time he made the Tykes pay. A long ball into the Leeds attacking left wing was headed back into the Leeds half but Eunan O'Kane lofted it straight back on the half-volley over the advancing Barnsley back line; Pablo picked out the trajectory straight away and he was suddenly one-on-one with Barnsley's keeper, Adam Davies. As Davies rushed out Pablo opened his body to get the ball onto his right foot and calmly curled it around the keepers stretching left hand; 2 – 0 Leeds and more than half an hour to go. For the first time in recent memory I had no concern that Barnsley could use that time to get back in the game and every belief that we'd go on and close it out, probably grabbing a goal or two more, such was the belief I now had in this Leeds team. Tim, who was stood next to me, was getting excited that he'd be in the money as he'd bet on a 4 – 0 Leeds win. I winked at my old mate Pete at that point and said I'd be well peed off if that happened; Pete knew full well that for years I'd had a quid on 4 – 0 to Leeds for every home game but I stopped mid-way through last season for obvious reasons.

For another ten minutes or so 4 – 0 looked a distinct possibility as Leeds started to look every bit the *"Super, Super Leeds, Super Leeds United"* we were now singing about. All over the pitch Leeds were brim full of confidence and with the 'magic hat' song ringing in his ears even Pontus was dazzling us with his footwork as he pulled off a move worthy of an appearance on 'Strictly' over in the south-west corner. But there was one aspect of this Leeds side that wasn't yet good enough; our finishing. Two more good chances went begging from the feet of Chris Wood, one with each foot and each time there were murmurs of *"For f*** sake"* coming from Tim who could see his 4 – 0 bet disappearing each time Wood aimed at goal. At 2 – 0 the missed chances were more annoyances than disasters but then, with 20 minutes to go, Barnsley were back in the game. A quick move down the Tyke's left wing over in front of the East Stand, a ball slipped in behind Luke Ayling and a fierce cross come shot went past Rob Green at his near post and ricocheted into the net off Charlie Taylor. As confident as we'd been a few moments earlier, a few of us were now thinking maybe this was that old Leeds tendency of foot-shooting reappearing.

Garry Monk responded strangely by immediately bringing off Hadi Sacko and bringing on Marcus Antonsson; I felt that Sacko, despite once again being a bit wasteful with his final ball, was still a very decent out-ball down that right wing. In fact Antonsson proved to be quite a handful himself and could easily have restored the two goal lead but for a strong left hand from Davies. With six minutes to go, Monk surprised me again by taking off Pablo and bringing on Kemar Roofe. Pablo had been instrumental in our second half dominance and I now thought we'd struggle to bring the ball forward. There was one final push from Barnsley as a few shots rained in towards Rob Green's goal but usually the body or head of Pontus Jansson was in the way and there were no more serious threats. Ronaldo Vieira replaced Stuart Dallas as Leeds wound down the final seconds.

2 – 1 was the final score and Leeds went into the next international break on the back of five wins in six games. We'd end this 11th round of games 11th in the table with 16 points; seven places and five points better off than last season. Huddersfield continued to lead the Championship with another eye-catching win at Ipswich that suggested they might well remain amongst the pace-setters all season, while more fancied Norwich were second, two points behind them. Leeds were a mere 4 points adrift of sixth placed Birmingham. At the bottom, Rotherham, Cardiff and Blackburn all lost again without scoring a single goal between them. Leeds were a full 8 points above the best of them, Blackburn.

On the mini-bus going home, the lads at the back of the bus kept us entertained with a full range of songs including one aimed squarely at Claire, the lady who made us stop umpteen times on the way up. *"Your bladder's sh**, your bladder's sh**"* they sang at the tops of their voices as she suggested we make another toilet stop! It was all taken in good spirit; it had been a good day despite all the distractions.

Leeds United 2 Barnsley 1 (**Bartley (36), Hernandez (54),** Taylor (70 og) 27,350 (**Barnsley 2,413**)

A Grand Day Out

The managerial merry-go-round was really starting to spin and was now centred on the Championship. As the next international break began and we eagerly (?) awaited the England-Malta and Slovenia-England World Cup qualifiers, England's first games post Sam Allardyce, Aston Villa announced that Roberto di Mateo was a gonner after just 121 days in the job. Villa had won only a single game this season and were languishing 19th in the Championship despite spending millions of their parachute payment to try to get back in the Premier League at the first attempt. The following day, Cardiff City ditched Paul Trollope as they contemplated their current position, second bottom in the Championship. They had two wins all season and the name being touted as a possible saviour was 'Red Adair' himself, Neil Warnock. How we'd love to see him back at Elland Road in the opposition dugout again… if only to hand him a good spanking. Sure enough, within 24 hours, 'Colin Wanker' as he is affectionately known by his own anagram, was appointed and another former Leeds manager, Kevin Blackwell, would once again work alongside him. One of their first signings was none other than Sol Bamba, now a free agent of course, having left Leeds for *"personal reasons"*. That ought to tighten up the Bluebirds' defence I thought sarcastically!

Within days, Derby County parted company with Nigel Pearson, meaning three of the bottom six in the Championship would soon be under new management. If anyone had been in any doubt how vital it was not to fall out of the Championship, they weren't now. The battle was on.

In another of those weird footballing coincidences, the third of the three Welsh sides in the English leagues, Premier League Swansea, also decided to make a change following Newport and Cardiff. They sacked Francesco Guidolin, a relative veteran of 259 days as they sat 17th in the Premier League. It was Guidolin who replaced Garry Monk as the Swans' permanent manager only last December. Swansea already had their next man lined up this time and quickly announced it would be former USA national team manager, Bob Bradley.

Just to make sure Leeds weren't kept out of the news by this managerial maelstrom, the journalist Simon Austin published an article this week in the football magazine 'Four Four Two' based on an interview with Neil Redfearn about his time working under Cellino. It didn't tell us anything we didn't already know but it contained reminders of many of the maddest episodes Massimo Cellino had brought to Leeds. The use of former furniture salesman Andrea Lore as a spy, reporting back to Cellino whilst the Italian was nominally banned by the FL was confirmed and we learned how Cellino once rang Redfearn from Miami to complain about an idea Redders had to play with four centre-backs. On another occasion Redfearn was baffled by Cellino's order that he must wear purple socks to the next game and ensure he sought out Eddie Gray and shook hands with him (Eddie's birthday is 17th January) to bring the team better luck! It was all the wacky stuff we'd heard rumours about many times before.

I spent the international break in Milton Keynes of all places, enjoying a bit of a meet up with some old school friends and their other halves. We had a day out at Bletchley Park learning that there was another Enigma in this world apart from Leeds United and we sought out a couple of excellent restaurants during our stay. The little story I cannot let go unrecorded though comes from the Sunday night as Mrs W and I sat in the bar of a hotel in Reigate. We'd driven on down after a couple of nights in Milton Keynes and were spending the Monday with our son Adam who was celebrating his 23rd birthday.

So, there we were enjoying a few drinks and catching up with the weekend's sport in the papers; England scraped a 2 – 0 win against Malta under then temporary manager Gareth Southgate while Nico Rosberg won the Japanese Grand Prix to inch ever closer to winning the World Championship. At a table over in the corner of the bar was a rotund bloke and an equally big woman and they were evidently on some sort of a blind date. The bloke was speaking far too loud for the type of conversation he was having and we could hear every word. It seemed he was keen on pursuing a relationship with the woman but he had some very specific requirements. *"There'll be plenty of kissing and cuddling of course"*, he explained, *"and if possible some mild bondage too, nothing dangerous of course but I promise that'll get the bulges appearing in all the right places!"* Mrs W and I exchanged glances and our eyes widened as the conversation went to places that got my imagination working overtime… as with Leeds United, so it is with life; wherever you are and whatever you're doing, expect the unexpected!

As we prepared for the trip to Derby, the Rams announced that the 'Wally with the brolly', Steve McClaren, would replace Nigel Pearson as their new manager just 17 months after he was sacked by them the last time. Down the road in Birmingham, Steve Bruce was confirmed as the new Villa manager. The music stopped and the seats were all filled for the time being.

The 12th round of Championship games began with a live TV game on Friday night. By Sky's good fortune they had long ago chosen Cardiff City v Bristol City, the so-called Severnside derby. It was Warnock and Blackwell's first game in charge of Cardiff and predictably the Bluebirds played like men possessed and won 2 – 1. But the real feature of the game was the performance of one of Cardiff's central defenders... a certain Sol Bamba. He played out of his skin, scored the winning goal and won the SkyBet man of the Match award. Don't you just love the irony of this game?

Saturday morning finally dawned and Kentley and I climbed aboard the Shropshire Whites' magic bus. It picked us up in the village, just a few hundred yards from my front door as we were en route between Shrewsbury and Derby. Kentley became a new member of the Shroppy Whites for the day as it was the only way he could get a ticket having missed out when the allocation was rapidly sold out a couple of weeks earlier. For me, with no driving involved at all today, it was a chance to 'fill me boots'.

First stop was The Old Swan, a Wetherspoon pub just off Market Square in Uttoxeter. We all piled off the bus and into the pub around 10am and I spent a very enjoyable hour and a half working my way through a Spoon's Large Breakfast and three pints of Sharp's excellent brew, Doombar. For a Saturday morning in a small town like Uttoxeter the place was nicely busy, boosted by a large number of Sunderland fans who'd stopped en route to their game later in the day at Stoke. When we saw them they were all in good spirits but they would no doubt have returned home in more morose mood as they went down 2 – 0 in an important bottom of the Premier League clash at the Britannia.

At 11:30am it was time to climb back aboard the mini-bus and make our way towards Derby, leaving crowds of those Black Cats' fans queueing at a cash machine in the high street. Goodness knows how much we football fans boost the national economy every weekend. Our next stop was a wonderful country pub in the village of Ingleby, a few miles south of Derby.

The John Thompson Inn and Brewery is home to the longest established micro-brewery in the UK and is one of only eight pubs to have been recommended in every annual edition of The Good Pub Guide. It was clearly a popular hostelry and was packed with folk enjoying an excellent looking carvery this Saturday lunchtime. Kentley and I took our beers outside where we sat in the autumn sunshine admiring a number of old classic cars. This is a regular meeting place for the Frazer Nash Car Club and several of their beautiful vintage machines were on display. If Carlsberg did pre-match meet-ups, this was what they'd be aiming for! The only slight issue with the moment was the beer itself. Kentley was adamant it didn't look quite right and when I tweeted a photo of my pint, quick as a flash @Peter83945514 aka SMILEY BADGE came back with: *"Make sure you have some Imodium handy if tha's supping that!"* I never tire of the humour our fans come up with!

Two more pints at the JT Inn and then we were off again. The lads had worked out that if we were quick we could probably grab one more pint at one of the pubs near the ground. Sure enough, we parked up in the industrial estate down the road from the iPro and we were in the Pride Park Harvester before 2pm. As always it was jam packed inside and out but we got another pint in and chatted with Chris and Phil M, Simon and Wayne and a few other lads until it was time to set off. It had been an excellent day; all we needed now was three points to round it off.

Derby had been a bit of a bogey side for us away from home with Leeds having just one win in the previous 11 visits but that one win was last season of course when Chris Wood buried a magnificent winner from outside the area. This season Derby had struggled but picked up in the last two games under temporary manager Chris Powell and now had the Wally at the helm. I hoped McClaren had been able to instil his own ideas on the side in the couple of days he'd had with them... you know, put them off their stroke a bit. Ironically, McClaren's first game in charge of Derby in his previous spell at the iPro was also against Leeds; Derby won that one 3 – 1 in October 2013. For Leeds fans it was a rare occasion when many of us travelled expecting at least a draw if not better on the back of our recent run of good results. The new Leeds defence, built on the sheer might of Pontus Jansson, the quiet cool of Kyle Bartley and the vast experience of Rob Green meant we no longer watched Leeds games with our hearts in our mouths. Admittedly we were still short of goals in the side but we usually conjured up one or two in most games. There were question marks today though. We never seem to do well after an international break and Garry Monk would be sat in the stand, his punishment for uttering obscenities towards the officials at Bristol. It's a good job fans aren't bound by the same restrictions or we'd have had no one at Derby at all when I remember the language we were hurling at Keith Stroud that night. As it was, Leeds sold out their entire allocation and we had 3,132 inside the iPro.

Another question mark was how we'd perform without Stuart Dallas; he picked up an injury whilst on international duty with Northern Ireland and Monk chose Alex Mowatt to fill in on the left hand side. We were still without Liam Bridcutt too and there had to be some concern over the fact Chris Wood had played two games for New Zealand during their recent tour in the USA. He was uninjured but must have been suffering some sort of jet lag. When the team was announced it was just the one swap; Mowatt for Dallas, the first change in four games.

Green
Ayling Bartley (Capt) Jansson Taylor
O'Kane Phillips
Sacko Hernandez Mowatt
Wood

Subs: Silvestri, Cooper, Vieira, Coyle, Antonsson, Grimes, Roofe.

Derby had some familiar faces in their squad including former Leeds favourite, Bradley Johnson, together with the likes of Will Hughes, Tom Ince, Matej Vydra and Scot Carson in goal. Craig Bryson and Johnny Russell were sat on their bench. It was a decent squad and it was hard to understand why they were struggling as much as they were.

A crowd of over 31,000 was inside the ground, not far short of their 33,597 capacity and the atmosphere was excellent as the game kicked off with Leeds in their all blue strip kicking towards us. Despite my record intake of ale, I felt surprisingly sober and as far I know I was still lucid as I chatted with Phil

B and Pete before kick-off. Despite the initial noise from both sets of fans everything quietened down as the game progressed and it was obvious, even from the early stages, that there was nothing between these two sides. Much of the game was being played in the middle third and chances were few and far between. Vydra and Bradley Johnson saw their long range efforts whistle over the Leeds bar while for Leeds, Chris Wood put a header wide as only he knows how after a lovely flowing move and cross from Luke Ayling. The best chance of the half came in the final minutes as Kyle Bartley was left all alone to meet an Alex Mowatt corner but the big centre-back got it all wrong and his powerful header hammered against the crossbar. He should have done better and on such things games are won and lost; it was the last action of the half.

The second half was only a few minutes old when proceedings were temporarily halted as Kyle Bartley nicked the ball away from Ikechi Anya and then clattered into him. It would be the end of Anya's participation and a significant moment in the game as he was replaced by Johnny Russell. Has anyone got the stats to tell us how often a substitute scores against us? Less than four minutes after arriving on the pitch, Russell had the ball in our net.

Pontus Jansson got the ball away for a corner to Derby on their right wing, over to our left. As the ball came down at the back post it seemed to get stuck in a melee of players before it suddenly appeared when Kalvin Phillips poked it tamely out towards the edge of the area. There was Johnny Russell running in to smash it at goal before Charlie Taylor could quite get to him to close him down. The ball seemed to take a ricochet on the way through before the net rippled.

Hadi Sacko had been particularly anonymous for some reason today and the goal was the signal for him to be replaced by Kemar Roofe who did offer a bit more as the pace of the game stepped up a notch. I still had the feeling that Roofe would become a different player if he could just get himself a goal to kick-start his confidence but sadly it wasn't going to happen today. Leeds were pressing so much that Derby inevitably had a few breakaways and we all thought they'd doubled their lead when Tom Ince, with a backing track of *"Your Dad's a c****

and so are you", raced down their left wing and sent over a low ball behind the Leeds defence. Vydra neatly completed the move by stabbing the ball home but the liner's flag saved us this time. As the Leeds fans taunted Ince some more he gave us a little wave. Matt Grimes replaced Mowatt and Antonsson replaced a visibly tiring Chris Wood as Leeds chased the game and the last ten minutes was our best spell as first Bartley had a weak shot saved and then Antonsson curled a delicious first time shot against the upright. The statistics showed that Leeds had the majority of the possession and more attempts at goal but of those 13 attempts only 2 hit the target as that old failing continued to hamper our goal scoring figures. We could rue those two attempts that struck the woodwork too; what a difference a couple of inches makes as the actress once said to the bishop.

There was genuine applause for all the Leeds players as they came across to us at the end of the game and Bradley Johnson joined them to show he still has fond memories of plying his trade in front of us. We knew we'd more than matched Derby today and with a bit of luck could have been returning home with at least a point. There had been no lack of effort from our players but I did have a sense that without Stuart Dallas the mobility of the side was a bit limited; Alex Mowatt covers nowhere near the ground the Irishman does. We had no way of knowing how draining that travelling had been on Chris Wood either but he'd done very little all afternoon. Equally though, Hadi Sacko had been very quiet and the only players who really stood out were Eunan O'Kane and Kyle Bartley who spent much of the last ten minutes as a makeshift striker. It was a tired looking performance despite the fact most of the players hadn't played in anger for a fortnight.

The news from Garry Monk after the game was that Stuart Dallas could be out for a few more games with a thigh strain and that was a worry. I'd come to the conclusion that Leeds had a pretty good first XI, capable on their day of beating anyone in this division with Jansson and Bartley often imperious at the back, Hernandez the magician in the middle and Sacko capable, at his best, of going past any defender in the Championship. But how were we fixed if any of the first

XI was missing? We were coping without Liam Bridcutt; O'Kane and Phillips were covering him OK, but we were pretty thinly covered elsewhere. The only real options to cover Dallas were Roofe or Mowatt, both totally different types of player. I concluded that Monk really needed to come up with a radically different formation as his plan B.

As we sat in the mini-bus for an hour after the game, inching away from the iPro, Kentley and I flicked through the reports of the game on our 'phones. Garry Monk was honest enough to admit that we probably didn't do enough to swing the game in our favour whilst acknowledging that on another day with a bit of luck we could have nicked it. He was disappointed that the goal was given away in the second phase of a set play but was now solely focussed on getting a reaction *"to the hurt"* on Tuesday night at home to Wigan.

Still inching along in the traffic, some of the lads taunted the locals through the bus windows and tried to get the attention of any good looking girls walking by or sat in the cars queuing next to us. It was all good natured but reports were also coming through about an incident outside the ground whereby a police dog had apparently bitten a Leeds fan waiting to board a supporters coach. There were other reports of over-zealous policing and it left a sour taste in the mouth after what had been, until then, a damn good day out.

In this round of games there were wins for Fulham, Newcastle, Forest, Norwich, Sheffield Wednesday, Cardiff and Derby of course, while the other 5 games were drawn. Norwich now topped the table with 26 points, 10 more than Leeds who were down to 13th. Newcastle, Huddersfield, Brighton, Bristol and Birmingham made up the rest of the top six. Wigan, Blackburn and Rotherham filled the bottom three places. With Villa, Derby and Cardiff all just above those bottom three it would now be interesting to see if under their new managers they could begin a sustained march up the table. As always, the Championship was turning out to be a fascinating competition.

Derby County 1 **Leeds United 0** (Russell (56))
31,170 (Derby 3,132)

Getting over the line

The Championship has always been about getting over the line; getting into those top two automatic promotion spots or getting into the top six for a shot at the play-offs. Indeed, in a league as fiercely competitive as the Championship, it's also about getting your noses ahead in each game and then working hard to keep it there. So many games are won or lost by the odd goal and those goals are so hard to come by that you just have to get over the line when it's in sight. Wigan Athletic were our next challenge and they knew all about how tight this league is.

Wigan were struggling in their first season back in the Championship after their one-year sabbatical in League One. The Latics had 10 points and only two league wins from 12 games but a closer look at their results suggested they were actually a difficult side to beat. All six of their defeats in the league had been by the odd goal whilst two of our six losses were by more than one goal – the opening day hammering at QPR 3 – 0, and our defeat at Forest 3 – 1. So, although many fans were going into this game confident that we'd get back on track with a comfortable win and a strong performance, I was still nervous. It didn't stop me slapping £2 on a 40/1 bet with William Hill though; Leeds to win 4 – 0. I know, I know, but I was working on the 'expect the unexpected' principle! We'd won the last four games at Elland Road so why not?

The challenge for Leeds would be all the more difficult as we'd go into the game still missing Stuart Dallas and as Saturday had shown, utilising Alex Mowatt out on the left simply doesn't work. When the team was announced in the

Pavilion ahead of the game, it was Kemar Roofe who'd been entrusted to fill the gap.

Green
Ayling Bartley (Capt) Jansson Taylor
O'Kane Phillips
Sacko Hernandez Roofe
Wood

Subs: Silvestri, Cooper, Coyle, Vieira, Grimes, Antonsson, Mowatt.

A few fans suggested that another way around the Dallas conundrum might be to bring back Gaetano Berardi and slot him in at left back now he was fit again. That would allow Charlie Taylor to play the wide left midfield role. I'd first seen the suggestion on LUFCTalk, the excellent fans forum, but in the Pavilion Peter Lorimer also mentioned it as an option. However, it was not to be, least not tonight anyway.

The first half-hour of the game was like any Championship fixture; as tight as the proverbial camel's arse in a sandstorm. A couple of shots from either side but nothing my Granny couldn't have stopped in her prime. Then, just after the half hour this happened: Eunan O'Kane brought the ball out of defence and slotted it into the path of Hadi Sacko on the Leeds right wing and he set off over the half-way line at pace. Unfortunately his first touch was heavy, allowing the ball to get about 12 yards away from him and Dan Burn was racing across now favourite to steal it or at the very least knock it into touch in front of the dug-outs. Somehow, Burn made a right mess of it though and although Sacko had given it up, Burn's sliding tackle merely knocked the ball against the Leeds man's legs and on towards the South Stand. With Burn now cartwheeling along the turf, Hadi was off after the loose ball and now he was behind the Wigan defence. He had all the time in the world to have a good look before launching a cross over to the back post where Chris Wood got himself a couple of yards of space about 8 yards out. Wood took the ball down on his chest and then on the first bounce lashed it back across the keeper into the far corner of the net. It was a fine goal and like that one he got at Derby last season it was one that got us all drooling at the thought that maybe he might start doing this every week! It was his eighth of the season already; Wood was on fire!

It was far too early to be thinking about getting over that line at 1 – 0 with only half an hour gone especially since there were signs that our recently improved, Jansson inspired defence, wasn't quite the fortress we'd seen of late. Wigan were next to go close as ex-Leeds man Stephen Warnock started a move that ended with Michael Jacobs pulling his shot wide from 12 yards. We'd have been moaning about such a miss had it come from Chris Wood. Seconds later there were questions being asked in our box again as an unchallenged Wigan header forced Rob Green into a save and then Chris Wood managed to hook the follow up shot off the goal-line. Leeds saw out the little flurry from the Pie Men and then had chances themselves before the half-time whistle.

At half-time we winced as we watched a big lad doing the dizzy penalty competition with so much arse-crack showing you could easily have parked your average mountain bike wheel in it. We were also treated to an interview in front of the Kop with Yorkshire born triathlete Jonny Brownlee. He was now fully recovered following his much publicised collapse towards the end of the recently held Triathlon World Series in the heat of Mexico where he was helped over the finishing line by his brother Alistair. Jonny had been leading the race with only 700 metres to go when he began weaving across the road and seemed on the point of collapse when Alistair arrived to prop him up and virtually drag him over the finishing line. The delay meant both were overtaken by South African runner Henri Schoeman. Jonny Brownlee was listed in the programme for the Wigan game as number 32, the latest name in that strange '32Red' innovation.

Twenty minutes of the second half came and went and Leeds were comfortably on top, although it was still frustrating that we couldn't add to the one goal lead. Chris Wood went closest with a looping header that had Bogdan scrambling along his line to claw it away from the top corner. It was looking for all the world that this was going to be our seventh game out of 15 where we'd only witness a single goal. Monk clearly thought so too as he began to make his substitutions which could in no way be construed as attempts to go for the jugular. First, off came the dangerous Sacko to be replaced by the more predictable Matt Grimes. In defending that move after the game Monk would tell reporters he was aware that Hadi had had enough or words to that effect. Well he still looked bright enough to me as he trotted off. The next change was even more perplexing as Hernandez was replaced by the far less mobile Alex Mowatt. Again, post-match Monk put the change down to tiredness.

The changes inevitably put us on the back foot and must have given Wigan the encouragement to have a go now they didn't have either Sacko or Hernandez prodding them. That finishing line was in sight now but how we could have done with an Alistair Brownlee to push us home as our players began to do a passable impression of Jonny, staggering along. With five minutes left, Monk gave Chris Wood the hook and Marcus Antonsson joined the fray; at least that was a positive change in terms of adding mobility and pace.

As we waited for the added time board to appear, I asked Kentley, *"It'll only be about three minutes won't it?"* *"Nah"* he replied, *"Bet you a quid it's four"*. A minute later I was handing him a quid and seconds after that Wigan equalised.

Pontus Jansson gave away a corner from a simple Wigan throw-in, down in the south-west corner. He looked totally knackered as he trudged to his place at the back post. The corner was launched long to the back post where Pontus would normally have been there to hammer it away with one of his trade-mark headers but this time we could see him dallying and not challenging his man. A Wigan head lobbed the ball back across goal and although an overhead kick missed the ball by miles it eventually landed in front of Shaun MacDonald and he rifled it into the net off the underside of the bar. We never did reach that finishing line, least not with all three points anyway. It was gutting and it reminded me of so many occasions in the past when we'd squandered good positions; this was what last season's Leeds were good at and we'd thought all that was behind us.

After the game, the BBC's Adam Pope put Monk on the spot about his substitutions, not for the first time this season. It had been Pope who rattled Monk with his questions about the team's *"identity"* a few weeks earlier. This time he suggested: *"Garry, do you feel that the momentum went out of the game once you took Hadi Sacko off?"* Monk clearly knew what Popey was suggesting. *"Well, the substitutions were kinda forcing our hands... physically those players needed to come off the pitch, so of course we'd have loved to have kept them on, he was a big threat for us, Hadi, with the pace and everything but sometimes you are forced in certain situations with certain substitutions so you have to do that. Errm, in terms of that, that's nothing to do with the game, that's just the way it was..."* It was a meaningless ramble from Monk that suggested to me he was flustered and I guessed he now regretted those changes. He got it back together as he focussed on what may have actually been the real issue; his team was still learning, *"Look, we want the best team right now that can do everything, can kill teams, can score four or five goals and make it comfortable, and clean sheets but this is not where the group's at you know, I think we've made big strides in a short space of time and they're improving on certain things. Other things need to be addressed and improved on and this group needs to understand that now the determination when you get that goal, to go on and dominate even more is what they need but that's for me to help them."*

It was a reminder to us all that it was still early days, albeit events elsewhere showed you just don't get a lot of time to perfect a squad these days. Rotherham went down 4 – 2 at Birmingham tonight and within hours Alan Stubbs became the next managerial casualty after only having 140 days to mould his squad. Kenny Jacket was announced as his replacement in another move that I really couldn't fathom. Had Kenny jacket not been jettisoned from Wolves because he couldn't cut it there? It's a funny old game!

Leeds United 1 Wigan Athletic 1 (**Wood (29)**, MacDonald (90+1) **19,861** (Wigan 326)

Back on track

Whilst the late Wigan equaliser was a blow to all Leeds supporters some of us older fans awoke the following day to an even bigger blow. News broke overnight that Gary Sprake, goalkeeper and member of the great Revie side of the late 60s and 70s, had passed away aged 71. To Leeds fans in their late fifties, Sprake was one of about 14 names inscribed on their hearts. Sprake, Reaney, Cooper, Bremner, Charlton, Hunter, Lorimer, Clarke, Jones, Giles, Gray, Madeley, O'Grady, Hibbitt, Belfitt, Johanneson, Bates and Harvey formed the squad that won the First Division title in 1969 and indeed formed the basis of our side for many years around that time. Sprake played in every one of the 42 league games in our first title winning season and kept clean sheets in over half of them. Yes, he earned a reputation for goalkeeping clangers – famously nicknamed "Careless Hands" by the Liverpool Kop who serenaded him with Des O'Connor's ballad following one such blunder in front of them – but he was also the most brilliant of shot-stoppers; the Marco Silvestri of my youth. At the end of his career he was ostracised by his former team mates and many Leeds fans for his allegations about Revie being involved in match fixing and bribing opponents although no FA charges were ever brought. But that was all put to one side on the news of his death. When someone just eleven years older than you passes on it's a reminder that life is not a rehearsal and that's part of the reason us oldies felt the loss so deeply but it was also because it was another face that once adorned our bedroom walls along with Bremner, Revie, Muhammad Ali and David Bowie.

No one had a clue what to forecast for the Wolves - Leeds game; both sides were so totally unpredictable. Wolves were without a win in four but that included narrow defeats to high flying Brighton and Norwich and a draw at Steve Bruce's reignited Villa. They'd also won 2 – 0 at Newcastle not long after being humbled at home by Barnsley 4 – 0. As for Leeds, our fans were looking for a result and performance that would confirm we were on the up and that the Derby and Wigan results were more to do with bad luck than bad football.

I was supposed to be joining Nigel on the 11:25 Stafford to Wolverhampton Cross Country service but, true to form, I got a text just as I arrived at the station to say he'd, *"Messed up the train times"*. So I made the short trip on my own and spent it chatting with a Villa fan and his two lads who were travelling to their home game with Fulham. He was from Stafford and knew a few of the lads from the Stafford Whites; everyone knows someone who's a Leeds fan.

From Wolverhampton Station I weaved through the streets towards the pre-match venue of choice today; the West End Working Men's Club on Merridale Street West. I was weaving not because I'd already had a few pints but because I was following the Google Maps' route on my mobile and the local landscape looked nothing like the map. After half an hour of walking I could finally see the tell-tale sign that Leeds were in town; a group of coppers stood outside the club. Some of the coppers were part of the Leeds contingent that travels around with the fans and they were brilliant, even suggesting I try to grab a lift back with one of the coaches as they could see I was sweating from the long walk in the sun.

The Shropshire Whites have been using this club for a few years. Gary, who pretty much runs the Shroppy Whites, knew of it as he's been known to DJ in there in days gone by and is very much a local. With drinking places in Wolverhampton for away supporters now hard to find, this place was absolutely perfect and when I arrived around 12:30 it was already packed with Leeds fans from all over the country. Bournemouth Whites, Keighley Whites and of course the Shroppy Whites all had their flags up around the walls and there was food, a big wall-mounted TV showing the latest Little Mix music video (OK you can't have everything!), beer at great prices and a pool table. Why can't there be places like this for us everywhere? The Club is said to be one of, if not the oldest surviving working men's club in the country, having begun life in 1893. It's been through difficult times recently as have most such places but with a membership in excess of 450, including over 100 women, it's now thriving and I'm glad we did our bit to help them out. In conversation with a chap serving behind the bar he told me the takings from our visit would be their best of the year other than New Year's Eve!

I chatted with Nick and Karen who were looking forward to a holiday in Iceland and met local Leeds fan Rob for the first time. All the Shroppies were in there of course and Simon W's usual car load. Chris, Phil and young Robbie were in and Nigel arrived eventually having sorted his trains. The always jolly Susan S from the Donny Whites came and said hello too, another face I could now put to a Twitter account. It was a brilliant, brilliant session and it reminded me why I love away days like this.

At 2pm the club began to empty and I opted to walk with some of the lads back to the ground despite having several offers of lifts. Gary, since he had the local knowledge, led the procession through the back streets to the Molineux. Gary being Gary though and Leeds fans being Leeds fans it was no surprise our procession got waylaid en route. As we were going right by the Combermere Arms it would almost have been rude not to call in. I felt we were on a bit of a history tour around Wolverhampton as the Combermere is a fascinating little pub, a former 'beer house' and one of the last remaining of its kind in the country being part of a pretty row of terraced houses. In one online review it's described as *"the epicentre of the 'thinking' Wolves support"* and it was predictably rammed full of both 'thinking' and 'drinking' Wolves fans. Everyone was friendly though and some of our lads managed to beat the scrum to get in an extra beer before we headed for the ground. The memory I'll take away from this pub is that there's a full size tree growing in the corner of the gents' toilet. The tree had protected status so they just built the toilet around it. If you're ever in the area it's a definite *"must see"*.

Inside Molineux I took my place alongside Kentley and Nigel as usual and then I surveyed the scene. The bright sun was almost blinding us as it often does here as we pretty much face due south looking towards the pitch from the lower tier of the Steve Bull Stand. I love this ground; the mighty Stan Cullis Stand towering into the sky to our right and old gold paint everywhere you look. It's been totally rebuilt since I first came here in the late 60s but it oozes nostalgia with the magnificent statue tributes to Billy Wright and Stan Cullis, the Steve Bull Stand and with Derek Dougan and Kenny Hibbitt in the hall of fame; Kenny being the bother of former Leeds man Terry who I mentioned earlier as one of the Revie squad. It's a great place to watch football but sadly there was one thing missing as I studied the players lined up in white shirts; Pablo wasn't there.

Green
Ayling Bartley (Capt) Jansson Taylor
O'Kane Vieira
Sacko Phillips Roofe
Wood

Subs: Silvestri, Coyle, Cooper, Grimes, Mowatt, Antonsson, Doukara.

Hernandez suffered a dead-leg in the Wigan game, thus explaining his substitution that night and so young Ronaldo Vieira got a recall in the Liam Bridcutt role with Kalvin Phillips moving forward into the Hernandez 'number 10' role. Stuart Dallas was still missing and so Kemar Roofe got a second consecutive start and of course Liam Bridcutt was still out injured. There was also still no sign of Gaetano Berardi even though 'Berra' was said to now be ready to return if needed.

It was a cagey start by both teams with Leeds kicking towards the Jack Harris Stand to our left where the noisiest Wolves fans were housed. An early wild shot from Hadi Sacko was greeted by taunts of *"You're fu***** sh**"* coming from that area. At the other end a sloppy header towards Rob Green by Eunan O'Kane was hopelessly short, giving Nouha Dicko a chance until the mighty figure of Pontus Jansson intervened with a trademark lunge that left the mighty Swede poleaxed on the turf for a while. Eventually he was repaired and seconds later performed more goal saving heroics again thwarting Dicko as he was clean through in the Leeds area. There was no doubt that Jansson and Bartley to a lesser extent had transformed the Leeds defensive capability this season. The game was only twenty minutes old and Wolves were now in the ascendancy and the supporters at both ends of the ground were making all the noise. Next it was Benfica loanee, Helder Costa hammering a long range shot just over our bar and I shivered as I spotted the number '17' on his back. The game was all about Dicko and Sacko in the first half with our man either terrorising the Wolves defence or giving up possession cheaply to send the home side away on another attack. In the final minutes, a long ball out of defence by Kyle Bartley gave Sacko a run and chase against full back Matt Doherty and this time Hadi's shot cannoned off the top of the crossbar. Sacko's battles with Doherty had already seen the Wolves man booked and it would prove to be the most important dual on the pitch as the game wore on. A brilliant save from Rob Green just before the break saw us to half-time at nil-nil.

The second half began with more half-chances and some ifs and buts but no attempts on target. A challenge on Chris Wood on the edge of the Wolves area looked a good penalty shout but nothing was given while that man Costa copied his first half shot and just skimmed Green's crossbar with another rocket. We were well into the second forty five minutes before Chris Wood registered our first shot on target despite Leeds now bossing the game in the middle of the park. This one was well saved at his near post by Carl Ikeme in the Wolves goal. Then, with just under twenty minutes left, Leeds grabbed a priceless lead.

It began as a carbon copy of Sacko's first half chance as Kyle Bartley once again launched a long diagonal ball into the Leeds right wing corner. Once again it was Sacko v Doherty and once again Doherty was being careful with his feet, so careful in fact that he forgot to take the ball and in an instant Sacko was behind him and into the box near the byline. At the perfect moment he squared the ball across the face of goal and a combination of Roofe and his marker Silvio slid the ball into the net at the near post. Roofe would later say he didn't touch the ball and it would go down as a Silvio own goal. The celebrations were manic as the Leeds players all ran towards us and Pontus Jansson hopped over the barrier and was orchestrating us as we all went mental. If we could hold onto this it would be a huge result and in a sense it would rescue the points lost on Tuesday. Had we learned how to hold a 1 – 0 lead though?

Well, just as against Wigan we had more than enough chances to make it safe but once again we couldn't finish them off. Sacko and Wood really do need to spend some time on the shooting range as both blasted decent opportunities over the bar whilst Costa did the same in the dying seconds at the other end. Monk worked his way through his subs bringing on Mowatt for Vieira, Liam Cooper no less for Hadi Sacko and Doukara for Wood as it was clear it was now all about holding the lead at all costs, crossing that invisible line.

We got there this time and at the final-whistle the players all came across to salute us and Pontus stripped off the remnants of a very ripped shirt and handed it to one of the disabled fans at the front of our section. *"All Leeds aren't we"* blasted out from the Steve Bull Stand and then all the way back to the coaches and the station. It had been a near perfect away day.

In a weird set of results today ours was one of eight games in the Championship that ended with just a single goal being scored and, being one of the winning sides, our position in the table was strengthened significantly. Newcastle were the only side to batter their opponents in this 14th round of games as they demolished Ipswich 3 – 0 at St James' Park to go three points clear of Brighton at the top. Leeds would end the weekend 10th but just three points behind 6th placed Bristol City. We were right in the hunt for the first time in seven seasons.

Wolverhampton Wanderers 0 **Leeds United 1 (Silvio og (73))**
23,607 **(Leeds 2,452)**

Magic Twosday

That managerial merry-go-round was now spinning out of control and it seemed that any gaffer whose team was flirting with the nether regions of the Championship was likely to be flung off into the distance. Championship managers number five and six were gone as we Leeds fans made our way to Elland Road for the EFL Cup game with Norwich. It looked like it was our fault that Wolves decided Walter Zenga was no longer the best bet for them following our win at Molineux on Saturday. Zenga was gone after only 87 days in post, having replaced Kenny Jacket (now at Rotherham of course) as recently as July. Wolves were in that risky bottom eight in the table as were Wigan Athletic who were next to twist. They were getting shot of Gary Caldwell, a relative veteran of 567 days. Only Ipswich, Forest and Blackburn of that bottom eight had not yet made a move. Leeds had finally heeded the call to reduce ticket prices for the EFL Cup and it seemed the fans were responding; over 20,000 were expected to turn up at Elland Road for the Tuesday night, 4th Round tie with the Canaries. It didn't appear to have done the job for the Shropshire Whites though and as there were only three of us travelling for this one – Gaz, Woggy and me – we were in Gary's little sports car again. It was another stop start nightmare of a trip up the motorways and we only just arrived in time for a couple of pints in the Pavilion. A ten minute debate with the bloke on the gate of the coach park didn't help to speed things up either. We eventually lost the argument this time that we were actually a mini-bus in disguise and it was *"more than my job's worth"* for 'Smiler' to turn a blind eye despite the fact there was loads of space left.

In the Pavilion we learned that Garry Monk had made eight changes to the side that fought so well down at the Molineux. It was a gamble no doubt that Norwich would also field a second XI and Monk called it pretty much spot on as Alex Neil, the Canaries manager, also made eight changes to the side that surprisingly lost 1 – 0 at home to a table-rising Preston North End.

Silvestri
Coyle Bartley(Capt) Cooper Berardi
Mowatt Grimes Vieira Roofe
Doukara Antonsson

Subs: Green, Ayling, Taylor, Wood, O'Kane, Phillips, Sacko.

In general, the Pavilion punters were disappointed. There was a feeling that we really ought to be going for this one but that number of changes suggested Monk had more of an eye on the visit of Burton Albion to Elland Road on Saturday.

Judging by the pile of stuff sitting on the items confiscated table alongside my usual turnstile number '30', there were a lot of Leeds fans getting in a sweat over the team selection. In particular I was surprised to see three cans of men's Sure deodorant and one can of air freshener! Come on lads, taking cans of deodorant to the footy? Whatever next, a change of underwear?

Owing to my late arrival in the Pavilion and the necessity of still taking advantage of the 'two pints for six quid' offer, I was late arriving in my usual spot on the Kop. The tribute to Gary Sprake was already underway in the form of a minute's applause while the two teams lined up around the centre circle. Sprake gazed down at us from the big screen, his famous hands out in front of him as if reaching down to us. Among the Leeds players was the figure of Marco Silvestri, dressed as Sprake usually was, in green, and actually looking not dissimilar to the Welshman in his very young days when he first joined Leeds. There were other similarities too in that both men were known to be superb shot-stoppers but also both had reputations for regular clangers; for Careless Hands read McFlappy Hands!

Despite the fact that the South Stand was closed and housed just a few Leeds flags fluttering in the breeze, the rest of the ground was pretty full and the atmosphere was excellent. The first twenty minutes or so were not good for Leeds though as Norwich looked a very useful outfit, knocking the ball about quickly and getting through on goal several times. Within 14 seconds of the start a loose pass from Liam Cooper was pounced on by Steven Naismith and his fierce shot was well saved by Silvestri. Seconds later and Naismith was firing a left-foot shot just over the crossbar into the Kop, This didn't look good at all. And it looked even worse in the 14th minute as Norwich unsurprisingly took an early lead.

Leeds were actually on the attack following a left wing corner and then suddenly Naismith was racing away with the ball. He exchanged a couple of passes with Robbie Brady who then swung the ball over to the back post. One of the smallest players on the pitch, little Alex Pritchard stooped to head the ball home in the bottom corner as he got ahead of young Vieira. It was a poor goal to concede from a simple move and cross. Bugger! Pritchard wheeled away celebrating by pointing at his head as if to suggest a headed goal from him was a rare thing indeed which I can well believe it is.

Norwich continued to dominate the game with shots raining in towards the Kop at regular intervals although Silvestri was having a good game and was getting to everything, including a fierce shot that he just got a finger-tip to, nudging the ball over the bar. Leeds did have the ball in the net and it looked a beauty from where I stood... a hundred yards away! A right wing Alex Mowatt corner seemed to be met by the head of Kyle Bartley at the near post and the ball was placed firmly past John Ruddy in the Norwich goal. Sadly, Kyle had pushed it in with an outstretched left-hand and eventually referee Andy Woolmer twigged and disallowed it, booking Bartley for good measure. It was something to get the crowd going again though as the clock ticked towards half-time. Then, out of nothing, Leeds had the ball in the net again and this time it counted.

Kyle Bartley sent a trade-mark diagonal ball deep into the Norwich box towards Kemar Roofe on the left hand side. He battled with Ben Godfrey and eventually clipped the ball over to the back post. Souleymane Doukara was there to side-foot the ball back along the goal-line and Marcus Antonsson was all on his own at the other post to tap it in. 1 – 1 against all the odds and as the half-time whistle went it felt like we'd dodged a bullet.

Whatever Garry Monk said to his players at half-time, it worked wonders. Right from the start of the second half Leeds took the game to Norwich and were actually the better team for the majority of it. Doukara thumped a header towards goal early in the half that Ruddy did brilliantly to keep out and then Silvestri was called on again to keep out an Oliveira shot. 67 minutes had passed and we were all starting to ponder the prospect of extra time. Garry Monk seemed intent on trying to get the job done in normal time though as he began to make his changes. Chris Wood was the first, replacing Marcus Antonsson. I wasn't totally in tune with that change as I felt Antonsson was doing OK and he was far more mobile than Chris Wood could ever hope to be but then again I couldn't deny Wood was a far better player now than he'd been back in August. The attendance was flashed onto the big screen: 22,222 – an excellent figure for an EFL Cup tie between two Championship sides although Mike and I debated whether the real figure was perhaps 22,221 or 22,223… if I was in the office I just know I'd fiddle it to read all the 2s!

Back on the pitch, Wood was determined to prove me wrong and within two minutes of his arrival he had a great chance as he tried to connect with a Doukara cross. Wood missed the ball completely but now it was bouncing along the six-yard line in front of the Kop and only Alex Mowatt was following it; he had to score! But no he didn't, he swung his right boot at the ball with eight yards of goal at his mercy and screwed it horribly wide. I did say his *right* boot. Later that night Alex would tweet: *"Wow, my right foot is shite..."* but for now he was looking up to the stars no doubt ruing the fact he'd not practised more with that right foot. It was a great chance and the inevitable thought was that it would be the *only* chance we'd get to put this tie to bed. The Championship had taught us that such misses are often the difference between getting something or getting nothing from a game.

Monk made his second change in the 76th minute and I was more in tune with this one; Sacko replaced Mowatt. Then in the 81st minute Kalvin Phillips replaced Doukara... quite why, no one really knew. Surely the game was going into extra time now. Mike was still going on about that crowd figure – 22,222. *"It's an omen"* he told us, *"game's gonna end 2 – 2 and then it'll be 2 – 2 in penalties and we'll lose it 3 – 2!"*

For the moment though we had a problem; Lewie Coyle was hobbling off the pitch with an injury and it looked like he wouldn't be back. It was that old Elland Road curse striking again, now we had no chance, heads went down.

The whistle went and I rushed off to the bogs, explaining to everyone in the row that I was actually coming back and it was just a call of nature; I was surprised so few were joining me; that's old age for you I guess. By the time I got back, the game was underway again and inevitably Norwich, with a man more than we now had, were piling on the pressure. I was resigned to losing the game now. Nine minutes of Norwich dominance at the start of extra time culminated in a corner kick which Robbie Brady was taking in the north-east corner, over to our left. He fooled everyone by stroking the corner back to Alex Pritchard who in turn hammered the ball into the middle. Nelson Oliveira was all on his own, five yards from goal and he steered his header past Silvestri. It was defending worthy of last year's Leeds defence, the one that had too much Wootton, Bellusci and Bamba in it. You could tell that most fans near us thought that was probably that as several slumped down in their seats and there was a momentary hush as we contemplated the enormity of the task of trying to get a goal back with only ten men. I was only saying it for something to break the silence really but I turned to Mike and told him: *"Well, I'm clinging to that prediction you made earlier Mike, it's going to be 2 – 2 and go to penalties!"* I didn't really believe that of course but as everyone knows, I do love the coincidence of numbers that often crops up in football. How many times has '17' featured since Massimo first brought it to our attention? So, might this not be Magic Twosday?

Half-time in extra time arrived and we were still 2-1 down but then as the last fifteen minutes got underway Leeds appeared to find their second wind. Suddenly Kalvin Phillips was making crunching tackles in midfield and he was winning most of them. Liam Cooper joined in the fun and he slid in to win the ball and then we winced as Phillips took a chunk out of someone and the ball broke to Matt Grimes. Every crunching challenge was met with a huge roar of approval; we may well be going down but we were going down with pride. Grimes took the ball on a pace or two and then, with the outside of his left boot, he played a sublime ball through the Norwich back line for Hadi Sacko to run onto. Sacko was too far out really to try the shot but being Sacko he tried it anyway and he hit it cleanly across the face of goal. It was probably going to beat Chris Wood who was lurking at the back post but then John Ruddy dived at the ball and got a hand on it and diverted it straight onto Wood's boot and he guided it neatly inside the post. What a reaction that got from the crowd! The noise was incredible, an outpouring of joy that you only get when you defy all the odds. Suddenly we could believe again, even ten men could probably hold on for another 11 minutes and then all bets were off in the lottery of a penalty shoot-out. I looked up at the big screen and nudged Mike; *"Leeds 2 – 2 Norwich"* it read. Chris Wood should probably have won it for us in extra time, never mind going to penalties. Roofe put over a fabulous cross that found him in acres of space but he got himself in a right old tangle and the chance was gone and not long after, with the time at precisely 22:22, Andy Woolmer's whistle signalled that it would indeed be penalties. Nigel turned to me and asked *"Would you rather have had Rob Green facing these penalties Sir David or are you happy with Marco?"* I thought for a moment and then replied, *"Silvestri, he's more unpredictable than Rob Green, more likely to come up with something spectacular"*. It did cross my mind though that it was Rob Green who got us through the shoot out in the 1st round tie up at Fleetwood, saving the 10th penalty brilliantly after all the previous nine had been scored.

Silvestri took his place between the sticks in front of the Kop and Graham Dorrans stepped up and slid the first kick neatly into the corner of the net despite several thousand Leeds fans going mental trying to put him off. Chris Wood was next and he went for the same spot, scoring despite Ruddy going the right way. Next up was the Norwich goal scorer, Alex Pritchard. What we didn't know then was that Silvestri had spent time before the game with goal-keeping coach Darryl Flahavan considering possible penalty scenarios and they'd agreed that if Pritchard took a kick Marco would stand his ground in the centre of goal. That was according to Garry Monk after the game. According to the Sun newspaper, Marco and his Missus, Sophia, sat down together and studied some Norwich penalties and it was Sophia who spotted Pritchard hit the ball down the middle.[1] At the time it looked incredible of course to see Marco apparently gambling that Pritchard would send it down the middle and easily punching the kick away! Marco would say later that it felt "horrible" not moving for a kick; first blood to Leeds. Next was Kemar Roofe and I can't pretend I wasn't a tad nervous. My favourite signing of the summer was yet to find the net this season but I was convinced he had cohonas the size of Halloween pumpkins. He smashed the ball into the same left corner Wood had chosen and Leeds were 2 -1 to the good. Steven Naismith was next and he looked a bit nervous to me. Once again the Kop was going berserk, jumping up and down, waving their arms, screaming, doing whatever they could to try to put the Norwich man off. Whether it was any of that or the brilliance of Silvestri we will never know but this time Marco dived to his right and pushed the kick away. Still 2 -1 to Leeds and now a chance to make it 3 - 1. It was in our hands, well, Kalvin Phillips' boot really.

---

[1] *https://www.thesun.co.uk/sport/football/2062517/*

He struck his kick well enough but Ruddy guessed right and pushed it away, diving to his right. Five of the six kicks had gone to that left-hand side as the penalty-taker would see it. Oliveira was next and he wasted no time in smashing the ball into the top left corner to even it up at 2 – 2 but crucially Leeds had the one miss less with Matt Grimes stepping up to the spot. Mike nudged me again and pointed at the screen; 2 – 2 it now read as the latest spot-kick was added to the penalty tally. Grimes was the first left-footer and he looked somehow awkward as he strode up to the ball. He blasted it over the bar. That was a bad moment; still 2 – 2 and that early 2 penalty advantage now gone. It was the latest twist in this topsy-turvy night and my head was telling me we'd probably blown it. The experience of the last few years has shown us that in these situations, more often than not the final blow would be against us and not for us. If anyone was to score a late winner it would not be us, if a mistake was to decide a game it would generally be our mistake or if a penalty was going to be missed it would be a player in white that missed it. Yet our most recent experience of a situation just such as this was up at Fleetwood and on that rainy night by the seaside Rob Green dived away to his left to save the final kick. And in general this season I'd started to sense that our luck was changing; maybe we were working harder or maybe it was just our turn. Another left-footer, Robbie Brady, was next. Brady hit the ball sweetly and accurately towards the bottom right corner of the net; the first attempt to go that way. What made Silvestri dive that way? If it was another bit of pre-match research then I'm very impressed but if it was Silvestri's spur of the moment decision then I'm even more impressed. It was a fine save, just getting a hand behind the ball and it ricocheted up and away past the post. After all his trials and tribulations, the barracking he's often received from Leeds fans for his poor handling and kicking and many, many errors, his part in the infamous sick-note six affair and his frequent verbal battles with fans on Twitter, tonight, for one night only maybe, Marco was our hero. And how spooky that this was the night that began with that tribute to another often maligned goalkeeper of ours, Old Careless Hands himself, Gary Sprake; spooky indeed and just a few days before Halloween. Suddenly we were one kick away from a cup quarter-final.

Cue one Ronaldo Vieira, just 18 years old, walking confidently from the half-way line towards us, the Elland Road Kop packed out and sensing a famous triumph, expectant. Now we are talking cohonas, don't disappoint us lad, please don't disappoint us! Marco Silvestri stood to one side with his back to the action; he couldn't watch. Garry Monk would tell us later he didn't watch any of the penalties; he never did as a player apparently. These were nervous enough times for the fans never mind young Ronaldo – the sweat was pouring off me and I concluded one bloke in front of me must have been the owner of one of those cans of deodorant confiscated at the turnstiles as I got a whiff of nervous BO. The rest is history as they say, the young man with the famous name became an instant legend as he calmly sent the veteran John Ruddy the wrong way whilst guiding his spot-kick in off the inside of the keeper's left hand post; an inch perfect penalty. Off he went to the now usual celebration spot down to my right in front of the Kop, savouring the adulation while the rest of his team-mates raced from half-way to join him. It was a moment right up there with the best we've had; possibly the best since that famous day we overturned the odds against Bristol Rovers to grab promotion back to the Championship. It was a magic, Magic Twosday after all.

Leeds joined an impressive roll-call of clubs that also went through tonight; Liverpool, Arsenal, Newcastle and Hull City while the following night Manchester United, West Ham and Southampton completed the quarter-final line-up. The draw was live on TV following the Man Utd win over Man City. Leeds were ball number '3'. The first ball drawn was number '4', Liverpool. Second, was ball number '3'.

Leeds Utd 2 Norwich City 2 AET (1 – 1 end of normal time) (Pritchard (14), **Antonsson (43)**, Oliveira (99), **Wood (109) 22,222** (Norwich 1,905)

Brewers Droop

Travelling on the Shropshire Whites' magic bus again for the latest trip to Elland Road, it was another painfully slow journey. It was nothing to do with the excellent driving of *"The Driver of our bus"*, the unflappable 'Humph' but everything to do with the Dayinsure Wales Rally GB taking place at Cholmondeley Castle, just off the A49 between Whitchurch and Warrington. It was the penultimate round of the 2016 World Rally Championship and it brought spectators in their thousands to the picturesque site in Cheshire, spectators whose cars clogged the A49 before turning into the grounds of the castle. Consequently it was another two and a half hour run this week meaning it was gone one o'clock as I entered the Pavilion.

This being our last home game before Remembrance Sunday, there were plenty of lads and lasses from the forces going round the tables selling poppies while the guests this week were two of our own old soldiers, Terry Yorath and Mel Sterland. 'Zico', as Mel was nicknamed in his playing days after the Brazilian of that name who also had a shot like an army tank, is these days a larger than life figure in every sense of the phrase. Comedian and compere Jed Stone introduced him with: *"You'll have spotted Mel's not exactly at his playing weight these days...*" Both Mel and Yorath were expecting Leeds to win against Burton with 'Zico' beginning his review sort of echoing that old Accrington Stanley milk advert with words to the effect of *"Blimey, no one back in the day would ever have thought we'd be here discussing the mighty Leeds United playing Bur-ton Al-bi-on would they?"*

But Burton Albion it was and no one around our table thought it would be anything but another close encounter of the Championship kind and no one thought it would be an easy task to get the Brewers over a barrel. Burton were no soft touch and had recorded decent results against some good sides on their own patch even though they were still to win on their travels this season. Before the game, Garry Monk was at pains to stress that sometime soon Burton were going to break that winless run and it was vital to ensure it wasn't against us. *"Focus"* he kept repeating in almost every sentence of his pre-match press conference and he was particularly insistent that no one in the club was thinking about that cup tie at Anfield until the next four league games were done and dusted.

Green
Ayling Bartley (Capt) Jansson Taylor
O'Kane Phillips
Sacko Hernandez Roofe
Wood

Subs: Silvestri, Berardi, Cooper, Antonsson, Vieira, Mowatt, Doukara.

Despite the heroics of the largely second XI players on Tuesday night, Monk predictably returned to his favoured first XI again for Burton. The one change from the side that beat Wolves at Molineux was the return of Pablo Hernandez in place of Tuesday's penalty hero, Ronnie Vieira. With Bridcutt and Dallas still not available, most fans considered this our best side. For the Brewers there were few familiar names, although Lloyd Dyer was known to us from his long spell at Leicester and more recently Watford while the dangerous Jamie Ward, currently on loan from Forest and another regular goal-scorer, was on their bench. Their manager was of course very well known to us; Nigel Clough, an eight year-old lad when his Dad, Brian, managed Leeds for 44 days back in

1974. Nigel was Burton through and through, having overseen their rise to the very top of the non-league pyramid during his first spell at the club from 1998 to 2008 and now he was back and last season guided them into the Championship. He was sure to get a 'warm' reception from the Leeds fans.

The teams lined up around the centre circle for the second time in a week, this time to honour the fallen heroes of our armed forces. The haunting melody of The Last Post was played by a lone bugler as 24,000 stood in silence while two soldiers marched across the pitch to lay wreaths of poppies in front of the East Stand. On the big screen a simple picture of poppies added to the solemnity of the moment. Later that evening pictures emerged showing Massimo Cellino up in the dignitaries' area of the East Stand, apparently taken during the minute's silence; he remained quite obviously sitting while his guests all stood politely to attention. Once again his PR skills were shown to be sadly inappropriate for his position and the picture did the rounds on Twitter alongside more pleas to Signore Radrizzani to complete the takeover that many still thought was imminent. One thing for sure, Cellino had been very quiet recently despite the Ross McCormack 'bung' case rumbling on in the background. The latest on that was a rumour in the press that the case against Cellino was collapsing, with the chief witness, former club official Graham Bean, having withdrawn his alleged damning evidence of the Italian's involvement because the FA had refused to pay a bean to Bean for his expenses! Not long after this was reported though, Bean apparently told the press his evidence still stood, so once again no one actually knew what the hell was going on. It could only happen in a case involving Leeds United.

Another cagey half of Championship football ended with no score as Leeds completed a nineteenth first half this season having conceded only 5 times. Burton came closest to breaking the deadlock with a looping header that came down on top of our crossbar in front of the Kop. My feeling at half-time was that a nil-nil draw or, God forbid, any sort of defeat, would prick our balloon and bring it down to earth like so many such small balloons we'd held briefly over the last few years. We had that precious thing called momentum at the moment but, just like helium, it leaks fast from a pricked balloon.

There was little change in the game until the hour mark. Until then both sides put together decent moves in midfield but both defences easily withstood anything thrown at them. The Leeds backline in particular looked impregnable and despite Burton amassing 22 shots, only two would trouble the gloves of Rob Green; the rest were blocked, missed or hacked away. Luke Ayling was having his best game in a Leeds shirt. Hadi Sacko looked our most likely prospect at the other end but time and again a promising break would peter-out as he ran up a blind alley. Even the crowd was starting to sound nervous as we saw the prospect of another opportunity to build something exciting begin to fade. Garry Monk presumably felt the same and on 73 minutes he decided it was time for plan D; Souleymane Doukara replaced Kemar Roofe. The crowd sensed this was make or break too and every challenge, every run, every touch of the big Frenchman was roared on. The more we roared, the more the Douk got stuck in and the more he strained every sinew the more we hollered and urged him on. He'd been on the pitch just ten minutes when he made the first dramatic intervention in the game.

Charlie Taylor came away from the Leeds area with the ball and clipped it forward to Chris Wood, ten yards inside the Burton half. Wood, racing towards the West Stand, caught the ball a bit heavy as he tried to steer it towards Pablo Hernandez, lurking on that touchline and the ball fizzed towards the Spaniard at a rate of knots. Incredibly, Pablo managed to hook his right foot around the ball first time on the volley and then, even more incredibly, sent it through a gap in the centre of the Burton back-line to where he could see Doukara racing onto it. The Douk sped into the box with the ball but he was being forced to the left and the Kop gave an audible sigh as it seemed the chance of a shot was lost. But Doukara suddenly put the anchors out and stopped in an instant; he stopped way quicker than his marker who slid in taking both ball and man and the referee was soon pointing at the spot.

It was only four days ago that we watched ten penalties in front of the Kop and now we had another. We were all nervous obviously, this was a huge moment in terms of that tank of momentum but Chris Wood looked confident as he waited for the signal from the referee. It was delayed for ages as the liner in front of the East Stand picked up a bottle of what looked like orange squash, apparently thrown from somewhere in the north-east corner; that brought boos from the rest of the Kop as we contemplated why any Leeds fan would want to do such a thing at such a vital moment. A bottle of water had been lobbed onto the pitch a few minutes earlier. We turned our eyes back towards Wood and waited for the whistle. Soon we were jumping around and shouting for all we were worth as Woody's spot-kick was drilled high into the centre of the net. The feeling that this was really not what we were accustomed to came back in spades; in previous years that challenge would have been waved away by the ref or if he'd given it, we'd have missed the bloody penalty. The Leeds planet was aligning with something somewhere. It was no surprise to see Pontus Jansson leading the celebrations in front of the Kop as he urged us to new heights with a series of Steve Evans-like gestures; his stock raised another few notches with us all.

Burton now had nothing to lose of course and they quickly had the kitchen sink loosened from its moorings and were hurling it at us. Pontus was equally determined to throw the fu**** back though and time and time again he and the rest of the defence would throw themselves in front of the shots that were raining in towards the South Stand goal. Leeds tried to break up the Burton flow with two more substitutions as Ronnie Vieira came on for Hernandez and then, with only minutes left, Mowatt came on for Hadi Sacko. Burton won a couple of late corners and then, now with seconds left, Vieira brought a man down right on the very edge of our penalty area. Vieira was booked and Leeds had every man back to defend the kick. Every Leeds fan was now whistling, trying to get the ref to end the game there and then but knowing he'd at least allow the free-kick. Matt Palmer thrashed the ball at the defensive wall and it came back, twice more shots were hammered towards Rob Green's goal but each was blocked and then finally Chris Wood could be seen bringing the ball away down the Leeds left, over to our right as we implored him to hang onto it and run it into the corner below us. We momentarily vent our anger as he suddenly clips the ball into the centre of the Burton defence but then we see why; the Douk was haring through onto the ball all alone! Now we were screaming at the Douk to *"Shoot, for fu** sake, shooooooooot!"* But the Douk doesn't shoot, he takes two, three touches even and now he's being closed down and finally pulled down and we're now screaming at the ref for another penalty. The keeper has dashed out and clattered into Doukara and his own defender and they're all in a pile on the floor but the ball's come free from the melee and rolls agonizingly towards goal. The Douk spots it and is first to react as he staggers to his feet and the ref is right there on top of the action waving and shouting, *"Play on, advantage!"* The defender is now also scrambling to his feet and we're going bonkers demanding that Souley get there first and then he does, just a toe to poke the ball over the line. The Kop exploded and all hell broke out in the corner near us. There were players and fans and stewards all bouncing around just as they did a few days ago when Ronnie put that penalty away. Oh I could get used to seeing this every week!

A 2 – 0 win was funnily enough what many folk predicted for this one but I'm sure they had a more comfortable 2 – 0 than this in mind. I'd wasted two quid with William Hill again on an 18/1, 3 – 1 to Leeds shot, but I didn't care.

Garry Monk again summed it up perfectly after the game when he told the BBC: *"It wasn't the best of performances, considering the context of the week we've had. We are not overly happy with the performance but are delighted with the desire to get the win…*

"We showed real character and determination to fight to the end. We had to scrap but we knew we would get chances and it was about taking those chances."[1]

We had a formula for success; a tight and resolute defence, a tremendous work ethic, and an ability to snaffle any chance offered… we'd literally made the Brewers droop.

---

[1] http://www.bbc.co.uk/sport/football/37736459

Suffice to say the Shropshire Whites' bus was a happy place to be for the two hour trip back to Whitchurch. Well, mostly...

We'd got as far as the first toilet stop; a lay-by just off the M56. Most of the lads piled off and headed for the bushes while one bloke propped himself against the front of the bus and treated us to the sight of his broad smile as he relieved himself against the front bumper. He was lit up like a Halloween pumpkin in the bus headlights. Suddenly, one of the lads who'd remained on board dashed off, ran round the front of the bus and jumped into the driver's seat. Then, to my surprise, he put the mini-bus into gear and began to reverse, leaving the poor bloke leaning on the front almost toppling over trying to grab the bus with one hand whilst hanging onto his todger with the other; the whole episode spot-lit for the amusement of folk going by in passing cars and the few of us still on the bus. Then there was an audible *"thump"* and I could see all the lads peering out from the bushes waving their hands madly trying to signal to our imposter driver. Either that or they were demonstrating a freehand peeing ability of Olympic qualification standard. Someone else shouted: *"What the f*** are you doing, you've fu**ing run over Humph you daft twa*, he's having a piss behind the bus!"* Poor old Humph, *"He's the driver of our bus; it turns like a tanker, Humph's a f*cking wan*er"*, had been knocked clean off his feet and was now lying prostrate on the tarmac behind the bus with his John Thomas hanging out! There were a few moments of worry as the full potential horror of the event was absorbed and the guilty party was now beside himself with fear of the damage he might have done to Humph but then, as Humph staggered to his feet and brushed himself down, everyone saw the funny side of it and we all fell about laughing. Humph got a huge roar of approval tinged with relief as he climbed back into the driver's seat and we got safely back on our way! It was a reminder to us all that, just like any Championship game, there is a fine margin between triumph and disaster!

Leeds United 2 Burton Albion 0 (**Wood pen (83), Doukara (90+6)**)

24,220 (Burton 699)

Bangers and smash

It seemed a very long time between the Burton game and our trip to Carrow Road. Apart from international breaks, we'd had a game every Tuesday so far this season. The only Championship activity this week was at Wigan where a new manager was unveiled; Warren Joyce, most recently head coach for Man United reserves. I thought this was a tremendous appointment for the Pie Men; so many teams go for big names who've recently been sacked elsewhere for failing in the same role, a policy that just makes no sense to me. Joyce had also held a coaching position at Elland Road in the past... that's Warren Joyce, not Joyce the tea lady who was rumoured to have been appointed to various senior roles at Thorp Arch under Cellino!

I was driving for the long 200 mile drag to Norwich and I picked Kentley up just after 8am. The first signs of winter were apparent as we sped down the A14 with lots of Guy Fawkes bonfires ready to be lit later that evening, the trees resplendent in their autumn coats and a touch of frost on the ground. For the first time in ages we had an untroubled journey and pulled into the multi-story car-park on Rose Lane just after 11:30am. We were heading for the Compleat Angler, a riverside pub on Prince of Wales Road but first we ate and grabbed our first pints of the day in a restaurant across the bridge. By the time we got back to the pub it was absolutely rammed full of thirsty Leeds fans, six or seven deep at the bar. We said hello to as many familiar faces as we could – Simon, Wayne, Phil, Chris, Paul and Dawn, Derek and Shirley, young Riley and Robbie, Marc and Shaun were all in there – but with no prospect of getting a beer this side of Christmas we soon beetled back to the bar in the Table Table and spent an hour in there with Nigel, Simon, Martin and his three lads.

The team news was received cautiously. Garry Monk had decided to reward Souleymane Doukara for his fine substitute appearances against Norwich and Burton last week; he'd start in place of Hadi Sacko. Otherwise it was the same XI that began the Burton game with still no sign of Liam Bridcutt or Stuart Dallas being fit to play.

Green
Ayling Bartley (Capt) Jansson Taylor
O'Kane Phillips
Roofe Hernandez Doukara
Wood

Subs: Silvestri, Berardi, Cooper, Antonsson, Sacko, Grimes, Vieira.

The walk to the ground was a lively affair. It seemed most of the 2,000 odd Leeds fans had decided to make the move at the same time... and there were some very odd Leeds fans! We sang and danced our way through the streets of Norwich while Saturday afternoon shoppers and passing motorists looked on with incredulity at this white, yellow and blue invading army. As we walked, a fabulous full rainbow appeared over to our left and a potential pot of gold awaited Leeds if they could do the business in the next couple of hours. When we arrived at the ground, the pat-down security checks at the turnstiles were some of the most cursory I've seen this season which surprised me at this time of year with fireworks so readily available. I did wonder if anyone would manage to smuggle any in. Inside the stadium it was the usual scene of pre-match hyperactivity with the concourse under the South Stand packed with Leeds fans enjoying more beer and rehearsing a few famous anthems; *"Pontus Jansson's magic..."* being the most popular ditty as I pushed and shoved my way through to the Gents. I was mid-stream when suddenly there was a blinding flash and an ear splitting *"boom"*.

In these terrorist strewn times, any loud bang in public places immediately has folk thinking the worst and I'm sure everyone stood near me was worrying, as I did for a split second; not only that we may have just peed down our trouser legs but maybe that a bomb had exploded in the vicinity. There was a deadly silence as everyone waited to see if there was a big cloud of dust and maybe the roof falling in…Thankfully there was nothing, and once our ears recovered from the initial numbness we all guessed what had happened. Some twonk had let off a banger in one of the thunder boxes. I thought back to the cursory checks being made at the turnstiles and shook my head at the futility of it; as Wham once said: *"If you're gonna do it, do it right – right?"* Gradually, the other blokes around me began to nervously laugh off the incident whilst surreptitiously brushing their trouser legs off but really lads, bangers in the bogs, flares, chucking beer around the concourse? Give it a rest eh?

Kentley, Nigel and I assembled at the east end of the South Stand, the regular away section here at Carrow Road. To our right, in the corner, was the very clever big screen they now have here; it can swivel through 180 degrees so that, in the rare event of a home goal, the action can be replayed to the folk in the Barclay End while the rest of the time it faces the other three sides of the ground. This new Epoch screen is a $45m^2$ high resolution affair, measuring a huge 400 diagonal inches and is the first in the world to be installed in a football ground. It was erected in the summer and I'm sure we'll see them at other grounds around the country in the near future.[1]

There was a bit of a crush around us and soon the whole stairway to our right was as full as the seating area; the stewards were fighting a losing battle to clear it. Hostilities were suspended while the minute's silence took place, this being the Canaries' Remembrance fixture, the third game running we'd had the sight of both teams lining up around the centre circle. When the referee's whistle blew, signalling the end of the tribute, the pushing and shoving recommenced but

---

[1]

http://www.fcbusiness.co.uk/news/article/newsitem=4538/title=norwich+city+showcase+world+football%92s+first+revolving+led+stadium+screen everyone soon settled down to watch the game. We were in great voice too, taunting the Norwich fans to our right with those old favourites, *"You've got six fingers, we've only got five"* and, referring to our EFL cup win ten days ago, *"You fu**** it up 2 – 1"*. *"You're just a small town in Ipswich"* went down well too. Our lads on the pitch were giving us plenty to cheer as well, as we dominated the early exchanges.

Pablo Hernandez was displaying all his silky skills as first he slid the ball across the face of goal for Kemar Roofe and then, picking up the rebound from Roofe's close range effort, he literally chasséd around a defender to cross it again. He was on fire. Wood was more of a slow burner, but in the 8th minute he leapt to head a Doukara cross down into the turf that was only just scrambled away. This was as good as we'd seen from Leeds this season. Within seconds another chance fell for Roofe but he hit the half-volley inches over and then another sweet move between Taylor, Hernandez and the Douk ended with a curling Kalvin Phillips effort that was well saved. Wood's header from the resulting corner was held by Norwich keeper McGovern. It was all Leeds but the worry was that we hadn't managed to break the deadlock. Incredibly, in the 24th minute the Canaries flew into the lead.

A rare Norwich shot was hooked away for a corner by Pontus Jansson. The left wing corner was lofted over to the near post where Robbie Brady jumped to back-head the ball towards the other post. As the ball lobbed towards goal Rob Green dived across his line and got finger tips to it but, as it fell, Luke Ayling could do no more than brush into his own net. It was a sloppy looking goal from a set piece that would no doubt annoy Garry Monk; it didn't do much for me either. It was classic Championship; if you don't take your chances the opposition will make you pay by nicking a rare one of theirs. Norwich 1 Leeds 0 at half-time.

During the interval, Keith appeared and we had a quick chat. He's seen plenty of football in his time and was full of praise for the Leeds performance in that first twenty minutes but we both agreed we'd lost our way after that.

Within a minute of the restart, Leeds seemed to have rediscovered their mojo. Roofe hammered a near post header just wide but then went down holding his head. At first he seemed to have come off better than his Norwich marker who was soon sporting a 'Kisnorbo' but some damage had been done to Roofe as well and as everyone knows, you have to replace a damaged roof quickly. Hadi Sacko was on five minutes later. It was a change that would turn the game.

Within seconds, Hadi was racing down the right wing exchanging passes with Luke Ayling and Pablo Hernandez and it was only a timely sliding intervention from the Kisnorbo'd Ryan Bennett that got the ball away for a corner. Hernandez trotted over to the Leeds right wing to take it, just twenty yards or so below us. The Canaries had conceded 23 goals in their previous 12 games and we were about to see why. As the corner floated across, Pontus Jansson got himself completely free of the group of players crowded at the back post. He was exactly on the angle of the six-yard box but he was all alone as he rose to gently nod the ball up and over the man guarding the far post. Cue delirium! We all knew what was coming next. Pontus ran in a zig-zag line across the pitch towards us, chased by the rest of the team with Hadi Sacko leading the pack. He didn't stop of course when he got to the advertising boards... oh no, not Pontus! Pontus was up and over and into the arms of his adoring fans. I was in self-protection mode; dozens of lads came tumbling down from behind, cartwheeling over seats and falling, domino like, along the stand. It was carnage for a few moments before everyone got themselves together again, settled down, and then turned their attention towards the Norwich fans who were, *"not singing anymore!"* It was some little while before Pontus could extract himself and when he did he was met with a yellow card in the upstretched hand of referee Andy Davies. It was Pontus's 4th yellow of the season; one more before the end of November and he'd be banned for a game; a sobering thought.

The game was set up now for a fight to the finish and it really opened up as both sides went for it. In another move that would later prove crucial, Garry Monk brought on Ronnie Vieira for the tiring Doukara. Leeds were playing some lovely stuff, keeping the ball on the deck and running it from deep. In

the 74th minute Rob Green grabbed the ball and rolled it out to
Eunan O'Kane. The Irishman touched it to Ayling and he set
off down the right wing. As he approached half-way he
clipped the ball down the line for Sacko to run onto. Sacko
toyed with Norwich full back Olsson, in the corner nearest to
us and then flicked the ball through some legs to Hernandez.
Pablo back-healed it to Ayling who'd continued his run all the
way from our box. Ayling took a couple of quick touches
before squaring it across goal and Chris Wood was there to
thrash the ball into the roof of the net. Oh my God! The
dominoes were tumbling again and there were tears in the eyes
of hairy arsed blokes who'd surely seen it all before. Chris
Wood thought about doing a Pontus as he raced over towards
us but instead slid down on his knees, arms stretched to the
heavens. It was another classic Leeds United celebration in
front of the fans to add to a fast growing portfolio. This was
getting hard to believe; it was just not what happened to
Leeds! Not in the last few seasons anyway. Oh how glorious
would this be if we could now hold out for the last twenty
minutes or so. A bloke next to me with a Norway badge on his
bobble hat told me in a thick Geordie accent: *"Howay man,
we're gannin up man, gannin up wi the Toon"*. I hugged him
whilst thinking what a decent book title that would make…
"Gannin up wi the Toon!"
We hung on for 14 minutes as Norwich threw everything at us
but then with two to go it was level again. A left foot cross
into the middle found Cameron Jerome who chested it on to
Kyle Lafferty. Lafferty, an 84th minute substitute, slid the ball
inside the far post. Have I mentioned how often a sub scores
past us? To have got so close to beating Norwich on their own
patch, only to give a goal away in the last minutes, was painful
but most of us were sanguine about it. A point here was still
going to be a great point and probably more than many of us
thought we'd get. We knew our performance probably
deserved more but hey, we were just getting greedy.
The Norwich fans were now singing again and cleverly turned
our earlier chant against us as they taunted us with; *"You
fu**** it up, 2 – 1 and you fu**** it up 2 -1"* while the man
with Norway badge told me, *"We're still gannin up wi the*

Toon!" That ruddy big screen was swivelling around showing exactly how we'd *"fu**** it up!"* In a move that seemed to suggest Monk was happy with the point, Matt Grimes replaced Pablo Hernandez. But did I mention that Ronnie Vieira was now on?

Rob Green gathered the ball from a weak Graham Dorrans shot and then lay on it for ages, clearly soaking up the final few minutes as much as he could. Eventually though he launched his clearance down the middle aiming for the head of Chris Wood. Wood did that thing where he jumps sort of bent over double so that the defender challenging comes right over his head. A shrill blast on the ref's whistle told us we'd won a free kick and we all hollered like mad thinking it would waste another few minutes; perhaps we could even send the ball into the corner. The board went up to signify there would be seven, FU***** SEVEN, minutes of added time, so we needed to waste as many seconds as we could. O'Kane stood over the ball and Vieira lurked a few paces to his right. We couldn't hear it, but later Ronnie would tell the BBC he was shouting *"Eunan, Eunan, I'll have it"*. Eunan pointed to his left and then flicked the ball to his right, a bit too hard if truth be told and Vieira had to stretch to trap it before knocking it another few yards ahead. Judging by the mower stripes on the pitch, he was around 38 yards from goal but he let fly anyway and the next we see is the ball sneaking under the outstretched hands of McGovern, right in the bottom left-hand corner and then flying up into the roof of the net! This was unbelievable! I looked to my left and somehow Nigel had been carried fifteen yards along the row. Norway badge was hugging me again and yelling *"I fu***** told yer mate, we gannin up!"* Quick as a flash we were turning to the disbelieving Canaries fans telling them they'd *"fu**** it up two-two"* while giving them an exaggerated 'V' sign each time we sang the word 'two'. They were now mostly heading for the exits shaking their heads in disbelief. This time we saw it through and at the final whistle our jubilant screams were momentarily drowned out by the booing from the home fans aimed at their own troops. Then, as the rest of the Canaries slunk away, we got into full celebration mode. *"Can we play you every week?"* we belted out, pointing at the Barclay End as it emptied quicker than a pub that's run out of beer and then, *"You're fu***** sh**!"*, over and over again just as teams sang at us last season.

Down in those banger bogs again after the game I could hear the Leeds fans still singing their heads off in the concourse and then it went quiet before another crescendo of cheering began, louder and louder until the walls were vibrating; perhaps that banger had loosened the brickwork. Eventually, there was an almighty roar and then, *"We are Leeds, we are Leeds, we are Leeds"* and *"Leeds are going up!"* echoed around the building. When I eventually got back outside the gents I saw crowds of fans watching the TV on the wall, it was showing the league tables and the big cheer had signalled the appearance of the Championship; Leeds sixth, with 26 points. Above us Norwich 27, Reading 28, Huddersfield 29, Brighton 34 and, top of the pile, the Toon on 37. Newcastle were our next opposition, at Elland Road, after the next international break; another test that would show just how far we'd come.

After the game, Garry Monk was trying to keep everyone's feet firmly on the ground when he told BBC Radio Leeds: *"That's one for the fans to enjoy. It's a great result, but there is nothing to be won yet. We know we are not the finished article yet, but we are making good progress."*

As we made tracks away from the ground, the singing continued despite the fact it was now pouring with rain. We were all getting soaked but a 5th away win of the season and 6th place in the table meant we were in 7th heaven. Elsewhere in the Championship, there were wins for Newcastle over Neil Warnock's Cardiff City, a home defeat for Wolves as Steve McClaren's Derby beat them in their first game under Paul Lambert, a 3 – 0 home defeat for Wigan under their new man Warren Joyce and a 3 – 1 home defeat for Rotherham under Kenny Jacket. A new coach did not seem to be working for every struggling Championship side but a 1 – 1 draw for QPR at Forest was the last act for Jimmy Floyd Hasselbaink as the Hoops decided it was worth a punt on a new man.

Norwich City 2 Leeds United 3 (Ayling (og 34), **Jansson (57)**, **Wood (74)**, Lafferty (88), **Vieira (90+1)**) 26,903 (**Leeds 1,931**)

Dropping the ball

During the next international break Mrs W and I flew to Italy for a final holiday of the year. We'd been invited to stay with friends who had an apartment near Genoa, on the Ligurian Coast. I tried to keep abreast of any Leeds news as best I could despite a very dodgy Wi-Fi connection in the flat; it was another week of celebrity deaths. Radio DJ Jimmy Young was first to leave us, on the Monday after the Norwich game; he was 95 mind as he said TTFN (Ta Ta For Now) for the final time. Later in the week the world lost Leonard Cohen, the influential Canadian singer and songwriter most famous for 'Hallelujah', which eventually became one of the most performed songs of all time. And then news came through that the actor Robert Vaughn had also passed. Vaughn is probably still best known for his role as the very suave Napoleon Solo in 'The Man From U.N.C.L.E' TV show and I, like millions of youngsters in the 60s, had gone out and bought myself a U.N.C.L.E fountain pen and a supply of invisible ink to be able to write and pass on secret messages at school just like our hero Solo.

Perhaps the biggest news this week though was that another part of my youth was being messed with in an unsavoury manner; Toblerone chocolate bars had been given a makeover to remove some of the famous triangles from each bar! How dare they! Oh, and over in the States, a Brexit like shock had occurred in the US Presidential election and Donald Trump had beaten Hilary Clinton against all the odds and defying all the pre-election polling data.

In the Championship, Ian Holloway was wheeled out of the TV studio to fill the managerial gap left at QPR while at League Two Mansfield Town, none-other than Steve Evans squeezed himself into their boss's big leather chair.

At Leeds it was all quiet. Pontus Jansson played for Sweden and Chris Wood turned out for the Kiwis and both were said to have come through injury free while Eunan O'Kane and Stuart Dallas were withdrawn from the Republic of Ireland and Northern Ireland squads respectively due to minor injuries. Tweets appeared sporadically from @andrearadri, (supposedly the Twitter account of Andrea Radrizzani); teasing us that he was progressing with some major deal which most Leeds fans hoped was the purchase of Leeds United. There was still no announcement from the FA concerning the Ross McCormack 'bung' case but Cellino was rumoured to have been in Italy, just north of where I was, apparently discussing a possible takeover of Brescia. That only served to heighten the anticipation that maybe he was on his way out of Elland Road but I didn't spot him to be able to ask the question...

The Toon weekend was a busy one for me; I'd been approached by the TV show, FAN TV UK, to go on their show on the Saturday afternoon to preview the game and then it was up to Leeds on Sunday for the live on TV game at lunchtime, the first of eight of our games out of the next 12 to be televised live. To get a cheap train ticket I was down in the capital early, very early; in fact I was in the Montagu Pyke Wetherspoon near Tottenham Court Road tube station by 9am. A Spoons' Large Breakfast and, once the 10am curfew was lifted, a few pints of Doombar and I was ready to face the nation.

Quite how much of the nation was watching Sky channel 212 at 4pm that Saturday afternoon I'm not too sure as it can only be described as a *"low budget"* operation! I was joined by eight other lads; fans from Ipswich, QPR, Man U, Norwich, Spurs, Swansea and two lads purporting to support the Toon. I say *"purporting"* as neither had a Geordie accent, both lived in London, and neither had been to a game all season! Anyway, we all squeezed into the 'green room', a box you'd struggle to get a pair of my lad's size 14 shoes in. The little beer fridge in the corner had a stock of six cans of Carling which we had to share round using a few china mugs while the tap in the two-man bogs next door had a propensity to hose you down if you weren't careful. One of the Toon fans was not careful and emerged with a distinctly not good TV look of a wet patch spreading across the crotch of his jeans. He was mortified, almost as mortified as the Swans fan was each time he spoke about Swansea's new manager, the American Bob Bradley; poor chap was suicidal (The swans fan that is, not Bob Bradley).The show passed off OK and I think I did the club justice, although it was hard when staring into the eyes of the show host, the lovely Kiri Bloore (now Kiri Day). Perhaps I ought to rewrite that sentence…

I didn't arrive home until after 10pm on Saturday, so it was a struggle being up again the following day to be at Whitchurch for 9:15 but I made it and was soon nodding off on the Shropshire Whites bus heading for Elland Road. There were lots of new faces on board the 52 seater coach, as indeed there would be at the game which was a sell out with 36,000 tickets having been snapped up weeks earlier. A chant of *"Where were you when we were sh**"* could be heard every now and again from the back of the bus aimed at all the *"part-time supporters!"*

The Pavilion was rammed full too, and half of it was taken over by 'Corporate Guests' enjoying a cooked breakfast, much to the chagrin of the rest of us who were spending most of our time queuing hours for beer. I guess it was a taste of things to come if we ever get back in the Premier League. I'm not sure I like the prospect.

Before the game, both sides warmed up wearing T-shirts adorned with the face of Gary Speed on the front and 'Speed' and the number '11' on the back. It was almost five years exactly since the popular Welshman took his own life in a tragic event that has never truly been understood. He wore the '11' shirt successfully for both Leeds and Newcastle and hence it was a day to remember and honour his contribution. A five page tribute began on page 11 in the programme and a minute's applause was planned for the 11th minute of the game. All eyes would be on our current number 11, Souley Doukara to see if he could score today. Doukara was perhaps a surprising inclusion with Hadi Sacko expected by most to play one of the wide roles with Kemar Roofe on the other side; Sacko would begin the game on the bench.

Green
Ayling Bartley (Capt) Jansson Taylor
O'Kane Vieira
Doukara Phillips Roofe
Wood

Subs: Silvestri, Berardi, Cooper, Dallas, Grimes, Berardi, Sacko, Antonsson.

It was unfortunate that for this, our biggest test of the season so far, against top of the table and much fancied Newcastle we were missing the likes of Pablo Hernandez (struggling to shake off a hamstring injury) and Liam Bridcutt who still seemed a long way off with that broken bone in his foot. Dallas would also most likely have started if he'd not just come back from injury.

Elland Road looked majestic as I took up my usual place at the front of the Kop. Even the top tier of the mighty East Stand, away to my left, was full to capacity. The only empty area was a small section at the west end of the South Stand, presumably to keep a respectable distance between the Leeds fans over there and the 2,700 Magpie fanciers. This is what it would be like every game if ever we get back to the Prem. *"MOT"* and *"We are Leeds"* belted out from the Kop and the South Stand and just to get us to try even harder, Pontus Jansson came over to urge us to make even more noise; he really gets it you know!

The 11th minute came and went and the whole ground stood and saluted Gary Speed, with the familiar *"Oh, Gary-Gary, Gary-Gary-Gary-Gary-Gary-Speed"* chant ringing out non-stop from most sections of the ground. On the big screen, pictures of Speed, alternating between shots of him in Leeds and Newcastle strips were shown and then one clever final shot of two merged photos showing him in the black and white of the Toon and the white of Leeds. On the pitch it was the rather gaudy black and orange away strip of the Toon that looked most lively, with the bald figure of Jonjo Shelvey putting himself about in midfield and the little scurrying figure of Dwight Gayle causing problems for the Leeds defence up front. It was typical of our luck that neither ought really to have been playing. Shelvey was facing an FA ban over alleged racist comments in a recent game against Wolves but he'd requested a personal hearing which had delayed the potential ban by one game. Gayle had reportedly lost four teeth when he was attacked at a Liverpool nightclub while out celebrating team-mate Jamaal Lascelles' 23rd birthday. Someone had reportedly taken offence when Gayle was spouting off about his £35,000 a week pay deal. Trust Gayle to have a speedy dentist![1]

Nothing changed in the score line in the 11th minute and the next thing we knew the clock was showing '22:00' Mike suggested maybe something would happen in the *"double eleven"*... Sadly it did.

Newcastle defender Jack Colback had the ball some 50 yards from goal, over in front of the East Stand and he must have spotted Rob Green off his line; perhaps he was even aware how our keeper was often unsure under a high ball... and how he often f***'s up in live TV games; QPR earlier this season and the time he earned the chant, *"You let your country down"* come to mind. So, Colback launches the ball half the length of the pitch and watches as it rises and then begins to drop; it was dropping right under Green's crossbar in front of the South Stand. Despite the fact that Green was back-peddling, it was a routine situation, either to catch the ball or to push it, volley-ball style, over the cross bar. Green did neither. Unaware that Dwight Gayle was lurking right in front of him, Green reached up and palmed the ball down in front of him. Gayle was onto it before it even hit the turf to stab it in the net... That hurt; it

---

[1]   http://www.mirror.co.uk/sport/football/news/newcastle-forward-dwight-gayle-loses-9289656

hurt a lot. It was always going to be a tough challenge to beat the Toon, especially without the invention of little Pablo in midfield but to hand them a goal like this was just so painful, and to do it in front of our first full house in donkey's years made it almost embarrassing. Gayle had scored but it was Green's keeping that was toothless.

Leeds brushed themselves down quite quickly and in the period up to half-time we were actually the better side. Luke Ayling forced a top save from Toon keeper Karl Darlow and Chris Wood had a couple of headed efforts at goal. Charlie Taylor had a half-hearted shout for a penalty too as he slalomed into the box before toppling over. Newcastle were not averse to the odd pull, shove and trip either. Leeds piled on the pressure with several corners in a sustained spell of pressure and from one an attempted Vieira volley smacked against the arm of Colback. Again the shouts went up for a penalty, none more loudly than from an irate Pontus Jansson. We all cringed as Pontus flew towards the referee and winced as he pushed him backwards with his chest. Another referee might well have sent him off but Graham Scott merely showed a yellow card. Sadly, it was a 5th yellow for Pontus and he was now banned for the Rotherham game. Leeds needed something to run for them in this spell but it didn't come and at half-time, after brief boos aimed at the officials, the Leeds players left the pitch to a chorus of cheers of approval. *"We always get sh** refs"* echoed around the ground.

There was more pressure from Leeds at the start of the second half but whereas Green let us down, Karl Darlow looked rock solid in the visitors' goal. He was down low to his right to keep out a close range effort from Eunan O'Kane. Then, in the 54th minute, the Toon as good as made safe the three points.

They probed and probed before a few one-two wall-passes created the opening for a simple low ball behind the Leeds defence and that man Gayle was there unmarked at the back post to slide the ball home. It was another cruel blow, with Leeds having looked so good for the previous twenty five minutes but it sort of summed up what you need in the Championship. The Toon had a rock solid keeper and defence, a midfield full of quality, accurate passers and a striker on hand to punish the slightest mistake; not that Green's mistake was slight obviously. Leeds made errors, failed to capitalise on a few chances and were wasteful with set-piece crosses and simple passes. It was a lesson for our young side but it was none the less still painful to see a game we had anticipated so much end so early. In replays of the second goal there was a case for saying Gayle was an inch or two offside too, but it was just not our day and that went un-noticed at the time.

Rob Green had another moment of indecision when he delayed and delayed with Gayle closing him down but this time he got away with it but Newcastle saw the game out with few real dramas. Sacko and Antonsson made late substitute appearances and in the short time he was on, Sacko proved to me he should have started; he has pace and invention in his game. But the final whistle blew with the Toon army singing *"We are top of the league"* and the Leeds fans left pondering what might have been. *If* we'd have had Pablo available, *if* Sacko had started, *if* the referee had been to Specsavers and *if* Rob Green wasn't camera shy... lots of ifs really. It wouldn't matter too much if we could go to the New York Stadium next Saturday and beat the Millers to regain our recent momentum but the post-match news was that we'd be going there still without Pablo and now without our brick-heading centre-back and crowd favourite, Pontus Jansson. With the Millers rock bottom with just 7 points, 8 adrift of the next side above them, Wigan, we all knew they would fight like crazy, particularly against their more famous Yorkshire rivals.

On the bus home, the Shropshire Whites collectively shrugged their shoulders and with a raffle, an attempt at a Mannequin Challenge (the latest social media craze), and the usual post-match banter, we all got ourselves ready for that trip to darkest Rotherham. Leeds were down to 7th after this, the 17th round of games... Ah yes, I'd forgotten this was our 17th league game, we probably didn't stand a chance did we Massimo? Equally I didn't win a sodding thing in the raffle on the coach either which was done on seat numbers... yes you guessed it; I was sat in seat '17'!

Leeds United 0 Newcastle United 2 (Gayle, (23 & 54))
36,002 (Newcastle 2,700)

3 points but no cigar!

The Rotherham game was always going to be a test of stamina... no, not for the bloody team, for me! I was picked up by the Shropshire Whites' mini-bus at 10:40am, yet the game, the latest in this string of eight in twelve Leeds games to be televised live on Sky, was a 5:30pm kick-off. Even taking the most scenic of scenic routes that Postman Pat might take over the tops it was only ever going to be a two hour run to Rotherham so that left almost five hours for drinking! FIVE BLOODY HOURS!

The rickety old mini-bus was alive with the sounds of clinking bottles, fizzing tinnies and a blaring soundtrack of 70s and 80s pop while the windows were soon running with condensation as the boozy breath of fifteen hairy-arsed blokes filled the air. We'd gone about twenty minutes when the first stop was made in Etwall, at the Seven Wells pub. It was billed as a twenty minute toilet stop but that was plenty of time to grab my first beer. For most of the lads on the bus it was a chance to supplement the bottled stock they'd been supping on the bus.

The main drinks destination was reached around 1pm; the Phoenix Sports and Social Club in Brinsworth, on the outskirts of Rotherham. They looked after us royally; the food was superb, the beer cheap, pool and snooker tables and Sky TV on several wall mounted screens. It was a pre-match heaven and by the time we left at 4pm most of us were seeing angels around every corner! I worked my way through several pints of Coors – experience has shown I can drink that 'til the cows turn for home' – before it was time to get back aboard the magic bus and head for the Aesseal New York Stadium; try saying that after a few pints!

I met Kentley outside the ground and then we fought our way through the crowds to get another pint at the little bar in the concourse. It was manic. There were three queues initially but Sods Law dictated that by the time we got to the front there were only two taps still on… and neither was ours! With a little help from Jack to one side and Dave R to the other who just happened to be alongside, we managed to charm the manageress to serve us. I would tell you how many pints that was for me for the day but honestly, by then I'd lost count. Suffice to say I glided up the steps to our seats in row 'O' overlooking the goal at the South End of the ground.

Green
Ayling Bartley Cooper (Capt) Taylor
O'Kane Phillips
Sacko Roofe Doukara
Wood

Subs: Silvestri, Berardi, Grimes, Vieira, Mowatt, Antonsson, Dallas.

It was no doubt a tricky team selection for Garry Monk who, regardless of what he said to the contrary, must have had one eye on the trip to Anfield coming up the following Tuesday. He'd face a similar dilemma for the following league game too, a tough looking encounter with improving Aston Villa that was arguably more important than the Anfield tie. One change was certain of course; Pontus Jansson was suspended following that 5th booking of the season he picked up against the Toon. Liam Cooper was the obvious and only real replacement for the magic hat man. In the event Monk made just one other change and I was very happy with it. He found space in the side for Hadi Sacko who replaced Ronnie Vieira and that in turn allowed Kemar Roofe to fill the so-called number '10' role. It was the role played by Pablo Hernandez when fit but it was proving hard to find a suitable stand-in now he wasn't. Kalvin Phillips tried against Newcastle but most folk reckoned he didn't do it justice.

Rotherham were struggling big-time, just one win all season, only seven points and well adrift at the bottom of the table. Having said that they did at least have history on their side; Leeds had not won a league game in Rotherham since 1982 and had never won at the New York Stadium. They had some danger men too and were not short of goals, boasting the likes of Danny Ward and Peter Odemwingie up front and the versatile Greg Halford at the back. They also had ex-Leeds man Tom Adeyemi on loan from Cardiff City and the experienced Lee Camp in goal. On paper they were a decent looking outfit but they were shipping lots of goals; 41 so far, more than any other side in the top four English leagues. I felt this was the archetypal must win game. We were allowed to give way to the Toon as they were simply the best but the Millers were threshing about amongst the almost dead men and if we couldn't beat them we really had no right to entertain hopes of promotion.

Leeds had around 2,200 fans at the game, around a fifth of the total crowd of 10,513 and, oiled by hours of ale supping, we were loud and proud. The first half went about as perfectly as any of us could have dreamt in our wildest of dreams.

Leeds hadn't scored a goal earlier than the 23rd minute all season but today we had one inside the first 15... just! 14 minutes were on the clock as Leeds took a throw in out on the right wing and patiently knocked the ball around looking for an opening. The ball was moved out to the left where Charlie Taylor held it while he assessed his options. Suddenly, he darted inside and between two Rotherham defenders who were doing a passable Mannequin Challenge. Another defender moved in slowly but Charlie was already whipping the ball across the face of goal some ten yards out and Chris Wood was there to stab it under Lee Camp. It was the perfect start and we celebrated with as much gusto as five hours of drinking would allow while some twonk over to our right hurled a smoking yellow flare into Rob Green's penalty area. Why any Leeds fan would endanger his own keeper is beyond me; at the very least the choking acrid smoke must have been getting in Green's eyes and throat just as it was in ours. We'd seen only last week how he struggles with high balls in crystal clear Yorkshire air so this wasn't going to help was it?

When the game finally restarted, Leeds were straight on the throttle again and Liam Cooper went close with a header that grazed the post. At our end, we got a reminder about that Rotherham strike force, as Odemwingie fired the ball under Rob Green but we'd already spotted a liner's flag up. Then, inexplicably, Odemwingie elbowed Liam Cooper in the face and was soon heading for the proverbial early bath. A goal down and now a man short, Rotherham were living proof of that football cliché that says when you're down nothing, absolutely nothing, goes your way. The Millers also lost Greg Halford to injury in the first few minutes and now, shortly after Odemwingie stomped off, goalkeeper Lee Camp was following as he succumbed to a knock while saving from Hadi Sacko. I swear if someone had brought on a packet of Treats they'd have melted in their hands...[1]

Kemar Roofe looked more at home in the number '10' role than Theresa May in this first half and it was fitting it was he who slotted the ball through to Doukara for a second goal just before the break. The Douk was his usual unerring self as he threaded his shot through a gaggle of legs into the opposite corner of the net. As the whistle went for half-time, many Leeds fans jogged down to the toilets to jettison some of the afternoon's ale, safe in the knowledge that this game was won. I'd not lasted that long and had nipped out and back just in

---

[1] *That's a joke referring to an old advertising campaign for the chocolate sweet brand "Treats" that went: "Treats, they melt in your mouth not in your hand!" for any younger readers who may not have ever seen it!*

time to see the Douk's goal. It was a long time since I enjoyed a half-time break thinking the points were already in the bag.

The second half began with no sign of the dramas to come; Leeds continued to dominate possession and Sacko, Phillips, Wood and even Kyle Bartley all had half-chances. Around the hour mark, Stuart Dallas got a welcome return to the side in place of Doukara and a few minutes later Antonsson replaced Roofe. It was all going to plan, well, nearly. The one problem was the accuracy of the Leeds passing or more specifically the lack of it. Time and time again promising attacks would end with a sloppy pass that went out of play or to the opposition. Eunan O'Kane was the main offender as he pushed forward; presumably trying to fill that Hernandez role now that Antonsson had taken over from Roofe. Eunan is no Pablo though and it became almost embarrassing for the lad as every pass he tried went astray. That in turn was allowing the home side to begin to sniff the scent of a comeback, as did the Millers' fans who were now roaring their men on. On the touchline we could see Garry Monk getting more and more animated, even taking his hands out of his pockets proving he did indeed have hands on the ends of his arms. Everyone was getting nervous and someone in our vicinity appeared to have let the nerves get to his bowels as the sulphur-like stench of a beery fart made the smoke of that earlier flare seem like the sweet scent of a spring flower. The Millers won a corner at the far end and we all cheered as it was headed away. Then it was headed back in and we held our breath before a Leeds head knocked it away again and we hollered our approval. But then it was headed back in once more and this time an Arsenal look-alike shirt rose and a head nodded the ball towards goal. Rob Green flew through the air and got a hand to it but it then smacked against the inside of a post and dropped into the net.

There were four minutes left, plus another four or five of added time and I'm sure every last one of our fans felt the same as I did; we were going to f*** this up.

The minutes ticked by and there was one moment when the ball seemed to defy the laws of gravity as it somehow stayed out of our net. Green stopped a shot on the line and then all hell broke loose as Leeds bodies piled in to try to keep the ball out and Rotherham bodies piled in to try to force it over the line. Eventually the ball broke free and we gasped as somehow Dominic Ball (ironically enough) smashed it over the bar from two yards. A long ball was played down the Leeds right wing and Chris Wood calmed our nerves by holding it up and then he got behind the defence and scuffed it across the face of goal; no one was there to tap it in but Charlie Taylor collected it the other side and he held it up again for a while and we began to relax. Time was nearly up. Then Charlie lost it and the fear grew again as red and white shirts flooded towards our goal. There was anger coming from our fans too, anger that we had allowed this ridiculous situation to have come about at all. They only had ten men for God's sake! It was a reminder of previous Leeds teams too, we've never been good at closing games out but we had thought this Garry Monk side was different. We got there this time and we had another three points but after the game Monk was clearly annoyed. He told BBC Radio Leeds:

"I'm happy with the three points and overall I thought we deserved them, but we made very hard work of it at the end.

"I spoke at half-time about not getting complacent, staying focused and aggressive, but the second half wasn't good enough.

"The last ten minutes was needless, we brought it on ourselves, if you give a team a sniff or chance in this league they will take it and we only had ourselves to blame...

"As the second half went on I wasn't happy, there were too many players doing the wrong thing and too many players giving the ball away and you can't have that against anyone, because any team can hurt you if you are doing that."

Even the Shroppy Whites' bus was a bit quiet on the way home and not only because we'd all supped vast quantities of beer; the win felt a bit hollow somehow. I guess it was worrying us that maybe we weren't as good as we thought we were; we still had 'sloppy' in our portfolio. We did manage one more pub stop mind, at Cherry Tree Farm on the Etwall Road, near the Derbyshire village of Willington. It's on the site of a service area with a massive car park. We had another quick pint before piling back on the bus and then we were all in hysterics as "Humph" went round and round the car park trying in vain to find the exit! Time and time again we'd go down a dead end and Humph had to carefully reverse the bus with the rest of us all making the *"peep-peep-peep"* noises of a reversing alarm or singing *"We're lost in a car park, we're f****** lost in a car park"* at the tops of our voices. When we did eventually get back on the road we gave 'Humph' a rousing rendition of his theme song: *"Humph is the driver of our ship, of our ship, Humph is the driver of our ship, our ship is a tanker and Humph's a f****** wan***, Humph is the driver of our ship!"*

When they dropped me off in the village, several of the lads got out for a pee behind the bus shelter in front of our village pub. I stood guard with my fingers crossed that none of the neighbours spotted us (or at least me!) while Humph tried to ensure the opposite as he cranked up the cd player volume and the old bus rocked to some 70s anthem or other. It was a fitting end to a grand day out. Thanks lads!

There were some strange scores in the Championship in this, the 18th round of games. Newcastle made six changes from the side that beat us the previous weekend for their home game with lowly Blackburn Rovers and paid the price with a shock 0 – 1 defeat. The other three sides now above us in the table all won, Brighton, Reading and Birmingham, as did fast improving Aston Villa, who we faced in seven days' time. Leeds were 5th, nine points behind second placed Brighton. Next up was that big EFL Cup tie at Anfield and I was on the Shroppy Whites bus again.

So, on the weekend that saw the death of Fidel Castro, the Cuban dictator, Leeds got another vital three points but there was most definitely no cigar for this performance.

Rotherham United 1 Leeds United 2 (Wood (14), Doukara (45+7), Wood (86)) 10,513 **(Leeds 2,277)**

Heads high at Anfield

Our win at the New York Stadium had more consequences than were obvious on Saturday night. By Monday morning Kenny Jackett had resigned and an appointment I never did understand came to an abrupt end after just 39 days and five games. Blimey, Brian Clough lasted longer than that at Leeds all those years ago!

Bigger by far though was the story of the exit of former Labour Shadow Chancellor Ed Balls from Strictly. Incredibly, Big Ed had lasted 10 weeks on the nation's favourite dance show, presumably due to vast numbers of viewers just having a giggle on a Saturday night as they phoned in to support him after returning from a skin-full down the local boozer. But the saddest exit of the week for me was the demise of Ola Jordan from I'm a celebrity… it had been a real chore watching her in that skimpy bikini in the Celebrity shower but… sorry, completely forgot what I was going to say there…

On the eve of our trip to Anfield a financial newspaper in Singapore, The Straits Times, broke a story that appeared to confirm that Andrea Radrizzani was indeed hoping to takeover Leeds. The key comment Radrizzani made and reported by the paper was: *"Massimo has 100 per cent now and if I do the deal, I will enter the club during this season with 50 per cent and have the option to buy him out completely in June next summer."*[1] OK, there was a huge 'if' in there but it was the first time either party had acknowledged publically that negotiations had taken place and Radrizzani was saying those negotiations were *"advanced"*. I still wasn't sure Radrizzani knew what he was trying to deal with here though and part of me felt this was more an attempt to flush out Cellino's true intentions; maybe discussions had taken place but as we'd seen so often in the past, Massimo is not averse to changing his mind. There was no comment from Cellino himself.

In the early hours of Tuesday 29th November, the day of our big game in Liverpool, reports began to appear on the BBC concerning a plane crash in Columbia. Very quickly it was established that the flight in question was carrying the players and officials of the Brazilian football team, Chapecoense, who were on their way to play in the final of the Copa Sudamericana against Medellin team Atletico Nacional. The plane crashed during its approach to Medellin airport. Of the 77 people on board, only 6 initially survived; three members of the team, two crew and one journalist.[2]

Football in the UK was back in the news too. The British football community was wracked with allegations of child abuse; several players had come forward to tell their stories of how they faced abuse from football coaches at clubs all over England during the 1970s and 80s. Even Leeds was mentioned by the Professional Footballers Association (PFA) as one of the clubs now facing investigations, although the club was quick to post a statement that they had *"not been made aware*

---

[1] *http://www.straitstimes.com/sport/football/leeds-poised-for-italian-switch*
[2] *http://www.bbc.co.uk/news/world-latin-america-38142998*

of any allegations regarding sexual abuse from the PFA or any other governing bodies to date."[1]

On the Shropshire Whites' bus travelling to Liverpool, I flicked through the latest news bulletins on the air crash and was heartened by the way the football world was coming together in support of the little team from Chapeco. The team they were due to play in the cup final, Atletico Nacional, had already suggested that the title be awarded to Chapecoense without playing the game while there were offers from many other clubs to loan players to help them continue in the short term. Liverpool had already announced that a one minute's silence would precede the Leeds game.

With a 4:30pm pick up in Whitchurch and then the usual rush-hour traffic, we were on a tight schedule but we did manage a 45 minute beer stop in Ellesmere Port. The lads had sussed out the pub whilst on the bus and even called out the directions to the bus driver who safely delivered us to The Thomas Telford on Whitby Road. There was just enough time for a couple of pints of Flintlock Ale and a superb Spoon's Ultimate Burger before we were herded back on the bus heading for the Mersey Tunnel and onward to Anfield.

We were on a hired bus with a driver for this game; it was a 32 seater booked in the expectation of around 25 making the trip but when several dropped out due to not getting tickets or not being able to finish work in time to make the bus's schedule we were stuck with it. It was almost brand new though and far too posh for us with reclining leather seats, an on board loo and even USB ports in the backs of the seats for mobile phones! The coach was decorated with tinsel and little Santa Claus pictures in all the windows ready for Christmas.

We slowly made our way along the streets surrounding Anfield looking for the away coach parking zone and at one point we drove right past Goodison Park. It was a real trip down memory lane for me. The first time I visited Anfield was back in 1976, over 40 years ago. That was for a Division One game with Leeds, that's the old Division One of course. We

---

[1] *https://www.leedsunited.com/news/club-news/21382/club-statement*

lost 2 – 0 that day. This evening there were crowds of folk everywhere you looked, hardly surprising as around 52,000 would be in the ground for the game, including well over 5,000 Leeds fans. As we inched along in the traffic jams I couldn't wait any longer and had to use those plush on board facilities. I was devastated when I got inside and saw how some of the lads had managed to pee all over the toilet seat and the floor was like a small foot spa… not that you'd have wanted to bathe your corns in this one! I wondered if we'd ever be allowed to get this particular coach again.

Eventually the driver parked up with dozens of other Leeds coaches on the roadside outside Stanley Park and we all clambered out into the dark cold night air and made our way across the park to the ground with thousands more fans coming from all directions. Over to our right we could just make out the stands of Goodison Park while some Leeds lads walking near us were telling each other stories about the bad old days when the Scousers would descend from the trees in the park and attack them with Stanley knives. Others were telling jokes about the little lads who used to, and possibly still do for all I know, greet you when you parked your car: *"Can I look after yer car mate?"* That was the cue to hand the little oiks a few coins to ensure you still had a full set of alloys when you got back after the game. I met Kentley inside and he'd heard a similar story: A bloke in a Range Rover pulls up outside Anfield and is met by one of the little oiks. *"Can I look after yer car mate?"* he asks in a squeaky Gerrard-like scouse accent, hand outstretched. *"No it's OK lad"*, the bloke explains, *"the dog's in the back."* The oik thinks for a second or two and then responds: *"So he can put out fires can he mate?"*…

Inside Anfield the atmosphere was tremendous; it was a glimpse into what the future might hold if we ever get out of this damned Championship. A packed house of over 52,000, the monumental new Anfield Main Stand to our right and the famous Liverpool Kop, filled with waving flags, at the far end of the ground. When the players emerged from beneath the Main Stand the ground erupted in a cacophony of noise and every one of the Leeds players turned towards us and applauded; quite what was going through their minds I have no idea, for some it would be a first experience of such an arena. While the home fans went through the ritual singing of *"You'll never walk alone"*, we Leeds fans did our best to drown it out with MOT, it was some contest but I reckon we won. Before the game there was that one minute's silence. As the PA announcer signalled the start of the tribute, applause broke out all around the ground and then everyone fell silent with the only sound being that of a police chopper buzzing above the stadium. In the Kop we could see a Brazilian flag as well as another paying tribute to the 96 Hillsborough victims. It read: *"We climbed the hill in our own way: justice for the 96"*... A tear trickled down the side of my face.

Silvestri
Berardi Bartley Cooper (Capt) Taylor
Vieira O'Kane
Sacko Roofe Dallas
Doukara

Subs: Green, Ayling, Phillips, Grimes, Mowatt, Antonsson, Wood.

Garry Monk definitely appeared to have one eye on that Aston Villa game coming up at the weekend. That was the only reason surely that he'd leave Ayling and Wood on the bench. The inclusion of Marco Silvestri was expected by us all as Marco's reward for his heroics in the previous round. We were told that Pontus Jansson was suffering from tonsillitis and of course Bridcutt, Coyle and Hernandez were still out injured so there weren't actually that many other options anyway so there was logic to Monk's selection. It did us proud too, against a Liverpool side that may have been young but which was full of promise and pace. Jurgen Klopp made 8 changes from the side that played the previous weekend in the Premier League win over Sunderland.

Liverpool would have 72% of the possession in this game but by the final whistle both sides managed 13 attempts on goal and both hit the target 3 times. There were few real chances in the first half but Hadi Sacko was put clear through by Stuart Dallas in the first few minutes; sadly, as we've seen a few times he doesn't yet have the composure to regularly finish off such chances and Mignolet saved in front of the Kop. At our end, Marco Silvestri pulled off one spectacular flying save turning away a shot from Wijnaldum that was otherwise destined for the top corner. At one point the Leeds fans began a chant of *"Stand up if you hate Man U"* and soon the other three sides of the ground were on their feet joining in; there is a mutual respect between the fans of our two sides and a mutual hatred of them over in Salford. Leeds played heroically and chased every ball but by the end of the half we'd succumbed to two injuries. Eunan O'Kane went off in the 27th minute and was replaced by Kalvin Phillips and then we noticed Liam Cooper was limping towards the end of the half. Coops didn't reappear for the second half and Luke Ayling, who we'd been told when he joined could double as a centre-back, filled in.

At half-time we marvelled at the fact that a solitary Leeds fan was sat quite calmly and openly wearing his white, blue and yellow scarf in amongst the Liverpool fans over to our left. He seemed to enjoy the limelight too as we serenaded him with a few songs. There was no sign of any animosity from the reds around him either. Very strange; *"He's Leeds United, he sits where he wants"* rang out from all around us.

If anything, the start of the second half was our best period of the game and only a few minutes in Kemar Roofe almost got his first goal for the club. Leeds were still harrying the home side at every opportunity and Kalvin Phillips was up on his man at the edge of the Liverpool area. The ball broke to Roofe on the left corner of the box and Roofe whipped his right foot around the ball in an instant. It curled deliciously and looked to be heading for the top corner, curling and curling, almost in slow motion... and then it thumped against the inside of the post and rebounded out. *"That's the chance!"* Kentley shouted to me and I nodded. That was probably *the* chance I thought to myself. Leeds were now dominating the game in an incredible spell of pressure and Kyle Bartley was next to hold his head in anguish. He rose to meet a right-wing corner but his glancing header flew wide. It was another glorious chance and soon Roofe was firing at goal again but this time Mignolet was down to stop it. We knew Liverpool would come again and soon they did.

A lightning fast break saw them fire a shot against a post and then minutes later they were ahead. A deep low cross from the right wing was aimed in towards that difficult spot in front of the near post. Ayling assumed Silvestri was coming, Silvestri obviously decided he couldn't get to it first but Origi was only focussed on the ball and he nipped in to poke it home. It was a poor goal to concede and the inevitable question was whether Rob Green would have had the experience and bravery to deal with the ball or whether the ball itself was just too good. We'll never know. What we did know was that we'd probably given the game away. Five minutes later and another quick break saw it confirmed.

A long clearance by Mignolet, a poor Leeds header, a quick exchange of passes and a back heel, and the ball was at the feet of 17 year-old Ben Woodburn who smoked it into the roof of the net to become the youngest ever Liverpool goal scorer, taking that accolade from Michael Owen. Football can be such a cruel game sometimes and it doesn't get much crueller than this; if that Roofe shot had been an inch more to the left, if Bartley had connected better with that header, if...

The Leeds fans sang to the end and if they were like me they believed to the end too. We thought we were back in it when Chris Wood steered the ball into the net but it was correctly ruled out for offside and Hadi Sacko showed that lack of composure again as he tried a shot when both Wood and Roofe were better placed. Wood should probably have buried a header he had too but once again his finishing let him down. It just wasn't supposed to be our night. As the game came to an end the Leeds fans chanted the name of Garry Monk and demanded he *"give us a wave"* which he did. It was a proud night to be a Leeds fan.

Now, if we could show that same commitment and heart against Villa on Saturday and maybe get just a bit of the luck now due to us, then maybe, just maybe there were plenty more big nights to come.

Liverpool 2 **Leeds United 0** (Origi (76), Woodburn (81))
52.012 (**Leeds 5,352**)

Villa collapse down to Wood n Roofe

It was like watching an Olympic high-jumper; each time Leeds got over the bar it was immediately put up another notch. We'd failed to get over Newcastle but then we slithered over Rotherham only to face Liverpool. We met that challenge head on and many considered we'd won a moral victory despite not actually progressing in the cup. But no sooner had the whistle gone at Anfield than we were thinking about the next hurdle; Aston Villa.

Villa were on a great run under new manager Steve Bruce, unbeaten in seven and climbing the Championship table in a manner many thought they ought to have done under Roberto Di Matteo. Followers of Leeds now saw the clash with the Villa as another yardstick with which to assess just how good we were; if we could beat them, the argument went; we could probably beat anyone in the Championship this season. The importance of the Villa game was clear for all to see by the sheer scale of ticket sales; like the Newcastle game, there would be well over 30,000 inside Elland Road even though it was yet another game to be screened by Sky, our fourth consecutive game to be shown live.

In an attempt to grab every last penny from another high profile game, the Pavilion was open from 12 noon, five and a half hours before the 5:30pm kick off; I was in there by 1pm! To be honest, there weren't actually many in there until the usual three hours before kick-off and annoyingly there were a couple of rock bands blasting away again which once again took the edge off the experience for me. As I've said many times before, we don't need music and we certainly don't need *loud* music as all we really want to do in there is talk football with our mates or watch a live game on the screens; the Man City v Chelsea crunch game was a 12:30pm kick-off that we were trying to watch today. Chelsea won it 3 – 1 to maintain their impressive run to the top of the Premier League.

Green
Ayling Bartley (Capt) Jansson Taylor
Vieira Phillips
Sacko Roofe Doukara
Wood

Subs: Silvestri, Berardi, Denton, Grimes, Antonsson, Mowatt, Dallas.

Garry Monk didn't have too many options for this one; there was still no Bridcutt or Hernandez and now Eunan O'Kane was added to the crocked list. Hence the two holding midfield players picked themselves and with Dallas only recently recovered the attacking midfield options were limited too. This was thus the side that won at Rotherham but with young Ronnie Vieira replacing O'Kane. Some fans were nervous that the baby faced assassins, Vieira and Phillips, would not have the experience to compete with an experienced Villa midfield. The good news was that Ross McCormack was out with an ankle injury so he'd watch the game from the stands although his little lad would take his place amongst the mascots… in a Leeds strip!

There was a minute's applause before the game to honour the memory of the Chapecoense players and officials and then we were underway although the action was frequently brought to a halt again by an overly fussy referee, not for the first time at Elland Road this season. It was a typically cagey Championship game between two teams that looked good at the back but lacked inspiration going forward and the bookies favourite outcome for the game, a draw, looked nailed on as the half-time whistle blew.

We, and the millions watching on TV, needed some action and we got it not long after the break. It wasn't perhaps what we had in mind though as we were treated to the sight of a scrawny lad in a pair of tatty boxers, a smile and little else, dashing onto the pitch. He came out of the East Stand and proceeded to entertain us all for a good minute or so as he expertly side-stepped and slalomed around numerous attempted rugby tackles from an ever growing number of red-faced stewards. He was good this lad and every missed tackle was accompanied by a great roar from fans all around the ground. Eventually, the sheer weight of numbers did the job and he was bundled over and escorted away. Apparently, this particular streaker was trying to raise money for charity and after the game social media devotees debated whether that fact ought to save him from a life-time ban or not. On the pitch, perhaps stimulated by the now enlivened crowd, the game began to come alive. After the game, Kemar Roofe would tell BBC Radio Leeds that Garry Monk had made a few tactical changes at half-time aimed at getting Leeds to press a lot higher up the pitch and it was certainly obvious that Leeds were now harrying the Villa players at every opportunity. It was one of those games though that was only ever going to be decided by a mistake or a moment of brilliance and fortunately it was Leeds that came up with the magic moment.

Villa had a decent chance when Albert Adomah got through but his shot struck the legs of Rob Green and went wide although referee Bankes missed that touch and gave a goal kick. But then another Villa attack petered out as Pontus Jansson appeared to accidentally knee the ball back to Rob Green. For the briefest of moments we held our breath wondering if referee Bankes might see it as a back-pass but as the game continued the South Stand covered Pontus's embarrassment with a few rounds of the magic hat song. Pontus saw the funny side of it and gave a little smile and a wave to the Villa fans suggesting he knew full well what he was doing all along. As play continued it was Leeds knocking the ball about patiently looking for an opening and eventually it arrived with Kalvin Phillips in the centre circle. Phillips purposely threaded the ball behind a couple of Villa players out to the left wing where Doukara had found a few yards of space. He checked inside onto his right foot and immediately curled the ball in towards the penalty spot. It was so casually done and yet it was a perfect ball, teasing the keeper to come for it. It still needed Kemar Roofe to be on the same wavelength though and he had to be quicker than the Villa keeper, Gollini. He was; Roofe ghosted in front of Gollini and headed it firmly past him leaving the Italian keeper clutching thin air. Of all the types of goals I thought Kemar might open his account with, a near post header wasn't on my list but it was a clear sign that there is more to Roofe than his trademark right foot thunderbolt. It must have been a huge relief to Kemar to finally get off the mark and the celebrations in the north-west corner were manic as they were all around us. Then Pontus Jansson appeared in front of the North Stand roaring at us to make even more noise. He ran to the other side of the Kop and then down in front of the East Stand waving his arms and imploring us get behind the side; the man was possessed! What a character he is, in fifty years of watching Leeds I don't remember any player who has been so willing to interact with the fans. The closest I could think of was Vinnie Jones but Pontus was taking fan interaction to a whole new level!

The goal meant Villa had nothing to lose now and they did their best to push forward in the remaining twenty minutes or so. But Leeds were set up as a counter attacking side with the pace of Hadi Sacko and inevitably Villa were leaving themselves open at the back. To be honest, Leeds looked more likely to score again than the Villa did to get back in the game and sure enough as the five minutes of added time was ticking down Hadi Sacko suddenly intercepted a poor Villa pass right on half-way. It was a straight dash towards the Kop now and Hadi just had the edge as he hit a right-foot shot at goal.

Gollini got something on it and the ball was still inches short of the goal line but Chris Wood slid in to scoop it into the net ahead of a defender's boot for his 13th goal of the season. The celebrations were unbridled now, as we all knew that was game, set and match to Leeds with literally only a handful of seconds left; it was a fantastic feeling.

Leeds moved into 4th spot in the table on 32 points and with the leaders Newcastle losing to Forest in this round of games we were now only eight points behind them. We were seven adrift of second placed Brighton and two behind third placed Reading and two of our next three games were against those sides.

Garry Monk was typically downbeat after the game suggesting: *"I don't think we played that well and we only really started to play better after our first goal.*

"We were doing things that we don't normally do, we weren't using the ball well enough and we were causing ourselves problems."

But he was gushing about Kemar Roofe's fine finish and told LUTV: *"... he has been excellent over the past month and I think he is getting better every time he goes on to the pitch."*[1]

It was hard not to get carried away with this win. Villa were a top side with a top manager and many thought they'd be an automatic promotion contender, yet a less than full strength Leeds, playing below their best, had seen them off efficiently. It was only one game but finally we'd shown we could compete, and beat, one of the best in class. In less than a week that bar would be raised again as we faced the prospect of second placed Brighton at the Amex where we'd never won. But before this season we'd not won at the New York Stadium either…

Leeds United 2 Aston Villa 0 (**Roofe (68), Wood (90+4)**)
32,648 (Villa 2,773)

---

[1]   *https://www.leedsunited.com/news/team-news/21403/garry-monk-the-crowd-got-us-through*

Too good to last

It was going so well, but we all knew it was probably too good to last. The latest rumour about Radrizzani was that he did, as he'd recently suggested, have an agreement with Cellino to buy 50% of the club but now it was being said that any option to buy the club outright, that is to get the other 50%, was purely dependant on Leeds *failing* to get promoted. If Leeds were in the Premier League next season, Massimo was going nowhere. He was going to stick around and enjoy the ride, not to mention the money.

There was also the small matter of that Ross McCormack bung case still occupying the FA that could potentially play some part in any future ownership discussions though. This week the Daily Mail was first to leak information suggesting that Cellino faced an eighteen month ban and a quarter of a million pound fine as well as the similar fine already handed out to the club. Cellino was quick to issue a statement claiming he was innocent and that if the Daily Mail report was correct then he'd be appealing the FA's ruling. The pro and anti-Cellino camps were immediately out in force again and at each other's throats on Twitter. Eventually, on the eve of the Brighton game, the FA confirmed the Daily Mail article adding:

"By 30 April 2017, he [Cellino] is to attend and complete an FA education programme covering the duties and responsibilities of an owner and director of an English football club."[1]

The prospect of Massimo turning up at an FA education course was, well, laughable but before we could see how that panned out we'd have to wait for the usual Cellino appeal.

Back to the football and BT Sport were now following Sky's lead and tapping into the viewing potential of Leeds United fixtures; the Cambridge FA Cup tie was already earmarked by BT as their Monday night game on January 9th. That made it nine live TV showings in 13 games; an incredible confirmation of the club's pulling power.

Brighton is a heck of a journey, even for me from the Midlands. Quite what it must be like on a supporters' coach from Leeds goodness only knows. Mrs W had agreed to come with me for this one; she wouldn't do the game but was quite happy to have a couple of days by the seaside, especially as the weather had turned really mild. It was around 15 degrees as we journeyed down the motorways, stopping en route to see son Adam in Reigate and then later pulling into the car park of The Brighton Hotel around 3pm. We managed a quick walk along the seafront and to the end of the Pier before making our way to the Fiddler's Elbow on Boyce's Street, the fabulous little traditional Irish pub I've been to many times before. The Guinness here is said to be the finest (and probably the cheapest) in Brighton and a lady I know reckons it's actually the best pint of the black stuff this side of the Irish Sea! We met Jo and Simon in the pub; they had a second good reason to be spending the weekend in Brighton; a wedding anniversary – and I thought I was the only bloke who could get away with taking the wife to football for a wedding anniversary or

---

[1] *http://www.thefa.com/news/2016/dec/08/leeds-united-and-cellino-fined-081216*

birthday! One Leeds fan I was chatting with in the pub told me how he worked in the submarine docks in Barrow and was currently working on the latest of the Royal Navy's Astute Class attack submarines, HMS Audacious. Leeds United had agreed an affiliation with HMS Audacious in the same way the club was linked with The Ark Royal a few years ago. A presentation was due to be made on the pitch at Elland Road before the Reading game, and this lad was part of it. *"Going to be the proudest day of my life"*, he whispered. I was glad his mind was very much on his big moment at Elland Road as I suddenly realised I'd picked up his Guinness off the bar and taken a big gulp; I carefully put the glass down, slid my hand along the bar and picked up my own without losing eye contact.

Nigel, Kentley and Lottie eventually joined us in the Fiddler's and we all sampled a few more pints of Guinness before it was time to make the walk up the hill to Brighton Station. There was the usual organised chaos as we were held in pens until the train arrived and then the Police ushered us through a Disney style queuing system onto the train.

Leeds had almost sold out the 3,000 ticket allocation for this one despite it being a Friday night live on Sky TV fixture some 270 miles from Leeds. We'd later discover that traffic delays had held up several of the Leeds coaches and many fans only took up their places in the stand just before kick-off.

Green
Ayling Bartley (Capt) Jansson Taylor
Vieira Phillips
Sacko Roofe Doukara
Wood

Subs: Silvestri, Berardi, Cooper, Grimes, Mowatt, Dallas, Antonsson.

It was the same side that saw off Villa last week and I'd guess that most Leeds fans thought this was our best chance yet of winning a game at the Amex; something we'd not yet achieved. Brighton would be no pushovers of course; they were second in the table behind the Toon and were on a run of 13 consecutive league games without defeat. In fact they'd kept nine clean sheets during that run. But Leeds had taken one more point than Brighton in recent games and we were above them in the six-game form table. I was happy that our defence would be more than a match for the Seagulls; after all, it had looked rock solid for months with this line up even without the steadying influence of Liam Bridcutt in front of it. But I was wrong…

The Leeds fans were in great voice as always and most of our affection was being expressed towards Pontus Jansson. The "magic hat" song got an early airing as did a rendition of Wham's 'Last Christmas' albeit with different words to those that George Michael and Andrew Ridgeley warble at us every year.

> *"Last Christmas I gave you my heart,*
> *But the very next day you gave it away.*
> *This year, to save me from tears,*
> *I gave it to Pontus Jansson."*

The problem was though; the Seagulls were crapping on our party, big time. With an attack led by the experienced and dangerous Glen Murray, on loan from Premier League Bournemouth, the Seagulls ripped into Leeds from the off. Luke Ayling had looked pretty untroubled by most wingers all season but now Jamie Murphy was roasting him at will. It was no surprise when, just 11 minutes into the game, Ayling had to resort to a rugby tackle on Murphy to halt him and got the inevitable yellow card. That was a worry with almost 80 minutes still to play. Ayling wasn't the only one struggling out there though, our cult hero Pontus was in trouble too. He also fouled Murphy and then had a go at Murray. The Brighton fans left Pontus in no doubt he wouldn't be on their Christmas card list this year but he did get an entry next to 'Ayling' on the ref's yellow card; 19 minutes gone and two of our back four in the book already. The ball was fizzing around our net at the far end of the ground with far too much regularity for my liking and no one seemed to be taking charge. Then, in the 22nd minute, Charlie Taylor conceded the first corner of the game. The ball came swinging in from the Brighton right wing and we could see Rob Green rooted to his line, even though we all judged he ought to have been claiming it. Then we spotted Lewis Dunk at the back post, all on his own. Dunk stuck out a leg to poke the ball towards goal and the next thing we see is the ball bouncing away and the referee holding up a red card! The shot from Dunk had eluded the panic stricken Rob Green but Kalvin Phillips had smartly shovelled the ball away with his right arm and he'd now been sent off for deliberate handball and denying a goal scoring opportunity.

Glen Murray stepped up to take the kick while Kalvin sloped off and in that moment most of us felt the game was probably lost if the spot-kick went in. I didn't have any hope that Murray would miss either as I spotted the big number '17' on his back. Rob Green made a magnificent flying dive to his left... but sadly Murray had clipped the ball straight down the middle; maybe Marco Silvestri might have guessed he was going to do that...

So, a goal and a man down with 70 minutes to go; it didn't look good. Leeds stoically battled away for the rest of the half and actually Brighton didn't really look like scoring again despite dominating the possession statistics. In fact, just seconds before the break Leeds had a glorious chance to equalise. Ronnie Vieira stole the ball out on the left wing and passed it infield to Hadi Sacko. Sacko scuffed his long-range shot horribly to the left but it went straight towards Chris Wood, 12 yards from goal. It was the sort of chance that Murray would have stuck away blindfold with leg-irons but Murray's mint while Chris Wood's finishing is not always as sweet and our man got his legs tangled a la Bambi on ice and the ball went past him untroubled. We were unlikely to get another opportunity like that.

Leeds brought on Matty Grimes for Sacko at half-time and we continued to toil for another 35 minutes. Kentley had mentioned earlier that our only real chance was to keep the score at 1 − 0 and then throw caution to the wind in the final ten to try to nick an equaliser. Well, we'd got to the last ten minutes and it was still 1 − 0. But then we had a mad few minutes or to be more specific, Kyle Bartley had a mad few minutes. First he tried an outrageous back heel, right on the edge of our penalty area that went terribly wrong, giving away the ball to the Seagulls. Eventually the only way Bartley could rescue the situation was to haul his man down and give away a free-kick. Inevitably Bartley was booked but more than that he looked rattled. Before the kick could be taken the ref had to talk to Bartley again and he'd clearly lost his focus on the game. As the free-kick swung in from the left, our right as we watched, Bartley was struggling on the wrong side of Lewis Dunk, even grabbing his hand at one point. Dunk did what any player would do in the opposition box, he theatrically went down and the referee bought it hook, line and sinker. Murray had been substituted by this time so it was Tomer Hemed who strode up and rolled the ball to the right as Green predictably dived the other way. That really was game up of course but the Leeds fans continued to recite the new version of 'Last Christmas' interspersed with a few *"We're Leeds United, we don't give a f*** "*s. We did of course, but it made the hurt go away for a few seconds. Proof that we did actually give a f*** came a few minutes later as a few Brighton fans sat in the hospitality area above us began to goad the Leeds fans below. Several of our fans began hurling their lose change up at the Seagulls and of course a few of the coins that made it up there accurately got returned with interest so we were all ducking and diving to avoid the little missiles. It pretty much went on for the remaining minutes of the game. The one thing that was obvious was that our lads' accuracy was as woeful as Chris Wood's and the fans in most danger of being hit were the Leeds lads stood at the back of our stand!

Many Leeds fans waited behind to salute a gallant effort by the team and then we slowly exited the stadium to do battle with the train queues again, carefully stepping over a couple of broken seats, ripped off by Leeds fans during those unsavoury final minutes. We always have trouble getting away from the Amex; for an almost brand new 30,000 capacity stadium the little Falmer station is woefully inadequate and, as in previous years, thousands of us were corralled outside while hundreds more were held on the platform. There was an added problem this season as we were informed by a bloke stood in the crush with us; there were fewer trains even than usual due to an ongoing train-drivers dispute. The wait went on and on and soon there was a separate queue of Brighton fans lined up along the other side of a barrier. A few insults were exchanged and then inevitably a scuffle broke out and punches were thrown. I was aware of the danger and was desperately trying to spot Lottie to try to get her away from the epicentre of the trouble but I couldn't see either her or Kentley anywhere. Eventually, when it all died down and the Police had done their bit in hauling out the troublemakers, we finally got on a train and I was reunited with Kentley and Lottie. *"When the fists started flying I grabbed Lottie and we pushed our way through the crowd out of the way"* Kentley explained. *"So I nearly got myself beaten to death for no reason at all then"* I quipped, tongue in cheek. God forbid what it'll be like if Brighton get back to the Premier League; it's an accident waiting to happen.

Brighton went to the summit of the Championship that night until Newcastle thumped Birmingham 4 – 0 the following day to regain top spot. There was no doubt this was the pair to catch. Leeds ended the weekend 6th, with Reading, Huddersfield and Derby also above us; we were the only top six side not to win in this, the 20th round of games.

Nigel, Kentley, Lottie and I all met up with Mrs W in the bar of our hotel once we eventually got back from the tortuous train trip and then the long walk back down to the seafront from Brighton Station. The following morning, Mrs W and I paid our £15 each to go up the brand new i360 tower that now occupies the spot that once housed Brighton's second pier. The West Pier was partially destroyed by storms in the winter of 2002/3 and was then finished off by two arson attacks in 2003. The new tower soars 162 metres above Brighton's seafront, cost £46 million to complete and is an entry in the 2016 Guinness Book of World Records as the *"world's most slender tower"*. As we gazed down from the all glass observation platform I contemplated that this was probably the only time this season we'd see Brighton below us...

Brighton 2 **Leeds United 0** (Murray (23 pen), Hemed (82 pen))
28,206 (**Leeds 2,736**)

Audacious!

I missed the parade around the pitch celebrating the club's link up with HMS Audacious; the Shroppy Whites' minibus, driven by the irrepressible Captain Humph, didn't get to Elland Road until after 7pm and by the time I'd had a pint it was as much as I could do to be in my seat for kick-off.

The Reading game felt like another 'marker'; another opportunity to test ourselves against a top side. The argument went like this. Reading were 3rd in the table, OK we'd slipped up against the top two, Newcastle and Brighton, but we didn't play to our potential against either. So, beating the Royals would put the record straight. It was not going to be easy though, no game in the Championship ever is and their outspoken manager Jaap Stam had put together a hard working if not always spectacular side. They were on a run of six wins in seven games, albeit the one they lost was a 5 – 0 thrashing at Fulham who themselves were starting to look likely play-off candidates. Leeds had a few injuries of course and were without the services of Kalvin Phillips who was serving his one match ban for that sending off at the Amex. Hernandez and Lewie Coyle were long term absentees while O'Kane was also out and now Antonsson was side-lined with a back spasm. The good news was that Liam Bridcutt was back in contention and would take his place on the bench after looking fit and ready to go in training this week. There was one surprise on the bench; Mallik Wilks, a 17 year-old striker who'd been scoring goals in the Under-23 and Development sides. BBC reporter Adam Pope had said of Wilks: *"He is a very exciting, raw, audacious talent,"* Pope told the BBC Leeds website. *"I've heard he's got a lot to learn technically but he's a real talent. He's exciting, goes past people and has a bit of bite."*[1]

Green
Ayling Bartley (Capt) Jansson Taylor
Vieira
Sacko Roofe Dallas Doukara
Wood

Subs: Silvestri, Berardi, Cooper, Grimes, Bridcutt, Mowatt, Wilks.

That bench showed again how wafer thin the squad was when carrying a few injuries and suspensions, as did the formation which sort of defined itself once the names were known.

This was not the most exciting game ever to have been played at Elland Road, far from it but the importance of the result to Leeds meant it was tense throughout. A crowd of just over 21,000, with a very meagre contingent travelling up from Reading, watched with nervous expectation.

The first fifteen minutes saw efforts from Roofe and Sacko while at the other end we had another heart in mouth moment as Rob Green messed up with a low cross that was eventually scuffed away to safety. Reading were showing how good they were with the ball, keeping possession for minutes on end but seldom doing anything positive with it. It was during one such spell of Reading possession that Jo and Elisa, aka Maria Sharapova, decided to pull my hair up into a little bun and

---

[1]   http://www.footballinsider247.com/reliable-journalist-tells-leeds-fans-expect-mallik-wilks/

hold it there with one of Jo's hair bands. I casually remarked that if Leeds scored while it was still like that I'd *"wear it for ever"*. When will I ever learn eh? Leeds scored!

A simple throw-in on Leeds' left found Chris Wood near the left corner of the Reading area and he slid the ball across the edge of the box to Hadi Sacko. Sacko tried to get past a defender but then pulled the ball across towards the penalty spot in front of the defensive line. It took everyone by surprise apart from Wood. He was lurking at the back post and was able to scoop the ball into the net from six yards. That was 14 for Wood for the season and his promise to get 20 didn't look quite as optimistic as some thought back in August.

Sadly, that was Wood's last action of the day as shortly afterwards he limped off with a hamstring injury. With Leeds a goal up it was the perfect opportunity to revert to the usual 4 – 2 – 3 – 1 formation with Liam Bridcutt making a welcome return and the Douk going up top. From that point on Leeds were back in counter attack mode and whilst Reading continued to enjoy the lion's share of possession they really didn't ever trouble us. That was partly due to the impressive way Leeds pressed and harried every Reading player on the ball giving them no time other than to play simple short balls to and fro across the pitch. At half-time the Leeds players trooped off to hearty applause from all around the ground.

The second half saw Reading continue to dominate possession but truth be told the rare Leeds counter attacks always looked more dangerous than the ponderous Reading moves which often saw them passing the ball along their back line to and fro just as Leeds often did last season. Reading recorded 77% of the possession but turned that into just 14 attempts at goal of which only two troubled Green. Leeds, with their 23% of the ball, conjured up 12 attempts and four hit the target. Mowatt replaced Roofe on 72 minutes and then Grimes replaced Dallas ten minutes later. There was always the fear that Reading would get lucky or come up with a moment of magic and hence the game held our attention throughout but most of us were thankful we didn't have to watch Reading every week if this was their usual MO. The final ten minutes did see the Royals get forward quicker and force a few corners and the

Leeds crowd got louder and louder as we urged our defence to stay focussed. The Pontus songs were prominent as it was often his head or body that came between Reading and glory. As the board went up to signify five minutes of added time, Matt Grimes brought the ball down cleverly about forty yards from the Reading goal and poked it out to Charlie Taylor on the left wing. Charlie gave it back to Grimes who himself had now ventured out wide. He was in a bit of a cul-de-sac, turning one way and then the other to try to run down the clock and then he managed to slip the ball back to Taylor, now being marshalled by two defenders near the touchline. Somehow he shimmied between the two and made a dart into the box where he had one more defender between him and goal. He shaped to get the ball onto his left boot but then felt the touch of a Reading player on his back and down he went. It looked soft to me but to everyone's joy and relief referee Geoff Eltringham was pointing at the spot. Taylor looked interested in taking the kick himself but eventually Souley picked up the ball and hammered it past Al Habsi in the Reading goal. No chance of Reading stealing an equaliser now and the celebrations could begin. There was time for one final Reading attack and that was repelled by a Jansson header and then a full body block by the big Swede to huge cheers from the South Stand and then the whistle went. Leeds had passed another examination with flying colours and the memory of Brighton was immediately a little fainter. As I nipped into the gents for a pee before going back to the mini-bus I remembered I still had my hair tied up in a bun; I surreptitiously removed it and no, I ain't keeping it for ever!

With Brighton, Newcastle, Huddersfield and Derby all winning their games, Leeds remained 5th in the table but were now just two points adrift of third placed Reading. A win against Brentford on Saturday and, if other results went our way, we could be third over Christmas!

Leeds United 2 Reading 0 (**Wood (19), Doukara (90+1 pen)**)
21,242 (Reading 280)

"Santa is a Leeds fan!"

I f anyone was still in any doubt as to how fragile a job in football management can be, Birmingham City's owners put them straight this week. The morning after the Blues managed a creditable 2 – 1 win over Ipswich to stay 7th in the Championship, Gary Rowett was sacked. In a little over two years Rowett had transformed Birmingham from a relegation haunted rabble to a side pushing for promotion, yet still the axe fell. The Blues' Chinese owners, Trillion Trophy Asia Limited, issued a statement saying: *"I would ask that our supporters trust our judgement and look forward to and embrace the future as we begin to implement the exciting vision of Trillion Trophy Asia Limited."*[1] It could be of course that the owners did have great vision and could see that Rowett couldn't deliver and that their new man, Gianfranco Zola, who was appointed within hours, could. A similar

---

[1] *http://www.bbc.co.uk/sport/football/38316110*

situation occurred a few years ago when Southampton got to the Premier League and then ditched Nigel Adkins in favour of the then relatively unknown Mauricio Pochettino. The Argentinian of course then pushed Saints on even further before leaving for Spurs. Time would tell if Zola could do the same for the Blues... but I doubted it.

At Leeds we still waited for an announcement to the effect that Cellino had sold out to Radrizzani; the Time To Go Massimo (TTGM) group was openly celebrating it as a done deal on Twitter but official notification was nowhere to be seen. Cellino was still keeping very quiet on all subjects but his name was still in the papers. This time it was a report in The Independent saying that eight months on he'd still not settled the £70,000 of legal fees due in respect of the Lucy Ward case.[1] He doesn't like paying his bills does he? The report went on to say that Ward was now urging the FA to look at the role Cellino played in the affair as well as that of Adam Pearson and former Club Secretary, Stuart Hayton. I wonder if those two now regretted ever hearing the name Massimo Cellino.

The final game before Christmas was the clash with the Bees of Brentford at Elland Road and I was on the Shropshire Whites' bus again. It was the same brand new bus we had for the Liverpool game and it still had the tinsel and little Santas in the windows. I daren't look in the on-board loo but a couple of ladies on board used it and there were no shrieks of horror so I guess they'd been cleaned up. Everyone was in festive spirits and all the classic Christmas tracks were blaring out from a mobile phone while Woggy passed round his Chocolate Bullets for a game of Russian roulette; some of the chocolates were milk chocolate but most were red-hot chilli flavoured ones that took the skin off the roof of your mouth! He'd brought some chilli flavoured vodka too if the chocolate didn't get you!

---

[1]   http://www.independent.co.uk/sport/football/news-and-comment/leeds-united-massimo-cellino-lucy-ward-unfair-dismissal-sacked-tribunal-a7477746.html

As it was the last game before Christmas, I was wearing my lucky antlers and it was apparently these that attracted the attention of the lovely Katherine Hannah from BBC Radio Leeds. I was sat with Derek and the County Durham lads in the Pavilion when Katherine and Adam Pope joined us. *"I simply cannot resist a bloke wearing antlers!"* she exclaimed. They wanted a bit of an interview about the prospects for the game and began with a question about the likely impact of not having Chris Wood today. Wood was rested having limped out of the Reading game with a tight hamstring. Neither Derek nor I were huge fans of Chris Wood although we both acknowledged he'd at least been in the right place at the right time to bang in 14 goals already this season. When I eventually got to listen to the broadcast a few days later it was clear that we were now in the minority as loads of fans called into the programme wanting to know who the *"numpties on the radio complaining about Chris Wood"* were! Look, for the avoidance of doubt, I accept that Wood had done well to score 14 goals and that those goals had been invaluable and I acknowledge that he'd improved greatly from a poor start to the season. But, he is, in my opinion, a limited player. He cannot head a football to save his life and had missed far too many relatively easy chances in front of goal. His pace is not great and nor is his ability to hold the ball up. In an article I wrote at the start of the season, I was asked which player I thought would be most influential this season and I had no hesitation in saying Chris Wood. I always felt he had the chance to get 20 goals or more this season and he was more than on track to do that. But, I still felt a better striker than Chris would possibly have scored a few more and would probably have converted a few of the many chances he'd missed. Neither do I buy the argument that many use who would tell you *"without Wood's 14 goals we'd be struggling to avoid relegation!"* Are they really saying that if Wood hadn't been there his replacement wouldn't have scored as many and overall we'd have scored 14 fewer? Nah, I'm not having that.

Anyway, it was good to have a chat with the Radio Leeds folk and we tried to get them to talk about a few burning issues of the day. Their fellow pundit, the previously popular Noel Whelan had blotted his copybook by posting a homophobic tweet ahead of the game in Brighton and was now suspended from the commentary team. *"We can't discuss it obviously"*, Katherine told us, but she stressed that he'd now apologised and hoped he'd get a reprieve. We pressed Adam Pope on the takeover rumours but again drew a blank other than to get Popey to confirm his belief that a deal must be in the offing. When the Radio team left us we were then joined at the table by John McClelland, the former Leeds centre-back who played under Howard Wilkinson. He's always up for a chat with the fans and he signed a couple of books for Tony. It all served to fill the few hours before kick-off as did a chat we had with the Pavilion manager as we once again complained that his bar staff were not all aware of the correct pricing of the beer in there. That old issue with the vouchers was still ongoing; sometimes they were accepted as worth £3.90 and sometimes only three quid. He said he'd get them together again to go over it once more but, as we'd guessed, he explained that every week there were many new agency staff who would probably only do one week and then disappear again.

Green
Ayling Bartley (Capt) Jansson Taylor
Vieira Phillips
Sacko Dallas Roofe
Wood

Subs: Silvestri, Berardi, Cooper, Mowatt, Grimes, Bridcutt, Antonsson.

It was perhaps a surprise that Liam Bridcutt didn't start since he'd done so well on Tuesday but it did fall in line with Garry Monk's very conservative policy of bringing players back from injury slowly. Phillips was back after suspension but Hernandez, O'Kane and Coyle were still out and Wood had that tight hamstring. Most of us thought this side ought to have enough to beat 14th placed Brentford.

I took my place in row GG of the Kop as normal and to my right there was a big group of Santas, all dressed in red. There must have been 15 of them altogether and as the teams came out and the cameras panned across the North Stand we had no trouble spotting ourselves for once on the big screen, right next to this sea of red. It was a stag party for a lad from Leeds who was in the middle dressed as a turkey. *"Santa is a Leeds fan"* belted out from our new friends while the rest of us were still mulling over whether even Santa should wear red in the Kop…

The first half passed quickly, not because there was loads of action on the pitch but because we spent most of the time talking. The match was another poor spectacle, with both sides cancelling each other out. The dangerous Scott Hogan had the ball in the net in front of the Kop just before half-time but thankfully that was ruled out correctly for offside. Apart from that the only entertainment in our section of the Kop was the regular ringing of the bells on my antlers every time I shook my head at a poor Leeds pass or a mishit shot. In fact the half-time penalty competition was more exciting than the game as a bloke dressed as a traffic cone tried, with varying degrees of success, to beat Lucas Kop Cat from 12 yards.

The second half was a slow burner too. In the 58th minute Charlie Taylor went off with what was assumed to be the after effect of a clattering tackle he got in the first half; Gaetano Berardi replaced him and that limited even more our aspirations down that left wing. But ever so slowly, Leeds started to fashion some decent chances and if any team looked likely to score it was us. A left wing corner from Stuart Dallas found Luke Ayling at the back post and he had time to chest the ball down but then snatched at the shot trying to blast it for all he was worth; it soared into the upper echelons of the Kop. Next it was Dallas again playing provider as he curled a perfect ball into the path of Souleymane Doukara, in the clear behind the Bees' defence. I would have put our house on the Douk slotting the ball inside the far post as he strode purposefully into the area but I'd have had some explaining to do to Mrs W and the kids; the shot slid agonizingly wide. Seconds later and Hadi Sacko chased a long ball to the byline and somehow kept it from going dead before finding Ayling in space in the box again. This time Ayling tried to curl the ball with the outside of his right boot but it just wouldn't curl enough and it flew past the left-hand post. These were good chances, chances that really ought to have been at least testing the keeper but all went begging. We sensed it was coming though and if the Leeds players ever slowed to draw breath we'd immediately urge them on again. *"Attack, attack, attack-attack-attack!"* we chanted, roaring with approval every time we won the ball. By this time Liam Bridcutt had replaced Kalvin Phillips and that added some impetus with Bridcutt much more willing to stride out of defence with the ball. Then Monk threw the dice one more time and sent on Marcus Antonsson for the now tiring Doukara. That was it now; we'd played all our cards.

Hadi Sacko had the beating of his full back every time and once again he was through but as so often his final ball wasn't quite right and it was easily cut out for a corner. He trotted over to take it with Stuart Dallas. There were several *"Oh for f***'s sake, get the f****** thing in the middle"* comments around me as Dallas touched the ball short to Sacko. But this time Sacko passed it back to Dallas again who whipped it across the area first-time with his left foot. Pontus Jansson was at the near post but just behind him Kyle Bartley raced in and jumped to meet the ball perfectly to glance a header past Daniel Bentley. Bentley was inches behind our Captain Cool with hands upraised ready to catch a ball that never quite got to him. Oh my goodness me did Elland Road erupt? The Santas all went bananas and I thought the Turkey was getting stuffed right there and then the way he was engulfed by his mates. This was a feeling we were not yet used to although we'd had a few late goals to confirm wins lately. Kentley turned to me and shouted: *"This is starting to feel like a promotion season…"*

It certainly did. We were winning our home games, scoring late goals to turn draws into wins; we were defending well and racking up clean sheets. We'd been strangely off the pace and nervous down at Brighton but apart from that we'd looked solid if not spectacular for several weeks. We had momentum and yes, for those of us that could remember back far enough, it felt like a promotion season should feel. And we still had the maestro, Pablo Hernandez to come back and we'd won this one without Chris Wood and Eunan O'Kane as well. We were rolling with the punches and we were usually hitting back harder.

Leeds saw out the final few minutes and then the inevitable roar of approval greeted the final whistle. Over the course of the whole game Leeds deserved the three points. We had much the better chances and, but for the want of a bit of luck and some more accurate finishing, we might have had another couple. Brentford played their part though and just shaded the attempts at goal statistics. At times our passing had been wayward and that finishing needs some work but it was another steady performance and above all else a vital three points to maintain our belief that this might finally be the season we have dreamed of since winning promotion back to the Championship in 2010. Oh yes, the stars were aligning.

The Championship was at last beginning to take shape and this round of games, the 22nd, saw wins for every one of the sides now in the top six. Leeds remained 5th with 38 points from their 22 games. Back at home, I looked at the table from this time last season and saw that in 5th place last year, also with 38 points from 22 games was Burnley who would go on to gather an amazing 55 points from their remaining 24 fixtures to win the Championship by a clear 4 points... I was dreaming already. Oh, and it did look like Santa was a Leeds fan after all!

Leeds United 1 Brentford 0 **(Bartley (89))**
25,134 (Brentford 384)

Big Splash at Deepdale

This really did prove to be the Last Christmas for George Michael; it was announced on Christmas Day that he'd passed away at the age of just 53 as the Grim Reaper continued to wreak havoc amongst the ranks of pop and rock stars just as he'd done throughout 2016. Rick Parfitt of Status Quo had been taken just hours earlier and it did seem that someone up there was planning the mother of all concerts. Never mind Live Aid; they were now planning Rock 'Til You Drop!...

Leeds fans were back on the treadmill on Boxing Day, as over 5,000 of us headed for Deepdale, home of Simon Grayson's Preston North End. I was on the Shropshire Whites' mini-bus, and we were a subdued band of merry-makers as we tried to shake off the excesses of too many Christmas beers. First stop was the Leyland Lion, a Wetherspoon pub in Leyland, about six miles south of Preston. We had a few pints there and then wandered up the road to the Market Ale House, a peculiar little bar that was more like a shop than a pub. They had an array of festive real ales on, including Skinners' 'Christmas Fairy' and Mordue's 'Howay in a Manger', the latter unsurprisingly hailing from North Shields. I'd steadily worked my way through four pints by the time the cue was given to make our way back to the mini-bus that was parked in a side street opposite Wetherspoon's.

The capacity of some of the other lads never ceases to amaze me and so it was no real surprise to see Gaz and another bloke stepping up into the mini-bus carrying two-pint carry-out cartons from the Ale House. It was a bit more of a surprise though to see several lads crossing the road coming towards us carrying glass pint pots brim full of the ale they'd just bought in Wetherspoon's! As calm as you like they clambered aboard, took their seats and then continued to sup their pints as Ash put the bus into gear and set off for Deepdale! They'll be few pint pots short when they come to do the washing up.

It was a gorgeous clear day although bitterly cold as the bus dropped us off outside the ground, right next to the famous "Splash" statue of Tom Finney. There was still half an hour to go before the 3pm kick-off but, weary from the exertions of too many Christmas get-togethers, I went straight to my seat up in the gods on row 35 of the Bill Shankly Kop. I studied the team sheet on my mobile.

Green
Ayling Bartley Jansson Berardi
Phillips Bridcutt (Capt)
Sacko Roofe Dallas
Doukara

Subs: Silvestri, Denton, Cooper, Vieira, Hernandez, Antonsson, Wood.

Once again it looked as though Monk was being ultra-careful in making sure he didn't bring players back from injury too quickly. Hence both Wood and Hernandez were not going to be thrown straight back in but might get a few minutes late in the game if all went to plan. Charlie Taylor was not being risked at all with his Achilles injury and Eunan O'Kane was also still on the side-lines. So, without Taylor, Hernandez, O'Kane and Chris Wood, all of whom I guessed would have started if fully fit and ready, I'd decided in my own mind that a draw would be a decent result against a Preston side that came into this game on the back of a couple of good results; a 1 – 1 draw at Forest and a 2 – 1 win at Bristol City. What I didn't factor in though was that the Preston defence was still very much in the festive spirit and would spend the afternoon offering us more space than Santa now had in his empty sack.

These were strange days for a Leeds fan; so used are we to seeing the rub of the green go against us and our own defence falling over themselves offering gifts to the opposition that despite the success we'd seen this season many of us were still looking over our shoulders expecting the footballing equivalent of the Grim Reaper to be there swinging his scythe. And what has happened to that number '17'? It was now more often than not a good number for us! In the 17th minute at Deepdale, Leeds went ahead.

A free-kick was lofted towards the back post and Pontus Jansson rose above everyone else to nod the ball towards the corner of the Preston goal. It may well have lobbed into the net anyway but Kemar Roofe was steaming in to make absolutely sure and he hammered the ball home with his head from about an inch. What a start that was! There were joyous scenes in the Bill Shankly Kop and the unmistakeable stench of a flare came from somewhere over to our left. For his part in the goal Pontus was serenaded once again with a rendition of his own Last Christmas song which also seemed somehow appropriate as our farewell salute to George Michael. I could see a bloke down at the front waving his own 'brick' hat too – a sort of white bowler with a red plastic brick stuck on top in honour of Pontus's fabled ability to *"head the fu**** back"* if you threw one at him. The man's cult status at Leeds (Pontus that is not the bloke in the crowd) was growing match by match with his fearsome defending but he was also becoming more and more of a threat in the opposition goalmouth these days; he has the presence and strength of one of Marvel's Avengers!

Preston were clearly stunned by the goal and it had already silenced their own sizeable crowd but just six minutes later they were even more stunned as Leeds took a two-goal lead. Hadi Sacko had been much maligned by some fans this season for frequently flattering to deceive. He'd often set off on a promising run only to fluff his final ball or put in a wayward shot. Now he'd claimed the ball just inside the Preston half and was scurrying along with it on one of his typical forays towards the opposition goal. This time though he played a delightful one-two with Kemar Roofe who back-heeled it straight into his path as he reached the edge of the penalty area and then he smashed the ball into the far corner of the net. It was a quality, quality goal but I have to say it all felt a bit surreal; 2 – 0 up away from home on a Boxing Day. A little bit of my mind was wondering when we'd all wake up and realise this was just dream!

Perhaps it was a good thing Preston then got a goal back, just to keep our feet on the ground. Four minutes after Sacko blasted us into a two goal lead, Marnick Vermijl latched onto a downward header in our box to steer the ball wide of Rob Green. Garry Monk would not be pleased with our defending for that one and for a while I did wonder if this was going to be one of those weird high-scoring games that you see now and again at this time of year; maybe a repeat of that infamous 6 – 4 home defeat we suffered at the hands of Preston at Elland Road in 2010. I was still thinking that a few minutes later as, unbelievably, Leeds restored the two goal lead. Once again the Preston defence gave a very good impression of pillars of stone as Souley Doukara trotted down the left wing. He got into the Preston penalty area, twisted right and left a few times and then hit a shot with his left foot from the tightest of angles. From 100 yards away we saw all that but weren't quite sure what happened next except that we could then see Doukara wheeling away towards the touchline where the Leeds bench was celebrating wildly. Replays would show that the Douk's shot beat Chris Maxwell at his near post and despite a defender's best efforts the ball squirmed over the line. 3 – 1 to Leeds and only half an hour gone.

That was pretty much it for the first half; Leeds had taken advantage of some very slack Preston defending without ever looking that much in control of the game. It did feel very much like that game at Elland Road when we went in with a 4 – 2 half-time lead but as fans we were still nervous we'd mess it up, which on that occasion we did of course. But this is a different Leeds United to that one and nowadays Simon Grayson was with the opposition. Grayson was sure to get his side a bit more organised for the second half and he still had Jermaine Beckford and Eoin Doyle to call on if needed.

Sure enough, Preston looked stronger after the break and there were times when Leeds didn't manage the game very well; our passing was wayward and we gave the ball away too cheaply and too often for my liking. Rob Green came to the rescue with a tremendous save down to his left as Preston took advantage of our carelessness. Perhaps in an effort to get more quality into the Leeds passing or perhaps just to give Hernandez some game time, the little Spaniard came on in the 54th minute, replacing Sacko. Pablo was clearly rusty as *his* passing wasn't very good to begin with but his movement was excellent and suddenly Preston were on the back foot again. Grayson tried to respond by sending on former Leeds man Jermaine Beckford, to a rousing rendition of the *"January 3rd remember the day..."* song and then, pointing at Beckford, we sang: *"You're Leeds and you know you are"*. I half expected Beckford to acknowledge our support with a little wave as he's done in the past but this time he kept his head down. Unfortunately for Jermaine and Preston though, he didn't keep his feet down.

Seconds after coming on, a long ball was pumped down the Preston left wing, aimed just past the dug-outs on that left-hand touchline. Beckford was there ready to challenge for the ball with Ayling but steaming in behind them both was Kyle Bartley who got his head to the ball first but in the process cleared the other two out. Once again I didn't see what happened next but what was clear was that referee Jeremy Simpson was holding up a red card to a white-shirted Preston player and soon the word spread around the stand that it was Beckford who was off! He hadn't even touched the ball yet and this was his first appearance since being sent off after a scuffle with his fellow Preston player, Eoin Doyle, a few games earlier. It was another example of how the luck, rub of the green, fate, whatever you want to call it, was running in our favour these days. Those stars seemed to be aligning.

With Leeds leading 3 – 1, Preston down to ten and only 20 minutes to go, there wasn't much fear in our hearts now. Leeds predictably dominated the possession in the latter stages and with Chris Wood now on to bolster the attack we never looked likely to throw this away. Two minutes from time, a crisp Leeds move ended with Wood gathering the ball and sliding it into the path of Pablo Hernandez who, with his experience, couldn't miss. He coolly knocked the ball low past Maxwell to complete a 4 – 1 rout of the Lilywhites on their own patch.

My caution had proved unfounded. I was the only one of the six members of the YEP jury not to predict a Leeds win; I went for a 1- 1 draw. At the end of the game it was all smiles for the players and the fans as each saluted the other in front of the Bill Shankly Stand. That chap with the Pontus hat with the brick threw it to Pontus and there was a huge roar as the big Swede put it on his head for a few seconds. The man is already a legend in his own lifetime and it is to be hoped that, like Vinnie Jones all those years ago, success for the team will help cement that status for ever.

Preston North End 1 **Leeds United 4 (Roofe (17), Sacko (23),** Vermijl (27), **Doukara (31), Hernandez (88))**
21,255 (**Leeds 5,689**)

Pos		Played	GD	Points
1	Brighton H A	23	24	51
2	Newcastle United	23	27	49
3	Reading	23	3	43
4	Huddersfield T	23	1	42
5	Leeds United	23	7	41
6	Sheffield W	23	4	40
7	Derby County	23	9	39
8	Fulham	23	12	36
9	Barnsley	23	5	34
10	Aston Villa	23	3	34
11	Birmingham City	23	-3	34
12	Norwich City	23	1	33
13	Preston N E	23	0	32
14	Brentford	23	-1	29
15	Wolverhampton W	23	-1	28
16	Ipswich T	23	-4	28
17	Bristol City	23	0	27
18	Nottm Forest	23	-5	26
19	Cardiff City	23	-12	24
20	Queens Park Rangers	23	-14	23
21	Burton Albion	23	-8	22
22	Blackburn Rovers	23	-12	20
23	Wigan Athletic	23	-10	18
24	Rotherham United	23	-26	13

The Championship table at the halfway point

Coops hands Villa late reprieve

Sky TV had picked out the Villa - Leeds game as their next live showing and so our game at Villa Park was moved forward from New Year's Eve to the Thursday night, 29th December. It was the sixth Leeds game out of nine to be shown live, going back to the Newcastle home defeat.

The Shropshire Whites decided to meet up in Wolverhampton for this game, at the Sunbeam, a Hungry Horse pub just up the road from Wolverhampton Station, in Victoria Square. I got the train from Stafford and arrived in The Sunbeam around 3pm, just in time for a pint of Abbot and an All Day Brunch. The mini-bus then took us to the Bentley Moor Social Club in Walsall where several other Leeds branches had arranged to meet. The club had done us proud by laying on plenty of food and the beer was cheap so we filled our boots while watching some of the second round matches in the World Darts Championship on TV. A big contingent from the Keighley branch filled most of the backroom with their huge flag tied on one wall while we camped in the bar with our flag hung between the dart boards on another. I chatted at one point with a couple of lads from the North Wales Branch, long suffering Caernarfon Town fans. We swapped non-league tales with me telling them about the financial woes of Worcester City and them explaining to me how Caernarfon had failed to win promotion to the Welsh Premier league due to them being struck off for failing to lodge accounts at Companies House. The Welsh FA said therefore that Caernarfon didn't exist and therefore couldn't be promoted![1]

It was gone 6:30pm when we all set off towards Birmingham – despite having seen tweets from the West Midlands Police asking supporters' coaches to be in the coach park no later than 6:15pm. Sure enough, when we arrived outside Villa Park in the dark the road to the coach park was closed off. Eventually most of the lads jumped ship leaving Humph and Gaz to sort out the parking.

I eventually tracked down Kentley who texted to say he was in the upper tier of the Doug Ellis Stand; Nigel and I were in the lower. I bumped into Mike and Paula on the long climb up to Row S and said hello to them, my pretext for catching my breath before going on up to my seat. Once there I took in the magnificent sight of Villa Park.

Villa Park was one of the first grounds I ever visited; when I was 14 I was considered old enough by Mum and Dad to make the trip up to Birmingham on my own. I'd get the train from home in Great Malvern to Worcester Foregate Street Station, walk down to the old bus station and then get on the Football Special that Midland Red used to run to places like Villa, St. Andrews, The Molineux and The Hawthorns. Back in those days Villa had fallen from grace and my first visit was for a Division III game against Swansea on April 3rd 1971 (Villa won 3-0); they were still getting crowds in excess of 30,000 though even then as they challenged for promotion back to

---

[1] *http://videocelts.com/2016/04/blogs/latest-news/welsh-fa-lay-down-the-law-and-refuse-promotion-over-licence-issue/*

Division II; they would achieve that the following season. I remember standing on the Holte End terracing marvelling at the sheer scale of the place and today, looking around the stadium, it was just as impressive and still has a capacity of over 42,000. It's been much redeveloped since I first went there of course and the four individual stands now soar up towards the sky. We were in the right hand end of the Doug Ellis Stand as we looked towards the pitch with the North Stand to our right and the massive Holte End away to our left. It was an impressive sight. Up on the big screens (there was one immediately to our right and another in the opposite corner, between the Holte End and the Trinity Road Stand) I studied the team listings.

Green
Ayling Jansson Cooper Berardi
Phillips Bridcutt (Capt)
Sacko Roofe Dallas
Doukara

Subs: Silvestri, Denton, Hernandez, Wood, Vieira, Mowatt, Antonsson.

Liam Cooper was drafted in with Kyle Bartley missing out due to a knock on the knee he'd suffered at Preston. Garry Monk told Sky that the game had come 24 hours too soon for Bartley to recover. Other than that it was the same side that started at Deepdale. Talking of Deepdale, the assistant referee on the touchline just down in front of us was one Sian Massey-Ellis, Sian Massey as she was up at Preston on that day when Billy Paynter broke his Leeds duck. She still wore her hair in the same pony tail she did that night making her look not too dissimilar to our own Luke Ayling.

There were definitely some nerves on show as the game kicked-off and judging by the smell around us it had got to the bloke in front of me big time. Nerves were affecting the players too and within the first minute we saw a shocking blind pass from Kalvin Phillips, right into the path of Jonathan Kodjia. Thankfully Pontus Jansson was alert enough to come sliding across and his block sent the ball wide. Minutes later and Phillips again put his defence in trouble as Kodjia snaffled the ball off him and put in a fierce shot that Rob Green pushed away one handed. It was all Villa in the opening ten minutes and the Leeds fans sensed the nerves the players were showing and tried to lift them with some rousing *"We are Leeds"* chants while the inventive chant of *"Villa, Villa, Villa"* seemingly sung by 30,000 Ozzy Osbournes came from the other three sides of the old stadium.

Leeds were pretty much pinned in their own half for the first fifteen minutes and some sloppy passing didn't help our cause at all; a third poor one from Phillips caused a few angry shouts from the Leeds section; Phillips is a bit of a Marmite player amongst Leeds fans. Around the twenty minute mark, Jansson frightened us all to death as he slumped to the ground with an injury... either that or he was taking the sting out of the Villa momentum by slowing the game right down. It coincided with a natural pause in hostilities in the stands too as both sets of supporters joined in a minute's applause for all those Villa fans who'd passed away in 2016. It was an idea suggested by Villa owner Tony Xia and began on 20 minutes and 16 seconds. During the tribute the Villa fans also sang the Villa Park classic *"Holte Enders in the Sky"*. Whether these things affected the Villa or not we'll never know but from that point on the Leeds players had much more of a say in the action. Even so, it took Leeds 30 minutes to give Hadi Sacko his first run in behind the Villa defence and that one came to nothing. His second came ten minutes before half-time and led to the first Leeds corner and a third came a few minutes later as slowly but surely we grew into the game. The first real shot in anger from Leeds came in the dying moments of the first half as Stuart Dallas volleyed over from out wide left. The best that could be said of Leeds was that defensively we were mostly solid and we stifled such ambition as the Villa could muster.

The second half started much more positively for Leeds with Dallas forcing his way into the Villa box in the first few seconds. He went down under pressure to half-hearted shouts for a penalty from the Leeds fans. It was the start of a prolonged period of Leeds possession and the Leeds fans sensed the tide might have turned. Our momentum was halted temporarily by an injury to Jack Grealish, an injury caused initially by a typically brutal Pontus Jansson challenge in the first half. Grealish was not the first opposition player to leave the pitch after a coming together with Pontus and I doubted he'd be the last. Ross McCormack jogged on to replace Grealish to a jaunty chant of *"Greedy bastard, da-da da-da"* from the Leeds contingent. It didn't seem to worry Ross who was soon firing in a dangerous cross-come shot that was parried away by Rob Green. But Leeds were now getting Sacko more into the game and in the 52nd minute he danced his way into the area below us winning a corner. Dallas walked across to take it to a rousing *"We are Leeds"*. The Irishman sent the ball curving out towards the penalty spot where Pontus Jansson met it firmly sending it down to Mark Bunn's left hand side. He seemed to have it covered but the presence of the boots of Kemar Roofe by his nose were enough to cause the ball to slip off his gloves and over the line. Jansson and the others all rushed to celebrate right in front of us but for once everyone stayed on the pitch and no one stripped a shirt off, sensibly avoiding the usual booking. It was a real smash and grab from Leeds and it seemed to stun Villa and their fans while Leeds just seemed to slip into top gear for the next twenty minutes or so. All that was missing was a second goal.

Within seconds of the Pontus goal, Kemar Roofe won another corner and once again Dallas swung the ball in. It was weakly nodded away by a Villa head straight to Pontus again, this time 15 yards out and unmarked. He had time to kill the ball first and then volleyed it with his right boot without it touching the turf but it had too much on it and smacked against the top of the bar and over into the Villa fans behind the goal. The corner was Dallas's last touch as he was replaced by Pablo Hernandez.

Still Leeds poured forward and yet another corner was the outcome of the latest run from Roofe. Then Sacko won another but Villa cleared it away. Villa were now playing on the counter attack and Liam Bridcutt had to take one for the team as he took out Bacuna over on the far touchline. The pace of the game had gone up several notches and it was mainly due to Leeds' play. On the TV replay when I watched the game back a few days later the Sky commentator described our play as "champagne football" as Pablo Hernandez linked with Sacko with a couple of delicious back-heeled flicks. Kalvin Phillips was even in the Villa box having a shot. It was as good a performance as I'd seen from Leeds in years. Bridcutt was controlling the area in front of the defence while Pablo was marshalling the area behind Roofe and Doukara. It was brilliant to watch. Another Villa breakaway saw Rob Green fly out to fist away another cross-shot but Leeds were dominating the possession. It was so far removed from what we'd grown accustomed to in recent years that it was actually quite emotional to watch.

On 68 minutes, Chris Wood made an appearance, replacing Kemar Roofe. Still Leeds pressed and the song now coming from all around me was, *"Leeds are going up"*. Playing like this we surely could. The Leeds fans had found their humour again too; as Luke Ayling stood alongside the pony-tailed Sian Massey-Ellis a little chant of *"There's only two Luke Ayling's"* floated up from the front of our stand. We were now into the last 15 minutes.

Hernandez put Sacko in again with a delightful ball in behind the Villa back line but Mr Bunn was off his line in a flash to spread himself and then hack the ball away. Meanwhile Villa made their final two changes bringing on Albert Adomah and Rudy Gestede and finally Villa began to make some headway as maybe Leeds began to tire. Adomah in particular was firing crosses in from both wings but Jansson was heading most of them away like the bricks in his song. We were now into the final ten minutes and Leeds made their last change bringing on the young legs of Ronnie Vieira for the older ones of Liam Bridcutt.

We had wondered if the absence of Kyle Bartley would affect us in this game; there was the inevitable thought, certainly in my mind anyway, that Coops was more 2015 Leeds than 2016 Leeds, part of a defence last season that underperformed on so many levels. Opinion on him is divided but there is no doubt that the Bartley-Jansson combo is a class above anything else we've seen at Leeds for many years. As the clock ticked into the 83rd minute, Coops gave away a needless looking free-kick on the Villa right wing. Adomah touched it to Bacuna who crossed. The ball was headed away by Leeds but Villa worked it back across the pitch to pretty much where the free-kick was taken from in the first place; Alan Hutton crossed it in again. This time Kalvin Phillips back-headed it away as far as Ross McCormack and he launched it back into the middle again over his own head. Several players went up to challenge for the ball and suddenly all the Villa players were running round with their hands in the air appealing for a penalty. The referee, Roger East, initially pointed our way giving a free-kick to Leeds but then, with four or five Villa players pushing and shoving him, he eventually went over to speak with the liner, Andy Garratt, who we could clearly see had been furiously waving his flag for quite some time. I knew damn well what was coming. This was an old Leeds feeling; that, oh so close but so far feeling; I don't think I've ever seen a situation like this played out with the ultimate decision going our way. Sure enough, after the briefest of chats with his liner, East points west, towards the Leeds penalty spot. Liam Cooper had gone up for the challenge with his hand in the air trying to palm the ball away and he'd obviously touched it. Andy Garratt's eyesight must be super-human but it was a basic error by Cooper, the sort of error that plagued us last season when Coops was a regular along with the likes of Bamba and Bellusci. I was convinced Kyle Bartley would have kept his hands down and it did nothing to dissuade me from my belief that Coops is not the sharpest tool in the box. Cooper was booked and old Kodjia put the spot-kick away to level the game up. For what seemed like the umpteenth time this season, Rob Green dived the wrong way.

Even after the penalty Leeds didn't let up trying to win the game and we probably should have done so. A long ball over the top saw Sacko dispossess Jordan Amavi but cutting inside he took just a split second too long to get a shot away by which time Amavi had got a boot in the way. The ball looped up and over the keeper but once again found crossbar not net and Villa got the ball away for a corner.

Both sides went for it in the final minutes like two ageing heavy weights in the final round of a world title fight; Cooper v Ali maybe. Our Cooper was having his own battle with Kodjia and missed another headed clearance allowing the

Villa man to fire in a shot that Rob Green did well to get in the way of. Then Kalvin Phillips sent Sacko away behind the Villa defence yet again. Chris Wood was screaming for the ball to be played across as he was also now in the clear but yet again Sacko couldn't find the killer ball and a defender got it away for yet another Leeds corner as the game moved into added time. Wood, not for the first time this season, gave Sacko some aggressive verbal advice. From the corner, Luke Ayling smashed in a shot that was blocked and cleared. Back up the other end and that man Kodjia was clearly no old codger as he broke free and fired wide of Green's left hand post.

And that was pretty much it. At the final whistle both sides were probably happy with the point, although it took a few minutes for most of us to come to that conclusion having bossed much of the second half and having played such flowing, attacking football. There was a definite sense of pride amongst the Leeds fans as we saluted our heroes; most of us waited while Pontus got his man of the Match award in the centre circle and then we applauded him as he walked over to us to throw his shirt into the crowd. It was as subdued as I'd ever seen him and I guessed he was just plain knackered.

The point took us up to 4th at least until the rest of the games were played on the Friday and Saturday. The only other game played this evening was a 2 – 1 home defeat for Rotherham against Burton. The Millers were still well adrift at the bottom of the table and they were our next opponents, at Elland Road on Monday 2nd January.

In the other games played this week, most finished level. Newcastle beat Forest 3 – 1 to go further ahead at the top of the table while second placed Brighton's home game against Cardiff was postponed due to thick fog across the South of England. The fog also caused the Reading game with Fulham to be abandoned at half-time. Leeds would go into the New Year 5th with 42 points; everything was still possible.

Aston Villa 1 **Leeds United 1 (Jansson (54)**, Kodjia (86 pen))
37,078 (**Leeds 2,407**)

Leeds grind down Millers

Interest in Leeds was starting to go stratospheric. Twitter was awash with pleas from fans trying to get hold of tickets by fair means or foul. It reminded me very much of the 1989/90 season when we last got promoted to the top division from the old Division II. At that time I was working in Bridgnorth in Shropshire but we had an office in St Helens from where our delivery driver would occasionally be despatched on an urgent mission to Elland Road... to pick up match tickets! These days I'm lucky, I have both home and away season tickets but for many fans it was getting nigh on impossible to see their heroes; even the Rotherham home game on the afternoon of January 2nd was said to be sold out.

I was in the capable hands of Mr Humph again today; he was at the wheel of the trusty old Shroppy Whites' mini-bus. I'd even been promoted to the front seat, squashed in alongside Woggy and Humph on the bench seat as even the mini-bus was full to its 17-man capacity. It was a frosty old morning as we tip-toed along the Cheshire country roads making for the

M6. The first toilet stop, taken in the car park of the Stretton Fox pub just off the M6, was an unusually quick one. Anyone hanging their todger out for too long in this weather was risking severe frost bite. There was that and also the fact that a bank of about half a dozen CCTV cameras was trained on the hedge where our lads were relieving themselves!

The mini-bus dropped me off outside Billy's Bar on Elland Road not long after noon and I jogged down to the Pavilion. Some problem on the motorways north of Leeds meant we were missing the lads from Durham but Steve was there as usual when I arrived and Kev, John, Alan and Smithy turned up eventually. There was the annoying noise from another rock band that interrupted the conversation for a while and Jed Stone, Pete Lorimer and Steve Hodge did the legends spot. Everyone was expecting a big Leeds win and I decided to turn the clock back and revert to my perennial 4 – 0 Leeds bet at 16/1. I even doubled up my usual quid I was so confident…

Green
Ayling Bartley Jansson Berardi
Bridcutt (Capt)
Sacko Roofe Hernandez Doukara
Wood

Subs: Silvestri, Denton, Cooper, Vieira, Dallas, Phillips, Antonsson.

It looked like a 4 – 1 – 4 – 1 formation to me but others had it down as a 4 – 4 – 1 – 1 with Roofe operating just in behind Chris Wood. My only concern was that we looked a little light in the middle of the pitch with only Bridcutt and Hernandez as what I call true midfield players. The likes of Sacko, Roofe and Doukara are strikers in my book, whether out wide as wingers or more central. The Rotherham side didn't look anything special although they did have an impressive looking bench which boasted Peter Odemwingie, Dexter Blackstock and Greg Halford among their number. Former Leeds man Tom Adeyemi started for them.

Leeds had started slowly at Villa a few days earlier and did so again in this game. In fact, the Millers were probably the better side in a mostly forgettable first half. They had the two or three best chances of the half with an Anthony Forde free-kick stinging the left hand of Rob Green before Adeyemi followed up to hammer the rebound against a post and then Izzy Brown fired a shot over the bar. For Leeds, not a single shot on target was recorded in the 45 minutes and not many that were off target either. In fact, so confident was I that nothing would happen that I disappeared off to the bogs with five minutes still to go and then watched the last few seconds on a TV screen in the concourse behind the Kop.

Garry Monk would tell the BBC after the game: *"The first half was as poor as I have seen us for many months."* He explained that he made a change at half-time and he thought that was the key to the improvement we saw in the second half. The change he made was to bolster that midfield area by introducing the effervescent Ronnie Vieira for a lack lustre looking Hadi Sacko. That looked eminently more balanced to me and I was quietly pleased with myself over my pre-match assessment of the lack of midfield manpower. With Vieira able to work alongside Bridcutt we were then back to the tried and tested and usually successful Monk formation of 4 – 2 – 3 – 1, with Hernandez playing the number '10' role and Roofe and Doukara out wide. It worked a treat.

Straight from the kick-off, Leeds won a corner-kick in the north-east corner and Pablo Hernandez trotted over to take it. It was a similar ball to the one Stuart Dallas put over for Pontus at Villa Park but this time it was Captain Cool, Kyle Bartley finding just a yard of space to climb and head firmly over the defender on the back post. There was a moment of concern as Pontus Jansson was left on the deck holding his head while Bartley and the rest of the crew set off towards the dug-outs to celebrate but with a bit of help from the physio and a few rounds of the 'brick' song from the Kop Pontus was soon on his feet gain.

Just as we did at Villa, we then seemed to relax and with the formation now working for us instead of frustrating us we began to dominate the game. Twenty minutes later and another sweeping move saw Liam Bridcutt swing the ball into the middle where Chris Wood, back to goal and seemingly tightly marked, was still able to take the ball on his chest, turn, and half-volley it high into the corner of the net for his 15th goal of the season. 2 – 0 and Leeds were cruising. I turned to Kentley and mouthed *"Gotta hand it to Woody he's proving us all wrong"* but Kentley was unconvinced: *"He's still f****** crap"* he whispered, shaking his head!

Everyone near us knew I was on 4 – 0 Leeds for my bet today and so now we were half-way there, there was a little chorus of *"He only needs two more, Dave only needs two more"* as we watched Leeds win the ball back yet again and begin another foray towards the Kop.

On 73 minutes, Stuart Dallas replaced Doukara and the fresh legs put even more impetus behind the men in white. A third goal followed with still more than ten minutes of the game remaining and it was Kentley's favourite player again, Chris Wood; this time bagging his 16th goal of this amazing season. Another classy Leeds move saw the ball pinging around in midfield before three one-touch passes saw Bridcutt, Ayling and then Roofe all involved in that north-east corner again. The final first-time ball was sent across the edge of the six-yard box by Kemar Roofe and Wood was there behind the bamboozled Millers' defence to side-foot the ball home. There were other chances to grab that all important fourth goal but it just wouldn't happen for us. A brilliant run from Gaetano Berardi of all people, almost Charlie Taylor like, saw him burst into the box in the inside-left channel only to see his right foot toe-poke come back off the left-hand post. Then, seconds from the end, a Pablo Hernandez free-kick smacked against the foot of the other post.

It finished 3 – 0 and I wasn't too bothered about the bet to be honest. Marcus Antonsson got a few minutes towards the end as Chris Wood took the plaudits for his two goals and at the final whistle all the players did a lap of honour around the pitch. Apart from that slow start, it was another efficient disposal of a very poor Rotherham side that still hadn't managed to persuade anyone to fill the gap created by Kenny Jacket's resignation several weeks ago. They looked doomed, although they were in a very similar position last season of course before 'Red Adair' Warnock stepped in to save them with an amazing run of results.

It was the last time we'd see the lovely Elisa at Elland Road at least for the foreseeable future; she'd been an ever present with our little band at the front of the Kop over the last few months but was shortly returning to her native Norway. We said our farewells and then we turned again towards the big screen at the far end of the ground to study the other results from today's Championship games.

There had been a full programme with all 24 teams playing today. Of the top sides, Newcastle surprisingly lost at struggling but unpredictable Blackburn who thus recorded an unlikely double over the Toon who fell to 2nd. The Seagulls of Brighton continued to fly with a 2 – 1 win at in-form Fulham which meant they leap-frogged Newcastle back to the top of the table. Reading were another side bang in form and they held onto their third place in the table with a 3 – 2 win at Bristol City. Huddersfield continued to defy all the pundits with a 1 – 0 win at Wigan that kept them 4th, a point ahead of us while Sheffield Wednesday continued their lack-lustre recent run with a goalless draw at home to lowly Wolves to stay 6th. Derby crashed 3 – 0 at Norwich but stayed 7th, now 5 points behind Leeds. It was tight but Leeds were right in the thick of the action. For now though, thoughts turned to the FA Cup and an interesting little trip to Cambridge.

The journey home was uneventful with the usual toilet stop, this time in our favourite lay-by just off the M56. We did then have to stop one more time… the lads had run out of lager! Boris saved the day with his knowledge that a Shell filling station en route back to Whitchurch sold beer, so Humph hurled the mini-bus onto the petrol station forecourt. It's a thirsty business this football fan lark!

Leeds United 3 Rotherham 0 (**Bartley (47), Wood (66 & 79)**
33,397 (Rotherham 414)

Monk's half-time miracle at the Abbey

During the week between the Rotherham and Cambridge games, our attention was all on the transfer window or more particularly the status of the various loan players at Leeds. The first critical issue was that of Pablo Hernandez who technically completed his loan period with Leeds after the Rotherham match. Then there was the issue of Pontus Jansson who Lorimer had reminded us before the Rotherham game would trigger an option to buy once he'd played 22 games which would be after the Derby home game on 13th January, assuming he played at Cambridge. That one was further clouded by the fact that big Pontus was now on 9 yellow cards for the season; one more and he'd be banned for two games and that option would be delayed. Would the methodical Monk risk him at Cambridge?

Some comfort on these questions was given by Garry Monk this week who, according to a tweet from Phil Hay, had told him there might be, *"One or two signings – and no one will leave"*. Fans hoped that meant Charlie Taylor would also be staying with the club, despite rumours that his recent lay-off was more to do with him moving on than an alleged Achilles injury. One issue was resolved before our trip to Cambridge; Pablo was secured until the end of the season with an option at that point for one season more.

Then, on Wednesday 4th January, we got the really big news that many Leeds fans had been praying for; Andrea Radrizzani had bought 50% of Leeds United. The Leeds official website announced the deal saying: *"Leeds United Football Club today confirms the completion of an investment by Aser Group Holding, through its acquisition vehicle Greenfield Investment Pte Ltd, in 50 per cent of the Club's share capital.*

"The agreement is between Massimo Cellino, and Andrea Radrizzani (42), who is Founder and Group Chairman of Aser Group Holding, the successful Co-Founder of international sports media rights company MP & Silva and a leading figure in the sports media industry over the past two decades."[1]

In a separate statement, also posted on the club website, Cellino told us (and it works better if you read this in a thick, unintelligible Italian accent with a bit of a slur...): *"I have worked hard for the past three years for Leeds United, we are a massive club, and I feel the only way we can get better is for me to bring in a new partner... Andrea is young and brings a new energy with him, as well as having a good experience in the football media business, which is the future for all clubs. I feel that bringing Andrea in as a 50% shareholder to work with me is the best choice we could have made. We will continue building a strong and healthy football club for the future."[2]*

It was time to draw breath. The talk was that this was just the first part of the deal and that the remaining 50% of the club would pass to Radrizzani in the summer with the only aspect then to be finalised being the price, which would obviously depend on whether we were still a Championship club or a Premier League club. Radrizzani made the right noises about being impressed by Garry Monk too, which again put most of our minds at ease. It was such a momentous announcement that any other news coming out of the club seemed somehow

---

[1] *https://www.leedsunited.com/news/club-news/21478/aser-group-holding-acquires-50-of-leeds-united*

[2] *https://www.leedsunited.com/news/club-news/21480/message-from-massimo-cellino*

irrelevant but there was still a football team to run and we were still only partway through the transfer window.

The first transfer news was that Luke Murphy had gone for a Burton. He was going out on loan to Burton Albion until the end of the season while the word was that the club would also be interested in doing the same with, or even selling both, Toumani Diagouraga and goalkeeper Ross Turnbull. In a way it was comforting that it seemed to be business as usual. The Leeds United ship was riding the waves untroubled at the moment and the last thing we needed was anything that rocked our great boat. Life as a Leeds fan felt very much like it must have been for a passenger who managed to get a ticket for the inaugural Titanic voyage, total elation… and yet we all know how that ended!

The third round of the FA Cup began on Friday night with Manchester City thrashing West Ham 5 – 0 in the London Stadium in front of a capacity 57,000 crowd. But then on Saturday we saw how the lustre of the cup is fading as several dire attendance figures were reported. Just 6,608 turned up to see the all Premier League tie between Hull and Swansea that the home side edged 2 – 0, while only 7,482 were at Loftus Road to see QPR dumped out by Blackburn. The way fans were deserting this once great competition must have been worrying the FA who were no doubt thinking: *"Where Do You Go To (My Lovely)"*, as Peter Sarstedt sang back in 1969. Sarstedt was the first celebrity from the world of music to cough his clogs in 2017 when he passed away on Sunday 8th January. We all hoped 2017 would not see as many celebrity deaths as 2016.

But there was no lack of interest in the Cup at the Cambs Glass Stadium, aka the Abbey Stadium, home of Cambridge United. Tickets in the Leeds end were as rare as hens' teeth while the last few tickets in the home sections had been gobbled up on the morning of the game. A capacity crowd of 7,973 would fill the little ground with the added spice that the U's manager was former Leeds cult figure Shaun Derry who said of Leeds in his programme notes: *"It's a magnificent club with a passionate fan base, who I'm sure will make themselves heard this evening."* Cambridge had every reason to go into the game in positive mood too, on the back of six wins and a draw in the league and a 4 – 0 win over Coventry in the 2nd Round of the Cup.

I was back in the driving seat for this one, a long three hour drag down the M6 and the A14. It was a wet old day with the rain lashing down most of the journey and only the tales of a myriad Christmas mishaps from my passenger and navigator extraordinaire, Kentley the Stokie, to stop me being hypnotised by the wipers. Between coughing fits he informed me he'd lost his expensive iPhone, scarred his arm for life by dripping boiling soup on it, cut the top off his finger whilst cleaning a wine glass, paid off a £100 parking fine and was now in the throes of man-flu. *"Good Christmas then?"* I quipped!

By 4pm we were circling the Abbey Stadium (I can't use that stupid sponsor title of 'Cambs Glass Stadium') looking for a parking space which we eventually found in a side street behind the ground. Using his Dad's mobile that appeared to have a battery the size of a small breeze block attached to it, Kentley got us to a bus stop where we caught the number '3' into the centre of Cambridge, alighting near our destination, The Regal Wetherspoon on St. Andrews Street. An All Bar One next door appeared to be empty but the tell-tale signs of a police van and a few burly coppers stationed outside the doors to the Regal told us we would more than likely find a few familiar faces inside this one.

As is the case with many of the Wetherspoon buildings we frequent on our travels with Leeds, this was another fine example. In 1937 the building was opened as the Regal Cinema, said to have been the most up-to-date cinema in the region at the time and regarded by Cambridge cinema goers as a veritable palace. It later became an ABC cinema and then recently was added to the Wetherspoon empire. It is a magnificent building. Inside we found a table on the balcony overlooking the bar downstairs and sat with Nigel, Heidi and Jo, chatting about all things Leeds United whilst a few Leeds lads below hammered their fists on a table as a makeshift drum accompaniment to a few all-time favourite Leeds anthems. A couple of coppers watched from a distance rolling their eyes.

The team selection appeared on Twitter as usual at 6:45pm on the dot.

Silvestri

Berardi Jansson Cooper (Capt) Denton

Grimes Phillips

Dallas Mowatt Doukara

Antonsson

Subs: Green, Wood, O'Kane, Vieira, Coyle, Roofe, Bartley.

Our initial reaction was positive; yes there were a lot of changes, eight in all from the starting XI against Rotherham, but these were all decent players with first team experience and Garry Monk had faith in them to step up to the plate. We were only facing League Two Cambridge after all although their recent form was pretty convincing evidence they were a useful outfit.

Just before 7pm we all set off for the ground; Jo and Heidi made their way back to their car while Nigel, Kentley and I took another number '3' bus. The driver of this one was a bit more rapid than the one we took earlier and as we all stood up ready to alight at the ground he slammed on the brakes. We were like human dominoes as we all skittled forward one into the other and it was only Kentley's quick thinking as he braced himself against the luggage rack that stopped Nigel crashing through the windscreen like the proverbial flying pig! Another chap, a Cambridge fan we'd been chatting to earlier was also involved in the shunt and he quipped, pointing at Nigel: *"You nearly lost him there"*. *"No chance"*, I replied with a wink, *"We've been trying for bloody years!"*

We tip-toed along the mud strewn path that runs between the ground and a bit of a rough narrow field leading to the away end and after the usual frisking we were in. It was as we made our way into the stadium that we overheard someone mention that the winners of tonight's game had been drawn away to either AFC Wimbledon or Sutton United in the next round. Those two would have to replay having drawn at Sutton on Saturday. The Dons had to be favourites now and I remembered from my visit there just last February that their Kingsmeadow ground had a capacity smaller even than Cambridge! I saw the Wombles beat Luton Town 4 – 1 in the

90th of my 92 grounds and it was memorable as yet another occasion when a post-match beer with the H brothers, Ricky and Mike caused me to miss my train home!

More familiar faces were gathered in front of an impressive looking burger van parked inside the ground and we said hello again to Paula and Mike and then Wayne who was munching his way through an equally impressive looking burger. Then we made our way into the South Stand along with 1,400 fellow Leeds fans. I had a quick chat with James on the way through and then Smithy nudged me in the back to tell me one of the Kaiser Chiefs was stood just along our row. Sure enough, as we peered along the row we could see Kaiser's bassist Simon Rix having a laugh with some mates while, uncannily, 'Ruby' belted out of the ancient and somewhat crackly PA.

The pitch was fully 20 yards away from the front row of our stand and one of those electronic advertising hoardings had been erected the full width of the pitch and around the two other sides facing the TV camera gantry over to our left. It was all part of the media package for BT Sport who were showing the game live – our 7th game to be shown live out of the last 11 played. No wonder Radrizzani had chosen Leeds; as a media rights expert he must have known full well there was more value to be extracted from the TV interest in his new baby. Sadly, the advertising strip at our end hid the bottom few feet of the net.

As Leeds kicked-off, the atmosphere around the ground was almost hysterical with all sections absolutely rammed to the gunnels. The Cambridge fans stood on the Newmarket Road End Terrace at the far end of the ground were passing a huge flag over their heads that read: *"Amber Army, Pride and Passion"*, while at our end we belted out the usual Leeds anthems. Cambridge, in their famous amber shirts and black shorts began at a whirlwind pace and were clearly determined to put on a good show for a rare full house in their own back yard. They seemed to cope with the bobbly pitch far better than we did too and showed that pride and passion in spades. The early action saw a plethora of mistakes from the all-in-white Leeds with Liam Cooper and Kalvin Phillips the chief culprits while the huge figure of the Us '26', Uche Ikpeazu, was looking a real handful. Another over-fussy Premier League ref, Craig Pawson, was in charge and he seemed intent on adding his weight to the Cambridge offensive against us. Time and time again Leeds tackles would be penalised whilst similar challenges, particularly from the giant Ikpeazu, were ignored. Both Kalvin Phillips and Pontus Jansson were booked in a frantic three minute period and moments later, the home side was ahead. It was though a poor goal to concede and one which really showed how much of a gap there was between our First and Second XIs.

Jansson's card came as a free kick was conceded just outside our box in the Us' inside left channel; Pontus allowing a stray elbow to clatter against a Cambridge head. Their danger man, the fifteen-goal Luke Berry stood over the ball. His shot was blocked by the wall but found its way to that other danger man, Ikpeazu. Tyler Denton was trying to stay with his man but looked like he was wading through pea soup as Ikpeazu got the better of him, albeit with the help of a hand as it looked to us. Ikpeazu rasped a shot at goal from an angle but with the bottom of the net obscured from our sight we all assumed the ball had rifled into the side-netting... well, after all, Silvestri was right there and had that near post covered... didn't he? So, why we wondered was three-quarters of the ground now screaming with delight? Oh bugger! Now we understood. Marco had been beaten at his near post and was now tamely pointing at his right hand with his left index finger appealing to the liner for that hand-ball decision that never came. We've seen Rob Green beaten at his near post too but... oh what the heck. Silvestri was poor throughout the game, constantly parrying and fisting balls he really ought to have been catching. Rob Green had a mistake in him but this game told us once and for all that he was a better all-round bet than Marco.

And that was pretty much the tale of the first half. If it could go wrong for Leeds it did and our lads trudged off the pitch 1 – 0 down and with the knowledge that we'd now be facing a rampant Derby County on Friday without our talisman, Pontus Jansson to deal with any flying bricks. The only hope we now had for today was that the methodical Monk could come up with another miracle change in tactics and formation that might see us salvage something from this particular Abbey. He didn't disappoint. It seemed it often took Monk 45 minutes to suss out the opposition but once he did he knew exactly what was needed. We'd seen it numerous times this season already and perhaps most vividly at Villa recently.

Lewie Coyle started the second half in place of Gaetano Berardi and I did half-wonder if that was Monk already thinking about Derby; Berardi to play right back perhaps with Luke Ayling alongside Kyle Bartley? Maybe Berra had picked up an injury, I wasn't sure. Anyway, I don't think it was that change that influenced the game so much as a different MO that the whole team was now adopting. Monk would tell us after the game that he felt we needed to get the ball out of defence much earlier, and if that meant playing the first ball longer and missing out some of the bobbly pitch altogether, then so be it, as long as it got the midfield battling for the ball much higher up the pitch. It sounded easier to say than do but whatever it was, it worked. Leeds suddenly began to assume the look of the higher placed team and Cambridge began to wilt. This was not the sheer dominance we saw in the second half at Villa Park or the quietly efficient display in the second half that did for the Millers but it was another strong second 45 minutes that just had Leeds fans wishing we could get it right from the start. Blimey, we'd be unbeatable!

Just 11 minutes after the break Leeds equalised and what a goal it was; another for the 'looks like Arsenal' collection. Coyle, Phillips, Dallas and then Matt Grimes moved the ball quickly across the pitch from right to left wing to Tyler Denton, then Doukara and then back to Grimes. Matty Grimes sent it back to Cooper and he slotted it through to Denton once more and he moved it on to Alex Mowatt who got a yard past his man to swing the ball across from the byline towards the back post. Stuart Dallas rose well above his marker to nod the ball back across the keeper into the far corner. A sweet move of ten Leeds passes; that was more like it! Everything looked a little more positive now and even referee Pawson was being fair with his decisions as the home side resorted to some agricultural tackling. Monk had worked one miracle at the Abbey and was now pushing for another as he sent on Kemar Roofe to replace a lack-lustre Souleymane Doukara. Tonight we'd seen the old Doukara; the one who always used to disappoint by being brushed off the ball and misplacing his passes and not the recently revitalised one. Minutes later and we'd completed the turnaround and led the game 2 – 1.

A Stuart Dallas cross from the left wing was headed out for a Leeds corner and Dallas himself jogged to the left corner to take it, our right as we watched the action. The ball curled into the box perfectly for Pontus Jansson to rise and hammer a header towards goal and Alex Mowatt adeptly got his head in the way to just nudge it up and into the roof of the net on the way through. Poor Pontus looked mortified that Alex had inadvertently denied him another goal or maybe he was still thinking about missing those next two games…

Talking of missing games, a couple of minutes later Liam Cooper went down injured and was soon limping away to be replaced by Kyle Bartley, now the only recognised centre back we had left for Derby. Garry Monk would joke later: *"I might need to dust off me boots"*.

Cambridge threw everything at us for a final all guns blazing raid on our goal but we survived and it would be Leeds heading for Kingsmeadow in the 4th Round, assuming Wimbledon could beat Sutton United in their replayed game. It would be a very similar challenge to this one with all the same selection headaches for Garry Monk to ponder. Meanwhile, at the end of this game we had the desperately sad sight of Pontus Jansson walking straight off the pitch and down the tunnel without so much as a wave to his adoring fans. He was still clearly devastated at that yellow card and it's ramification of a two game ban. That Derby game now looked tougher than ever.

What had we learned tonight? Well, for me the key point to sink in was that, outside of our best XI or maybe 12 or 13 players, we were not actually very strong. Of the 8 who came in tonight I only rated Stuart Dallas and Alex Mowatt (who many reckoned was the man of the match) amongst our best, the rest were average, squad players, journeymen at this level and if we were not lucky with injuries and suspensions we'd struggle without a couple of new arrivals coming in during this transfer window; that and the fact that the methodical Monk is a great tactician.

On the long drive home I had the inevitable Kentley toilet stop request, just as we were about to get onto the M1 at junction 22. Kentley had spotted on Google Maps what he thought was a service station so we pulled off the road but ended up in a very dark car park in front of a Travelodge surrounded by trees. We couldn't fathom where these services were but a police car happened to be parked in the middle of the car park (it didn't cross our minds why at this point) so we slowly did a full circle and then pulled up right next to it. The two coppers eyed us suspiciously as Kentley lowered the passenger window. The windows of the police car were already down and the copper in the passenger seat appeared to be writing some notes. *"Where's the service area mate?"* asks my Stokie friend of the copper nearest to us. *"There's no service area"* he tells us, still looking us up and down suspiciously. *"There's a filling station just up that lane behind us with toilets and a coffee machine, that's all"*. It's at that point that I suddenly realise there's a scantily clad fit looking woman sat in the back of the police car and as we pull away Kentley blurts out: *"Oh bloody hell, I think we just interrupted an arrest or maybe a surveillance job!"* We speculated that the only thing this woman could possibly have been done for in this unlit car park in the middle of nowhere was as the main attraction of the local dogging club! It was, after all, gone 1am in the morning. *"Let it never be said, the romance is dead, Ruby, Ruby, Ruby, Ruby!"* was in my head, no doubt a consequence of hearing the song earlier. We used the gents at the filling station, Kentley loaded up with a takeaway coffee and a pack of four Crunchie bars to keep him going and we sped off up the road hoping we were now not listed on some police computer record as a suspicious vehicle. It's all just part and parcel of the rich tapestry of life you get to see as a footy fan travelling around the country in the dead of night!

Cambridge United 1 **Leeds United 2** (Ikpeazu (25), **Dallas (56), Mowatt (3)**) 7,973 (**Leeds 1,407**)

Coming of Age

Graham Taylor
1944-2017

The seemingly relentless stream of celebrity deaths appeared to know no end as, on the eve of our game with Derby, the death of former England manager Graham Taylor was announced. Taylor, a gentleman by all accounts, was just 72 years of age. *"Do I not like 2017"* I could hear him saying to Saint Peter at the Pearly Gates.

At Leeds, Andrea Radrizzani was going through the less pearly gates of Thorp Arch, to be introduced to the players and to inspect the facilities. While in the press, several papers were reporting that Leeds had turned down offers of around £7m for Charlie Taylor from Middlesbrough, West Brom and Crystal Palace. Boro's war-chest was probably greatest as they'd recently let go of David Nugent who'd then signed for Derby in time to be included in their squad for our game on Friday 13th... don't worry folks, it's the 17th we have to worry about, not the 13th, ask Massimo!

It was the start of another long weekend for me, beginning with the drive up to Leeds with Mrs W. The good lady was being dropped off at Leeds station from where she was heading up to our friends Sheila and Brian's place in Darlington for the weekend; I was driving up there after the game. Predictably, Friday afternoon on the M6 was chaos so we slogged our way up the back roads to Junction 17 to avoid the first of several accidents that would blight the journey. I was still knocking on the door of the Pavilion three hours before kick-off though. Steve, as always, had somehow bribed his way in early and so I joined him while we waited for the rest of the crew to arrive. Eventually Tony, George and Trevor bowled in and then Kev, Alan, John, Nigel, Simon, Mick and Jacqui all squeezed in around our usual table as did former Leeds player John McClelland who often comes for a chat with us now that he knows our little group. It was Graham Taylor of course who signed John for Watford back in 1984 where he played for almost five years before joining Leeds in 1989.

All the pre-match talk was about how Leeds would set up defensively in the absence of Pontus Jansson, especially if Liam Cooper also failed to make it. Coops was suffering with a dead leg while word also came through that Hadi Sacko wouldn't make it either due to an unspecified injury and Charlie Taylor was still not apparently fit to resume. Inevitably, the speculation that Taylor was about to depart the club would not go away despite Garry Monk saying no one would be leaving. I made no secret of the fact that I'd be happy to see Luke Ayling fill that centre back slot alongside his mate Kyle Bartley rather than Liam Cooper who, for me, was still prone to too many unnecessary errors such as we saw at Cambridge.

Green
Coyle Ayling Bartley Berardi
Bridcutt (Capt) Vieira
Doukara Hernandez Roofe
Wood

Subs: Silvestri, Denton, O'Kane, Mowatt, Phillips, Dallas, Antonsson.

So I got my wish; it was Luke Ayling who filled in at centre-back with young Lewie Coyle getting a well-earned start after his good showing at Cambridge and 'Berra' switching to left-back. Effectively therefore we started the game with three right-backs in the back four. The rest of the side picked itself with the possible exception that a case could've been made for Eunan O'Kane to start in place of Ronnie Vieira instead of being on the bench. Derby would start with Scott Carson in goal, Darren Bent and Tom Ince up front and former Leeds man Bradley Johnson in midfield while new boy Nugent and the unmistakeable white-haired Will Hughes would both start on the bench. A minute's applause was held before the game to honour Graham Taylor and then the action began.

Leeds kicked-off attacking the South Stand in their usual all-white strip while Derby defended in a kit of turquoise blue; I've got a bathroom painted the same colour... not that it helps you visualise it if you haven't been in my bathroom. It was a near perfect first half with Leeds bossing the possession and playing the 45 minutes almost entirely in the Derby half. The only annoyance was some fat bloke in a donkey jacket who kept disappearing every ten minutes presumably for a pee; every time he slowly squeezed himself along our row there was almost an impasse as his bulk met the immoveable object that is Nigel aka Paddington (for his general shape and fondness for marmalade sandwiches). *"He's in the way, he's in the wa-ay, his name is Paddington and he's in the way"* could be heard in our vicinity every time the big bloke shoved his way past.

For 44 minutes Leeds attacked, playing the most dominant and attractive football we have seen from a Leeds side for more years than I care to remember. It must have been pleasing Sky TV's customers and was probably condemning us to many more rescheduled matches as TV bosses no doubt scoured the fixture list looking for yet more Leeds game to show. We ought to have been three or four goals to the good as we racked up corner after corner and shot after shot. Doukara, Bridcutt and Bartley two or three times ought to have scored but the finishing touch was not ever quite there. The best chances came when Ronnie Vieira charged down a Scott Carson clearance only to see the ball squirt off to the right and then when Kyle Bartley got his legs in a tangle at the back post from one of our many corner-kicks when it looked like he could walk the ball into the net. Derby were clearly rattled and ought to have been down to ten men when Craig Bryson elbowed Pablo Hernandez giving the Spaniard a bloody nose. Referee Scott Duncan awarded the free-kick but nothing more. It must have been good viewing for Messrs Cellino and Radrizzani too, sat together high up in the East Stand but the one lingering doubt was that Derby, having got away with it so far, might still grab a break-away goal, however undeserved that might be. *"Deserved"* is not really a footballing term. Thankfully, as the metaphorical clock ticked into the 45th minute, Leeds scored.

It was from another of those many corners (we'd total 16 during the whole of this game) that we finally got the breakthrough. In an interview after the game Chris Wood told us how Kyle Bartley, annoyed at the three chances he'd already fluffed, told Chris Wood to swap with him and take up position at the near post for this corner. As the ball from Hernandez floated across, Wood timed his jump to perfection to steer a header across the face of goal and inside the back post for his 17th goal of the season; I made a mental note to never, ever, criticise the big Kiwi again. Even more satisfying was that the twonk in the donkey jacket had just gone out for another pee and presumably missed the goal... *"Leeds are going up, na, na-na, na-na-na, Leeds are going up"*, echoed around Elland Road and two Italians high up in the East Stand must have been rubbing their hands. There was still time before the break for a scare in front of the Kop as Tom Ince burned the fingers of Rob Green with a shot but Green pushed it away safely and that was half-time.

Derby made a double substitution at half-time to try to stem the tide, bringing on Will Hughes and Matej Vydra who has scored against us in a previous reincarnation at Watford. It nearly worked too, as for a few minutes Derby forced us back. Darren Bent even had the ball in our net in front of the South Stand as Rob Green almost copied what Carson did in the first half, taking too long over a clearance that cannoned off Bent and back into our net. For a second or two Green looked crestfallen at what he'd done but then his blushes were saved as referee Duncan ruled it ricocheted in off an upraised arm. It was just another little reminder as to where one of the last few weaknesses in this current Leeds squad still lurked. Neither Green nor Silvestri is 100% reliable.

But that was the extent of the Derby fightback, after that initial five minutes Leeds took control again and but for some weak finishing should have scored more. We didn't and that is something else to work on in the future. Bradley Johnson picked up two yellow cards and walked off before Duncan could even show him the red that followed to round off a miserable evening for the Rams. It was as dominant a display as anyone could remember and by the end of the weekend, with defeats for Brighton at Preston, Reading at home to QPR and Huddersfield at Sheffield Wednesday, Leeds were firmly bedded into the first play-off spot, 3rd behind new leaders Newcastle and second place Brighton. Leeds were a full 8 points ahead of Derby in 7th now, albeit with 20 games still to play. No one could now deny that, if Leeds could avoid too many injuries and suspensions, and if we could continue to play like we had recently, then a play-off spot was the minimum we ought to achieve come the end of the regular season. This young Leeds side had come of age.

I had a leisurely drive up to Darlington after the game and then had the delight (?) of watching Darlo play Gloucester City in a National League North fixture the following afternoon. It was a bitterly cold day and for 80 minutes there was precious little going on out on the pitch to warm the 1,800 crowd who'd braved the arctic temperatures. Then, a tiny lad called Nathan Cartman came on and he changed the game with his darting little runs. He scored one and set up another to win the game for Darlo 2 – 0. Funnily enough, Cartman graduated through the Leeds United Academy before being released presumably because he's only about two feet tall! Leeds fans everywhere this weekend were feeling ten feet tall.

Leeds United 1 Derby County 0 (**Wood (45)**)
25,546 (Derby 870)

Tykes in La La Land

When I got home from our Darlington trip (which incidentally was mainly to be present at Brian's Mum's 90th birthday celebration and not solely to stand on a freezing field watching Darlington beat Gloucester) I watched the press conference that had been held at Elland Road unveiling Andrea Radrizzani as the new co-owner of Leeds United. Leeds' CEO, Ben Mansford was flanked by Cellino and Radrizzani like the ham in an Italian sandwich. Mansford and Radrizzani both looked nervous every time Cellino spoke, wondering no doubt what clanger the maverick mad-man was about to drop. As Mansford read his introduction from some pre-prepared notes, Massimo, true to form, leaned across and turned the paper over giggling like a naughty schoolboy. Mansford looked even more uncomfortable as he handed over to Cellino to introduce Radrizzani. Massimo didn't disappoint and soon had everyone squirming as he told the assembled press (and remember to say this aloud in that thick, slurred Italian accent): *"It's a been a long time since I speak with the press, the last time I 'ad this experience it was with a beautiful journalist but she was 'iding a camera... in da purse..."* I think Mansford, like me, was wondering during that slight pause exactly where that camera was hidden! Mansford looked to the floor while Radrizzani's eyes widened with fear. Cellino told us how the money needed to be successful in the Championship was *"scary"* and hence why he needed to share the load with a partner. We'd learn from Radrizzani during another interview he gave to the Guardian this weekend that his interest in Leeds was sparked by a chance encounter with Kenny Dalglish at the Champions League quarter-final between Manchester City and Paris Saint-Germain.[1] The former Liverpool legend had commented how Leeds was one of the last few giants of the game with scope to return to its former glory days and as a result of that comment Radrizzani made contact with Cellino. One comment that perhaps sent a shudder down the spine of many Leeds fans was when Radrizzani told the LUTV cameras: *"From the beginning it was clear to me that Massimo didn't really want to sell entirely the club, because he has a passion for Leeds and he's a fighter and he wants to do something good for the club before he gives up so he will never give up the club…"* Most of us just shrugged and hoped that last bit got confused in translation. Mansford shifted in his chair again.

A direct question from the floor, asked to Radrizzani about funds for the transfer window, was intercepted by Massimo: *"I don't let him invest nothing, we are 50-50 I told him we no spend nothing, we have too many players, don't get in a mess, because sometimes we want to help too much, as an owner sometimes we want to participate to the winning of games and instead of help we make disaster. So, when the team is playing good you just have the wish that nobody gets injured. We have good players and they are growing as a young team…"* Both Mansford *and* Radrizzani shifted uncomfortably this time and as soon as Massimo paused for breath Radrizzani was quick to jump in. *"I think we are aligned completely, me and Massimo and Garry in what we need, the idea is to touch as less as possible because we don't want to touch the balance of the team and the performance and not only on the pitch also in the locker room everything is working very well. The group is very united so I think we are aligned. We are looking potentially at one or two players that Garry mentioned last night and Ben, our CEO is working on that…"* Massimo's eyebrows gave the lie to the fact that this was an area the two owners were already at loggerheads over. I hoped Radrizzani's view held

---

[1]   https://www.theguardian.com/football/2017/jan/15/leeds-united-andrea-radrizzani-dalglish

sway as I reckoned, like Monk, we needed a couple of new faces as cover.

While Leeds had apparently found the Holy Grail of success, other Championship clubs continued to search for it. While Leeds were unveiling Andrea Radrizzani as their new joint owner, Nottingham Forest were sacking their manager, Philippe Montanier after less than seven months in the job. Montanier was the 10th Championship manager to bite the dust this season.

This week we learned it would be Sutton United and not the favourites Wimbledon who we'd face in the 4th round of the FA Cup. Sutton beat the real Dons on their rented Kingsmeadow pitch 3 − 1 with a bit of help from Wimbledon defender Paul Robinson who got himself sent-off in the 15th minute. So, it would be a trip to the Borough Sports Ground in Gander Green Lane, Sutton, for as many of us that could beg borrow or steal a ticket. Their tiny ground only holds 5,013 and we'd been allocated just 755 hen's teeth.

In another of those football coincidences that I love so much, Lincoln City, the only other non-league side still in the Cup, pulled off a shock by beating Ipswich Town in their replay with a last minute goal. Lincoln City had not reached the 4th round since 1975-76; their manager that year? Graham Taylor.

And in another strange but sad coincidence, Taylor's great friend and former England Women's Cricket player Rachael Heyhoe Flint died this week aged 75 as the Grim Reaper showed no sign of taking a winter break.

In one more replay this week, our next league opponents, Barnsley, were knocked out of the Cup in another shock result; 1 − 2 at home to League Two Blackpool. The winner came in the very last minute of extra-time, so hopefully there were going to be some very tired legs in their XI at Oakwell on Saturday evening. For once the timing of the games was to our advantage. If we could now press home that apparent advantage by repeating the sort of display we conjured up against Derby, then the whole of the Leeds United family would be in La La Land.

Mrs W and I went to see the film of that name on Thursday evening and I have to admit it sort of set the tone for the year we all hoped we'd have; a joyous and vibrant riot of song-and-dance with a happy ending and not to mention the uplifting sight of Emma Stone dancing in a flouncy yellow summer frock. The following day we watched transfixed as Donald J. Trump was sworn in as the 45th President of the United States and then listened to one of the most impassioned and patriotic speeches I have ever heard from a politician taking office as he promised to create a new USA, a sort of Utopian State of America; a walking, talking, living and breathing La La Land. He pledged to stamp out *"the crime and the gangs and the drugs"* as well as putting America first in every sphere of life. If he was in any doubt about the scale of his task, as he spoke, two blocks away anti-Trump protesters went on the rampage, smashing shop windows, hurling trash cans into the streets and pledging to oppose him at every step.

It was the Shropshire Whites' mini-bus again for me on the Barnsley trip and it picked me up right on my doorstep in the village. Surprisingly it was not full, only eleven lads and one lass making the journey to South Yorkshire. We had the first toilet stop at McDonald's on the A50 near Uttoxeter and the staff must have thought they were in for a bumper sales day as everyone trooped in. But then they must have been scratching their heads as everyone went straight through to the bogs and then straight out again afterwards. The stop was only really made for our one lady passenger, Claire, as the lads are all quite happy using the bin they always have propped in the rear corner of the mini-bus… well it's only like being on an Easy-Jet flight!

The next stop was The Prospect Tavern in Hoyland on the outskirts of Barnsley. We were joined in there by a coach-load of the West Midlands Whites whose bus we'd followed virtually all the way from Stoke. We were in there from about two o'clock 'til after 4pm enjoying a few pints and watching the TV as the afternoon's 3pm kick-offs got underway and the scores flashed up. The pub even laid on free pork pies and mushy peas. Then it was back on the bus and off up the road to Oakwell.

Just driving into Barnsley it was crystal clear that a 5:30pm kick-off on a Saturday was never a great idea for this game.

The kick-off was dictated by Sky TV of course (this was now our 9th live TV game out of our last 13 and our 11th televised game of the season so far) but it was a chance for fans of both sides, like us, to have been in the pub all day long. As we pulled up in a queue of traffic we could see scuffles breaking out on the pavement and there were police everywhere on foot, bikes and horses. It was dark too of course and that always seems to intensify the aggression. Once the mini-bus parked up I set off up Belgrave Road heading towards the away end. That was manic too; an insane crush of humanity all pushing and shoving to get to and then through the donkey's years-old turnstiles and on into a concourse far too small for the 5,000 odd Leeds fans who'd be packed into the Palmer Construction Limited North Stand. Maybe Palmer Construction could actually do something useful for the club and build them a new stand that was actually adequate for the twenty first century. Just to get to the bogs under our stand took me ten minutes, carefully pushing through the crowds and trying to keep children and womenfolk safe in the crush. The Leeds fans weren't helping of course as a big group of lads was gathered in the middle singing and dancing about with scant regard for the toes they were stepping on and the folk they were pushing out of the way. Several Leeds lads had climbed up onto one of the steel beams above our heads and were now sat up there orchestrating the singing. I was pleased to finally get out of it all and up to my seat in row Z, up above the goal at the north end of the ground. I was soon joined by Nigel and Kentley as always and we settled down to await kick-off.

Green
Coyle Ayling Bartley Berardi
Vieira Bridcutt (Capt)
Doukara Hernandez Doukara
Wood

Subs: Silvestri, Denton, O'Kane, Phillips, Mowatt, Dallas, Antonsson.

It was exactly the same side that started against Derby and why not? That side played the best football we've seen for years, it was an obvious choice if they were all fit. We were told that Charlie Taylor and Hadi Sacko were still unavailable through injury and for Pontus Jansson this was the second of his two-game ban. For Barnsley, Marc Roberts had recovered from the injury that saw him limp out of their cup tie in mid-week and Conor Hourihane played up front despite being linked with a big money transfer to Aston Villa. They'd already lost Sam Winnall to Sheffield Wednesday in the current window and they seemed to be a club facing a bit of a crisis. Hourihane would join Villa a few days later. Old Leeds 'favourite' Aidy White was on the Tykes' bench and we'd been allocated the Premier League's 'celebrity ref' for this game; Mike Dean.

As expected, the first ten minutes saw Barnsley throw the kitchen sink at the makeshift Leeds defence and it was a nervy old time as we wondered if we could survive without the steadying might of Pontus. Against Derby, Leeds had dominated the midfield so much that there was very little pressure on the back-line but this was a whole different scenario. We wobbled a bit and Lewie Coyle showed those nerves as he completely sliced an attempted left foot clearance but we came through it and slowly began to get our own game together. With 18 minutes gone, a quick Leeds breakaway down the right wing with Hernandez ended with Marc Roberts heading the ball away for a Leeds corner. Pablo himself swung it in from the right wing at the far end of the ground and Chris Wood met it with his knee at the front post to bundle it into the net. There were the inevitable scenes of joy at our end with a couple of flares going off down to our left while we could see some trouble erupting at the far end; presumably due to a few Leeds fans being in there. Police and stewards waded in and for a few minutes you could easily have thought you were back in the bad old days of the 70s and 80s. There was a bit of a scuffle in the corner to our left too as fans from both sides puffed out their chests and gestured to each other. The arrival on the scene of a long line of police in full riot gear seemed to calm everyone down and with typical humour the Leeds fans broke into the Laurel and Hardy tune as they marched military style across in front of our stand.

Once the fighting subsided it all felt very comfortable; a goal up and in a good run of form and playing a side that must have been low in confidence after that Blackpool cup defeat here the other night. Leeds were going for it too, we forced six corners in the next twenty minutes or so with a Chris Wood header and a fierce shot from Doukara going close but blocked away. Each time the ball came over Marc Roberts had great handfuls of Kyle Bartley's shirt and at one point appeared to push him to the ground with a hand-off to the face. Despite Bartley's protests Mike Dean seemed unimpressed and waved him away theatrically. It still looked comfortable as we entered the last minute of the half. Doukara then put in one of his typical challenges deep in Leeds territory on the Barnsley right; shoving his man over while showing no interest in the football at all. Mike Dean gave the inevitable free-kick.

Part of the solidity of our defence this season had come from the fact that we always seemed to be on our toes, alert and watchful but for once we went to sleep. The free-kick was rolled down the inside right channel into space while Adam Armstrong dashed from the crowd of players in the middle to collect it. No Leeds player spotted his run and he had time to check, get the ball onto his left foot and curl it in towards the near post. Tom Bradshaw did the rest, getting a yard in front of Kyle Bartley to steer a header just wide of the diving Rob Green. It was a sucker punch and just shows that in the Championship you must put your chances away when you're in control of a game as the opposition is always likely to go down the other end and nick one. Predictably Oakwell erupted on three sides, no doubt in disbelief and relief more than anything else. As the sides trooped off down the tunnel to the dressing rooms below our stand it was with a jaunty step for the players in the red shirts. That season long failure to bury enough of our chances had come back to haunt us again while perhaps we'd finally seen how this makeshift back-line wasn't quite the beast we were more used to with Pontus and Charlie Taylor in it. That became even more apparent in the opening minutes of the second half.

Pablo Hernandez had looked strangely subdued in the first half and straight-away he was easily caught in possession and the ball was hooked up the Barnsley right wing. Luke Ayling was under it but seemed to think it was going to make the penalty area where Rob Green was waiting, so he let it bounce. But it was still a yard outside the right edge of the area as we looked on from 100 yards away. Now, neither Green nor Ayling quite knew what to do so they both let it bounce again before Green finally took matters into his own hands, or at least his head, and nodded the ball out for a throw-in near the corner flag. Ayling was clearly rattled. Barnsley took a quick throw and after two or three short passes the ball was crossed to the far side of the area where Liverpool loanee Ryan Kent controlled it with his back to goal as he was marshalled by Lewie Coyle. You had to wonder if Luke Ayling or Gaetano Berardi would have done it better than Coyle as Kent turned on a sixpence to his right and then lashed the ball left-footed across Rob Green into the far corner of the net. 2 – 1 to Barnsley and suddenly promotion looked a damned sight more difficult than it had twenty minutes earlier. We'd been cruising, not only in this game but in all seven games we'd played since that previous aberration down in Brighton. Only that lack of accuracy in front of goal had prevented us beating Villa and making it a magnificent seven. Now our defence looked wobbly, we were 2 – 1 down and the Oakwell crowd smelled blood; our blood. This was going to be a tough challenge as suddenly, backed by their own fans, the Barnsley players looked a foot taller and a yard quicker than ours all over the pitch. And six minutes later it got worse as the confidence just surged through the veins of those red shirted Tykes.

Josh Scowen raced away from us towards the edge of the Leeds box and Kemar Roofe slid in from behind and brought him down for a free-kick about 25 yards from goal. Roofe was booked. Conor Hourihane tapped the ball a couple of feet to Scowen on his left who stopped it dead by putting his foot on the ball and Hourihane then swept it left-footed around the Leeds wall into the corner of the net. It was a near perfect shot that started a good yard outside the post but curled and curled and just nicked the inside of the woodwork before rippling the net.

Leeds didn't give up of course, that's not in the make-up of this side and we kept plugging away. We pulled a goal back too in the 68th minute when Marc Roberts stuck out a hand to push away a long diagonal ball from Kyle Bartley that was otherwise destined to land on Chris Wood's boot. Wood efficiently smashed the penalty to the keeper's left as he dived away to his right but we couldn't find another to level things up and the game ended 3 – 2 to Barnsley. It was the third time this season we'd conceded three goals, the others being the 3 – 0 opening day defeat at Loftus Road and the 3 – 1 loss at Forest. The only positives to come out of the game for Leeds were that Wood got his 18th and 19th goals of the season and of course Jansson's suspension was now out of the way. With Huddersfield beating Ipswich 2 – 0 this weekend they now went third in the table with Leeds slipping to 4th but still 5 points ahead of Derby in 7th. Newcastle and Brighton continued to lead the way with Reading and the Wendies completing the top six. Barnsley would no doubt think they were still in the hunt too as they'd end this 27th round of games in 8th, only four points outside the top six. It would look and sound like La La Land in South Yorkshire tonight as they sang and danced in the cobbled streets.

The mini-bus was quiet on the way home with hardly a song as we contemplated the battle ahead to secure a play-off place. A couple of lads had already booked hotels in London for the play-off final but were now pondering their options. This game provided a bit of a reality check; I knew we'd easily make those play-offs or even catch Brighton or the Toon if we could play like we did against Derby every week but that was the point, it just isn't possible to do that every game. At our best we're good, but Barcelona we are not; at least not yet.

The only humour on the bus going home was provided by Claire as she contemplated whether she could use her 'Shewee' to go in the bucket the lads use at the back of the bus; Ash, the driver for the day, was determined to stick to his one stop each way rule. The lads were obviously keen for her to try… but common sense prevailed and she hung on 'til Market Drayton. Mr Ash reminds us all the time: *"If you can't hold it, don't drink it!"*

Barnsley 3 **Leeds United 2 (Wood (18)**, Bradshaw (45), Kent (48), Hourihane (54), **Wood (68 pen))** 17,817 (**Leeds 5,241**)

Doukara's Forest Fire

Toumani Diagouraga was the next Leeds player to leave during this latest transfer window; he went off on loan for the rest of the season joining Mick McCarthy's Tractor Boys. Meanwhile, as we prepared for the home game with Forest, there was still no news of any new players coming in. Whenever asked by reporters, Garry Monk would stick to his story that he expected two players to be joining and he was confident the club was doing everything to ensure the deals happened. He always stressed though that it was important any players coming in fitted into the squad both from a football and social point of view; he didn't want anyone who might upset his well-balanced apple cart.

The Forest game had been rearranged due to our FA Cup run; brought forward from the weekend to accommodate our trip to non-league Sutton the following Sunday. So Forest and Leeds were the first teams to play in the 28th round of games. The night before our match, both Brighton and Reading played their games in hand with both winning 1 – 0 against Cardiff and Fulham respectively. Brighton thus went back to the top of the table ahead of Newcastle while Reading went third. Next came Huddersfield and then Leeds in 5th. Seeing the table with every team having played the same number of games brought home how difficult it was going to be to catch either Brighton or Newcastle to nick one of those automatic promotion spots. Newcastle were ten points ahead of Leeds and Brighton had a 12 point advantage. But as Monk kept telling us, all we could do was focus on the next game.

Forest arrived at Elland Road in some disarray, but then again we said something similar ahead of our trip to Barnsley and look how that ended! Forest had sacked Philippe Montanier a couple of weeks earlier and would travel to Leeds under the temporary charge of their Academy Manager, Gary Brazil. They were only five points above the drop zone currently occupied by Burton, Blackburn and Rotherham and had only one win in their previous nine games, albeit that did come in the most recent, a 1 – 0 win at home to fellow strugglers Bristol City. Forest's owner, Fawaz Al Hasawi, was under similar pressure from fans to that which Massimo Cellino had felt at Leeds and had seen two recent attempts to sell the club stall at the last minute.

For Leeds, it was vital we got back on track to ensure our confidence wasn't undermined following the Barnsley defeat which everyone was putting down as a one-off, an aberration caused by Barnsley being fired up for a Yorkshire derby and the makeshift Leeds defence showing itself to be more fragile than we first thought.

Green
Ayling Bartley Jansson Berardi
O'Kane Bridcutt (Capt)
Dallas Hernandez Roofe
Wood

Subs: Silvestri, Coyle, Mowatt, Vieira, Phillips, Doukara, Antonsson.

When the team was announced on Twitter there were many heads nodding in approval in the Pavilion. Most reckoned this was the strongest XI we could field with the players currently available. Charlie Taylor, and to a lesser extent Hadi Sacko, were names most thought to be in contention for a place in our best XI but both were still said to be struggling with injuries so didn't even make the bench. For Forest, former Leeds man Eric Lichaj was still their regular right-back while the only real danger man I could spot in their line-up was Britt Assombalonga who, for a spell last season, was in scintillating form until he suffered a serious knee injury. They did also have former Arsenal striker Nicklas Bendtner on their bench but none of their three scorers in the reverse fixture were even in their squad this time.

The first half was a cagey affair with very few clear-cut chances for either side but the one big chance came for that man Assombalonga. A long diagonal ball into the Leeds area beat Kyle Bartley and the Forest man took it neatly on his chest before blasting a shot that Rob Green managed to tip over the bar. I made a mental note to remember how important that save would be should we go on to win the game. Chris Wood did have the ball in the net but that one was correctly flagged for offside as he latched on to a knock-down header following a Hernandez free-kick. Other than that we were restricted to watching a few long range efforts soar into the stands at both ends.

After the game, Garry Monk admitted that Forest's game plan worked well for them in the first half: *"Credit to Forest in the first half - their game plan to slow the tempo was lowering our intensity and pace of play, which was making it difficult for us and making it a much more even game.*

"I said at half-time that we needed to up our intensity and we made a couple of tweaks..."[1]

The need for another clever half-time tweak by Garry Monk was evident to us all but we'd seen several times this season how astute he was in assessing what changes were needed to

---

[1] *http://www.bbc.co.uk/sport/football/38659680*

grab the initiative and so it was no surprise when Leeds began to dominate the game in the second half. Finally, I began to relax as it looked as if we'd rediscovered the magic formula that was so evident against Derby, although I was still none the wiser to really understand where it disappeared to up at Oakwell.

In the 55th minute, Leeds won the third of three corners in the space of a few minutes and Pablo Hernandez jogged over to the north-east corner to a backing track of *"Pab-lo Her-nan-dez"* from the Kop. When the ball came over, Kyle Bartley nodded it down and there was 'Jonny on the spot' Chris Wood to control it with his left knee before prodding it home with his right boot. It was his 20th goal of the season, a target that for the first few weeks of the campaign looked hopelessly unlikely but now it seemed he could do no wrong. He was now scoring more regularly than he was missing... It was Leeds 38th league goal of the season and of those an incredible 12 had now come as a result of set pieces, either corners or free-kicks. Contrast that with previous seasons when we used corner kicks as a time to check our mobiles for messages so rarely did anything come of them! The arrival of Bartley and Jansson meant we now had a real threat from any high ball into the box and in Hernandez we had someone who knew how to deliver them. The tension was released immediately, in the stands as well as on the pitch, as everyone began to dream again and we could all chuck that Barnsley result in the 'aberration' file. A chant of *"Woody, Woody, Woody"* rang round Elland Road and the ear-cupping nonsense from the Fulham game here back in August was not even a distant memory any more. We were confident enough to sing *"Leeds are going up"* too, a chant that was conspicuous by its absence in the first half.

Leeds continued to dominate as it looked as though the goal had sucked out the last vestiges of resistance from a deflated looking Forest side. With 72 minutes showing on the big screen, Souleymane Doukara replaced Stuart Dallas as Monk made his first change. Souley obviously has a superstition and we watched as he did his familiar little hop onto the pitch. Leeds immediately attacked again and won another corner and once again Pablo trotted over to that north-east corner and once again the Kop chanted his name to the La Bamba tune. This time the out-swinging corner was powerfully headed away by a Forest defender but waiting exactly where it was flying to was a certain Souley Doukara. Douk was stood just about where Sol Bamba was when he hit that screamer against Wolves last season, the one that would have taken my head off had the net not stopped it. It was a case of déjà vu; I stood with mouth open as Doukara watched the ball all the way onto his right boot and then smashed it on the volley straight into that same top corner. Once again I couldn't stop myself just ducking slightly as I watched, mesmerised and unable to believe the net would stop such a rocket. Our little gang of folk at the front of the Kop went absolutely mental. *"Oh my f****** God"* I remember shouting at the top of my voice as I turned to share the moment with the others. Everyone was jumping up and down and punching the air, not only because it was such a tremendous strike but also of course in the belief that the three points were now secure. It was right up there with my all-time memorable moments at Elland Road. *"Was it his first touch?"* was the question being asked as the hubbub slowly subsided and to this day I still don't know the answer but most people reckon it was. It was so reminiscent of a certain Tony Yeboah in his pomp banging in those goals against Liverpool and Wimbledon that it was no surprise the Kop was soon chanting, *"Tony, Tony Yeboah, Tony Ye-bo-oh-ah"* and then for the rest of the game every time Douk got the ball they roared, *"Shoooooooooooooot!"* regardless of where he was on the pitch.

Most of the crowd was now ready to party and out on the pitch the Leeds players were clearly enjoying the atmosphere as they began to knock the ball about in 'champagne football' mode. As pass followed pass the crowd began to sing out *"Olé!"* and I'm sure many fans, like me, had images going through their minds of that great Revie side toying with Southampton all those years ago with Bremner and Giles back-heeling the ball to each other. In that game Leeds got seven of course whereas tonight we were still only two goals to the good. Mind you, by the end of this game Leeds *ought* to have bagged at least a couple more and it was only down to some wayward finishing from Chris Wood that we didn't. Leeds introduced Vieira and then Alex Mowatt for the last ten minutes or so and Ronnie was soon snapping at the heels of any Forest player who dwelt on the ball for more than a nano-second. Eric Lichaj did exactly that and Vieira was able to toe poke the ball from under his nose and then as Mancienne switched off momentarily, Chris Wood was in behind the Forest defence with just the keeper to beat. It was the sort of chance that a top striker would bury 99 times out of a hundred. But one thing about Wood that I've noticed is that the more time he has to think about a goal-scoring opportunity, the less likely he is to knock it in the net. This time he tried to lob the keeper from 20 yards out but ballooned it horribly over the bar into the disbelieving Kop. Minutes later he was at it again as he should have completed a stunning Leeds break with a tap-in goal. Luke Ayling brought the ball quickly out of defence, played a one two with Alex Mowatt and then clipped over a perfect ball to Wood, all on his own, ten yards from goal. Somehow, Wood got his feet in a tangle and instead of tapping the ball past the keeper merely allowed the ball to hit him and bounce safely into the keeper's hands. I couldn't help wondering what the Kop's response would have been to the two misses had the game still been nil-nil; it was so much like the Chris Wood we saw back in August...

As it was it didn't matter. Leeds closed the game out safely and the three points took us back into third place in the table albeit having now played a game more than the rest of the teams in the top half. It was a sixth straight home win to nil as well. We'd given the response Garry Monk wanted to the Barnsley defeat, we were back on track and I for one was convinced we could still catch the top two, just as Burnley did the previous season when they had a storming end to the campaign. Everything was still possible but first we had another tricky little FA Cup obstacle to negotiate; Sutton United down Gander Green lane.

Leeds United 2 Nottingham Forest 0 **(Wood (55), Doukara (74))** 24,838 (Forest 667)

Sweet f a cup success

On the Friday before the Sutton United cup tie, just as Garry Monk was giving his pre-match press conference, the BBC confirmed that a young man, Raheem Wilks, was killed in a shooting incident in the Harehills area of Leeds. He was the 19 year-old brother of Leeds player Mallik Wilks.[1] I suppose such things do affect other clubs in equal measure and I just don't get to hear about them but tragedy and bad news does seem to be never far away from Leeds. Incredibly, in his press conference at Thorp Arch, Garry Monk told reporters that Mallik would be involved with the squad to travel to Sutton saying: *"Mallik feels the football will help."*

One player who would not now be involved was Alex Mowatt as the final touches were put to a transfer to Barnsley. Monk confirmed that the deal was, *"All but done"* while he still

---

[1] *http://www.bbc.co.uk/news/uk-england-leeds-38767596*

seemed confident players were coming in, saying: *"I can only assume that the players that the club have talked about will come through the door as soon as possible"*. It did strike me as a funny way of putting it though, almost as if he was challenging 'the club' not to balls it up. On the other hand, and remembering how Cellino blurted out that he'd told Radrizzani *"to spend nothing"* in that initial press conference, it was not surprising to see another player go as I guessed they were making room for new players on the wage bill. That was Mowatt, Diagouraga and Luke Murphy removed in recent weeks. Leeds fans on Twitter were rattling their sabres believing that Cellino, and now by implication Radrizzani too, were refusing to support Garry Monk. There were still a few days of the transfer window left though so time to do the right thing.

Just as we were absorbing all that, another statement popped up on the official club website confirming that Massimo Cellino's appeal against his 18 month ban for his alleged part in the Ross McCormack bung case was still ongoing and therefore any sanction from the FA would remain on hold. This basically meant that the originally stated start date of any ban, February 1st, had now been pushed back until the outcome of the appeal was known. Goodness knows when that might be. And of course the day all this happened was the first day of the Chinese New Year... the year? The year of the cock of course! As always, the football would be a pleasant relief from all the off-field stuff... wouldn't it?

Kentley picked me up in the BMW just before 8am and then we set off on the 180 mile journey to Sutton, a London borough situated about ten miles south-west of Charing Cross. Sutton has a long list of famous sons and daughters including singer-songwriter Joan Armatrading who lived here in the 1970s; David Bellamy, the TV botanist, who studied at Sutton Grammar School; James Hunt the racing driver and Katie Melua who lived in Gander Green Lane not far from the football ground. The Rolling Stones also got their first big break at a pub in Sutton in the early 60s and of course Don Revie's Leeds United legends were here for a 4th round FA

Cup tie in 1970 when we triumphed 6 – 0 with four goals from Allan Clarke and a couple from Peter Lorimer.

We were heading for Sutton Cricket Club which had been designated as a meeting place specifically for travelling Leeds fans. It was only a ten minute walk to Sutton United's ground, had ample car-parking and was not far from the West Sutton railway station. We slotted the BMW into a space in the car park around 11:15am.

Inside the cricket club it was like a who's who of Leeds United away fans. Tickets had been allocated on the basis of the number of away games attended this season (a minimum of 14 games out of the first 16 of the season was required); so all the regular faces were there. The bar must have done a roaring trade and they had bacon and sausage baps at £2 a time to help soak up the beer, all enjoyed whilst looking out of the full length windows at the cricket outfield where back in the 1890s W. G. Grace used to ply his trade according to the club website.[1] If I had a quid for every cricket club that claims to have had W.G. Grace playing on its pitch I'd be a wealthy fellow!

Just after 1pm, Kentley spotted a tweet from @PhilHayYEP listing the Leeds team.

Silvestri
Coyle P.McKay Cooper (Capt) Denton
Phillips Grimes
Dallas Doukara Whitehouse
Antonsson

Subs: Peacock-Farrell, Ayling, Roofe, Sacko, Vieira, Wilks, Vann.

All Leeds fans knew that Monk was going to make a lot of changes; he'd spoken before the game about how he needed to *"balance"* his squad and ensure he had a strong, fresh team for the vital league game at Blackburn in three days' time as well as picking a side to go to Sutton *"and win the game"*. But was this team he'd picked really capable of beating Sutton? I

---

[1] *http://www.suttoncricketclub.com/history/*

had my doubts. I thought it was going to be difficult for us if we picked a 2nd XI but this wasn't a 2nd XI, it was more like a 3rd XI! Paul McKay, Billy Whitehouse, Jack Vann and Mallik Wilks were not even listed in the first team squad with squad numbers and didn't have a single appearance between them, while Tyler Denton and substitute keeper Bailey Peacock-Farrell had three career appearances between them. Cooper and Sacko were coming back after very recent injuries and of course Mallik Wilks had only a few days earlier suffered the death of his brother. I doubted if our named starting XI would have ever played a full 90 minutes as a team together before and I was seriously concerned we could even put up a fight against an experienced Sutton side with plenty of league football experience that was far more used to playing on a plastic pitch than we were and which had been playing together all season. There was the added fact that the little ground would be packed to the rafters and that the Sutton players would be selling their talents to a live TV audience. Only Stuart Dallas remained from the starting XI that faced Forest the previous Wednesday.

It was a damp, miserable afternoon with rain coming down on-and-off all day and we trudged, hunched against the weather around the corner to the little ground. A huge queue had formed at the home turnstiles snaking all the way down Gander Green Lane, presumably as everyone had turned up at the same time and every ticket had to be checked and one end torn off by a turnstile operator. Kentley and I checked with a steward where we needed to head and he said we could try going round the ground in an anti-clockwise direction but we might find it blocked and have to come back. We had plenty of time so we tried anyway but sure enough our way was blocked by the BT Sport TV paraphernalia. Retracing our steps we spotted Alan Pardew arriving in a shiny black Range Rover, presumably to do some punditry.

Around 750 Leeds fans were either packed into the tiny 5-step terrace which was just about under cover or lined up along the boundary fence around one corner which was open to the elements. Just as the game kicked-off the rain started again and it was an appropriately miserable evening that became ever more miserable as the game progressed.

To be honest, Leeds were never in this game and my worst fears were proved well founded. It was a game that would prove beyond doubt that good as our first XI or maybe XII or XIII is, beyond that we are poor and it was easy to see why Garry Monk was urging the club to bring in a couple more quality players that we so desperately needed to support our good first half of the season. We were sloppy, slow, and weak in the challenge and in all respects inferior to a Sutton side that oozed passion and aggression. They had some big lads too and they were quick to close us down to thwart any possible progress towards their goal. Within minutes of the start they had the ball in our net as a lofted pass found Paul McKay and Cooper wanting and Roarie Deacon got behind them both to smash the ball high into the top corner. This time Leeds were saved by a liner's flag but replays would show it was a borderline decision. An acrobatic dive and save from Silvestri was then needed to keep out another powerful shot from the lively Deacon who was running rings around the Leeds back line. Liam Cooper then lost his man again but this time pulled him down and got a booking for his efforts. The problems were mounting for Leeds. Another good run and shot from Deacon was then followed up by Bedsente Gomis and Silvestri somehow stopped his shot going in with his legs. It was all Sutton with just one half-chance from Stuart Dallas troubling the home keeper and that he dealt with easily. Before the half was over that man Deacon had tested Silvestri yet again with another fierce shot that was heading for the top corner. I did wonder if Garry Monk might be making an offer for the Sutton striker just as Don Revie bought John Faulkner after that game in 1970. We could do worse on this performance.

We got to half-time still level but as I made my way to the very rudimentary bogs in the corner of the ground where ivy was growing through the roof, there was lots of head shaking from Leeds fans. The second half started in the same manner with the amber and chocolate shirts of the home side usually first to any second balls and looking far and away the better side. Just eight minutes into the new half, the inevitable happened. It was another long ball over the top of the Leeds defence, this time down the Sutton left wing. It was a ball that we've seen Marco Silvestri struggle with time and time again, especially last season when Bellusci and Bamba were in front of him. *"To come or not to come?"* that was his question. He chose to *sort of come*, out to the corner of his box as Lewie Coyle similarly dithered. Maxime Biamou wasn't dithering though, he kept going but as he made to go past Silvestri the keeper pushed him to the ground. The ball had now broken free and Deacon was after it but Lewie Coyle got to his feet quick enough to stick out a boot and down went the troublesome Sutton striker. It was all a bit theatrical but there was an argument for at least two penalties either for the Silvestri push or the clipping of Deacon's heels. Referee Stuart Attwell pondered for a second or two and then pointed to the spot. The Sutton skipper, Jamie Collins stepped up to take it and as Silvestri went full length to his right Collins stroked the ball inside the other post. Nightmare!

Leeds threw on Hadi Sacko and then young Mallik Wilks and finally, with twenty minutes left, Kemar Roofe. But truth be told Leeds were no better and Sutton could now see and smell a big money 5th round tie; they were not going to be denied. A second yellow card for Liam Cooper meant he departed the pitch before the rest and in hindsight he was the lucky one. At the final whistle many Leeds fans hurled abuse at their own players and eventually that awful *"What the fu***** hell was that?"* chant broke out just as it did so often last season in our worst moments. In fact, in so many ways this Leeds performance mimicked many we saw last season when Silvestri would blunder and our centre backs would dither. For me though it was still distasteful to show hostility to our own players, I felt many of our own fans were actually missing the point. It was not that this team of ours today had played badly; it was more a case that they just were not good enough and had so little experience of playing together. Garry Monk, by throwing so many youngsters together in such a difficult atmosphere was the real cause of this defeat. When many of the fans around me then started hurling abuse at Luke Ayling who was walking towards us to throw a shirt to the crowd I almost lost my temper. Come on lads, he didn't even get on the pitch! Show some effin respect to a bloke who has helped transform our defence this season. Ayling looked shocked at the response he was getting.

As Kentley fired the BMW back up the motorways on roads awash from the pouring rain, we listened as Garry Monk gave his post-match reactions. *"It was a very disappointing result and a very frustrating performance,"* said Monk.

"Nothing went right for us, that is what led to the defeat, a poor performance and a poor result.

"I take full responsibility, I am the one who selects the team and I made a lot of changes, it didn't work out, it backfired.

"We have a game against Blackburn Rovers in three days' time and I had to try and get the balance right to make sure there is a freshness and energy."

Fair enough, Monk was taking the responsibility but I was still angry. I know it's not just Leeds that have become afflicted by this *"promotion is everything"* attitude but I felt cheated. Seven hours in the car in the pouring rain and having splashed out £70 on the trip. I'd spent the afternoon watching a bunch of U23 players that in the main, we will never see regularly turning out for the first team. Even Neil Redfearn would say publically after the game that he didn't understand why the likes of McKay, Whitehouse, Vann and Wilks were included when there were *"plenty of better players than them"* fresh out of the Leeds Academy: let's face it, he should know.

On Monday night, sat at home I watched as the 5th round draw was made by Gareth Southgate and Robbie 'my hair is ridiculous' Savage. They picked out the ball of Sutton United and then that of Arsenal. I felt cheated again; that would have been some tie had it been the Arsenal at Elland Road instead. As it was, it would be yet another season of sweet f a cup success for Leeds United.

Sutton United 1 **Leeds United 0** (Collins (53, pen))
4,997 **(Leeds 739)**

Turnips or Swedes?

Although our game at Blackburn was on Wednesday this week, several Championship games were played on Tuesday including Barnsley's home game with Wolves. Barnsley quickly went two goals down inside 36 minutes and then, three minutes before half-time Alex Mowatt, on his Barnsley debut, was sent off for a lunging two footed tackle! It seemed like the football gods were all aligned against the Tykes at the moment as news had also come through this week that former Leeds man Aidy White was out for the foreseeable future with a recurrence of a groin injury. The lad seemed to be almost perpetually injured when he was at Leeds.

Tuesday was also the final day of the transfer window and during the day we finally got news of a new face arriving at Leeds. The Leeds official website announced: *"Leeds United are delighted to confirm the transfer deadline day arrival of Spanish winger Alfonso Pedraza. The talented 20-year-old joins United from La Liga outfit Villarreal CF on loan until the end of the season, with an option in place to sign permanently in the summer.*

Pedraza has spent the first half of this season on loan at Spanish Segunda División outfit CD Lugo, where he made 23 appearances, with his final game coming in last Sunday's 1-1 draw with Real Zaragoza."

Then, while we were still absorbing this news, just like those flipping London buses, along came a second signing, another loan and blow me down, another winger; 24 year-old Modou Barrow from Swansea. I just hoped he was going to prove to be the wheel deal... Monk first signed Barrow when he was manager at the Swans back in 2014.

Neither player was signed in time for the Blackburn game but both would be available for Huddersfield the following Sunday. It reminded me very much of that ill-fated game at Hillsborough in January 2014 when, a few days after being dumped out of the FA Cup at Rochdale, we lost 6 – 0 with two debutant wingers; Jimmy Kebe and Cameron Stewart. I sincerely hoped this wouldn't be history repeating itself. Oh, and if anyone was still superstitious over that number 17, Pedraza wore 17 for the Spanish U19s when they won the European Championship last year while Barrow wore 17 in pre-season last summer for Swansea; anyone superstitious?

I was flying solo for the Blackburn trip – Kentley and his lady friend Lottie were meeting me in the pub before the game. As always I left super early and with no delays was parking up on Blackburn Road around 4:30pm. In the pub, the Golden Cup, at the top of the hill, there was a handful of folk to begin with but it steadily filled up and by the time Kentley and Lottie arrived it was steaming as usual. A couple of pints of Thwaites Original helped to wash down two of the pubs excellent cheese and tomato baps and I was ready for the game.

Green
Ayling Bartley Jansson Berardi
O'Kane Bridcutt (Capt)
Sacko Roofe Dallas
Wood

Subs: Silvestri, Coyle, Vieira, Phillips, Hernandez, Antonsson. Doukara.

As everyone expected, not many that started at Sutton were in the XI tonight; just Stuart Dallas in fact. The only surprise was that Hernandez was only on the bench, while I could have made a case for the inclusion of Vieira instead of O'Kane and maybe Doukara for Sacko. Those four seemed to have one good game and then one poor one so it was just a matter of hoping when they were picked they did the business. There was no one player who stood out to me as particularly dangerous in the Rovers' squad and they were still in serious trouble; three points adrift of the safety zone. They did have the experienced Danny Graham in their side; Leeds fans with long memories would remember him making three appearances for Leeds while on loan from Middlesbrough back in 2006.

We had to meet up with Kev at the ground; he'd kindly offered to swap his lower tier ticket for Kentley's upper tier one so that Kentley and Lottie could stand together. I chatted with Humph the Shroppy Whites' mini-bus driver and then Gaz S while Kev and Kentley did the swap. The fan-zone was in full swing just outside the away entrance and seemed to be popular with the huge contingent of Leeds fans; almost 6,000 of us would be filling the Bryan Douglas Darwen Stand.

Kentley, Lottie, Nigel and I all squeezed into row 29 and we took in the view. It was a great position, near the top of the lower tier behind the goal but Kev shouted down from the upper tier that his view was better; he was on the front row up there! I was amazed how few Blackburn fans had turned up; the upper tier of the stand at the far end was completely empty, presumably closed, while the rest of the ground was only sparsely occupied. I'd learn after the game that many Rovers' season ticket holders boycotted this game in their ongoing protest against the Blackburn owners, Venky's, the Indian chicken meat processing outfit. The attendance would be reported as 17,026 but there was *no way* there were that many in the ground and local media would suggest it could have been nearer 12,000, with the official figures boosted by those season tickets that are these days included whether the holders are at the game or not. It meant that we had pretty much half of the support in the ground and it must have felt more like a home game for our lads. The only noise coming from the Blackburn supporters was a lone drummer over to our left who did his best to comply as we periodically demanded: *"Drummer, drummer, give us a song"* throughout the game only to then drown out his beats with: *"We don't need a drum, we're Leeds United, we don't need a drum!"*

The first half of this game is best left unreported; it was a poor example of Championship football. Leeds had got a mixture of the away kits on today; the shirts and socks of the yellow strip and the shorts from the blue strip. We thus looked very much like the Swedish international side which must have made Pontus feel at home but truth be told we played more like turnips than Swedes. Rovers predictably began strongly and even had the ball in our net as early as the 4th minute when we witnessed again how Rob Green is not the best under a high ball. This time he was saved when the referee adjudged he'd been fouled as he jumped. For us Leeds fans, it was particularly disappointing to see Leeds perform so sluggishly when we all expected a fresh, vibrant display courtesy of the fact that almost all of these players were not weighed down by the fatigue of playing at Sutton. In fact, probably the brightest of our players was Stuart Dallas who *did* play there. That completely blew the theory that players need to be rested and I did begin to wonder again what the benefit to the club was of that ridiculous strategy. But not only were we sluggish, we were weak, often being brushed aside in the challenge by the Rovers' players and losing out to most second balls. Eunan O'Kane was the main culprit, too often easily knocked off the ball and then feebly misplacing his passes when he wasn't. We were desperately missing Pablo in the middle too, no one was controlling and directing that area in behind our front line, probing and testing the Blackburn defence. For whatever reason, Hadi Sacko was seldom in the game either. It confirmed to me that Hernandez for his creativity, Doukara for his strength and Ronnie Vieira for his youthful aggression should probably have started instead of Sacko, Roofe and O'Kane. We needed to tighten up down our left flank too; Blackburn got through time and time again to knock crosses over including the one in the 4th minute that got Green in a tangle.

Garry Monk was thinking along the same lines too and during the interval it was clear that Pablo at least was coming on, as he was put through his paces with one of the coaches while the rest of the subs knocked a ball about. Sure enough, when the teams emerged after the break there was no Hadi Sacko and Leeds reshaped with Pablo in his usual advanced midfield role. It took him a while to find his range as we've noticed before when he comes on but gradually Leeds started to look a much more joined up outfit. We'd got to the hour mark though without a single shot on target and at that point Souley Doukara was sent on to replace the ineffective Kemar Roofe. Predictably, every time Souley got the ball an impassioned plea of *"Shooooooooooooot"* rang out from the Bryan Douglas Stand.

We got to the 74th minute and the only effort on target from either side was a fierce left wing free-kick from Blackburn that Rob Green did well to palm away. But then Leeds got the break they needed. A long high clearance by the home defence was deftly brought down by Gaetano Berardi who immediately slid the ball further right to Liam Bridcutt. He looked up and hit a long diagonal ball over to the left side of the Blackburn area, over to our right. Chris Wood was there and he just nudged a Blackburn defender out of the way but let the ball run on to Stuart Dallas who took it down on his chest. The ball ran another couple of yards and took two bounces before Dallas put his left boot through it sending it across the face of the keeper to nestle in the bottom corner. The celebrations were predictably manic on and off the pitch. On it, Dallas was mobbed down in the right hand corner below us with most of the players joining him there; all apart from Pontus Jansson who was doing his own thing pretending to be the conductor for our orchestra. A couple of flares hurtled down onto the edge of the pitch from somewhere in the Leeds crowd and soon we were all engulfed in the smoke. There was only a quarter of an hour to go and Blackburn had shown as little as we had up until this point so the Leeds fans were celebrating what they assumed would be three points and another step towards promotion. What could possibly go wrong?

A few minutes passed and then Monk made his final change sending on Vieira for O'Kane. That really did look like the final piece of the jigsaw as young Ronnie set about snapping at the heels of any Rover that came near him. With that bite now restored at the back of the midfield, Pablo now getting in his stride further forward and Souley Doukara now throwing his weight around on the Leeds right we looked dominant for the next few minutes and the celebrations continued unabated. Then, disaster struck.

Kyle Bartley harried and chased Craig Conway back towards his own goal, forcing the midfielder to retreat thirty yards or more before he managed to slip the ball inside. Then, horror of horrors, a Blackburn player hit a low bobbler from more than thirty yards out and it bounced twice on its ragged journey before nestling in the bottom corner of our net. *"Gordon Bennett, what the f*** is going on?"* I cry. Well, actually it was Elliott Bennett and now for the first time all night there was a bit of noise from the home fans. We'd managed to snatch a draw from the jaws of victory with a sloppy, sloppy goal. What a waste of two points.

But to paraphrase the great Benny Hill, *"Strange things are a happening in and around Leeds this season; is that the wind a rustling or the hinges on the gate to promotion? Or Leeds' ghostly glory days stirring up a commotion?"* Pablo Hernandez is suddenly slaloming through the Blackburn defence and a little dinked left-foot shot is blocked away for a corner, over to our right. Pontus Jansson, Kyle Bartley and Chris Wood gather in the middle, six footers all, as Pablo jogs over to take the corner. It's going through my mind that Leeds now regularly score from such situations; 17 set pieces so far this season had brought us goals in league games, a win today would be our 17th league win of the season…hmmmn 17… Pablo delicately places the ball on the very edge of the quadrant, it takes him ages to get it right then he takes five steps back and holds his right hand in the air to signal he's ready. When I watched the replay back on LUTV a few days later, Thom Kirwin says on commentary: *"Imagine the scenes if we could score a winner from this…"*

We watch transfixed as Pablo runs forward and clips the ball into the middle and then we can see the giant figure of Pontus Jansson hurtling through the air to meet it full tilt with his forehead. It absolutely ripped into the net and Pontus didn't break stride as he continued his run until he was stood on the byline in front of us. *"Imagine the scenes…"* Pontus went right to the corner before stopping to perform a perfect military salute to us all and then was buried under a pile of yellow and blue as the rest caught up with him. The Leeds fans all around were going absolutely mental; Kentley sweeping

Lottie off her feet and Nigel doing a sort of Paddington Bear jig while all I could do was keep mouthing *"Oh my God this is unbelievable!"* I had flashbacks of that oh so similar moment at Norwich not so long ago when Ronnie Vieira walloped that long range shot home in injury time to win that one. All that was missing was my mate with the Norway bobble hat screaming *"We're gannin up wi the Toon!"* What a moment this was. Leeds saw the game out professionally as Chris Wood won a couple more corners and then kept the ball there with a little help from Pablo. All around the ground the Rovers fans were now streaming away much like those Norwich fans did on Bonfire Night, while the Leeds fans sang and danced until the final whistle and beyond. At the end of the game the big screen showed the scores in the other two Championship games being played tonight; Fulham had won 2 – 0 at Burton and the Toon were leading 2 – 1 at home to QPR.

As Kentley, Lottie and I wandered back up Blackburn Road we were passed by the long stream of Leeds' coaches heading back to the motorway. The Shroppies' mini-bus went slowly past with Humph at the Wheel and we all gave each other the Leeds salute. The sound of, *"Leeds are going up",* could be heard as another coach went by. Back in the car I switched on the radio just in time to hear that QPR had grabbed a late equaliser at Newcastle; the night was getting better and better! Garry Monk's summary of the game was spot on as usual, we'd got away with one.

"It wasn't pretty by any stretch of the imagination. Neither team got control of anything. (It was) a bit to and fro, a bit of a grind. We defended our box very well, stayed strong when it was difficult and in those crucial moments we scored two good goals. Yes (we were) a bit lucky to come away with the three points but the mentality and character is what I was pleased with."[1]

Blackburn Rovers 1 **Leeds United 2 (Dallas (74)**, Bennett (83), **Jansson (89))**

17,026 (Yeah, as if!) **(Leeds 6,402)**

---

[1] *http://www.bbc.co.uk/sport/football/38740344*

John Smith's bitter atmosphere

The night following our game at Ewood Park, Huddersfield Town convincingly beat Brighton 3 – 1 but the Seagulls remained top with 60 points, a point ahead of Newcastle. Then came Reading, 55, Leeds, 54 and Huddersfield, 52. Derby completed the top six with 46. Leeds and Reading had both played a game more than the others.

On the same night, the Leeds website announced the news we'd all wanted to hear for weeks. Pontus Jansson had agreed a deal to complete a permanent transfer in the summer. There were still other issues we wanted settled – a new longer contract for Garry Monk and one for Kyle Bartley in particular – but this was a big comfort to us all. To know that the iconic figure of Pontus was now going to be around until 2020, other things being equal, was great news indeed and I raised a glass of malt to that.

Hard on the heels of that good news came another statement on the Leeds official website. The FA had finally pronounced judgement on Cellino's appeal against his ban in relation to his part the Ross McCormack transfer case. The fines and the length of Cellino's ban were all reduced with Cellino now due to be suspended from all football activity for 12 months (originally 18 months) from 18th February 2017. Ironically therefore, his last day in office could well be the *17th* of February. You couldn't make this up could you? The Leeds response was as follows:

"Decision of the Appeal Board Regarding the Transfer of Ross McCormack

Leeds United Football Club can confirm that it has today been partially successful in its Appeal against the original decision connected to this matter. The Club's fine for allegedly breaching FA Agents Regulations has been reduced from £250,000 to £200,000.

Although the Appeal has been successful, the Club remains disappointed by the outcome and the size of the fine that remains.

The Club are also incredibly disappointed by the fine and ban imposed upon Mr Cellino, despite reductions following the Appeal. Mr Cellino is responsible for significantly reducing the Club's debt and wage bill as well as the appointment of Garry Monk. Mr Cellino has been the integral leader of the Club's re-emergence this season.

The Club will now consider all options with its legal team before making any further comment." [1]

After a couple more days, a further statement was published confirming that Cellino was to take his appeal to the next stage – the so called rule K option. It was also confirmed that his fine had been reduced to £100,000 from £250,000 and his ban to 12 months from 18 months as a result of the initial appeal. The first appeal was clearly well worthwhile and did now make the initial punishments seem a little over the top. Back to court everyone!

Huddersfield was next on our fixture list and all Leeds fans were nervous. Even Garry Monk confessed the Terriers were favourites on their own turf having just beaten the league leaders. I was driving again for this one and having picked up Kentley just after 8am we had a trouble free Sunday morning journey up the M6 and M62, arriving in Huddersfield at 9:45am. It being Sunday, we were able to find roadside parking not far from the ground; this was another live on Sky

---

[1] https://www.leedsunited.com/news/club-news/21576/leeds-united-decision-of-the-appeal-board-regarding-the-transfer-of-ross-mccormack

TV game kicking-off at 12 noon. We optimistically tried the Yorkshire Rose pub but that was closed, so the next best thing, without walking miles, was a Costa Coffee outlet just a bit further along the main road. Predictably it had a fair few Leeds fans in there and I had a quick chat with Andrew L at one point – he mentioned that Kyle Bartley was a doubt due to a bug of some sort.

Green
Ayling Bartley Jansson Berardi
Vieira Bridcutt (Capt)
Doukara Hernandez Dallas
Wood

Subs: Silvestri, Coyle, Pedraza, Barrow, O'Kane, Cooper, Antonsson.

We were still in Costa when we spotted the team on @PhilHayYEP's Twitter feed; it was the XI that were on the pitch at the end of the Blackburn game, so Hernandez, Doukara and Vieira got to start this time. It was the team both Kentley and I expected and wanted to start and obviously Kyle Bartley had got over his bug sufficiently to take his usual place alongside Pontus. The word was that Kemar Roofe was struggling with a rib injury while Sacko and Phillips were left out altogether. The two new boys, Pedraza and Barrow were on the bench. Huddersfield manager David Wagner raised a few eyebrows by leaving Nahki Wells and Izzy Brown on their bench but their main driving force in midfield, Aaron Mooy did start.

As we stood looking down at the pitch there was plenty of noise coming from the Terriers' fans over to our right who were sharing the Chadwick Lawrence Stand with us. Somewhere among them was a drummer who seemed to have boundless energy as he banged his way through virtually the whole game. Just before kick-off a huge blue and white striped banner was unfurled covering most of their section and held aloft over their heads. At the bottom were the words: *"WE BLEED BLUE AND WHITE"*. The Leeds fans predictably scoffed at that with a rousing chant of *"What the f****** hell is that?"* Not long after the start we spotted the red and white flag of Turkey in the Huddersfield section over on the left-hand touchline and several Leeds fans including my old mate Phil B shouted at the stewards to get it removed which it eventually was. By the following Tuesday, Huddersfield had tracked down the bloke waving the flag and had issued him with an indefinite ban. It was no young yobbo; it was a 59 year-old bloke who should have known better. For obvious reasons it remains the most hurtful thing opposition fans can display when playing us and it was one of several things we'd witness today that let the home club down. The stadium itself though looked magnificent and with 22,400 inside it was pretty full; the capacity these days is 24,500 and Leeds had sold out their 1,958 tickets long ago. Leeds once again wore the Sweden-look yellow and blue strip they sported at Blackburn and as the sun broke through the clouds it looked pretty smart.

Leeds' football was looking pretty smart too in the early stages as we won three successive corners in the first ten minutes but Huddersfield had chances too and it was a decent game between two skilful sides. Chris Wood was put through by Hernandez and Wood's fierce left foot shot on the angle was only just parried away by the Terriers' keeper, Danny Ward. Then Rob Green did the same with a shot from the German Collin Quaner who was making his Terriers debut. On 25 minutes a tackle by Liam Bridcutt left Kasey Palmer on the turf and soon he was limping off to be replaced by Izzy Brown. Have I mentioned before how often we get stung by opposition substitutes?

Next, Rob Green was left helpless as an attempted clearance from Pontus Jansson smacked against Quaner's boot and looped up over the Leeds keeper but thankfully landed on the roof of the net with Pontus giving a little prayer to The Almighty. A few minutes later though and Leeds luck was all out of town.

Izzy Brown's first touch was a midfield header to Aaron Mooy who was starting to see more and more of the ball. He lifted it out to the Town right-wing where Berardi and Elias Kachunga tussled for it. Berardi got it all wrong as the ball slipped under his foot and Kachunga was away on his bike. Meanwhile Izzy Brown trotted down the middle following the play. Berardi went with Kachunga but Pontus came sliding across to prod the ball away from both of them but only as far as Tommy Smith who was following up. Smith toe-poked the ball first time across the area and then it was a case of whether Green or Izzy Brown got there first. Brown's outstretched right boot just touched the ball into the net ahead of Green's gloves; it was only Brown's second touch. Once Berardi had made the initial mistake it was a real rapier like attack from the home side and now their fans were going mental all around the ground, or at least they did for eight minutes...

Huddersfield scored in the 27th minute and now, in the 34th Pablo Hernandez was being bundled over by the man of the moment, Izzy Brown, over on the Leeds right wing at the far end of the ground. Pablo himself stood over the ball as the big men arrived in the box and then the Spaniard raised both arms above his head to signal his intentions. The initial cross was poor and it was easily headed straight back by the first Huddersfield defender but Pablo brought it down and immediately swept it back into the middle. This was a much better ball and it found Kyle Bartley's head and he in turn spotted Chris Wood just a yard or two away and in behind the Huddersfield defence. Wood took one touch to knock the ball towards the left post while Danny Ward was now wrong-footed and stranded at the other. It was then a simple tap-in for Wood just inside the other post. There were lots of blue and white arms in the air appealing for offside and boos rang out from the home crowd but replays would show that Bartley and Wood were both well onside and in fact it was a brilliantly placed header from Bartley to pick out the Leeds centre forward.

There was still time before the break for another of those lightning quick Huddersfield attacks and this time Mooy picked out Kachunga at the back-post but somehow Berardi dived in to block the shot and save the day. The Swiss full-back had made up for his earlier faux pas with that one. From the resulting corner, Quaner got free one on one with Green but once again our man spread himself to save a certain goal. It had been a thrilling first 45 minutes.

The second half wasn't quite as frenetic but such chances as did come went the way of the home side and then with an hour on the clock Leeds made their first change; our first look at Alfonso Pedraza who replaced Doukara. It was the signal for the pace to pick up again and first we were thanking Rob Green once more for another point blank save as Quaner found himself six yards out with only Green to beat. As Leeds brought the ball out it found its way to Pedraza on half-way. He cruised towards us with the ball at his feet and then, with nothing much on in the way of a pass, he put his left foot through the ball and only the big right hand of Ward stopped it smashing into the top left corner just below us. Leeds made two more changes; Barrow was wheeled on (I hope you are getting these!) for Stuart Dallas and then Eunan O'Kane swapped with a visibly shattered Pablo Hernandez. We were into the final ten minutes and I was ready to accept the point.

The clock ticked on to 89 minutes and Mo Barrow's first real contribution was a foul challenge just outside our own box. Nahki Wells fired in the free-kick but Leeds headed clear and then Huddersfield recycled the ball back into the middle with a cross that Kyle Bartley again headed away. This time, Kachunga gathered it and after turning and twisting on the Town left wing he played it back to Mooy, 30 yards from goal. We could see Mooy getting the ball onto his right foot and we could hear the Town fans shouting *"Shoooot"* but then we breathed a sigh of relief as he horribly mishit it. It was running tamely to the left of the goal at the far end of the ground and the Leeds fans were just starting an ironic cheer. Then, to our disbelief, Luke Ayling sticks out a boot and deflects the ball in behind our back-line. It ran perfectly to Michael Hefele, all on his own, six yards out and he stabbed the ball past Green. The John Smith's Stadium erupted in pandemonium all around. To our right the vocal section of the home crowd were now celebrating like they'd won the FA Cup while over to our left their manager, David Wagner, was racing across the corner of the pitch to leap upon his players who were all bouncing up and down in a group hug and fist pumping for England. Finally, Wagner turned and walked back across the corner of the pitch to the touchline and then continued to fist pump and celebrate all the way back to the dugouts. As he tried to walk across the Leeds technical area though, Garry Monk took a step forward to block his way and the two collided with a bump before grappling with each other. In seconds all hell broke out as the staff of both teams got involved in some handbags at dawn. Then, spotting what was happening, all the players of both sides came racing across to join in! It was all jostling and tugging rather than punches being thrown but it got both sets of fans going and for a few minutes it was as hostile an atmosphere as I can remember. Watching replays of the fracas later, the funniest thing was seeing Garry Monk quickly walk away and shove his hands back deep in his pockets, seconds after he stepped into Wagner's path leaving all sorts of mayhem in his wake. He couldn't have caused more disruption if he'd have pulled the pin from a grenade and lobbed it into the Terriers dugout!

Eventually the referee sent both managers to the stand and the game got underway for the final few minutes but there was little more football action and Leeds were beaten 2 -1. It was a cruel way to lose it, so late in the game and with an unlucky break of the ball but in truth Huddersfield probably deserved the three points for their second half display and they looked a class outfit once Izzy Brown and later, Nahki Wells took to the pitch. Aaron Mooy was also the controlling influence in the middle third all afternoon.

I have to say the celebrations in the John Smith's were way over the top; it was three points folks not the World Cup Final! I wondered whether Leeds may yet have the last laugh if the two sides met again in the play-offs; Huddersfield versus Leeds at Wembley maybe? Outside the ground the hostilities continued as the home fans hurled abuse at Leeds fans waiting to board the coaches. There may not have been any beer on sale in the John Smith's today but the atmosphere was decidedly bitter!

Huddersfield Town 2 **Leeds United 1** (Brown (27), **Wood (35)**, Hefele (89))
22,400 **(Leeds 1,958)**

Only human

The big tune of the moment was "Human" by Rory Graham, aka 'Rag'n'Bone Man'; whenever you listened to the radio or switched on the TV its main lyric – *"I'm only human after all"* was there; an annoyingly stubborn lyric and tune that stuck in your head.

One bloke we all thought was *not* human, our very own superhero, brick-heading, Viking warrior, Pontus Jansson, was ill. No one knew quite what superbug it was that had the audacity to strike him down in his prime ahead of an important game but as we sat shielding our ears from another incredibly loud band in the Pavilion, Derek spotted this perturbing tweet from @PhilHayYEP: *"Illness is what we're hearing with Jansson. Definitely out today. #lufc"* A general mood of cautious optimism suddenly turned to nervous apprehension and even a 3 – 0 to Leeds pre-match forecast from Steve Hodge, who joined Lorimer and Mel Sterland with Jed Stone in between ear-splitting sets from Apollo Junction, failed to improve our mood. Inevitably the conspiracy theorists were soon at work spinning possible alternative reasons for the giant Swede's absence; a big fall out with Kyle Bartley was the main one touted during furtive conversations in dark corners of the Pavilion. Much as there had been a bright new Monk-inspired positivity about the Leeds United dressing room this season, it didn't take much to bring out the sort of rumours we heard regularly when we were crap every week!

Green
Ayling Bartley Cooper Berardi
Vieira Bridcutt (Capt)
Dallas Hernandez Pedraza
Wood

Subs: Silvestri, O'Kane, Barrow, Coyle, Sacko, Doukara, Roofe.

Very few fans had confidence in Liam Cooper anymore and even those that did would still admit he was nowhere near as commanding in the middle as the magic hat man. I would have preferred us to put Luke Ayling back in the middle and use Lewie Coyle at right-back as we'd done in the past when both Pontus and Coops were unavailable. But with Cooper fit, I never thought Monk would do that as it really would've been a signal that even Monk had lost faith in him. The rest of the team was pretty much what most fans thought it would be, although everyone had their own preference as to who'd play out wide; in my view there wasn't much to choose between Dallas, Sacko, Doukara, Roofe or either of the new recruits, Pedraza and Barrow. They all had their pros and cons. The Cardiff side, now managed by Neil Warnock of course, included Sol Bamba but there was no Lee Peltier who was injured. Familiar names from previous encounters were scattered throughout their squad including Sean Morrison, Greg Halford, Craig Noone, Peter Whittingham, Rickie Lambert and Junior Hoilett, albeit the last two were only on the bench.

Sol Bamba had been the mainstay at the heart of the Bluebirds' defence since Warnock arrived in South Wales and that was despite the two falling out big-time when Bamba lost his head against Ipswich in December. Warnock explained ahead of our game how the many messages on Social Media from Leeds fans about Bamba had helped in his pre-match motivation for the erratic defender. *"They were saying 'You Cardiff fans, wait until you see him make a blunder'. I keep pinning them up on the board and letting him read them every week just to remind him to play the game simple. I owe Leeds fans quite a lot for the way Bamba is playing at the minute."*

Leeds had not really played well since we beat Derby on 13th January. In the five games since then, we'd lost to Barnsley and Huddersfield, beaten Forest and Blackburn and of course the Third XI had gone out of the FA Cup at Sutton. Many Leeds fans still bemoaned the decision to effectively forfeit the Sutton game as they saw it as halting the valuable momentum we had going before then but that really ignored the fact that the defeat at Oakwell came a week earlier than the massacre at Gander Green Lane. For me, I just wanted a solid win over Cardiff to maintain our top six position and to confirm that a play-off spot was rightly ours; we *were* one of the top six sides in the Championship. All the top sides were now winning regularly and you had to believe they would all come through fairly easily against the likes of Cardiff. Less than a win and the doubts would creep in and we'd all be thinking that maybe the wheels were coming off. *Well, we were only human after all.*

We were in the middle of another cold snap so we were all wrapped up in scarves and woolly hats as we took our places on the Kop. Elland Road was busy and over 31,000 were in the ground; there were new faces everywhere I looked. One face I couldn't see was that of Kentley the Stokie, but he regularly arrived a few minutes after kick-off. I hoped he'd taken heed of my tweet warning folk about the annual Valentine's fun-fair that was taking up much of the club's car park space though…

Actually he hadn't! He pushed his way along row GG to take his place beside me at 3:26pm precisely! When there was a break in play he explained, *"All the bloody car parks are full because of that ruddy fun-fair, I've just had to dump the car in a bush down a side street"*. I rolled my eyes but told him he hadn't missed much. I suddenly realised that I was almost whispering and then it struck me why. Elland Road, despite being pretty full in most parts was doing a passable imitation of a library. It was really quiet and there was hardly any singing coming from either the Kop or the usually prolific South Stand. There were probably two reasons for this; one, there must have been a hell of a lot of non-regulars in the crowd and, two, there wasn't actually much to sing about.

Leeds started well and looked determined to avoid back-to-back defeats, something we'd managed since we lost to Forest and Huddersfield back in early September. Pablo was far more involved than of late although he still didn't appear to be at his magical best and little came of his many forays into Cardiff territory. Alfonso Pedraza seemed a bit out on a limb too and saw precious little of the ball; he was doing nothing in my mind to show he was any better than any of the other wide players we had in the squad. Chances at either end were few and far between but the best went to the Bluebirds just as Kentley arrived. A Craig Noone free-kick found the head of Greg Halford in acres of space in the Leeds area in front of the Kop but fortunately Halford was as surprised as the rest of us by his good fortune and he headed straight at Rob Green. Kyle Bartley looked even more laid back than he usually does as Halford got away from him. The Leeds defence all looked at each other as if wondering *"Where the f*** is Pontus!"* Another fickle referee, James Linington, was also helping to slow the game down and such noise as the Leeds crowd did muster was mostly aimed at him. The half-time whistle was a bit of a relief to be honest.

The second half began much the same as the first ended, with Leeds upping the tempo and looking neat and tidy in possession but it didn't last long and soon Cardiff's plan to smother us took effect again. Referee Linington's long disciplinary interventions also continued to damp down any momentum the game threatened to generate. Then, less than ten minutes into the new half, Cardiff silenced the already quiet Elland Road completely. It was really a case of déjà vu as Craig Noone swung a long diagonal ball into the Leeds penalty area from out on the Cardiff right wing in front of the West Stand. Just as we'd seen Greg Halford all on his own in the first half, now it was Sean Morrison looking like a leper with BO ghosting in to head past a static looking Rob Green with Luke Ayling two yards behind the action.

Leeds were not making any impression on what looked to be a fairly ordinary Cardiff side. If anything we still seemed more concerned to protect our own back-line as Liam Bridcutt went deeper and deeper, often playing behind Cooper and Bartley. With thirty minutes left, Garry Monk made his first change; Hadi Sacko for Stuart Dallas. Within seconds of coming on he set up a decent near post chance for Chris Wood but sadly Wood hammered the ball low into the side netting from a tight angle. Then, a few minutes later, the game was as good as over.

You had to wonder about those rumours about Bartley and Jansson falling out; something wasn't quite right with Kyle today. Maybe he was just missing his right-hand man but he also had words with his good mate Luke Ayling as the two of them messed about with the ball in front of the East Stand. Eventually they got the ball back to Liam Bridcutt, almost on the Leeds byline and he lofted the ball down the right wing. It bounced once and Hadi Sacko lost the challenge in the air to Aron Gunnarsson who then skipped away from a knackered-looking Pablo Hernandez. Ronnie Vieira came across to make a tackle but it was half-hearted and Gunnarsson came away from that challenge with the ball and with Ronnie doing that old Leeds defensive thing; sitting on his arse on the turf. The Cardiff man then accelerated first past Luke Ayling and then our out of sorts looking Kyle Bartley. It was like school rugby; you know, when the really big lad in the opposition gets the ball and suddenly half your team stop and rub their legs feigning a pulled thigh muscle! I used to do it all the time! Kenneth Zohore was waiting on the edge of our area with no Leeds player within spitting distance and when Gunnarsson laid the ball back to him he steered it accurately into the corner of the net . With the Leeds defence looking around at each other, arms limply by their sides, looking dazed and bewildered it really did have the look of a wagon with the wheels coming off.

Roofe replaced Pedraza and Doukara came on for Vieira in the final minutes and Leeds did finally seem to understand the urgency of the situation. Hadi Sacko and Pablo had a few excursions down the right wing and they fashioned half-chances for Wood and Roofe and we won a couple of corners that resulted in headers that gave the Kop some catching practice but we never looked remotely like scoring. To add insult to the injury our promotion hopes had already suffered, Liam Bridcutt picked up a second yellow card near the end and he would now miss the Bristol game next Tuesday. For the last few minutes Pablo was our only central midfield player, and he was totally shattered.

At the final whistle there were boos from some folk in the Kop but even the booing was half-hearted to be honest. The match statistics would later show that Leeds bossed the possession to the tune of 71% to 29% and had 17 attempts on goal but only three of them hit the target; I couldn't remember the Bluebirds' keeper having to stretch himself once. It was a limp display and almost gave the impression that maybe it wasn't only Pontus, maybe all the others had the early symptoms of some debilitating virus or other. Leeds held onto their 5th spot in the table but with wins for Newcastle, Brighton, Huddersfield, Wednesday and Norwich, and draws for Reading and Derby, Leeds were the only side in the top eight to lose in this round of games. The teams that were going to finish in the top six would not be losing many more games this season; they would just keep getting stronger as the finishing line approached. Leeds had to sort themselves out quickly and come out fighting against Bristol or they'd rapidly be overtaken by the likes of Derby, Norwich and Fulham.

Kentley left a few minutes before full time, eager to get his car extracted from those bushes and to get back on the road home before the inevitable post-match traffic chaos. I was sat on a very quiet Shropshire Whites' coach as we inched our way through the roadworks on the M621 when my phone buzzed; it was a text from Kentley that read simply: *"And a parking fine to finish the afternoon off."* I wasn't sure if it was prompted by Kentley's text or the memory of our defensive lapses against Cardiff but that bloody song came back into my head:

I'm only human
I make mistakes
I'm only human
That's all it takes
To put the blame on me
Don't put the blame on me[1]

Leeds United 0 Cardiff City 2 (Morrison (53), Zohore (71))
31,516 (Cardiff 433)

---

[1] *Human (2017) Written by Rag'n'Bone Man & Jamie Hartman, Sony Music Ent.*

A bit more like it

Spirits were lifted soon after the Cardiff game as Pontus and Kyle Bartley posted a tweet with them both smiling together and the legend *"We only fight together bro"*. That was enough for most of us to ditch any thoughts that the two had fallen out. Garry Monk was also suggesting that the throat infection that kept Pontus out of the Cardiff game had improved sufficiently to mean the big Swede was in contention for the Bristol home game on Valentine's Day.

It was another nightmare journey for Kentley and I that took the best part of two and a half hours to do the 100 miles from Stoke to Leeds. There was very little of the motorway network we use for this trip that wasn't now covered with roadworks and a 50mph speed limit but Kentley's weak bladder also cost us a few extra minutes. Kentley was driving and the old BMW was heading up Windy Hill on the M62 near Saddleworth when he suddenly announced he was desperate for a pee having unwisely necked a bottle of orange Lucozade early in the journey. *"Well you'll have to hang on a while there's bugger all round here mate"* I laughed. *"No, we're alright"* he replied *"I'll come off at Junction 22, there's a bit of a track across the moors that I've used before".* Sure enough he took the slip road off the motorway and then turned right up the A672 towards Saddleworth and at the top of the hill there was this little track off to the right, a dead end that led to some sort of communications mast. He jumped out, ran behind a hut underneath the giant grey steel pylon and then disappeared! If a passing cop car had spotted us I'm sure they'd have arrested us, probably having cross-checked us against that previous episode when we were coming home from the Cambridge game. Back on the motorway and we both chuckled as we overtook a white van with *"Monk's Security Systems"* emblazoned across the rear doors. *"I bet he's got Bartley and Jansson trussed up in there"* Kentley quipped!

We took our places at the usual table in the Pavilion with the three Durham Lads, Steve and Kev and discussed the likely team selection. If Pontus was fit and if the white van had safely delivered him and Kyle then there was no doubt what the defensive five would be while Wood and Hernandez we assumed were definite starters too. With no Bridcutt, who was suspended following his two yellows on Saturday, we guessed it would be two out of Vieira, O'Kane and Kalvin Phillips behind Pablo and then it was anybody's guess who the wide men would be.

Green
Ayling Bartley (Capt) Jansson Berardi
Vieira O'Kane
Sacko Hernandez Roofe
Wood

Subs: Silvestri, Cooper, Dallas, Pedraza, Barrow, Phillips, Doukara.

So Monk opted for Sacko and Roofe with Pedraza on the bench following his first start on Saturday. It was probably the XI I'd have come up with to be honest.

Having taken Mrs W to Wetherspoon's in Market Drayton for a romantic Valentine's Day breakfast in the morning (I am the last of the true romantics!) I was teetering a bit when I finally left the Pavilion to go across to the ground. I'd had a couple pints of draught Spitfire in Spoon's and had topped that up with four pints of Fosters in the Pavilion so I pretty much floated along the alleyway between the back of the North Stand and the fence behind which the Valentine's fun-fair was eerily silent and brooding in the early evening darkness. I remember thinking *"I hope Leeds bloody well score tonight... 'cos as sure as hell I won't!"*

Leeds started well and within the first couple of minutes Pablo weaved his way into the box and just hit his cross an inch or so too high for Roofe to make good contact at the back post in front of the Kop. Bristol had obviously won the toss and had turned us round and next David Cotterill hit a twenty five yard free-kick that Rob Green did well to save in front of the South Stand. Back came Leeds and Hernandez again set up Roofe but this time Kemar pulled his shot wide. Then we had the delight of seeing Pontus Jansson playing on the right wing as he raced to collect a ball that was headed clear from another Pablo corner. He jinked past his marker to get to the byline and then dinked a perfect little cross onto the head of Roofe who this time saw his effort scuffed away for another corner. The crowd loved that piece of Magic Hat Man magic and then a few minutes later we were up and celebrating the first goal of the night.

Eunan O'Kane was getting some unwanted Valentine's Day attention from Josh Brownhill and Jens Hegeler that left the Irishman prostrate on the turf as referee Jeremy Simpson blew for a free-kick. O'Kane got to his feet holding the ball and was still chatting to the ref about his mistreatment as he placed it back down on the grass. Pablo strolled up, bent down and moved the ball a foot further forward and then, on the blind side of the ref who was still talking to O'Kane, stabbed it into the Bristol penalty area to find Chris Wood in the inside right channel. Wood appeared to just nudge his marker who went tumbling to the ground and then swept the ball past Fabien Giefer in the visitor's goal. Nine times out of ten I'm certain the ref would demand the kick be taken again but ref Simpson must have been on a promise this Valentine's evening and he signalled the goal despite wild protests from the Robins that they weren't ready! It's that sort of quick thinking that Leeds miss when Pablo isn't out there.

The goal came in the 27th minute (Leeds had still only scored one goal in the first fifteen minutes all season) and things got better for us ten minutes later when the dangerous Tammy Abraham limped off with an injury. Abraham, a season long loanee from Chelsea, was the Robins' top scorer this season with 21 in all competitions; only Newcastle's Dwight Gayle and now our own Chris Wood had scored more in the Championship.

And right at the start of the second half it got even better as Pablo Hernandez took a pass from Luke Ayling, turned onto his left foot and struck the ball at goal. Aden Flint stuck out a boot to try to stop the shot but only managed to divert it wide of his own keeper and Leeds were 2 – 0 up and coasting. It was probably too comfortable for Leeds, we hadn't had a two goal lead this early all season, and slowly Bristol began to press despite Mo Barrow and then Kalvin Phillips being introduced to try to get the impetus back. My mind went back to the game at Bristol at the start of last season when we were also 2 – 0 up with one minute of normal time to go... we drew that one 2 – 2! The ref wasn't going to help us again either, as a blatant hand-ball by a Bristol defender in front of the South Stand was waved away denying Leeds a stone-wall penalty. Bristol got more and more of the ball and half-chances came fairly regularly but they were running out of time and Rob Green was blocking everything they threw at him.

We were well past the 89th minute now and no one expected or wanted any late drama but we still contrived to hand Bristol the merest glimpse of a comeback as they grabbed a consolation goal in the 6th minute of added time. A Matty Taylor shot was saved at the foot of a post by Green who shovelled the ball away for a corner on the Bristol left. When the ball came across it was met at the front post by the head of Milan Djuric who glanced it across the face of goal inside the back post. No sooner had the ball crossed the line than the ref was blowing his whistle to end the game but it took a bit of the gloss off an otherwise efficient night's work. The Leeds defence in particular looked really depressed; a clean sheet bonus payment was lost of course.

It was still a decent night for Leeds though; the top two, Newcastle and Brighton, only managed draws against Norwich and Ipswich respectively although the other three top six sides all won; Huddersfield, Reading and Sheffield Wednesday. Every game was a cup final now and the expectation was that losses for the top six would be rare between now and the end of the season. If Leeds were to be one of those top six we had to keep winning but the prospect of going to Portman Road on Saturday to get three points didn't fill me with great confidence. Having said that, our narrow defeat to Cardiff on Saturday looked a little less shocking tonight as the Bluebirds came away from Derby with another three points courtesy of a 4 - 3 win at Pride Park; there were no easy games in the Championship and Neil Warnock's Bluebirds were now the form side in the division.

The following day the Leeds OS posted another statement confirming that Massimo Cellino's ban had been stayed pending the outcome of his latest appeal under the FA Rule K process. It was another blow to those fans who thought this was going to be his last week at the club. Meanwhile the BBC reported that goal-line technology would be introduced in the Championship from next season with all the Championship clubs having agreed it in principle at a meeting this week. Leeds fans were already hoping they'd see it at Elland Road anyway, in the Premier League!

Leeds United 2 Bristol City 1 (**Wood (27), Hernandez (47),** Djuric (90+6))
22,402 (Bristol 330)

Ipswich

There were now just 14 games to go in the regular season: a massive 42 points still to play for and the next three on offer were at Portman Road. Leeds had recorded only one win in their previous nine trips to Suffolk and Mick McCarthy's lads were on a decent little run having drawn with both Brighton and Reading and won at Villa Park in their three most recent games. I wasn't confident as I fired the Audi down the A14 with Kentley in the passenger seat.

Parking in Ipswich is a real ball-ache; we drove from car park to car park trying to find one without a five hour maximum stay restriction and it took us the best part of half an hour to locate the Spiral Car Park under the New Wolsey Theatre where a stay of up to six hours would set us back £7. The good news though was that we could see the floodlights of Portman Road from the entrance to the car park. First job was breakfast though and Kentley soon located the nearest Wetherspoon pub, The Cricketers in Crown Street. On the door were a couple of notices from the Suffolk Constabulary informing us that the pub was for "Home Fans Only" but since we had no obvious Leeds colours, in we went. Quite what purpose the notices were serving goodness only knows as inside there were several Leeds fans openly sporting Leeds tops and Leeds tattoos! I enjoyed yet another 'Spoon's Large Breakfast with a pint of Adnams Ghost Ship Ale while Kentley had his usual Chicken Strips with a Chicken Panini. The pub was a little tatty by Wetherspoon standards and unusually for their establishments the building has always been a pub, dating back to the 1930s when it was built as a Tollemache inn.

With breakfast done we then walked around the corner and up the hill to the Greyhound, where Keith had told us he was drinking with his mate Bob. Keith had been unable to get tickets for the Leeds section and had therefore had to rely on an Ipswich season ticket holder to secure seats in the home end. We chatted with them while sinking another pint and then waited for the team to appear on Twitter.

Green
Ayling Bartley (Capt) Jansson Berardi
Vieira O'Kane
Sacko Hernandez Dallas
Wood

Subs: Silvestri, Cooper, Bridcutt, Barrow, Roofe, Pedraza, Doukara.

That meant there was just the one change from the side that beat Bristol City on Tuesday; Dallas replaced Kemar Roofe who dropped to the bench. The surprise was that Liam Bridcutt, now available again following his one match ban, was only on the bench. The two new loanees, Barrow and Pedraza, joined Bridcutt in the dugout and I did wonder again quite what the logic was of bringing those two into the club; they didn't seem to add any particular attributes that we didn't already have. Tom Lawrence, the Ipswich winger and leading goal-scorer, missed this game through suspension which was a bit of good fortune for Leeds. The Leicester City man, on loan with the Tractor Boys, picked up his 10th yellow card of the season in their 1 – 1 draw at Brighton on Tuesday.

Kentley's ticket was for a different section to mine so we went our separate ways at the turnstiles. My seat, part of the away season ticket allocation, was in a section that was part home and part away fans, separated only by a row of stewards and police. I was in the upper tier of the Cobbold Stand, about midway between the goal to our left and the half-way line, so I had a good view of the teams as they came out of the tunnel in the corner on the opposite side and to my left. For some reason Leeds had decided to wear the yellow away top with white shorts and socks making them look rather like eleven fried eggs. I could only assume that the plan had been to wear all white but then maybe the ref decided there would be a clash with the white trim on the otherwise blue Ipswich Town shirts. The other thing I had a good view of was the playing surface; it was threadbare! I could well imagine that the Tractor Boys would enjoy playing on it as it looked more like a ploughed field than a Championship quality pitch.

Whether it was the pitch or whether we were just having an off-day I'm not sure, but from the start Leeds' passing was atrocious. Leeds couldn't get going; every time we won the ball we'd give it straight back with a wayward pass. Ipswich meanwhile were finding their men with unerring accuracy and it was no real surprise that as early as the 9th minute they were ahead. It was a sweet move too. Pablo Hernandez gave the ball away with one of those sloppy short passes that was easily intercepted by Emyr Huws and then Huws jinked past a half-hearted attempt at a tackle by Ronnie Vieira. On he went towards the Leeds area down to my left before sliding the ball wide to Grant Ward. Ward clipped the ball into the middle first time and Freddy Sears got to it before Luke Ayling to crash a right foot volley past Rob Green. It would have been a lovely goal had we scored it.

For the next half an hour, Ipswich had numerous chances to increase their lead as Leeds continued to give the ball away cheaply. Stuart Dallas was caught in possession twenty five yards from his own goal and was relieved to see Grant Ward fire his shot over the crossbar and then from the first of many corners, Knudsen somehow contrived to lift the ball over our bar when it looked easier to score. Rob Green then had to act smartly to push another corner out from under his crossbar. Tempers were fraying in the stands as our fans got frustrated by the poor Leeds passing, two blokes standing a few feet away traded blows with each other when one took exception to something the other said. A steward waded in to sort it out and eventually a reluctant truce was brokered and we all turned our attention to the game again. Half-time was nearly upon us and Leeds had a free kick over on the far touchline; Hernandez took it quickly as he often does and moved it inside to Eunan O'Kane who in turn moved it out to Luke Ayling on the touchline down below us. Ayling played it short to Hadi Sacko and we all groaned as he decided against trying to beat his man. But instead he checked and then lifted the ball awkwardly in towards the penalty spot with his left foot. Chris Wood challenged for the ball in the middle and just got the slightest touch allowing it to travel on behind him towards the back post. Stuart Dallas was grappling with Jordan Spence in much the same way those two Leeds fans were a few minutes earlier and somehow Dallas was able to stretch out his left boot to poke the ball between the goalkeeper's legs to equalise! It was way more than Leeds deserved at that point and we celebrated knowing that we might just have got away with one here. Out of the corner of my eye I could see the two Leeds fans that were fighting with each other only moments ago now embracing each other like two long lost lovers and I smiled as the steward looked on shaking his head in disbelief. A Leeds goal soon mends a broken relationship between fans. Half-time; Ipswich 1 Leeds 1.

During the break, Garry Monk obviously decided it was time to see if Liam Bridcutt could improve our quality; we all knew he was coming on as he was warming up throughout the half-time interval without his tracksuit, but most of us thought he would replace Eunan O'Kane who, to put it politely, had been uninspiring during the first 45 minutes. In fact it was Ronnie Vieira who didn't come out after the break. For twenty minutes or so, the change appeared to have no impact at all as Ipswich continued to dictate play and several times the Leeds net appeared to be living a charmed life as the ball ricocheted around Rob Green's ears. But we survived and in the latter stages of the half we were probably the better side as we finally seemed to get to grips with the bobbly pitch. Sadly, for all the possession we had, we didn't carve out a single chance as the home defence snuffed out every attack or sometimes our final ball was too long or too short or too wayward. Throughout the whole of the game Leeds would manage just one shot on target – that Dallas goal – and only three other attempts. Ipswich managed 10 attempts of which three hit the target; Sears' goal and two decent Rob Green saves. At the end of the day, a 1 – 1 draw at Portman Road was a fine result. In the bogs on the way out, I struggled to get the hand dryer to work and after several seconds trying I gave up and made way for an old fella who was waiting patiently behind me; he was an Ipswich fan wearing their blue, white and red colours. *"It's a bit temperamental is this one"* he called after me, giving the unit a bash with his fist. Straight away the dryer fired up and he winked. *"Local knowledge you see"* he said, wringing his hands under the powerful draft of air. Local knowledge is indeed all important and the Tractor Boys had it in spades knowing how to pass the ball on that tricky pitch.

It was FA Cup 5th Round weekend so there were only seven Championship games today; Brighton and Sheffield Wednesday both won while Huddersfield were on Cup duty against Manchester City. They played out a creditable 0 – 0 draw to earn a replay at the Etihad that we all hoped would clog up their fixtures. Newcastle United played on the Monday night in front of the Sky TV cameras, comfortably beating Aston Villa 2 – 0 to return to the top of the Championship leapfrogging Brighton. On Tuesday night, Huddersfield showed little sign of fatigue as they grabbed a late winner against promotion rivals Reading but Sheffield Wednesday, our next opponents, surprisingly lost 2 – 1 at home to Brentford. The top six were now: Newcastle with 69 points, Brighton on 68, Huddersfield 64, Reading 60, Leeds 58 and Sheffield Wednesday 58. The top three also had a game in hand over Leeds, Reading and the Wendies who'd all played 33 games.

Ipswich Town 1 **Leeds United 1** (Sears (9), **Dallas (42)**)
18,748 (**Leeds 2,013**)

Staring at the play-offs

Blackburn Rovers didn't play this week, their last game being a 2 – 1 defeat at Hillsborough on Valentine's Day. Whether it was that specific result I'm not sure but finally the Venky's came to the conclusion I reached months ago; Owen Coyle was not the man to save them from relegation. Coyle was sacked and within hours they had a new man installed in their big leather chair; Tony Mowbray. No doubt they hoped Mowbray could do something similar to what Warnock had achieved at Cardiff. Cardiff were now one of the form sides in the Championship, with seven wins from their last ten including a 5 – 0 thrashing of Rotherham this weekend. Only Huddersfield had a better record in the last ten league games. Coyle wasn't the only manager to feel the hook this week; Claudio Ranieri followed two days later. Ranieri led Leicester City to the Premier League title less than twelve months ago but now, with the Foxes in a hole near the foot of the table, his time was done.

Andrea Radrizzani displayed Cellino like tendencies this week as he took to Twitter to refute a message that appeared to come from the Instagram account of Charlie Taylor. In response to a fan who suggested that Taylor *"...can go for all I care, any offers above 7mill in the summer I'd bite there* [sic] *hand off"*, Taylor appeared to reply: *"I'm out of contract in summer so good luck with that one"* Radrizzani told his followers that this was *not* from the hand of Charlie Taylor despite the account in question carrying the usually definitive 'blue tick'. No one really quite knew what to make of it all.[1]

I had company for the trip to Leeds for the Sheffield game; Red Russ and his lovely lady Fi were stopping the weekend with Mrs W and I and I'd secured Russ a ticket for the game. Having enjoyed a few ales and a bit of whisky sampling from my collection of single malts on the Friday night, it was a pain having to be up so early for the trip to LS11. It was yet another TV game, the 14th of the season and it was another one of those ridiculous 12:30pm kick-offs. We dropped the girls off in the centre of Leeds around 10am and then drove back to Elland Road. Russ filled the minutes of the short journey with the story of his brother, Steve.

Russ's brother is a minor celeb; he was the lad once famously given a second half run-out for West Ham by Harry Redknapp, in a pre-season friendly. It was July 1994 and Steve was with his fellow Hammers on the touchline behind the dug-out as they played at Oxford City. Steve had been giving former Leeds striker Lee Chapman plenty of abuse during the first half, calling him *"a donkey"*. Eventually, Redknapp, who was running short of players following a number of injuries, turned to the mouthy Hammer saying: *"Oi, can you play as good as you talk?"* They found Steve some boots and gave him the number '3' kit and he came on as a substitute for Chapman playing alongside the Hammers debutant that day, the £1.2m Joey Beauchamp. Steve even got the ball in the net, although the fairy-tale didn't quite end perfectly as the 'goal' was

---

[1]   http://www.footballinsider247.com/radrizzani-wades-taylor-instagram-row-leeds-fans/

disallowed.[1] What would any of us Leeds fans give to turn out for the Mighty Whites? As Russ finished regaling me with the story of his brother's 45 minutes of fame, I brought the car to a halt in my usual spot on Lowfields Road.

Elland Road was busy, really busy. There was still more than two hours 'til kick-off but when we tried to get in the club superstore it was mobbed and we quickly gave up on that idea; Russ would have to go without any Leeds memorabilia. It was the same in the Pavilion too but we managed to squeeze in alongside the usual crew. It was hardly surprising it was busy everywhere as we'd been told the game was almost a complete sell out and over 35,000 tickets had been sold and all this for a Saturday lunchtime game in February that was being shown live on Sky. As the business end of the season drew closer, the interest in the club was getting to levels not seen since our last promotion back in 2011; that was from League One of course.

There was plenty going on in the Pavilion to keep the big crowd occupied too; Comedian Jed Stone had Peter Lorimer, Andy Couzens, John Hendrie and Terry Yorath as guest legends – all of whom forecast a 2 – 1 win for Leeds – while the music was supplied by The Pigeon Detectives, the Indie rock band that hails from Rothwell in West Yorkshire. They famously played in the Pavilion once before of course, at the end of season Awards Dinner in 2014 when Massimo Cellino joined them, playing guitar on a version of Jimi Hendrix's *Hey Joe*. They appeared to have brought enough kit to fill Wembley Stadium with sound and after their brief three-song gig we were all stone-deaf.

Green
Ayling Bartley Jansson Berardi
O'Kane Bridcutt (Capt)
Sacko Hernandez Doukara
Wood

Subs: Silvestri, Cooper, Vieira, Barrow, Pedraza, Dallas, Roofe.

---

[1] *https://www.theguardian.com/football/blog/2013/sep/05/harry-redknapp-played-fan-west-ham*

Garry Monk was continuing to stick with the tried and tested, refusing to utilise his new wingers, Pedraza and Barrow. Why should he anyway? The only game when either started, at home to Cardiff, we lost. This was despite the fact we'd looked well below par in recent games and were still struggling to create much in the way of chances; getting by with the odd goal and relying on The Famous Five in our usually rock-solid defence. The chatter in the Pavilion had been mostly about what the hell we'd do if we lost any of that defensive unit through injury or suspension. Ayling, Jansson and Bartley were all collecting cards like kids collect Panini Stickers in a World Cup year and we'd been amazingly lucky with injuries thus far. Surely we'd lose one or more of them for at least some of the remaining dozen games after today. Luke Ayling's lady was expecting a baby any time soon and if that happened to fall near a game Luke would surely want to be there. At least Charlie Taylor was said to be nearing full fitness.

Elland Road burst into life as the two teams appeared and Russ was clearly impressed with the sights and sounds he was witnessing. It was a more usual experience for me of course and I was more interested in familiarising myself with the Owls and in particular their two danger-men, Jordan Rhodes and 'Fessi'; Fernando Forestieri. I shuddered as I spotted Rhodes with a big white '17' on the back of his black and orange kit. Jordan Rhodes had faced Leeds ten times before, with Huddersfield, Blackburn and Middlesbrough and was yet to finish on the losing side. Mind you, I also remembered that 17 had become a more favourable number for us this season; this 2017 season. Wednesday's squad was packed full of expensive strikers, with Sam Winnall and Steven Fletcher on their bench along with former Leeds loanee, Barry Bannan. Another former Leeds man, Tom Lees missed out through injury.

While Liam Bridcutt was doing the honours with the coin toss in the middle, Kyle Bartley came over to stand in front of the Kop, just a few yards in front of me. Each game recently he had started this sort of 'psyching himself up' routine, staring towards the Kop whilst bent over with a hand on each knee.

Today he appeared to be staring straight at me and it was a bit intimidating. If looks could kill I'd be lying on the floor to paraphrase an old Heart song.

This would prove to be yet another of those titanic struggles between two closely matched Championship sides; not surprising really as their records after 33 games were near identical. Wednesday annoyed us by winning the toss and turning the sides around, so it was Leeds attacking the Kop in the first half and some early excitement was caused by Hadi Sacko as he nutmegged a defender on the byline but then failed to pick out either Chris Wood or an unmarked Doukara. It was just one more of Sacko's 'nearly' moments. At the other end we saw a flash of a '17' swivelling in the Leeds box to thump a snap-shot just over Rob Green's bar. 23 minutes had gone with neither side hitting the target as Leeds began another sortie towards us.

Bridcutt brought the ball away from defence and played a one-two with Ayling on the right, in front of the packed East Stand. Bridcutt then moved it left to Hernandez and then on to Chris Wood who touched it further left to Doukara again. Gaetano Berardi went to overlap but as he took the short pass from the Douk he cut back onto his preferred right foot and fired the ball across the Owls area. Vincent Sasso appeared to be in pole position to head the ball away for a corner but for some reason known only to him he missed the ball and it flew straight onto the right foot of Chris Wood, six yards from goal. A tap with his right foot to control it and a poke with the same boot and the ball was in the net with several Owls defenders appealing for offside. Everyone in the Kop thought Wood was probably offside too and we all turned our heads towards the liner over to our left but after a bit of a dither he ran off towards the half-way line. Replays would show conclusively that Wood was being played onside by a defender out on the touchline in front of the West Stand. Chris Wood loves playing the Wendies as much as Rhodes enjoys playing us seemingly and Wood thus kept up his record of scoring in every game he'd ever played against them.

Leeds should have gone in two goals to the good but Hadi Sacko again left us open-mouthed with another piece of indecision. Chris Wood had brought the ball away from deep in the Leeds half to put Sacko away in the inside left channel. Wood then raced down the middle screaming for Sacko to slide the ball in behind the Owls defence where he couldn't fail to score but Sacko dithered and pondered and dithered again and eventually ran out of pitch. Wood, not for the first time this season, spent several seconds raging at the young winger who merely jogged away trying not to look in the direction of the furious striker. That was the last first half action and Leeds left the pitch with the cheers of Elland Road in their ears. It had been a good first half for the home side with the only negative being that persistent lack of accuracy in some of our passing that sometimes needlessly puts us under pressure, particularly as we fiddled about near our own box. To be fair, each time it happened our Famous Five would then make amends with a crunching tackle or a lunging block but I'd rather we just launched the ball away in the first place.

Another thing that had worried us all through the first half was the refereeing of Michael Jones. He was clearly well aware that he was live on TV as he took ages with his talks to players after minor indiscretions and his whistling appeared to be totally random. His decisions also showed a marked tendency to go against us too. Early in the second half, Eunan O'Kane was tackled from behind in the Owls' box by Sam Hutchinson and he went down; it's not easy to run without your legs but Mr Jones waved play-on with a wild gesture no doubt aimed at the millions watching at home. Minutes later and a Sheffield corner floated into our box and the merest touch from Souley Doukara appeared to pole-axe the same Sam Hutchinson but this time, as Hutchinson did a passable impression of a dying swan, ref Jones blew for a penalty! *"We only get sh*t refs"* blasted out from the Kop as Jones held up a yellow card to Doukara to add to our woes. Jordan Rhodes picked up the ball ready for the penalty. Have I mentioned how the number 17 appears to be more in our favour this season?

The noise was deafening as the Kop tried its best to put Rhodes off his stride. We all knew the likelihood was he would score; the bugger always scores against us but still we felt duty bound to do our best to help Rob Green. I'm sure a few fans, like me, did just fleetingly recall that image of Green diving away to his left up at Fleetwood all those months ago to save the final penalty that put us through that tie. Funnily enough that was a game when 17 wasn't particularly good to us. The noise continued to build and build and then just as Rhodes was about to strike the ball we hollered for all our worth as we stood on tip-toes trying to get a good look where it was going. Then we could see that Green had at least guessed the right way and then, incredibly, we can see the ball bouncing back from goal and Berardi and Jansson both sliding in like synchronised swimmers to block a follow up shot. Green had indeed guessed right and, just as he did at Fleetwood, he pushed the ball onto the post and eventually it went away for a corner. We celebrated just as we'd do for a Leeds goal; it was another of those top one hundred all time moments, total joy and total delirium.

The penalty save would prove to be the match winning action, there were just two shots on target in the whole game; Wood's goal and Rhodes' penalty and thus the three points came our way. The win would take us up to fourth in the table, now three points ahead of Wednesday in sixth. Later in the day the results in the other games would pretty much all be favourable to us, with Newcastle, Huddersfield, Reading, Fulham and Norwich all dropping points. In fact only Brighton, who now went top again after beating Reading and Preston who moved up into ninth, won this weekend out of the top ten. Automatic promotion now looked unlikely for Leeds as with a dozen games left we were still nine points behind the Toon who had a game in hand but the play-offs remained very much alive. The next test was another live TV game; Friday night at St. Andrew's, home of Gianfranco Zola's mid-table Blues. This is what football is all about; expectations high but fear of failure too. I was almost fearful of hoping for too much in case we failed to deliver but Leeds were staring at the play-offs with as much intensity as Bartley showed staring at me earlier. Now, where's that whisky?

Leeds United 1 Sheffield Wednesday 0 (**Wood (24)**)
35,093 (Sheffield Weds 2,748)

Banish the Blues

On the Tuesday after the Wendies game, Newcastle scored two late goals to pull off a vital (for them) win at Brighton that meant they leapfrogged the Seagulls back to the top of the table while Derby lost at Mowbray's new Blackburn charges to all but end the Rams play-off dreams for another year. It was another reminder that there is no such thing as an easy game in the Championship... well, apart from playing Rotherham anyway!

The FA concluded their investigation this week into the fracas that took place at the end of the Huddersfield game. David Wagner was handed a two game touchline ban and a £6,000 fine while Garry Monk would have to sit in the stand for one game and hand over three grand. In an interview this week with Adam Pope of BBC Radio Leeds, Monk put a brave face on the punishment, noting he was still allowed to give pre-match and half-time team-talks so it would have little or no impact on his plans for Birmingham. He had to do the same for the game at Derby back in October of course so the omens weren't exactly good; we lost that one 1 – 0. But the most difficult decision, Monk joked, was to choose what colour kit the team would wear as we faced yet another side that played mainly in blue; the fried egg special we wore at Ipswich or maybe the Swedish replica we sported at Blackburn and Huddersfield.

Kentley was joined by Lottie again for the 45 mile trip down to Birmingham and they picked me up around 3:15pm. It was the usual Friday afternoon grind down the M6 but we were parked up behind the McDonalds on the Bordesley Circus roundabout by 5pm. Kentley tapped *"Wetherspoon"* into his 'phone and we were soon on board the number 60 bus to the Moor Street stop just a few hundred yards from the Square Peg, a J D Wetherspoon outlet on Corporation Street. From 1885 until 1991 this was the ground floor of the Lewis's department store and consequently it's a very peculiar shape; very long and narrow. In fact it's said to have once been the longest pub in Europe. Now it was just the longest to get served in! To be fair it was busy, full of folk en route to the game and I was surprised by the number of Leeds fans in there; we found one table that was vacant next to a family kitted out in Leeds clobber, one of them I recognised as one of the blokes dressed as monks down at Sutton not long ago. It's a funny old world this Leeds United planet!

As we scoffed our Spoon's meals and I downed my usual pint of Doombar, the unmistakeable sound of Leeds anthems began to waft from the other end of the bar. Then we heard some Brummie accents responding in kind with their own chants. It wasn't long before there was a bit of a scuffle and some raised voices and then we could see a few Leeds fans being frog-marched out of the pub by some of the doormen. We decided it was time to move on.

For old time's sake the three of us had another drink in the Cricketers Arms in Little Green Lane, not far from the ground. It's where I've had a beer on most of my visits to St Andrew's and as usual it was packed out with fans of both sides but with no sign of the bother we'd just witnessed in the Square Peg. Maybe the latter was just in the wrong place... a Square Peg in a round hole? Nigel joined us in the Cricketers for a quick pint before we headed off to the game.

It was Nigel who gave us the team news and there was just the one change from the side that started against Wednesday.

Green
Ayling Bartley Jansson Berardi
O'Kane Bridcutt (Capt)
Dallas Hernandez Doukara
Wood

Subs: Silvestri, Cooper, Phillips, Sacko, Roofe, Barrow, Pedraza.

The erratic unpredictability of Hadi Sacko was replaced in the starting XI by the non-stop workaholic attributes of Stuart Dallas. That undoubtedly made us more resilient but there was the inevitable question as to who was going to get behind the Blues' defence. Leeds kit choice was the standard all white home ensemble.

We took our places up behind the goal in the Gil Merrick Stand along with over 3,000 other travelling Leeds fans on a miserable, wet Friday night; amazing support once again for yet another live on Sky televised game. Before kick-off we stood and applauded as the players lined up around the centre circle but I confess I had no idea what or who for as the crackly PA message was impossible to decipher. I did feel a bit of a plonker though when I turned to ask Julie T, who was stood just behind me, what it was all about. With a look that suggested I'd gone completely mad, she merely pointed to the big screen away to our left and there was a huge head and shoulders picture beaming back at us of Roger Hynd, with the legend '1942-2017' underneath. Hynd was a centre-half for Birmingham in the early 70s who passed away in February; he was also a nephew of the great Bill Shankly.

With the pre-match tribute completed, we were up and running and of course Garry Monk, like the rest of us, was watching from the stands. Down on the touchline we could see Monk's opposite number, the unmistakeable figure of Gianfranco Zola, prowling in the Blues technical area with a nervous looking James Beattie also down there for Leeds. Monk was sat up in the front row of the stand alongside Leeds Performance Analyst, Ryan Needs. It had been a troubled time for Zola; he came in when Birmingham surprisingly sacked the popular Gary Rowett back in mid-December with the Blues then in 7th place in the table, only a point behind Leeds at that stage. Since then the Blues had won only two games and they'd sunk perilously close to the relegation places although the second of those wins came only a week ago at Wolves. The way the Brummies started this game though you would have thought they were still a team in the top echelons as they ripped into us with full-back Emilio Nsue in particular causing havoc on their right wing and giving Berardi a real headache. Time and time again the ball would be pumped out towards Nsue and he'd try and get the ball into the middle. The Leeds players seemed to take longer to get used to a very soggy pitch too as the rain continued to drift across the ground and Leeds' passes went astray far too often; a trait that was becoming much too regular. The support from the fans was superb though, with an early rendition of *"We're not famous anymore"* almost lifting the roof off.

Kyle Bartley clearly sensed something was not quite right as he had a bit of a paddy when Craig Gardner hammered a shot into the side netting and then another Nsue cross was headed away by Jansson for the first corner of the game; nothing came of it. Minutes later and a sliced clearance from Jansson landed on the right boot of Che Adams and only a strong hand by Rob Green kept his shot out, giving away another corner. It was all one way traffic and the nerves were starting to tell as a few angry comments could be heard from the Leeds fans around us. But then, in the blink of an eye, Leeds were ahead.

Green rolled the ball out to Liam Bridcutt who knocked it out to the Leeds right where Luke Ayling made a few yards before launching it towards Chris Wood. It was actually an identical ball to the one we'd just seen Pontus Jansson mess up offering Adams his chance. The difference with this one though was that the defender, stretching, got nothing on the ball and on the first bounce Wood stuck out his right foot and perfectly lobbed it over the advancing Tomasz Kuszczak! Amazing, and completely against the run of play and the celebrations were therefore all the more sweet... well, apart from the stench of a yellow flare, the smoke from which was now engulfing us. *"Leeds are going up"*, a rather coughing, spluttering rendition, broke out all around us followed by a *"Garry, Garry Monk"* as we all searched the faces in the stand behind the dugout trying to spot him. It was slightly spooky to me that two such similar chances had ended so differently; a Rob Green save at our end but a Leeds goal at the other. It really did feel as if the football gods were behind us and all those stars were finally aligning. Chris Wood had a golden touch these days too and I could vividly remember very similar scenarios Wood often found himself in those first few weeks of the season when he was more likely to plant the ball in row Z rather than the opposition net. Now there were just 6 teams left in the Championship that Wood hadn't scored against this season... and we still had to play them all. That would be some record.

The goal didn't change the nature of the game mind as Birmingham continued to attack and we continued to offer up easy interceptions through poor passing. The Blues had plenty of half-chances but a combination of terrible finishing and heroic defending by the Famous Five kept the score at 1 – 0 through to half-time. A Robert Tesche rocket thumped against our crossbar just before the break to remind us there would be plenty of work to do in the second half.

We were kept amused during the interval by the sight of Leeds fans singing and chanting and trying to bang on the windows of the Sky Sports studio where Peter Beagrie and Gary Rowett were trying to give their half-time analyses. Whose bright idea was it to site it there behind the Leeds fans? Bet he's been sacked by now. When I watched the recording a few days later you could clearly see the stewards behind Beagrie trying to keep the fans away from the glass while a muffled *"All Leeds aren't we"* and then *"Sky TV is fu***** sh**"* could be heard in the background. As they went for another advert break, the TV host, Scott Minto, rather meekly told viewers, *"Well, apologies for any choice language you may have heard..."*

The second half began much as the first had ended, with the Blues enjoying most of the possession and Pablo Hernandez spraying the ball in all directions but seldom to a Leeds player. The only noise in the stadium was coming from the 3,281 Leeds fans. Brum were restricted mostly to long range efforts and most of those flew into the stand behind the far goal but Bartley cleared a Che Adams header off the line and Rob Green pulled off a great save within five minutes of the restart. Green had become a revelation in recent games and many commentators reckoned he was in the form of his life; it was a sign Leeds were fading though that he was having so much work to do.

Whenever Leeds won the ball back we'd give it up again within a few passes and there was a feeling it was only a matter of time before we conceded, despite the heroic defending from *"Luke Ayling and Berardi, Pontus Jansson Kyle Bartley"* as we sang for minutes on end. Another corner for Birmingham went straight to Pablo Hernandez and even his attempt at a clearance sent the ball back over his own goal line for another corner; he was having a stinker. Just before the hour mark and Monk had clearly seen enough, but it wasn't Pablo who came off, it was Eunan O'Kane, with Kalvin Phillips coming on to add more physicality to our midfield. At this stage we were only just hanging on. Zola then made his first change, bringing on the tall figure of Lukas Jutkiewicz armed with a piece of paper which he shared with Tesche. It must have been an important note as within sixty seconds the Blues were level.

A right wing free-kick just eluded Jutkiewicz at the back post but he chased it down and passed back to Keita who crossed from the left. Doukara headed away but a shot came straight back in that Stuart Dallas blocked. This time it went to Craig Gardner and his first-time left foot shot found its way through a crowd of players to nestle in the bottom left corner of the net as we looked on from the opposite end. We had a great view of the shot and could follow its trajectory all the way from boot to net just clipping Dallas's arse on the way through which may have been enough to deceive Rob Green. It was no more than the home side deserved and for a few minutes it was the Blues singing celebratory songs... but only for a few minutes.

We were still coming to terms with the goal and I was starting to think a point would still be a great return if we could just hold on when Leeds won a throw-in near the half-way line over to our right. Phillips got the ball and glided over to the Leeds right wing, our left as we watched and he played a neat little triangle of passes with Luke Ayling and Souley Doukara. As Phillips swung in a curling cross we were just happy to be enjoying a spell of possession while we all gathered our thoughts. The ball was headed back out to Phillips again, now forty yards from goal. He played a one-two with Pablo and then another with Doukara and suddenly Kalvin was behind the Blues backline, seven yards from the byline to the right of goal. The pitch was particularly slick in that area and Kalvin slipped on his backside as he squirted the ball along the edge of the six–yard box and then those footballing gods dealt us another ace as a covering defender also slipped allowing the ball to arrive with Chris Wood, now unmarked, seven yards out. It was uncanny; it seemed once again that all the good luck we'd been denied for years and years was now being repaid in spades. Wood poked the ball home and pandemonium broke out in the Gil Merrick Stand. If this season wasn't destined to end in promotion then someone somewhere was being particularly cruel, teasing us in this way. Birmingham were level for just three and a half minutes.

St Andrew's was understandably stunned and the home fans were silenced once more while we Leeds fans were still celebrating wildly; we knew we hadn't played that well but as we've said many times before it's often better to be lucky than good. We certainly weren't good and Pablo continued to look like a fish out of water, totally unable to find his passing boots; everyone near me was moaning about him and Kentley and I were sure he'd be going off soon. But it wasn't Pablo who was next to feel the hook, it was Stuart Dallas. The good news was that the man coming on, Alfonso Pedraza looked fired up as he raced across the pitch to take up his position on the left wing; a left footer on the left wing... whatever next?

Pablo was now causing us aggravation in defence as well as he gave away a needless free-kick out on the Birmingham left wing and another murmur of discontent rumbled around the Leeds fans. Fortunately the free-kick came to nothing. More Birmingham pressure followed and then Che Adams was going down in the Leeds box under the slightest touch from Kyle Bartley. It was no more than Doukara did on Hutchinson last week and that cost us a penalty but the referee today, the excellent Chris Kavanagh, gave this one to us, a free-kick for hand-ball as Adams grabbed it expecting his reward. Kavanagh is only 26 years old but I have been impressed every time I've seen him and I'm convinced we'll see him in the Premier League next season. There were just two yellow cards in this game too, showing that a top ref doesn't need to be always resorting to cards to control a game. David Davis got one for a poor challenge on Pedraza in the 78th minute, as finally Leeds got the measure of the home side. It was now Leeds knocking the ball about and the Blues chasing shadows, probably as the last bit of stuffing had been knocked out of them with the second Wood goal. They knew full well that this wasn't destined to be their day. Even Pablo was now getting his second wind and he fired in a shot that Kuszczak did well to save. Maybe a younger Pablo would have buried it though. I still wanted him subbed and was saying so to Kentley as Leeds attacked again with Kemar Roofe stood in front of the dugout ready, presumably, to replace Hernandez. Phillips won the ball in midfield and touched it to Pablo who played a one-two with Chris Wood who then sprinted towards the box pointing where he wanted the return pass. Doukara was free on the right too, maybe Pablo would play him in...

But this is exactly why Pablo is so useful; it's why he breaks so many eggs before he makes the perfect omelette. This time he did a 360 degree pirouette, just having a quick look to assess Doukara's position before opting instead to slide the ball through onto the left foot of fellow Spaniard, Alfonso Pedraza. It was the least likely ball... but it was devastating and Pedraza did the rest taking one touch before rifling it low across Kuszczak into the far corner of the net. Game, set and match to Leeds.

Three blue flares came raining out of the Leeds section somewhere over to our left, landing near the byline but Leeds had banished the Blues tonight with a display of clinical finishing. We hit the target six times from just ten attempts and three of those went in. By contrast Birmingham amassed 27 attempts but they too only got six on target and only the one went in.

In the final minutes, Leeds really came alive with Roofe finally replacing Pablo as we expected and as each pass found a man we cheered with an *"Olé"* and then, slightly tongue in cheek, we sang *"If Berardi scores we're on the pitch"*; everyone wanted Gaetano to break his Leeds duck this season. He'd epitomised the fight and determination of our back five, The Famous Five as I'd taken to calling them and it would be a magic moment if he got one... maybe a 25-yard screamer at Wembley to win the Play-Off Final... I can dream. *"Garry,*

Garry Monk" then rang out from the ranks of the Leeds supporters while around the other three sides of the ground there was a steady stream of Bluenoses heading for the exits.

Garry Monk must have had an excellent view of the game from up there in the stand and he summarised it perfectly speaking to the BBC:

"I didn't enjoy the first 60 minutes. Birmingham were excellent and it was tough for us.

"We were second best, especially in the first half. They will feel aggrieved that they did not capitalise on the chances they created.

"But we showed a strong mentality and, in that last half-hour, we were excellent. We scored some very good goals and in the end won comfortably.

"The subs made a good impact, Pedraza scored his first for the club and we had two great finishes from Chris Wood, especially the first - great improvisation. "

Yep, that was the game I saw too. It was Friday night of course and so the journey home was tortuous with more motorway closures and a few wrong turns from Kentley but we didn't mind. The following day the results elsewhere showed the top sides continuing to forge ahead with more wins for Fulham, Reading, Wednesday and Newcastle who beat third placed Huddersfield. The only surprise was that Brighton went down three-nil at Forest. There were now only seven teams I could see that could make the Play-Offs; it would be six from those seven. On Tuesday night Leeds would travel down to London to take on 7th placed Fulham knowing that anything but a defeat would leave Leeds at least 8 points ahead of the Londoners with just ten games to go. It was another huge, huge game.

Birmingham City 1 **Leeds United 3 (Wood (14 & 67),** Gardner (63), **Pedraza (81))**
20,321 (**Leeds 3,281**)

London's Galling

I was driving for the long trip to Craven Cottage and I was joined once again by both Kentley and Lottie who was now becoming a regular. I picked the two of them up at a layby just off junction 15 of the M6 and we were searching for a place to drop the car in Wandsworth by 4:45pm. Kentley eventually directed us to the Southside 1 NCP, next to the shopping centre of the same name. Then it was a brisk 20 minute walk to The Railway, a Wetherspoon pub next to Putney rail station.

We'd used this pub many times before and it wasn't long before I spotted a familiar face; my old pal Andy W. Keith, Bob and Steve were next to arrive and we all found a table towards the rear of the pub where we set up camp. We'd later be joined by Adam and Connor and a couple of mates of theirs and, late as usual, Nigel bowled in when we were just about thinking it was time to set off to the ground. This game was all about London; Kentley had played us numerous songs from Apple Tunes on the drive down that included references to

London including the Fulham anthem, 'London's Calling' by The Clash and one of my favourites, 'London Traffic' by The Jam. I kept the theme going by sticking to London Pride as my beer of choice.

The night before the game I'd spotted a few tweets suggesting that Chris Wood and Luke Ayling might not feature against the Cottagers and while we were chewing the cud in the Railway confirmation came through courtesy of Phil Hay's Twitter account that Luke Ayling had been left back (strange as he's a right back...) in Leeds to be at the birth of his daughter while Chris Wood would miss out with a slight calf strain.

Green
Berardi Bartley Jansson Taylor
Phillips Bridcutt (Capt)
Sacko Roofe Pedraza
Doukara

Subs: Silvestri, Cooper, Vieira, Barrow, Dallas, Barrow, Antonsson.

It was a very different team and it would test to the limit Garry Monk's contention that everyone had their part to play this season; five changes from the side that began at Birmingham just four days earlier. The defence looked as strong as always, as long as Charlie Taylor could hit the ground running but with Hernandez rested we were playing four attacking players in the front third of the pitch. How was that going to pan out?

The general consensus was that if we could escape with a point then it would be a very good point indeed. That would leave Fulham still 8 points adrift of Leeds albeit they did have a game in hand. I was convinced that other than the current top six – Newcastle, Brighton, Huddersfield, Leeds, Reading and Sheffield Wednesday – only Fulham could break into this elite club by the 7th of May. Hence, by my reckoning, as long as we finished above Fulham, we were in. Importantly, when Leeds were playing a seemingly winnable game against QPR at Elland road in a week's time, Fulham had a daunting trip to Newcastle. Hence, as long as Leeds got that point here, I fully expected us to be 11 points ahead of Fulham by then with only nine games left after that. Surely that would be Leeds secure in that top six bar a complete disintegration of our form. But we were getting ahead of ourselves...

Looking through the Fulham side the only name that really bothered me was Tom Cairney; yes, he's that lad who Leeds decided was too small when he was allowed to leave the academy. Ever since then he's always played out of his skin against us as he did back in August when only a late, late Chris Wood overhead kick salvaged a point after Cairney had scored earlier.

It was a damp but warm evening as we all made the walk from The Railway, over the Thames and along the edge of Bishops Park. The bright lights of Craven Cottage, reflecting in the dark waters of the Thames in the distance at first, were soon right over our heads as we jostled for position outside the turnstiles at the Putney End. It was being said that Leeds would have over 7,000 supporters inside the ground, the majority with tickets bought from Leeds but a significant number alongside us in the so-called 'neutral' section. As I took my place the atmosphere was something very special. It reminded me of a night at Barnsley in September 2010. That night we also took around 7,000 fans and I stood amongst them next to my eldest lad, Mark and we were gobsmacked. This felt just as incredible. I could only hope the result wasn't similar; we lost 5 – 2 that night at the Tykes. Funnily enough though, Jonny Howson had put us ahead as early as the 3rd minute at Oakwell, tonight it took us only five...

I was still settling myself in, on Row LL up behind Rob Green's goal at the Putney End when Kemar Roofe was bundled over just inside the Fulham half. Kyle Bartley stood over the free-kick. Then, with almost a carbon copy ball to the one Luke Ayling played through to Chris Wood on Friday, this time it was Fulham defender Tim Ream stretching out a boot to try to stop Souley Doukara repeating Woody's trick. But all he managed to do was slice the ball past his own keeper into the net! It took a few seconds for the Leeds fans to work out what had happened but as the Leeds players gathered together to celebrate, we soon got the gist. The celebrations around me were absolutely mental, it was as much as I could do to stay on my feet as bodies were flying everywhere and the floor of our stand was rocking like a cork a stormy sea. I love Leeds like a secret mistress but seldom had the earth moved for me like this.

The rest of the first half panned out much like the game at Birmingham; Leeds were under the cosh. Fulham are a very good side, indeed some Leeds fans had openly acknowledged that they were probably the best team we'd seen at Elland Road this season and they were now living up to that tag. They moved the ball about sharply and accurately. That man 'too small' Cairney had a shot scream narrowly wide and then Neeskens Kebano rattled the crossbar with a shot that appeared to have crossed the goal-line as it bounced down. Replays would later show us that it most definitely *did* cross the line and once again the luck had gone with us as referee Lee Probert waved play-on. Leeds were doing that horrible thing where we could only string a couple of passes together before surrendering possession too, we seemed to always be trying to pass the ball too quickly, often first time when there was no real need. I could only assume it was part of the counter attacking MO we were set up for. In reality it was just bringing more and more pressure on the back four and Rob Green, albeit they were performing their usual heroic miracles in repelling the Cottagers thus far. Similar to that Blues game though, on the rare occasions Leeds did break away we did go close to extending the lead. Pedraza found himself in the same position he scored from on Friday but this time his angled shot was well saved. It was a damn good game but too much of the action was at our end of the pitch.

During the interval, hundreds of Leeds fans made merry on the concourse behind the Putney Stand while one jolly chap, seemingly a Leeds fan, was conducting them from his vantage point high in a tree on the other side of the stadium perimeter fence! Another Leeds fan was being wheeled around in a wheelie bin to the amusement of all. Kentley came back after a trip down there to report: *"Nothing to see down there, just a normal Leeds away day!"*

The second half began with a typical Charlie Taylor run into the opposition box that ended with a wild shot that was high, wide and not particularly handsome but it was good to see him back in the fray doing what he does best. But that was an exception; the rule was pretty constant pressure on our own goal and some rash tackling from Leeds. Kalvin Phillips got his usual yellow card just five minutes after the break. Leeds were all so deep that any clearance was merely mopped up by the Fulham defence and back they would come like a tidal wave but fortunately Rob Green was having another fine game as were the back four. Even so, another rare Leeds foray towards us found Pedraza yet again free in the box on his left foot but this time he crashed his shot against the post. Had our finishing been as clinical as it was at St Andrew's the score could well have ended the same. We did our bit to try to keep our troops on their toes as we continued to make more noise than I could remember at any recent game; we sang *"Luke Ayling and Berardi, Pontus Jansson Kyle Bartley"* non-stop for about ten minutes. But all the time I had the feeling Fulham would get a goal just as Brum did last week but we should have had a couple more by now to make that irrelevant. Time was starting to run out for Fulham but events were about to turn in their favour. Mo Barrow replaced a very poor Hadi Sacko on the hour and Fulham had used all three of their subs including the teenage sensation Ryan Sessegnon and the veteran Scott Parker. Barrow didn't look any more useful in this situation than Hadi Sacko but he did get his name in the book as he halted one Fulham attack. We were looking more desperate by the minute.

Leeds began the run-down to the end with two more very slow substitutions as Dallas replaced Pedraza and Vieira replaced Roofe. If bums squeaked ours would have sounded as if they needed a squirt of WD40.

We were into the last two minutes of normal time as Kalvin Phillips launched himself into a tackle on the edge of the Leeds box and it was no surprise to see another yellow card and then a red one held up in his direction. No one worried about that too much; surely we could see out a few minutes of added time couldn't we? My mind flashed back to the Fulham game at Elland Road as we moved into that added time, five minutes of it. I'm fascinated by the way football frequently throws up moments of irony, coincidence and symmetry.

Wood equalised at the death in that reverse fixture to grab a 1 – 1 draw.

And so it proved to be. With the very last kick of the game, just seconds after another fine Gordon Banks v Brazil look-alike save from Rob Green; "Tiny" Cairney whipped a left footer into the top corner.

It was annoying, damn annoying, galling even but most fair minded Leeds fans knew it was the least Fulham probably deserved, not that 'deserved' is a term that features much in football as I've said before. Many others, like me, also recognised that we'd negotiated a tricky game at one of the best sides in the Championship and had maintained that 8 point gap. They did have a game in hand though and that was an easy looking encounter with lowly Blackburn Rovers if any game can ever be described as 'easy' in the Championship. There was a reminder how tight the division is with tonight's other results; seven of the 12 games played tonight ended all-square and only one ended with a two-goal margin; Brighton's 2 – 0 victory at poor old Rotherham. Huddersfield were the only other winners out of the top ten, doing them no harm at all. In fact the Terriers would only be three points behind second placed Brighton if they could win their game in hand. Leeds were still fourth.

	P	GD	Pts
1 Newcastle	36	40	77
2 Brighton	36	29	74
3 Huddersfield	35	7	68
4 Leeds	36	14	65
5 Reading	36	3	64
6 Sheff Wed	36	13	62
7 Fulham	35	19	57
8 Norwich	36	7	53
9 Preston	36	3	53
10 Derby	36	6	52

Fulham 1 **Leeds United 1 (Ream og (5)**, Cairney (90+5))
22,239 **(Leeds 2,951)***
*NB. The Leeds figure excludes the Craven Cottage Neutral Area which was probably all Leeds as well!

Jumping through hoops

Massimo Cellino had been very quiet in respect of matters Leeds United but he was still working his way through various outstanding legal cases unrelated to the club. This week he and his sister Lucina were finally cleared of any wrong doing in a case going back twenty years. The case related to claims against the family firm, SEM Molini Sardi, which at one time had been ordered to repay £30 million of export subsidies and pay a fine of around £200 million.[1] This week the High Court in Rome wiped it all away. Cellino and his legal team clearly never give up and are obviously experts in jumping through hoops.

Behind the scenes at Leeds things appeared to be very stable and this week the club announced that the Clipper Logistics sponsorship had been extended for another season. Steve Parkin's Clipper logo would remain on the East Stand and on the back of the shirts although there was no mention of the sums of money involved.[2]

---

[1]   http://www.yorkshireeveningpost.co.uk/sport/football/leeds-united/leeds-united-co-owner-massimo-cellino-secures-another-acquittal-in-italian-courts-1-8432413

[2]   http://www.yorkshireeveningpost.co.uk/sport/football/leeds-united/leeds-united-whites-extend-partnership-with-parkin-s-clipper-firm-1-8432101

There was no end in sight to Championship managerial sackings even though the season only had a few weeks to run. Norwich City's Alex Neil held his Friday press conference as normal ahead of his team's home game with Blackburn and then four hours later he was sacked! Blackburn themselves swapped Owen Coyle for Tony Mowbray only three weeks earlier and were actually unbeaten in four as they attempted to defy all the odds and avoid relegation. Norwich confirmed they were looking to get a new man in ready for the important summer transfer window which at least looked like they were planning ahead. It confirmed that they, like me, considered Norwich were too far behind to make the play-offs despite currently occupying 8th spot. I still felt it was six from the current top seven.

News also broke on Friday of the death of yet another iconic name from my youth; racing driver John Surtees passed away at the age of 83. I was seven when Surtees won the F1 World Championship in 1964 having already won the Motorcycle World Championship four times; the only man to win world titles on both two and four wheels. Surtees' F1 triumph came in a Ferrari and I've followed them ever since. In fact, I was looking forward to the start of the new F1 season, especially as I'd be there, in Melbourne, watching the first race; but more of that later.

Our next test was a home game with fast improving Queens Park Rangers; the Hoops. Ian Holloway replaced Jimmy Floyd Hasselbaink at Loftus Road back in November and after a slow start they'd run into a bit of form, winning four of their last five games albeit none against a top team. I was absolutely convinced Leeds had enough to beat them and I was equally certain Newcastle would beat Fulham this weekend, a combination of results that would surely mean the Cottagers couldn't catch us.

I was with the Shropshire Whites again, on another big bus for this one as the fans continued to flock to Elland Road in their thousands. Another 30,000 plus crowd was expected for a rare Saturday 3pm kick-off. In the Pavilion everyone, like me, saw nothing but a strong performance and another home win as the order of the day. Our pleas for a music free session in the

Pavilion were once again ignored but at least I had to admit the band, 'Mod Revue' was half decent. They ran through a whole host of 'mod' and 'ska' tunes ranging from the Kinks to Madness via The Jam and The Who. Like John Surtees, these were all names that featured prominently in my youth.

Green
Ayling Bartley Jansson Berardi
Vieira Bridcutt (Capt)
Roofe Hernandez Pedraza
Wood

Subs: Silvestri, Cooper, Taylor, O'Kane, Dallas, Doukara, Sacko.

When our little group in the Pavilion learned of that team we were mostly happy, although Kev was adamant he'd have rested Luke Ayling. Ayling and Bartley were both on nine yellows and one more today for either would mean they faced a two game ban. With Charlie Taylor fit, why risk Ayling? That was Kev's considered view.

The game was not the most inspiring I've ever seen as Leeds huffed and puffed trying to break down a resolute QPR back five and midfield four. We had the lion's share of the ball for a change but really didn't do much with it while QPR were content to play on the counter which on occasions they did very well. The only significant event in the first half was the oh so predictable Ayling booking; that meant no Luke Ayling against Brighton next Saturday nor for the away game against Reading after the international break.

The second half was no better and Leeds continued to pass the ball without getting behind the QPR defence. Chris Wood was left isolated, chasing lost causes, while Roofe and Pedraza were totally ineffective out wide. Monk changed it round on the hour by trying Sacko instead of Roofe and while that did at least put a bona fide winger on the right, Sacko was his usual indecisive self, refusing to try to get past his man despite being given numerous chances to do so. Doukara would eventually replace Pedraza on the other wing and then an out of sorts Vieira gave way to Eunan O'Kane. None of the changes gave us any more potency and the game ended as it began with neither side scoring nor a single shot on target from Leeds. At the end we waited for the results of the other games to appear on the big screen over in the south-west corner; there was good news and bad. Reading had been soundly beaten at Preston and Sheffield Wednesday lost at Villa but that rock solid home win for the Toon turned out to be a fairly comfortable 1 – 3 away win for Fulham who were thus only two points behind Wednesday in sixth and they had a game in hand. They'd gained another two points on us too of course and would only be three points behind us if they won their game in hand. The Shroppy Whites' coach was a quiet place for a few miles until we'd all rationalised the day's events but then, as we always do, we managed to look on the bright side of life. We were still fourth, we'd stretched our lead over Reading and the Wendies and at least Kyle Bartley had got through without a ban and could now afford six more before the season end. Some of the lads at the back of the bus began to sing while the rest of us continued to study our mobiles and the upcoming fixtures. Nine games of the regular season left and every single one of them was a cup-final.

If we thought we were starting to stall a bit we needed only to look at Derby to feel better. In another sign that they'd already thrown in the towel this season, they sacked Steve McClaren who they only brought back as recently as October; he'd overseen just 29 games. Then, knock me over with a feather; Wigan sacked Warren Joyce after only four months; the Latics occupied the third of the relegation places. One possible reason for these sackings was that there were now some really big names available; Garry Rowett was soon snapped up by Derby in what looked like a great move; Rowett was one of the few 'successful' managers who'd been sacked this season and was available. Forest finally appointed Mark Warburton as their new man; Warburton parted company with Rangers in February. Wigan decided to go with Graham Barrow (who?) as their interim manager until the season end and more than half the Championship teams had now swapped horses this season; some more than once. Leeds was one of the elite few that hadn't.

Leeds United 0 QPR 0 **30, 870** (QPR 720)

Wood is all you need!

As soon as Sky picked our home game against high flying Brighton as another live on TV game and moved the kick-off from 3pm to a ridiculous 5:30pm, I knew my presence at the game was unlikely. Mrs W and I were due to leave home at 4am the following day, heading for Manchester Airport and ultimately Australia. Initially, I booked myself on the Shropshire Whites' bus, another big bus with most seats filled but as the day drew nearer I realised it was madness to travel up to Leeds and risk a late night return with that early start looming on the Sunday morning. In the end I saw sense and decided to join the ranks that would be *"...watching on the telly..."*

During the week, there were three significant games involving teams fighting with Leeds for one of those top six places and all three went in our favour. On Tuesday night, Fulham surprisingly dropped a couple of home points in a 2 – 2 draw with Blackburn Rovers although maybe 'surprisingly' is to understate the recent upturn in Rovers' form since Tony

Mowbray got hold of them; since then they were unbeaten. Then, on Friday night, I watched on TV as Huddersfield came unstuck at Bristol City, losing 4 – 0. On the same evening another Yorkshire club, Sheffield Wednesday, also came unstuck at home to Reading in an all top-six six-pointer. Were those stars aligning in our favour again? Well, if they were then you would have to believe that we'd beat the Seagulls in *our* crucial game.

After sorting out some last minute shopping and packing I got myself settled on the sofa to watch the afternoon scores coming through on Gillette Soccer Saturday, something I seldom get to do of course and I couldn't believe the results I was seeing; none of the top sides won! Newcastle drew 0 – 0 at Birmingham while Fulham, incredibly, lost 1 - 3 at home to Wolves, another side, like Blackburn that was now zooming up the form tables and putting some distance between themselves and the bottom three. It seemed amazing to me that just a couple of weeks ago Fulham looked the main threat to our play-off hopes but they had now won just one game in their last four albeit that, again unbelievably, was that win at Newcastle! This year's Championship was proving even more unpredictable than ever and it was earning its title of the most competitive league in Europe. Contrast that with the fact that Chelsea won 2 – 1 at Stoke today to go 13 points clear of Spurs at the top of the Premier League. All that was left now for Leeds was to capitalise on all these results by pulling off a win at Elland Road. I got myself a beer and got comfortable on that sofa…

The team news coming out of Elland Road though suddenly made me very uncomfortable.

Green
Berardi Bartley Cooper Taylor
Bridcutt (Capt) Vieira
Sacko Hernandez Pedraza
Wood

Subs: Silvestri, Jansson, O'Kane, Barrow, Roofe, Dallas, Doukara.

We knew Luke Ayling and Kalvin Phillips were both suspended so we expected them to be absent but why was

Pontus Jansson on the bench? He was on 13 yellow cards which meant he faced a three match ban if he picked up two more before the end of the season, but this was a huge game and surely one where we needed the big Swede. There was no reason given in the opening minutes of the TV show and there was no clue on Twitter, although it was awash with fans asking the question. The Brighton defence was described as *"makeshift"* on the TV coverage but all the usual forwards were there including Sam Baldock and Glen Murray. In goal for the Seagulls was Yorkshireman and big Leeds fan David Stockdale who'd shown he could separate his own career from his love of Leeds with a 100% record against us thus far.

It was fascinating listening to the Leeds crowd singing; it was pretty much non-stop and of course on TV I could hear the South Stand just as loud as the Kop rather than hearing them from 100 yards away. Garry Monk had specifically called for the Leeds fans to raise the roof for this and all the remaining home games.

It was a cagey opening to the game, fifteen minutes passed quickly but without either keeper troubled. The Leeds fans could clearly be heard singing about that *"f****** great goal"* scored by Dom Matteo in the San Siro and how they considered Sky TV *"is f****** sh** "*!

Leeds' best opportunity came from the first corner, in the 21st minute, but Bartley's looping header dropped wide as the first attempt from either side was registered. A second corner followed 3 minutes later as Leeds began to dominate but nothing came of that one either. On commentary we were told Leeds had scored more goals from corners than any other side in the division just as this one was safely cleared away. On 27 minutes a Hernandez cross was put out for yet another; it was all Leeds. We saw a flashing glimpse of the old Chris Wood as he completely missed his kick when the corner dropped perfectly at his feet, six yards out. We then saw a glimpse of Leeds fans of the dark old days as a Brighton player was shoved by a fan as he marshalled the ball out of play in front of the Kop. *"No need for that"* muttered Don Goodman on commentary.

As Leeds continued to press, Brighton got ragged, as did their tackling. Liam Rosenior saw yellow for a nasty over the ball challenge which left Hadi Sacko limping badly. On TV they debated whether it could even have even been red. Half-time came and it was still nil-nil with the only slight worry being a couple of miscues from the clearly rusty Liam Cooper, one of which almost beat Rob Green. There were no shots on target from either team though in a chess match of a first half and two of the best defences in the Championship looked comfortable. In the studio Kelly Dalglish had her work cut out to come up with incidents that Dougie Freedman and David Prutton could argue the toss over... the advert break was necessarily a long one!

The second half began in much the same manner and with few goalmouth incidents to cheer the Leeds fans sang *"If Berardi scores we're on the pitch"*... he did have one long range effort blocked in the first half but that was optimistic thinking.

Chris Wood then had another moment to forget as the ball came through to him from a Berardi cross, again only six yards out. It came quickly but at his best he'd have buried the chance. As it was he limply hit it at Stockdale. Wood was not on fire today... or was he?

In the 64th minute Leeds broke down the left hand side with Pedraza and his low cross was scuffed away out of the Brighton area. Ronnie Vieira risked life and limb in winning a strong tackle and eventually the ball landed with Pablo. He twisted and turned and twisted again before firing in a shot that once again was blocked away. Leeds were going for the jugular now and Charlie Taylor picked up the rebound this time and took his man on and got to the byline. A lovely clipped cross floated towards Chris Wood and this time he got it right. Despite being grappled by a defender he pushed his man away and rose to meet the ball perfectly to guide a looping header out of the reach of Stockdale into the opposite corner of the net.

After a brief explosion of noise as most of Elland Road celebrated, the mood soon turned nervy again; having got the lead in this oh so important game, every Leeds fan was now concerned that we'd give it up, I know I was. Eventually a rousing MOT broke out but it was cut short as Glen Murray got free in the inside-left channel but pulled his shot wide. You could hear the intake of breath come out of my surround sound speaker system! Mrs W arrived just in time with another beer...

74th minute and Akpom replaced Baldock for the Seagulls and Pedraza gave way to Souley Doukara. A bit like Chris Wood got from the visitors earlier, Leeds were now offering Glen Murray some shooting practice. Somehow he was suddenly free, 12 yards out and he absolutely thundered a shot at Rob Green's goal at the Kop end. Green somehow got his gloves in the way but it nearly knocked him over. Brighton were now collecting the kitchen sink and preparing to throw it.

Ten minutes to go and Hadi Sacko gave way to Stuart Dallas, no doubt for his better tracking back and defending but four minutes later and it was our first sub, Souley Doukara, with the ball at his feet driving powerfully into the left side of the Seagulls' area. Fikayo Tomori slid in to try to take the ball but missed it by a fraction and instead collected both ankles of the flying Douk who went down in a heap. Experienced Premier League ref Lee Mason pointed at the spot. It was left to that man Chris Wood again to try to beat Stockdale from 12 yards and this time he did it emphatically in Bing Crosby fashion; straight down the middle! OK he'd missed a couple of decent half-chances but he'd put away a tremendous header and his penalty taking has been A1 all season. Now the noise blasting out of the TV speakers was phenomenal; it wasn't long before the home fans were chanting *"Leeds are going up"* and then in playful manner they turned to the Brighton fans in the West Stand and sang *"You'll f*** it up again!"*. Last season of course they only missed out on automatic promotion by goal difference and then lost to Sheffield Wednesday in the semis.

Leeds took up some seconds by substituting Pablo Hernandez with Eunan O'Kane and then a Glen Murray header went close but that was it. At the final whistle an ear-splitting roar erupted from the TV and I slumped back on the sofa more in relief than excitement really. It was hard to believe we were now so close to a shot at those play-offs but in his post-match interviews Garry Monk was having none of it, telling the viewers it was *"just another three points"*.

Leeds ended the weekend back in fourth spot; eight points behind second place Brighton but more importantly, eight points ahead of seventh placed Fulham who now had no game in hand. Only eight games to go but still 24 points to play for; nothing won and nothing lost yet. We moved into the next international break and a two week suspension in Championship hostilities and I was going off in the same direction as Chris Wood. He was destined to jet out to New Zealand to join up with the All Whites who had home and away 2018 World Cup qualifiers against Fiji during the break while I was on my way to Oz.

It wasn't all good news today; England's rugby team had a chance to record an all-time record 19 consecutive test victories if they could beat the Irish in Ireland on this St. Patrick's Day weekend; typical of the Irish they spoiled that party with a 13 – 9 win, albeit England had already won the Six Nations Championship. In France there was another terror attack with a lone attacker shot dead at Orly Airport. And then, just before I turned in for the night ahead of the long journey to Australia, news came through that the legendary musician, Chuck Berry had passed away; another of those iconic names from my youth. *"Roll over Beethoven"*, make room up there for Chuck.

Leeds United 2 Brighton and Hove Albion 0 (**Wood (63, 85 pen))**
29,767 (Brighton 1,545)

Down Under

I was dreaming; I knew I was dreaming. In my dream I was in the crowd in a marquee near the finishing line and a horse called Mighty White was carrying five thousand quid of my hard earned cash. It started as a 20/1 shot but he was leading the race and was only a furlong from home. Bizarrely, I was with Kev W and Tony who I often sit with in the Pavilion and several school mates and we were all going ballistic. Then something woke me...

A siren was blasting out in the street below, 12 floors below. I was having trouble opening my eyes. My head was thumping and my mouth felt like I'd been chewing dry cement all night. I tried to open just one eye, just a fraction but then the blurred image I saw made me shut it again rapidly, not quite believing what I was seeing. I processed the information; a bloke with a beard appeared to be asleep in bed with me where Mrs W ought to be. I vaguely recognised my new bed fellow, he looked a bit like Kentley, so for a brief moment I thought I'd been on some wild drunken Leeds away game and maybe we'd had to find a hotel room. I thought some more. Finally, it all started to come back.

I was actually in our Airbnb apartment in Melbourne. The day before had been my 60th birthday and it had been a whirlwind day of sightseeing, celebrating and beer drinking. My lad Mark and a work colleague of his, Adam, had flown over from Perth on Thursday night to join us for my birthday and then for a weekend at the Australian Grand Prix in Albert Park. The bloke in bed with me, I now recognised as Adam and he was dead to the world and smelled like he'd just climbed out of a vat of beer. I still had no idea what he was doing in my bed or for that matter, where the wife was but slowly the mists were clearing and I pieced together the events of the previous 24 hours.

We began the day with breakfast at the hotel around the corner and then the four of us, Mark, Adam, Mrs W and I made our way across the city to the MCG (Melbourne Cricket Ground) for a guided tour; Mark's birthday present to me. It was brilliant, an amazing stadium with a capacity of exactly 100,000. As well as the cricket it's used in winter for Aussie rules football. It was here in summer 2013 that Liverpool played a pre-season friendly against Melbourne Victory in front of 95,000 fans and the whole stadium famously sang *"You'll never walk alone"*. Google it and watch the video; it's stunning.

After the tour, we had our first beers of the day over lunch and then Mrs W and I went back to the apartment to change while the two lads went to find a bar for the afternoon. We were due to meet them again a couple of hours later at another bar in the City, Young and Jackson's Hotel, opposite Flinders Street Station, where I'd arranged to meet 'Deebo' and 'Mr Russell', two Leeds fans who live and work in the Melbourne area and who I know from the LUFCTalk forum. I'd had another couple of beers with them by the time the boys arrived and clearly they'd had several more than I had. The details of what happened next are pretty sketchy in my mind but Mrs W has filled in the blanks and has dined out on them during numerous dinner parties and family gatherings ever since!

The beer count accelerated at dinner at the Meat and Wine Co. on The Southbank looking out over the Yarra River and the city skyline and I was already nearing my limit. But the night was yet young.

Mrs W continued the story of the remainder of the madcap evening once I'd slipped out of bed and found her awake on the sofa; Adam was still comatose in our bed. Apparently, the next port of call was another riverside bar where Mark had arranged to meet Jess, now a teacher in Melbourne but also a family friend who hails from our village back home; it is a small, small world that we frequent. I vaguely remember having a few more beers at some big trestle tables in that bar and then being disappointed when last orders were called. Mrs W explained that Mark and I were by this time getting rowdy and we had a barman almost pinned against a wall as we demanded to know where we could get more beer. *"The Casino, The Casino"* he apparently blurted out, no doubt fearing for his life. So, you guessed it, off we all went to the Casino. The next thing I remember is Mark passing me a handful of chips (the round plastic kind) and then him snatching a couple back and slamming them down on the roulette table just seconds after the ball had clattered to a halt. Before I had chance to pick them up, the croupier had swept them away with the rest of the losing chips. Well, all hell broke loose at this moment apparently with Mark and I demanding the croupier hand back the chips as they'd clearly gone down after the game had ended. Mrs W reckons we soon had everyone around the table crying foul and demanding our chips be returned while at first the croupier was adamant the chips had been placed in time. There was such a commotion going on that it wasn't long before security were called and a big crowd of people was now gathered around the table. Mark then demanded they review the CCTV footage. A manager arrived, duly watched a replay and was soon handing our chips back. Vindication of a sort but Mrs W then went on to explain that due to the noise we were making we were then asked to leave! There was a problem though; we'd lost Adam.

Mrs W openly admits she was now struggling to control the rest of us and she was rightly nervous to let Mark and I free again in the Casino while she went off to find Adam. Eventually she got us all back together like a shepherd herding a flock of naughty sheep and she tried to find the exit. The security people were still monitoring us and they pointed out the lift and somehow we all piled in. I wish I could remember the next bit as it sounded hilarious. Mrs W and Jess apparently strode out of the lift when it arrived on the ground floor, expecting us three blokes to follow... but, now in totally uncontrollable and mischievous delirium, we three musketeers refused to get out of the lift and then Mark pushed the button for the top floor. Suffice to say the doors closed with the three of us hollering *"Leeds are going up, na-na-na-na-na, Leeds are going up"* and, complete with silly grins, we waved the girls adieu as the doors slid together! Apparently, we went up and down several times and each time the doors opened at the ground floor the girls tried to coax us out of the lift but each time we refused and went back up again, still singing *"Leeds are going up"* at the tops of our voices!

Somehow, more through good luck than judgement, Mrs W found Jess a taxi and the rest of us apparently walked home arm in arm singing a full repertoire of Leeds songs. Several police monitored our progress but Mrs W persuaded them she was in control. The final part of the story of course was just how Adam came to be in our bed. Mrs W explained she'd been woken in the early hours to find him at the foot of our bed and had politely suggested: *"Adam, go back to bed"* only for him to slump across the bottom corner of our mattress. *"He wasn't doing any harm"* my good lady explained *"so I decided to leave him"*. *"But"*, she went on, *"The next thing I know he's crawling up the bed and squeezing himself in between you and me!"* At that point she decided a threesome was not an experience she had on her bucket list so she retreated to the sofa!

It was a mad, mad day but a birthday I will never forget. In fact the whole three weeks of the holiday was unforgettable. Despite our sore heads, Mark, Adam and I eventually recovered to enjoy two great days at Albert Park for qualifying and the Grand Prix and of course we were all over the moon that Ferrari's Seb Vettel won the race. We are huge Ferrari fans despite the fact they race in red (don't tell Gary Edwards or he'll be nipping over to Maranello to paint the cars white). On the Saturday night we rushed back into the city for the AFL game at the MCG between Essendon Bombers and Hawthorn Hawks; what an experience that was; 78,294 noisy Aussies and all the razzmatazz of Aussie rules footy. Essendon won a thrilling game 116 to 91.

Mark and Adam flew back to Perth a few hours ahead of Mrs W and me as we began the second leg of our tour spending a week in Mark's fabulous apartment overlooking the Swan River. Inevitably, once I got to Perth my thoughts began to turn to the Reading game, one of two away games I was missing, including the Brentford game on April 4th. Sky had annoyingly picked our trip to the Mad Stad for yet another live TV slot at 5:30pm on the Saturday evening... that's 12:30am Sunday morning in Perth. It was our 17th live TV game this season. 17, argh, that wasn't ever going to go well was it?

I put a few feelers out on social media to see if Perth Whites were doing anything for the game but it seemed none of the usual establishments were running with it due to the time slot. I did get a lovely offer from one Perth White though, offering to fetch me to his place to watch it although he cautioned: *"You'll have to get a Uber back though as I'll be having a beer!"* I thanked him for his offer but Mark also had the BeIN TV channel that was showing the game in Oz so we decided to watch it in the apartment.

There were just eight games of the regular season to go and Reading were one of the five teams that looked to be fighting for the four play-off spots assuming Newcastle and Brighton didn't stumble badly and miss out on automatic promotion. Leeds went into the game with a two point advantage over Jaap Stam's Royals but more important was the eight point gap we held over 7th placed Fulham. The teams below Fulham – Norwich, Preston and Derby – all looked too far adrift to worry about. It was a crucial game, a game where a win for either side would be hugely significant with so few points left to play for. I sat down in front of the gigantic 70 inch TV in Mark's flat thinking a draw would be an excellent result. There were some worries though; the main one being that we had an appalling record in the games immediately following international breaks. This season there had been three previous breaks and we'd lost all three games that followed them – Huddersfield and Newcastle at home and Derby away – and we hadn't scored a single goal in any of those and had conceded four. They just happened to have been difficult games against top teams of course but Reading fell squarely in that category too. It was a worry.

The Leeds game was the final one of this round of matches so I already knew the other results. Derby kept their faint hopes alive beating QPR while Fulham won at Rotherham and Wednesday drew 1 – 1 at Barnsley. Huddersfield somehow lost 0 – 1 at home to Burton in the shock result of the day. The top two, Brighton and the Toon, both won to make it look almost certain they'd go up together automatically and it still looked like four from the following five – Huddersfield, Leeds, Reading, Wednesday and Fulham – to make the play-offs. The draw I was hoping for would pretty much do the job while even defeat for Leeds wouldn't be a disaster as long as we could get something at Brentford a few days later.

Green
Berardi Bartley Cooper Taylor
Bridcutt (Capt) Vieira
Sacko Hernandez Pedraza
Wood

Subs: Silvestri, Phillips, O'Kane, Dallas, Doukara, Barrow, Roofe.

Pontus Jansson, having been benched for an unspoken misdemeanour for the Brighton game was now missing altogether. He'd travelled with the team but was out with a slight hamstring strain, albeit Monk told the media he'd planned to use Coops anyway. As much as I respected Garry Monk's support for Coops, I'm no fan of the defender. I've always felt Coops is not the sharpest tool in the box in both senses of the phrase. The rest of the team selection looked OK though – I liked the idea of having Pedraza and Taylor together on the left as that looked an attacking combo and of course Luke Ayling was still suspended otherwise I'd have liked to see him with Sacko on the right. Berardi had done a great job defensively all season but he was not a threat going forward and I didn't see much chance of us ever getting *"on the pitch if Berardi scores"* as we keep singing. We got an unexpected bonus this week when Chris Wood was allowed to travel home early, missing the second New Zealand game against Fiji with a minor injury. It would have been a tall order for him to make the Reading encounter if he'd played the second game as he'd have been flying halfway around the world just a few hours earlier and I know what that's like!

Mrs W had long since gone to bed, grateful no doubt to have it to herself for once. So it was just Mark and me sat on the long leather sofa in front of that giant TV with the dark waters of the Swan River in the distance behind us. I'd spent an hour or so earlier watching the Chelsea v Crystal Palace game that ended with a shock 1 – 2 win for Palace. That was all action in the final few minutes as Chelsea tried to rescue a point. Our game, by contrast, was a slow burner, with the early stages seeing the familiar Reading passing game we witnessed at Elland Road in December; back and forth along their defensive line the ball went and the Leeds fans were soon audible through the TV speakers with their sarcastic shouts of *"Olé"* each time a pass was completed. Loud blasts of MOT and *"We are Leeds"* could also be heard in the opening minutes. Leeds, in the fried egg yellow shirts and socks with white shorts, patiently tracked their men and kept them mostly away from our goal. Leeds had three decent half-chances in the first twenty minutes with a Hernandez flick, a Bartley header and a Pedraza shot that, with more care, might have got us a goal but then, with 22 minutes on the clock, Leeds fell behind. A quick Reading throw-in was intercepted in their right wing corner by the head of a stretching Charlie Taylor but it only went straight to Kermorgant who blasted it home. Rob Green got a glove on it but it was going so fast he merely deflected it in. The flow of the game didn't change much and Leeds continued to fashion better half-chances than the home side but the luck just wasn't going for us. We could have done with a ref with better eyesight too as Chris Wood was smashed in the jaw by a forearm from Reading's innocent looking defender, Tyler Blackett. Sadly, Premier League Referee Keith

Stroud clearly hadn't had his annual visit to Specsavers. A few days later, Stroud committed a major blunder at Newcastle, awarding Burton a free-kick when a Toon player encroached into the area during a Newcastle penalty, instead of ordering a re-take. If he doesn't even know the laws what chance did we have? Anyway, Blackett escaped with hardly a word. Reading had the better of the final minutes of the half and that luck did start to even up a bit as Kermorgant's late shot found the post. The second half ebbed and flowed with Leeds probably just shading it without ever looking likely to score. Doukara, Phillips and Roofe got minutes towards the end and Liam Cooper disgraced himself when he planted a boot squarely on the head of the prone Reece Oxford but, despite a long chat with his liner, Stroud once again, fortunately this time, hadn't seen what happened. It convinced me once again that Coops is more of a liability than an asset and he's the one link remaining with our catastrophic defence of last season. Mark and I looked at each other and Mark muttered something about *"He'll get a ban for that when it gets reviewed after the game"* and sure enough a few days later Cooper was banned for six games, effectively leaving us with just Bartley and a hamstrung Jansson who was also flirting with another ban for the final games. Yeah, brilliant Coops. The ban for Cooper was fully justified but Leeds fans generally were a bit put out that Blackett escaped any post-match sanction for his forearm smash on Wood; the video evidence was considered inconclusive. Some Leeds fans also embarrassed us by throwing bottles onto the pitch, presumably aimed at the Royals' keeper Al-Habsi. There was one funny moment though as Al-Habsi emptied the contents of a bottle in his area and then proceeded to slip on it as he cleared the ball up-field. The game ended 1 – 0 and Reading thus leapfrogged Leeds into 4th place. We remained six points ahead of the seventh placed side, now Sheffield Wednesday, with everyone bar Huddersfield having played 39 games. The Terriers had a game in hand but it looked unlikely they'd catch the top two.

Flicking through the BBC news on the Kindle, I spotted that the comedian Ronnie Corbett had died the previous day, yet one more name that was a constant of my first 60 years;

Corbett was 85. I closed the Kindle and tip-toed off to the bedroom leaving Mark asleep on the sofa: it was goodnight from me and goodnight from him...

Reading 1 **Leeds United 0** (Kermorgant (21))
23,055 (**Leeds 3,546**)

Mrs W and I spent the week in Perth doing all the tourist stuff; we had a long drive north to see the amazing Pinnacles in the Nambung National Park near the town of Cervantes; visited the Crystal Caves near Yanchep; Mark took us for a drive in Swan Valley, famed for its many wineries; we walked around Perth and marvelled at the views from up in Kings Park, had a tour around Fremantle Jail and we spent a day on Rottnest Island, home to the strange little squirrel-like Quokkas. We also drank many, many beers and I have to admit Mrs W and I were beginning to flag a bit as Mark dropped us at the airport for the final leg of our tour; Hong Kong.

We arrived in HK early Monday morning and had five full days there before we were due to fly home on the Friday night. Our game at Brentford was on Tuesday night in England; 2:45am on Wednesday morning for us. The game wasn't on TV and I have to admit I didn't investigate too closely what the options were to listen to it. In fact, I went to bed Tuesday night just hoping for a pleasant surprise in the morning, maybe another Wood moment... perhaps I should rewrite that.

When I awoke, the first contact I had was a Twitter message from Nigel: *"Put that one right up there amongst our worst performances of the season!!!"* I clicked on BBC Sport and soon found the Tuesday night Championship results. Leeds had lost 2 – 0, with the Bees grabbing two first half goals and the report on the game suggested it could have been much worse. *"Brentford, 12th in the Championship, could have won by more as Green made a double save from Vibe and Florian Jozefzoon, while Chris Wood had a late penalty appeal waved away for the away side."*[1]

---

[1] http://www.bbc.co.uk/sport/football/39414036

That was disappointing, Brentford were a decent side but I still felt we ought to have had enough to get at least a point. I studied the team Monk put out and I shook my head.

Green

Ayling Bartley Jansson Berardi

Bridcutt (Capt) Phillips

Barrow Hernandez Dallas

Wood

Subs: Silvestri, Taylor, Vieira, O'Kane, Roofe, Doukara, Pedraza.

There were five changes from the side that started at Reading albeit Jansson for Cooper was enforced now that Coops was banned. It disappointed me that Monk changed both wide men and that Charlie T was benched again; surely we'd be better picking two wingers and sticking with them, give them time to work with the full-backs? It suggested to me again that Monk didn't know who his most effective wide men were; he'd given them all game time in the two defeats and most reports suggested none had really shone. I studied the other results and noted that Wednesday had nicked 6th place again from Fulham with a 2 – 0 win at relegated Rotherham while the Londoners went down 4 – 2 at Derby. Both the top two won; Newcastle in that game v Burton where Stroud messed up and Brighton against Zola's Birmingham, who were sinking ever closer to the relegation zone. Huddersfield beat Norwich 3 – 0.

	P	GD	Pts
Newcastle	40	40	84
Brighton	40	33	83
Huddersfield	39	6	74
Reading	40	5	73
Leeds	**40**	**13**	**69**
Sheff Weds	40	11	66
Fulham	40	18	64

Our margin over Fulham was still five points and that seemed to me the only important statistic as we headed into the last six games. A play-off spot was the only target now.

Brentford 2 **Leeds United 0** (Sawyers (18), Vibe (34))

10,759 (**Leeds 1,656**)

Back Home

Our 13 hour flight from Hong Kong touched down at Manchester's terminal 2 a few minutes early; it was 6:40am. Predictably our two suitcases were among the last to appear on the carousel but we were still in the car heading down the M6 by 7:30am and we pulled on to the drive at home just after 8:30am. I had time to sift through the post, file away the tickets for Newcastle and Burton, have a shave and a shower and I was back on the road heading for Leeds by 10am. I didn't feel too bad, not too bad at all considering I hadn't slept in the previous 34 hours. I have to say there was plenty of leg room on our Cathay Pacific flight but I find it really difficult to sleep on a plane, or any form of transport for that matter.

I spent much of the flight watching movies and made a few notes for the book. Earlier, whilst whiling away a few hours at Hong Kong airport, Leeds fan Mike T, alias Adrian Teakdesk, thought he'd help me out by tweeting a brain teaser to keep me *"occupied during the flight"* – *"If Pontus + Green = 154"* he tweeted, *"what does Pontus + Vieira = ?"* I couldn't crack it to begin with and thought it was something to do with squad numbers but then Mike hinted, *"It's far simpler than that, primary school level in fact"* and I was away. He sent me further questions including *"Which two players = 178"* and the task filled an hour or so but I'd completed the puzzle before we'd even taken off.

I was wandering down Lowfields Road in glorious sunshine by 12:15pm and everything bar the weather looked pretty much as normal. Surprisingly, the Pavilion was already busy when I walked in, a sure sign of another big ER crowd and Steve, Trevor, George, Tony, Shirley and Derek were already ensconced at our usual table. The gist of the conversation was that the game against Preston was a 'must win'.

It was my view too; our progress had stalled in the two games since the international break and the gap to 7th, currently Fulham, was now only 5 points. Like me, Leeds were now 'back home' and we needed some confidence back in the squad with another home win. Our points tally at Elland Road was second to none and we needed to keep it that way against a Preston side that could still catch us and grab their own play-off spot theoretically although they'd need a miracle set of results to achieve that.

As we waited for the announcement of the team, we struggled to discuss the possibilities amongst ourselves as another bang average rock band was blaring away on the little stage. I confess I did have a bit of a headache... but that was probably the lack of sleep as well as the band.

Green
Ayling Bartley (Capt) Jansson Berardi
Phillips Vieira
Roofe Hernandez Pedraza
Wood

Subs: Peacock-Farrell, Taylor, Coyle, Doukara, O'Kane, Dallas, Barrow.

With Liam Bridcutt injured, this was probably the side most fans would have gone with although I still felt Charlie Taylor would have helped us be more aggressive in a game we really had to win. For a third consecutive game, Garry Monk changed the man playing wide right; Kemar Roofe got the call this time following less than average performances from Barrow and Sacko. The wide men continued to be a major source of debate among Leeds fans. Marco Silvestri was missing for Leeds with a knee injury that would require an operation and see him missing for the rest of the season. Young Peacock-Farrell filled in. On the bench for Preston was a certain Jermaine Beckford and another former Leeds man, Paul Huntington was named in their defence.

As I queued at my usual turnstile, number 30, the lad in front of me was taking an age; the card reader seemed to be having a problem with his card. Again and again he offered the plastic to the reader and each time the little green light refused to illuminate. Then, all of a sudden, he smacked himself on the forehead and pulled another card from his wallet. *"For f*** sake, I'm trying to use me bloody bank card"* he exclaimed. I sympathised, having recently tried in Perth to pay for a meal with my season card!

I took my usual place on the Kop alongside Nigel and Kentley and in front of Jo and Mike with the sun threatening to blister our noses. It would take another fifteen minutes or so for it to disappear over the roof of the Kop to give us some respite. We squinted as we applauded in memory of Chris and Kevin, the Leeds fans killed exactly 17 years earlier in Turkey. As the PA announcer so movingly put it; *"We will never forget them"*.

There was an early scare when Tom Barkhuizen got between Bartley and Jansson to thump in a header that Rob Green had to tip over the bar; we weren't used to seeing Barts and Pontus caught like that. Barkhuizen had another opportunity when he got behind the Leeds defence but this time screwed his shot wide. But Leeds soon hit their stride and everyone was playing their part. In particular, Pablo Hernandez seemed to be enjoying playing with the sun on his back and was much more like the little midfield general we'd seen earlier in the season. That man Roofe was also enjoying his role on the right side, either on the wing or, just as often, cutting inside. Phillips and Vieira were pushing forward strongly too and urging Luke Ayling and Berardi to do the same. It looked promising and on 18 minutes the promise was fulfilled.

Kemar Roofe had almost got himself a chance a few minutes earlier when he just failed to get on the end of a Pedraza pass, Alfonso having run from the edge of his own box to deliver it. Now Kalvin Phillips had the ball out on the Leeds left attacking the Kop; he stopped and played it back to Vieira who in turn gave it to Bartley who played it out to Luke Ayling. Leeds were probing, looking for an opening. Ayling passed inside to Vieira who slid the ball forward centrally to Kemar Roofe, back to goal. Suddenly the opening was there, Roofe clipped the ball first time towards Chris Wood, behind and on his left and immediately spun to his right looking for the return pass. Wood was in tune and laid it right into Roofe's path and he was through on goal. He took two touches, one more than was ideal to be honest but as two defenders slid in he finally hit the ball with his left foot. The Roofe I saw last season at Oxford would have buried the ball in the roof of the net but this Roofe still hasn't quite found his touch and his shot cannoned off a defender's boot and looped up over the goal keeper. It seemed to take an age and at one point it looked like it might balloon over the bar but eventually it just crossed the line under the bar and Elland Road erupted. It was an eruption founded on relief more than anything else, relief that we were back on track and en route to win this 'must win' game.

The rest of the half saw Leeds mainly in control although, typical of any Simon Grayson side, Preston were always looking to go forward when the opportunity arose. Leeds fashioned the better chances though and Hernandez was really enjoying himself slaloming past player after player although often without reward. Chris Wood just failed to connect with a Vieira cross and then did the same as a Luke Ayling shot fizzed across the area. We needed that second goal to really settle the nerves and we thought we had it too as finally Wood did connect. Again it was a lovely Leeds move. Vieira and Ayling between them ambushed a Preston forward to win the ball back deep in Leeds territory before Vieira knocked it short to Kalvin Phillips and then Pedraza. Alfonso rolled the ball through the centre of the Preston defence where Kemar Roofe appeared to jump over it allowing it to run on to Chris Wood and Wood side-stepped his man before firing low past Chris Maxwell in the visitor's net. It was another great move and the celebrations were well underway before we noticed the ref trotting over to the liner in front of the East Stand. I knew damn well how this would end; it always goes against us. And it did again, despite initially signalling a goal the ref was now signalling offside! The decision was that Roofe had got the slightest of touches on the ball as it went past him and when he touched it Wood was inches offside. Bugger!

Still chances came for Leeds though and usually they involved Roofe. Minutes later he ought to have scored when he scuffed a low Pedraza cross wide with his left foot but he made amends right on half-time. A Maxwell goal kick was headed forward by the Leeds defence to Chris Wood whose first header back to Hernandez on halfway bounced back up to him. He jumped a second time to nod it back to Roofe and this time Roofe cracked it first time down the inside right channel where Pablo Hernandez was now haring after it. It was now just a matter of whether Pablo could get to it before Maxwell who, spotting the danger was now charging out of goal. With a mighty lunge Pablo just got a toe on the ball to knock it past the keeper and it rolled just quick enough to beat the covering defender. 2 – 0, half-time and all was good in the world. Pablo would celebrate his 32nd birthday in a couple of days and it would prove to be a memorable weekend all round for his family as his brother in law, Sergio Garcia, won the US Masters golf on Sunday.

At half-time, the scores went up on the board from the other games going on around the country. There was a muted groan as we spotted Fulham were two goals to the good against Ipswich and then a bit of a cheer as we saw Huddersfield were losing at Forest. But then there was a gasp of incredulity and we all rubbed our eyes not quite believing the score at Norwich; *"Norwich 6 Reading 1"*. That gave us all as much pleasure as seeing Jermaine Beckford signing autographs for Leeds fans during the interval.

In the second half, Preston started strongly and even with a two goal lead I was still anxious. Had Preston scored during that period the game might have turned on its head but thankfully we held out and then began to dominate again ourselves. There were several half-chances and Chris Wood hammered a close range shot against the bar as did that man Barkhuizen at the other end but it seemed likely we'd seen all the goal action for the day. Leeds left the first substitution until the 70th minute when Stuart Dallas replaced the cramping Kemar Roofe. Shortly afterwards Jermaine Beckford entered the fray to cheers from the Leeds fans and chants of *"January 3rd..."* and *"You're Leeds and you know you are"* which must have irked the Preston fans almost as much as the chance he then missed. Then, as the game appeared to be winding down, Doukara replaced Chris Wood. Charlie Taylor came on for Pablo Hernandez as Garry Monk was clearly protecting his most valuable assets for the trip to St James' Park the following week. In the final moments, Alex Baptiste was sent off for kicking out at Pablo off the ball. The two had been tussling with each other all game.

So, the game was winding down but no one told Souley! Seconds after coming on Doukara found himself on the end of a Dallas cross with only Maxwell to beat but the keeper's boot nudged Souley's shot wide of the post. But then, after a quick exchange of passes between Ayling, Berardi, Vieira and Phillips, Phillips clipped a perfect curling ball around the back of the Preston defence to send Souley away on his own. He drove on into the box and then blasted the ball inside the near post to grab his 6th goal of the season and complete a pretty good day for the majority of folk inside Elland Road.

Fulham did go on to beat Ipswich, Huddersfield did lose at Forest and Norwich eventually went on to demolish Reading 7 - 1 while Sheffield Wednesday surprisingly beat Newcastle 2 – 1 at Hillsborough in the late kick-off. Brighton won 2 – 1 at QPR the previous night. All that meant the top of the Championship now looked like this:

	P	GD	Pts
Brighton	41	34	86
Newcastle	41	39	84
Huddersfield	40	4	74
Reading	41	-1	73
Leeds	41	16	72
Sheff Weds	41	12	69
Fulham	41	20	67

Leeds United 3 Preston North End 0 (**Roofe (18), Hernandez (45), Doukara (90+3)**)
31,851 (Preston 817)

Good Friday

Five games to go in the regular season and Good Friday saw Leeds facing automatic promotion contenders Newcastle United at the magnificent St. James' Park. It was arguably the most difficult of the five, on paper at least.

The Toon needed a maximum of 8 points from their final five games to be mathematically certain of promotion with only Huddersfield in a realistic position to deny them and the Terriers were ten points adrift, so even that was an unlikely prospect. Leeds of course were still looking over their own shoulder with Fulham now only 5 points behind but they had a difficult looking run-in facing Norwich, Villa, Huddersfield, Brentford and, crucially perhaps, Sheffield Wednesday in their final game. Surely they couldn't win them all? Could they?

Mrs W and I were taking the opportunity of another game in the North East to visit our friends in Darlington, Sheila and Brian, so we motored up there on the Thursday. Then, on Friday, Sheila, Mrs W and I took the train to Newcastle; we were going to have a mooch around the city together before I went off to the football. The train was a small three carriage affair that started out from Liverpool and came via York. It was no surprise then that it was jam packed with Leeds lads getting in some pre-match tinnies before hitting the Toon for plenty more beer of the draught variety. It was standing room only but the lads were all well behaved and eagerly gave up their seats to any fit looking girls who boarded the train. As one big lad brushed past me en route to the on-board toilet I could see *"Marching on Together"* tattooed on his forearm. I pointed at it and gave him a Leeds salute and he burst into a slurred rendition of MOT. The Whites' army was on the move.

The weather was uncertain; it didn't know whether to rain or not but it was chilly when the sun went behind any of the dark clouds shrouding the Tyne. We stopped at a little café for lunch, Violet's, just under one end of the old green Tyne Bridge and later crossed the Millennium Bridge to visit the Baltic Centre for Contemporary Arts. Some of the art was, well, 'far out man' but there was a magnificent view to be had along the Tyne back towards the City from the viewing deck on the fourth floor. To the left of the Tyne Bridge, as we viewed it, was the Sage Gateshead, the distinctive silver clad concert venue described by punk queen Patti Smith back in 2007 as *"A huge, silver, shining peanut"*!

As the clock ticked on towards 5pm I said farewell to the girls and headed to the Mile Castle, a Wetherspoon pub I went to before our League Cup game against the Toon back in 2013. It wasn't a particularly good omen as we lost that game 2 – 0; it was the one where McCormack chipped onto the bar in the first five minutes and then we did little else all game. I headed there as it was the only Toon pub I was even vaguely familiar with. I checked out all three floors while supping my first pint of the day but didn't spot anyone familiar. I'd seen Simon W and Wayne heading away from the pub earlier so I messaged Simon to see where he was heading; he came back: *"We are in Union Rooms mate but it's an arsehole to get in"* I decided to head instead to the Bridge Hotel, right next to the High Level Bridge and Castle Keep; Jo messaged to say she was in there. I joined Jo and MuckyFat aka Martin and kept an eye on the Wolves v Brighton game on TV while working my way through another three beers. Brighton won comfortably to make it a clean sweep for four of the top seven sides so far in this 41st round of games. Huddersfield sneaked past Preston 3 – 2 with a disputed late penalty, Fulham won 3 – 1 at Norwich and Sheffield Wednesday beat Cardiff 1 – 0. Reading were due to play at Villa the following day. Leeds really needed a win to maintain position but that was asking a bit much so most folk reckoned a draw would be OK. Kentley and Mike arrived together in time for a last pint before we all set off on the short walk to the ground.

I never fail to be impressed with St. James' Park (SJP); it's a monster, towering into the sky over the shops and houses in the area. Kentley, Mike and I stopped to admire the statue of Jackie Milburn outside the Gallowgate End where the great man's ashes were scattered following his death in 1988. Then we made our way to the ginormous Leazes Stand and climbed 14 sets of steps to the top of the world.

If anything, the view inside is even more awe inspiring than the view of SJP from outside. Our seats were nowhere near the top but the pitch still looked tiny from our vantage point up in the gods. Over the roof of the East Stand, to our left, we had a view of the city and immediately on our left, high up on the massive Perspex weather protection was a huge video screen. The ground was almost full with over 52,000 packed inside and as the teams came out, the Toon in their classic black and white stripes and Leeds in all blue, the atmosphere was as good as anything I'd come across. Over in the Gallowgate End, several huge banners were unfurled proclaiming *"We are United"* and *"Geordie Pride, One City, One Club, One Life"* together with large flags bearing the unmistakeable face of their manager Rafa Benitez. The centre circle was filled with a giant advertising banner for the Newcastle sponsors, Wonga and Puma. It was some sight but the sound track was all Leeds; over 3,000 Leeds fans had been on the ale all day and our voices were in grand fettle.

Green
Ayling Bartley Jansson Berardi
Bridcutt (Capt) Phillips
Roofe Hernandez Pedraza
Wood

Subs: Peacock-Farrell, Taylor, O'Kane, Vieira, Dallas, Doukara, Sacko.

Ronaldo Vieira was said to have a touch of illness but was still named on the bench, otherwise this was pretty much the side everyone expected.

Newcastle attacked our end in the first half but in the first few minutes all the action was taking place in front of the Toon Army at the Gallowgate End. Pablo Hernandez floated in a free-kick from the right but pulled it badly and Luke Ayling chested it down on the edge of the box before returning it to Pablo as if to say, *"Try that one again mate!"* His second effort was much better and was headed away from near the penalty spot to Chris Wood who chested it down before laying it back to Pedraza on the left corner of the area. Alfonso shifted the ball to his right and then thundered in a shot that rattled the Toon cross bar. It bounced down right in front of Kemar Roofe and although keeper Karl Darlow was back on his feet in a jiffy, Roofe only had to nod his header into one of the corners to beat him. As we've seen so often this season though, Roofe's finishing has left a lot to be desired and his weak header was swatted away by Darlow to safety. My mind immediately raced back to that Ross McCormack effort here in 2013 that smacked the same bar and I remembered with a shake of my head that we didn't get another chance after that. As Newcastle eventually cleared the ball away, Jonjo Shelvey caught Pablo Hernandez on the back of the head with a high boot. Shelvey escaped with nothing more than a word from referee Chris Kavanagh but Pablo needed a Kisnorbo wrapped around his head to stem the flow of blood. At least there was now one player out there who was easily recognisable from our spot in up the clouds.

Pedraza would have another decent shot that fizzed across the face of Darlow's goal but the rest of the action was then at our end as Newcastle started to boss the possession, force many corners and give Rob Green several opportunities to show us what a great keeper he is. A combination of good fortune and heroic defending somehow got us to half-time with the score still at nil-nil and I wandered off for a half-time secondary smoking break in the nearest bogs. Most of us queued and choked quietly while one lad just inside the door decided it was OK to pee in the waste bin, oblivious to the fact there were holes in its base!

The second half followed the same general trend as the first with Newcastle now attacking towards the Toon fans at the far end. Shelvey, who arguably shouldn't even have been on the pitch, was orchestrating every move. But still Rob Green was solid and still Pontus Jansson was like a colossus in the centre of our defence, throwing himself in the way of any shot aimed at Green's goal and heading away every cross. It was a mighty defensive display. Newcastle's corner count was now in double figures as Matt Ritchie placed the ball once more in the quadrant on the Toon left wing. Once again it was the head of Pontus Jansson who knocked the ball away but this time it was collected by Vurnon Anita who shifted it out to the right wing to Yoan Gouffran. His lofted cross to the back post was, for once, not attacked by either Bartley or Jansson leaving Aleksandar Mitrovic to rise and head it back into the centre of the six-yard box. Jamaal Lascelles jumped highest to glance a header down to Rob Green's left hand and the keeper's glove just failed to stop the ball going over the line. Leeds were behind with half an hour or so to go.

The support from the Leeds fans was immense; other than a brief eruption when they scored we really couldn't hear the home fans at all over the noise we were making. Our behaviour wasn't impeccable mind; a few bottles were thrown one of which seemed to come from way up above us and it ricocheted off one unfortunate Toon's head onto another as it reached terra firma below. Our behaviour on the pitch was causing a few worries too, in the space of two minutes both Pontus Jansson (handball) and Kyle Bartley (foul) were booked and for Pontus that meant he was now just one booking away from his 15th of the season and a three match ban. That would no doubt occupy much thinking time at Elland Road as they tried to work out if it was better to get another booking in say, the Wolves game, so Pontus would be available for the play-offs or whether we just trusted to luck remembering that the only centre back cover available was Luke Ayling as Cooper was still banned. Kalvin Phillips also picked up another booking as the pressure mounted.

Just before the Newcastle goal, Hadi Sacko surprisingly replaced Pedraza who I thought was playing well and then with 15 minutes left Monk made another strange substitution by bringing on Doukara for Bridcutt. Monk then made his final throw of the dice sending on Charlie Taylor for Berardi in a change that I was much happier with although it baffled me that Monk didn't do it to pair up Taylor and Pedraza which I thought was the most obvious partnership on the left. There was not much sign that the changes improved anything. Newcastle were just starting to ease off and were thinking more about time wasting and keeping tight at the back but Sacko looked no more effective than usual while Doukara lofted one cross way too long and out of play after a promising move. We were into added time and Newcastle were now intent on keeping the ball in the Leeds defensive corners. As they won their 19th corner of the game (Leeds had none!) Jonjo Shelvey finally got his name in Kavanagh's little book as he tried to waste yet more time. Colback was then booked as he cynically brought down Kemar Roofe who was breaking from midfield. Anything was acceptable to them now to protect their valuable three points that would leave them just one more win away from a return to the Premier League at the first attempt. Hernandez lofted the free-kick towards the edge of the Newcastle box, miles below where Kentley, Nigel and I were standing. Leeds had everyone bar Green forward and the Toon had everyone back. Consequently when the ball was headed clear it was only Leeds players in position to collect it again. Sacko raced back and collected it out on the Leeds right wing over to our left. Sacko lofted it back towards goal with his left boot and Jansson back-headed it further on but it was headed away again. Once more there were no Newcastle players outside their own defensive area so Leeds collected the clearance, Pablo Hernandez this time centrally. Hernandez suddenly looked inspired and he jinked past one player before stabbing the ball through to Kemar Roofe, back to goal on the left corner of the area. Roofe stopped the ball and then swivelled to swing it into the middle and incredibly we could see it coming down between two Toon defenders, neither of whom had spotted Chris Wood steaming in. The cross was inch perfect to land on Wood's right boot and he was able to side-foot a volley into the top corner giving Darlow absolutely no chance. It was apparently the first attempt Chris Wood had managed in four games but he was deadly with it.

The Leazes Stand erupted in amazing scenes as hairy arsed blokes hugged and kissed each other and punched the air while the Leeds players gathered below us to take our plaudits. The rest of the ground was on the move, thousands and thousands of Toon fans were streaming towards the exits knowing there were only seconds to go. Even Garry Monk allowed himself a little jig of delight over on the touchline as he too knew we had snatched a point from the jaws of defeat. It was one of those magic moments that footy fans live for; out of the blue, unexpected but so, so important... possibly. We all knew this was the most difficult test we faced in these vital last five games and we'd come through it with a point. If we could now beat Wolves on Easter Monday then we'd surely have one boot in the play-offs. It was that important.

Garry Monk told the BBC: *"What an amazing mentality they have created. We have played better but you need both. You need the mentality, the spirit but also the quality and we were able to show that quality in that single moment, which was important and sometimes that's all it takes."*

The celebrations carried on all the way down those 14 flights of steps with the new Ronnie Vieira chant accompanying us all the way down. *"Ronaldo Vieira, he's just a teenager, he never gives the ball away... One-two-three-four"*, on and on it went until we could hardly speak let alone sing. It continued in the streets of Newcastle too as we passed scantily clad girls and lusting Geordie lads heading for the bars and clubs in the city. Kentley had parked just outside the city and by the time we reached the car all was quiet. The Leeds fans were now either on coaches or trains heading home or they'd be ogling those Geordie girls with their high heels and micro-skirts in the many city centre bars. There would be some sore heads in the morning!

Kentley drove us back to Darlington where the wonderful Sheila and Brian had offered to let Kentley stay the night; Sheila put on one of her impromptu meals when she realised we'd not eaten since lunchtime although we had to wake her first; she'd drunk far too much wine with Mrs W! All in all this truly had been a very, very Good Friday.

Newcastle United 1 **Leeds United 1** (Lascelles (57), **Wood (90+5)**)

52, 301 (**Leeds 3,169**)

I don't like Mondays

I don't think anyone expected anything other than three points for Leeds from the home game with Wolves on Easter Monday. Everyone was still buzzing from that last gasp equaliser up at St. James' Park and somehow that was seen as a sign that this was going to be our year. Wolves were no mugs of course; under manager Paul Lambert they'd pulled away from the relegation zone and were now pretty comfortable in mid-table having recently been on a five match winning streak including very impressive victories at Brentford and Fulham. They'd slipped up in their previous couple of games at Bristol and at home to Brighton but even so we all knew any Lambert team would be no easy meat. Three points for Leeds though was a must to keep that cushion between us and the two teams capable of stopping our progress into the play-offs; Fulham and Sheffield Wednesday. With those two playing each other on the final day the anticipated three points from Wolves would surely get us very close to a certain top six spot come May 7th.

Another big crowd was predicted at Elland Road and that had been obvious to me as despite arriving in Lowfields Road at noon, cars were already parked half-way down towards the stadium, whilst in the Pavilion we scrambled to get enough chairs around the table for the latecomers. As a reminder it was Easter, Jacqui gave us all a little chocolate football each to savour with our beer but the really big news in the Pavilion was that they now had plastic two-pint beakers to accommodate the 'two for six quid' deal. Progress!

There were no particular nerves amongst the Pavilion regulars although in the back of most fans' minds there was the knowledge that Leeds seldom do anything in a straightforward manner and a stumble today would be a typical Leeds scenario. When the team was announced there were few dissenters as it was the same starting XI we saw take the field up at Newcastle although I was still disappointed that Garry Monk didn't opt to pair Taylor with Pedraza. Berardi continued to get the shout despite his limitations going forward.

Green
Ayling Bartley Jansson Berardi
Bridcutt (Capt) Phillips
Roofe Hernandez Pedraza
Wood

Subs: Peacock-Farrell, Coyle, Taylor, O'Kane, Doukara, Dallas, Sacko.

Ronaldo Vieira, he that *"never gives the ball away"*, was missing altogether now with the mysterious illness that kept him benched at SJP. The big question on everyone's lips was whether Pontus would opt to get himself his 15th yellow card this afternoon to ensure his ban would only cost him the last three league games but clear him to be available for the play-offs. Most money was on a last minute winner from the big man and then a booking as he whipped off his shirt to celebrate in front of the Kop...

Once I was settled in my place in row GG, I took in the vista of another bumper crowd in the old stadium. The only visible spaces were over in front of the Wolves fans at the far end of the West Stand and a few in the upper tier of the East Stand.

32,531 were in Elland Road today and it was a magnificent sight; not a sell-out but yet another attendance over 30,000.

Wolves annoyed us by winning the toss and electing to have Leeds attack the Kop in the first half; as soon as we saw the teams changing ends the usual chorus of boos went around the ground. Someone always comes up with a positive slant though and a voice was soon heard to say *"Preston did it too lads and it didn't help them!"*

Had Leeds come out and played as we did against Preston then perhaps it wouldn't have mattered but it was very quickly obvious that we were not on our A game today. Wolves started brightly and, as you'd expect, they hunted in packs, while Leeds were doing that annoying thing of misplacing passes all over the pitch and failing to get on each other's wavelength. The almost celebratory atmosphere that we began the game with soon turned to one of nervous annoyance. A very weak referee, Jeremy Simpson, didn't help our cause either. He refused to penalise an obvious push in the back on Kyle Bartley at a Leeds corner and then annoyed the whole of the Kop as he overruled his assistant to award Wolves a goal-kick. Nothing was going right and the tension increased.

Leeds were not totally without chances; former Leeds keeper Andy Lonergan cut out one dangerous ball that Kalvin Phillips fizzed across goal but Rob Green was much busier at the other end pulling off two excellent stops as his good form continued. The first should really have been scored by Andreas Weimann as Berardi and Jansson got in a tangle on the edge of the Leeds box. It left Weimann all alone, 18 yards out, but Green was there in a flash to block the shot. The second was a save low down to his left from Dave Edwards.

Then, with 38 minutes on the clock Pontus Jansson tried to push forward. With few options available, Pontus weaved past two or three Wolves players as the Kop hollered for him to have a shot at goal but then he was outnumbered and lost possession. Wolves quickly moved the ball forward with Ben Marshall and he slid the ball through the Leeds defence, bisecting Liam Bridcutt and Gaetano Berardi to find a Pontus Jansson shaped space. Nouha Dicko was onto it like lightning to tuck it away in the bottom left corner. It felt like a turning point in this so far successful season. When the half-time whistle blew there were plenty of boos but most were directed at the referee who'd given a performance more akin to Homer Simpson than Jeremy. The verbal assault continued as the officials were shepherded off the pitch to the safety of the dressing rooms with the players all long gone.

The second half was better by Leeds but never good enough. It was not for lack of effort but there was a definite lack of quality, particularly in trying to create anything positive in the final third. Garry Monk produced his usual array of unusual substitutions as first Hadi Sacko replaced Bridcutt and then, just after the hour mark, we finally got Charlie Taylor on for Berardi; the move I'd been calling for. Straight away Charlie was involved in the game bombing down the left wing in front of the East Stand but then Monk baffled me as he withdrew Pedraza, an obvious link for Taylor on the left and brought on instead the right footed Souley Doukara. Very strange!

Pontus Jansson did his best to get that 15th yellow card as he argued with Homer and knocked the ball away having conceded a free-kick but it was almost as if old Homer knew exactly what game Pontus was playing and he merely gave him another stern talking to. Leeds won several corners late in the game and with Bartley up supporting the attack a few headers went close but it was all too little too late and at the final whistle there were more boos and this time they were squarely aimed at the Leeds players.

I trudged wearily back up Lowfields Road after the game with Kev and Nigel and when I got to the car I slumped down in the driver's seat and switched on the radio to hear what BBC Radio Leeds made of it all. Noel Whelan and Katherine Hannah sounded as miserable as the rest of us. In his post-match interview with Adam Pope, Garry Monk remained upbeat and promised his players would give everything they had to try to achieve a play-off spot that had been so tantalisingly close before this set-back.

"We didn't want that to happen at this stage of the season but we've had the mentality for so long where we've been in the play-offs quite comfortably and have kind of been in that protective mode of trying to stay in there.

"Now we have to change that mentality to be a team that goes on the hunt and lets it all go.
"It's still a really good situation for us. We've got no time to feel sorry for ourselves, that doesn't get you anywhere."[1]

Leeds had indeed been safely in that group of six at the top of the Championship since 26th November, 26 games ago and now, with all the other relevant results today going against us, we'd sunk to 7th, overtaken by both Wednesday and Fulham. It had been a rotten day; boy, do I not like Mondays.

	P	GD	Pts	
Brighton	43	37	92	Promoted
Newcastle	43	37	85	
Reading	43	2	79	
Huddersfield	42	5	78	
Sheff Weds	43	14	75	
Fulham	43	24	73	
Leeds Utd	**43**	**15**	**73**	

Leeds United 0 Wolverhampton Wanderers 1 (Dicko (38))
32,351 (Wolves 1,172)

---

[1] *http://www.bbc.co.uk/sport/football/39549519*

Going for a Burton

One result on Easter Monday that didn't really affect Leeds directly was at St. Andrews where Birmingham City lost yet again. This time they went down 0 – 2 to Burton Albion, coincidentally our next opponents and managed of course by Nigel Clough. The result left Blues 20th in the Championship, only 3 points above the relegation zone with three games to play. Since Gianfranco Zola took the Blues' hot seat back in December the Midlands side had won only two of 24 games and they'd slipped from 7th, where Garry Rowett left them, to that precarious position of 20th. Since Zola arrived they really had gone for a Burton and now Zola himself waved the white flag. He resigned after the Burton game saying: *"I sacked myself. I am sorry because I came to Birmingham with huge expectations. It is not that I like quitting, but Birmingham deserves better."*[1] I should be running a club; I knew it was a mistake back in December! The appointment of Zola ranks amongst the most spectacular own goals of all time and it might well mean Birmingham face life in League One next season. So, who did they turn to in an effort to avoid that fall from grace? None other than Harry Redknapp; one could only guess at the scale of the bonus Redknapp had been offered to keep them up; he was telling the media he'd get nothing at all if Blues went down. I guess Rosie the dog was already dusting off her doggie passport in preparation for another visit to that bank in Monaco. And while we were all absorbing the news of Harry's Houdini attempt, the nation was plunged into election fever yet again as Theresa May called a snap election to get the nation's backing for her Brexit negotiations and believing presumably that the Labour Party had also gone for a Burton. And if that wasn't enough excitement for one day, Leeds announced they'd frozen the prices of their season ticket renewals for next season yet again regardless which division we'd be in. Mine

---

[1] *http://www.bbc.co.uk/sport/football/39628280*

would actually be over a hundred quid cheaper than last year as now being 60 years old I was entitled to the senior citizen concession. It was just £316 for me next season for a home season ticket for another year of excitement and frustration. The question was though would I be watching Championship footy or Premier League footy? The assumption I'd made, along with most Leeds fans, was that we ought to at least be in the play-offs so there would be no question of that partial season ticket refund we'd been promised by Massimo if we missed out on the top six... All we had to do was to win three games, against Burton, Norwich and Wigan and we'd be in the end of season lottery. Most Leeds fans were confident we could do that, despite having struggled to find our form in recent weeks and in any case we were all certain Fulham couldn't possibly win all their remaining games as they faced high flying Huddersfield, London rivals Brentford and finished with a trip to Sheffield Wednesday who we also fancied we could overtake; after all, as we'd said many times, they can't both win that one! First though we had to beat Burton and they themselves needed one more win to just about guarantee Championship football next season. With football finances as they are these days that was a huge incentive that shouldn't be underestimated. Anyway, I made the relatively short drive along the A50 to Burton full of confidence; it was a lovely day too, what could possibly go wrong?

I parked in the little industrial estate opposite the ground and then walked down Wetmore Road to the Great Northern, a little pub I'd visited on previous visits to the Pirelli. I was here near the end of the 2009/2010 season with my old mate Brian, watching his beloved Darlington beat the home side 1 – 2 in an unlikely away win that still wasn't enough to save them from dropping out of the football league that season. I was also here when Leeds came for a pre-season game in August 2012 when Leeds ran out 0 – 1 winners. The ground was only opened in 2005 and it is tiny with an official capacity of 6,912. There would only be around 6,000 in it today for our visit even though Leeds had sold out their 1,600 allocation. Another few thousand Leeds fans would be watching the game on 'beam-back' at Elland Road such was the interest. It was a game as

I've said already, we all thought would see us get back on the winning road.

I wandered into the pub at 12:30pm and there was only a handful of fans in there by then; a few Leeds and a couple wearing Burton's yellow colours. I worked my way through a few pints of Bridge Bitter (4.2% from the local Burton Bridge Brewery) and one of the pub's tasty cheese and onion baps while I awaited the arrival of Kentley the Stokie. I was getting bored watching a preview of the FA Cup semi-final between Spurs and Chelsea on a TV screen up on the wall; they covered everything from a tour of the Wembley changing rooms to how they paint the lines on the pitch. I wandered outside to stand in the sun.

It wasn't long before a familiar face arrived; Alan, who is in the Pavilion at Leeds with his mate John before every home game. Today he was with another old pal of his, Gordon, who lives not far from the Pirelli; Alan stopped with him the previous night. I'd not really had a long chat with Alan before but it was fascinating listening to him and Gordon's stories; they were both schoolboy footballers together at Leeds back in the late 60s and early 70s and Gordon then actually lived on Elland Road in a house just behind the chip shop. He told us how his mum will fondly relate the tale as to how she once sewed up John Charles's trousers when he split them but the tale I liked most was when Gordon was unexpectedly called into the club for a pre-season game one summer.

The boots he'd used for the previous season were totally shot, so he'd thrown them out but he hadn't yet bought new ones so he turned up at Elland Road without any. The coach looking after them at the time was Bob English, a well-known figure from the Leeds back room staff in the days of Don Revie and Bob was incredulous at this stupidity. *"What sort of a footballer turns up without any boots?"* he roared. English had been known to send young players home for having dirty boots let alone arriving with none at all. *"What size are you lad?"* asked Bob. *"Five and a half sir"* Gordon replied and off went Bob to see if he could find any. He returned after a while with an old pair of size five Adidas boots that were well worn and handed them to the young Gordon who managed to squeeze them on. *"You'd better play well in them son"* Bob English told him, *"Them's Billy Bremner's boots!"*

The time passed quickly listening to Gordon and Alan's tales and we were soon drinking up and heading back up the road to the Pirelli. Kentley and I were in the East Stand terracing and we had to push and shove a bit to get ourselves a spec; there was also a section of seating in our end of the South Stand over to our left; I could see big Tim and Clive in there. On the pitch, the players of both sides were just entering the arena with a guard of honour of a group of cheerleaders decked out in very unglamorous black and gold uniforms. They shimmied with their silver pompoms as sexily as their drab outfits would allow. You don't see many American cheerleaders in black and there's a reason for that! The Burton mascot, Billy Brewer, dashed across the pitch looking like he'd had a few too many Bridge Bitters but there was no sign of his usual side-kick Bettie. A chant of *"If you're watching on the beam-back you're a c***"* broke out from the other end of our terracing just to let our mates back in Leeds know we were thinking of them.

Before kick-off the two teams – Leeds in all white and the Brewers in yellow shirts with black shorts and socks – lined up around the centre circle. I'd lost count of the number of times this season we'd observed a minute's silence or applause but once again today it was with heartfelt sympathy for the bereaved families that we stood to attention in complete silence once we all understood it *was* a silence and not an applause tribute; the PA at Burton was very difficult to understand. The tribute was in honour of the 20 year old student from Burton, Hannah Bladon, who was killed in a senseless knife attack in Jerusalem on 14th April and two footballers from vastly different eras. Former Leeds player Ugo Ehiogu suffered a cardiac arrest and died on Thursday 20th April at the age of just 44 while former Burton player Dave McAdam did at least reach the ripe old age of 94 before he passed away recently. McAdam was also at one time on Leeds' books. As always, as the referee's whistle brought the silence to an end the whole stadium erupted in a cacophony of roars, hoots and hollers.

Green
Ayling Bartley (Capt) Jansson Taylor
Vieira Phillips
Roofe Hernandez Doukara
Wood

Subs: Peacock-Farrell, Berardi, O'Kane, Dallas, Antonsson, Pedraza, Sacko.

I'd forgotten all about checking to find the team selection earlier on so I was only now absorbing this line-up as I mentally checked off the names I could see on the pitch. There appeared to be three changes from the starting line-up against Wolves; Doukara was in for Pedraza while Taylor came in for Berardi and Vieira replaced Bridcutt who was said to have another Achilles injury... it certainly was his Achilles heel! Once again I was a bit perplexed by Monk's selection; he'd now done what most folk had wanted by bringing Charlie Taylor back but rather than pair him with the left-footed winger Pedraza he was now hooked up with the right-footed Doukara. Burton were without their Leeds loanee Luke Murphy who was not permitted to play against his parent club while another ex-Leeds Luke, Luke Varney was on the bench. You could say they would be missing their 'Lukes as aids energy'.

Leeds started well, with Hernandez firing over and Chris Wood even having the ball in the net inside ten minutes; sadly it was ruled out by referee Darren Bond for some reason that has remained a mystery to this day. Pablo Hernandez looked mildly uncomfortable taking a corner in front of three of the scantily clad cheerleaders but he swung the ball across and Pontus Jansson rose to head down and towards goal from 12 yards. The ball bounced up and was further headed into the air near the right hand post as we looked on from the other end. Kyle Bartley jumped with the goalkeeper and won it cleanly to knock it towards the other post where Chris Wood nodded it home. I've watched it a dozen times and can't see what the issue was. It sort of took the wind out of everyone's sails as for one brief second we thought we were on our way. Now we had to start again and both teams seemed to have settled into their respective rhythms, trading corner kicks in the main with seven to Leeds and six to the Brewers during the first half. Worse still was the news filtering through from Huddersfield where Fulham had now taken a 1 – 2 lead after initially falling behind. There was no score in the other game that had meaning for Leeds; Sheffield Wednesday were still nil-nil with Derby. By the time the half-time whistle blew at the Pirelli, Fulham had blasted into a 1 – 4 lead. As I trudged off to fight the battle of the bogs, where a pair of waders would have come in handy, the conversations amongst the Leeds faithful were pretty pessimistic with phrases like *"I f****** knew this would happen"*, *"We've no f******* idea out there have we?"* and *"At least I'll get me 90 quid back on me season ticket"* being the order of the day.

The second half was very much like the first but without the corners and neither side looked very good. Leeds in particular looked bereft of ideas, energy and at times ball skills while the Burton manner of defending was similar to that of Peter Kaye… *"'av it!"* The hour mark ticked by and Leeds made their first change; Sacko replaced Doukara. It almost brought immediate rewards too as Charlie Taylor stabbed the ball into the middle with the outside of his left boot and Pablo Hernandez only had to steer the ball past Bywater in the home goal. Somehow, Pablo made a complete cods of it and glanced it wide. Pontus Jansson then had a similar chance and did exactly the same as Leeds almost profited from the only corner of the second half. The Leeds fans were now getting frantic and some were hurling abuse at the players as the news came through that Wednesday were now 2 -1 up against Derby. Leeds were mired in 7th if it stopped like this. But it didn't stop like this.

Leeds brought on Pedraza for Kalvin Phillips as the urgency of the situation had clearly been relayed to Garry Monk. Leeds were now going 4 – 4 – 2 with Roofe and Wood in attack and Pedraza and Sacko on the wings. Burton brought on the dangerous Michael Kightly. Have I mentioned how substitutes always seem to score against Leeds? Of course I have, a thousand times.

Actually, this time he didn't score, or at least not yet, but he was the assist as Burton scored and 1,600 Leeds fans at the Pirelli and countless more watching at Elland Road had their hearts broken. It was so simple too. A shocking pass from Sacko, deep in his own half, was intercepted by the aforementioned Kightly who looked bright as a button. He jabbed the ball forward to Marvin Sordell on the edge of the Leeds box with Kyle Bartley tight behind him; but not tourniquet tight. Sordell held Bartley at arms' length and then got himself a yard in which to swivel and hit a curling right foot shot just inside the post. The Burton players all celebrated over in the north-west corner, to our right at the far end, just where three of those cheerleaders were now 'shakin their asses' in tune with the Burton goal-music rasping out over the crap PA system.

The Leeds fans tried to regroup and go again with some lusty *"We are Leeds"* chants as we realised those play-offs were fading away faster than my 'Man from Uncle' invisible ink used to but the Leeds players looked shell-shocked. A bloke next to me was imploring them to *"get up off your f****** arses and give it a go for f*** sake, it's not over yet!"* but then even he was rocked back on his heels as Burton scored again.

Bywater hit a long goal-kick deep into Leeds territory and Vieira and Bartley jumped with Atkins. Atkins won the ball and headed it on, right into the Bartley shaped gap now yawning in the Leeds defence. Sordell was onto it in a flash, poked it through to Kightly and with Charlie Taylor momentarily stopping, Kightly buried the ball in the corner. The Piranhas' 'Tom Hark' blasted out again, the Burton players and fans went mad and the cheerleaders shook their booties again with tutus twirling while several Leeds fans pushed past me heading for the exit. It was a bad moment, it felt like the end.

It took the Leeds players a few minutes but eventually they must have decided there was no point in being cautious now and everyone piled forward. Kyle Bartley in particular was more often than not up with the attack as he took his 'lead from the front' mentality literally. With Sacko on the right and Pedraza on the left and Hernandez now spraying the ball wide at every opportunity, suddenly and almost for the first time this season we started lobbing bombs into the middle for Bartley and Wood to attack. Why oh why didn't we do this earlier though? Burton looked shaky too and no more Leeds fans left the terracing for the moment at least. So often has the improbable afflicted Leeds that I'm sure many of us actually believed Leeds would turn this around. Even the bloke next to me was up on his toes again yelling *"There's plenty of time lads, come on we can f****** do this"*. And for a few brief moments it looked like we might; in the 80th minute Leeds had one back.

Hernandez launched in a free-kick from out on the Leeds left which was headed clear but only as far as Ronnie Vieira. Vieira launched it straight back with his left foot towards Chris Wood who was now behind the Burton defence. As he headed across goal, Kentley and I were directly behind the flight of the ball and we could see it was going in anyway but Kyle Bartley made sure with a flying kick to smash it home. Now the Leeds fans were up for a battle and belief was suddenly restored. Leeds immediately won the ball back from the restart and were straight on the attack. It was all hands to the pump for Bywater and his merry men in the heart of the home defence.

Another cross, this time from Luke Ayling, found the head of Bartley again and the ball dropped at the feet of Kemar Roofe, inches from the line. We thought he was bound to score and we were already celebrating madly but in a comedy moment that sort of summed up Kemar's season he couldn't apply the finishing touch and with the ball actually on the goal-line the next boot to it was a big Burton one and with that clearance our season probably went for a Burton too.

At the final whistle, Kentley flopped down onto the crash barrier overcome by the emotion of it all while I stood silently watching the Leeds players all drop to the turf. It was clear that everyone thought this was the end of our challenge for the play-offs and of course that meant no play-off final trip to Wembley and no Premier League football next season. Some Leeds fans were angry and a few blokes behind me started to abuse the players as they came across to salute us. I turned and shook my head at them and drew angry glances so I turned back towards the players, held my hands high in the air and clapped them as best I could muster. Several of the players quickly went off towards the dressing rooms but Pontus and Luke Ayling went right along the width of the Leeds support applauding and Hadi Sacko even threw his shirt into the crowd. Just as it wasn't acceptable at Sutton to abuse our players, it wasn't acceptable now. They'd done their best.

Quite where the fault lay I wasn't sure but it was hard to resist the temptation to think that these last few games had just pushed our young squad too far. We almost certainly would have coped better with a few more quality additions in the January window and we still didn't really know why that didn't happen. The two players we did bring in, Mo Barrow and Pedraza were no better than we already had. Their arrival seemed to put uncertainty in Garry Monk's mind too as he chopped and changed his wide men every game trying to find the best combination. Our players looked jaded and it was probably as much mental fatigue as physical that had drained the youngsters as they tried to cope with the pressures of getting across the line. As is usually the case, the real reason was probably a combination of all those factors. A bit of luck wouldn't have gone amiss either, especially with that early 'goal' that was disallowed today. The first goal is always crucial and who knows what the outcome might have been had that counted. At the end of the day though, it was hard to come to any conclusion other than we were just not good enough.

Fulham clearly *were* good enough as they held on to that 1 – 4 lead to make even more secure their top six status, while Wednesday also saw off Derby. I'd certainly felt there was no way Fulham would win all their final few games which looked, on paper, really difficult but so far they'd swept away all before them. It was not technically over yet of course; if Leeds could win their final two games against Norwich and Wigan and if either or both Wednesday and Fulham did stumble then we could still climb back above them. The problem was neither I, nor most Leeds fans at this time could see how Leeds could get their winning mojo back; everything seemed so flat out on the pitch.

As I walked back to the car I bumped into several folk I know and to a man, and a woman, they were all talking about it being over. Most were sanguine about it, acknowledging what a great job Monk had done to get a limited and inexperienced squad even this far and being optimistic that, as long as we could keep Monk and the nucleus of the side then next season could well be 'the one'. It was that typical football fan's optimism; the season is dead, bring on the next season and we'll go again. We do it every year.

Garry Monk summed the game up, as he always does in a positive manner, believing his side didn't deserve to lose but looking at the match stats, despite having the bulk of the ball we had one fewer attempt on goal and one fewer on target than Burton and that sort of told the story of our season; we don't create enough. I saw somewhere that Leeds had created fewer attempts on goal than any other Championship team, including bottom side Rotherham. Monk assured the fans though that his players would give absolutely everything they had at Elland Road against Norwich and would keep going while there was still a sliver of a chance of success, small as it maybe. Once again we faced two more must win games and this time, we actually had to win them. If we could, then our fate was in the hands of Fulham and Wednesday and less so Huddersfield and Reading who could mathematically still be caught if they lost all their remaining games. The odds were on our season going right to the final game at Wigan, but without a miracle it wouldn't see us in the play-offs.

Burton Albion 2 **Leeds United 1** (Sordell (75), Kightly (77), **Bartley (80)**)
6,073 (**Leeds 1,641**)

Must Win

On Monday night, Newcastle beat Preston 4 – 1 at St. James' Park to secure promotion, while on Sunday, Villa had beaten Harry's new boys 1 – 0 to leave them deep in trouble.

	P	GD	Pts	
Brighton	44	35	92	Promoted
Newcastle	44	40	88	Promoted
Reading	44	1	79	
Huddersfield	43	2	78	
Sheff Weds	44	15	78	
Fulham	44	27	76	
Leeds Utd	44	14	73	

The objective for Leeds against Norwich was simple; it was the definitive 'must win' game. We'd talked about 'must win' games for weeks but until the maths tells you that if you don't win then it's over, then it's not really a 'must win'; it's more 'a win would help us enormously' game. Today the maths was clear; defeat would end our season, while a draw relied on Fulham losing to Brentford. Even a Leeds win would only keep the season alive if Wednesday lost or if Fulham dropped at least two points. It was most definitely a 'must win' game.

Around two o'clock, the Leeds team selection was being scrutinised on mobile phones all around the Pavilion. Garry Monk promised us nothing would be left in the dressing room today; his players would go for broke in search of the win that would hopefully take the season to the final game, at Wigan next Sunday. Yet the team he picked didn't exactly exude the *"shit or bust"* philosophy I was expecting.

Green

Ayling Bartley (Capt) Jansson Berardi

Vieira O'Kane

Roofe Hernandez Dallas

Wood

Subs: Peacock-Farrell, Coyle, Taylor, Phillips, Doukara, Pedraza, Sacko.

The midfield choices were limited by the fact that Liam Bridcutt was still suffering some discomfort from his Achilles but the rest of the squad was said to be fit and available. Yet Monk was sticking with his 4-2-3-1 formation despite seeing us far more positive at the end of the Burton game with a 4-4-2 line up. In particular I'd expected Charlie Taylor to continue in tandem with Pedraza, as I still saw that as the most logical option on the left. The inclusion of O'Kane was surprising too; he hadn't started since early March although interestingly that was at the end of a run of four consecutive starts during which we beat Bristol, Wednesday and Birmingham and drew at Ipswich. Leeds fans had been calling for him to be brought in perhaps with that knowledge in mind.

Elland Road was a sell out again for this, the final home game of the season and as we all stood to applaud in memory of all Leeds fans who'd passed away during the season, a tradition of a few years now, I breathed in deeply and enjoyed the vista of a glorious looking football scene. Everything was set for the last big push.

Our usual little gang – me, Jo, Lynn, Nigel, Mike and Kentley - was boosted by Mrs W on my right and Lottie on my left; the two ladies were joining us at the Awards Dinner later and hence their attendance at the game. Leeds won the toss and Norwich, in their usual yellow shirts and socks and green shorts, attacked the Kop in the first half; it all looked and felt very much like that Bristol Rovers game back in 2010... I wondered... I hoped... Jonny Howson was in yellow and green this time though of course.

There was no early sign of the drama to come as almost half an hour passed in the usual Championship manner with few real chances for either side. Norwich looked sharp and relaxed though; relaxed no doubt as they'd only been playing for pride for the last few weeks with none of the pressures the Leeds lads had been under to fight for every point. They were quick too, very quick. For Leeds there were a couple of crosses sent in from wide positions towards Chris Wood but both were more suited to an adult giraffe than our top marksman and both sailed away off the top of Wood's head. Then, in the 28th minute, we were stunned.

The Canaries were walking the ball to and fro just on half-way before eventually spraying it out to the left wing where Pritchard and Dijks exchanged a couple of passes. Pritchard then tapped it into the path of Steven Naismith and he had time to trap the ball, move it onto his right foot and then strike a perfect shot just inside the post to the right of the diving Rob Green. The Leeds defence just stood off Naismith allowing him pretty much to pick his spot. It was a rare piece of sloppy defending from Leeds with Pontus Jansson being the nearest when the ball was struck. Elland Road was silenced, this wasn't in the script at all and it looked as if the players were as shocked as we were. Some half-hearted *"We are Leeds"* chants rose from the depths of the Kop and then from the South Stand but it was as if the breath had been knocked out of us like a heavyweight boxer taking a blow to the midriff, a bit like we'd see Anthony Joshua and Klitschko knock six bells out of each other later that night. Six more minutes passed with most of us watching trance-like as Norwich moved the ball about at pace, running off the ball, creating patterns on the spring turf and then suddenly Jonny Howson was in possession on the half-way line. He touched it to the tiny figure of Alex Pritchard and Pritchard played it forward bisecting a line of three white shirted defenders for Josh Murphy to run onto with Jansson once again left on his heels and young Vieira watching on as if only mildly interested. In the middle, Oliveira made a dash for where he knew the ball was about to be played and we watched in horror as it arrived on his left boot just three yards out with Rob Green now in no man's land scrabbling along his line. The net rippled and Leeds were 2 – 0 down. A few boos rang out from the Kop while the 900 or so Norwich fans broke into a chant of *"Easy, Easy"* from their section of the West Stand. This now felt a bit like that first day of the season down at Loftus Road when we'd turned up in our thousands in the sunshine, full of hope, expectation and optimism, only to find ourselves being played off the park and a goal down inside four minutes. It was a bad moment and with only 34 minutes on the clock I could see streams of Leeds fans already jogging up the steps to the exits over in the East Stand for an early half-time cuppa. The pain became even more acute as news filtered through that Brentford had equalised at Fulham meaning Leeds still had that slim chance of catching the Londoners if that game stayed level but only of course if Leeds could win. That was looking out of the question the way our defence was performing. Straight from the restart Leeds gave up possession and Oliveira ought to have scored an identical goal as Pritchard blocked a Jansson clearance and crossed but this time the ball was scuffed wide of the post. But then, in the 45th minute and just as many more Leeds fans began to retreat to the concourses, things got even worse.

Jonny Howson waltzed along the touchline in front of the West Stand before sending the ball along the turf inside to Oliveira. He turned Jansson one way, then the other and then curled a lovely right foot shot into the far corner of the net. This was a Pontus Jansson none of us had seen before and it was worrying, although that man Oliveira looked a class act up front for the Canaries. Three-nil down as we moved into one minute of added time and all was lost. Or was it?

There were now loads of empty spaces where I stood with many more fans having given up and sloped off to the bogs or the concourse snack bars. Kentley pointed over to the Cheese Wedge and muttered something about Swiss cheese... (So many fans had left that section that it looked full of holes). I was only half listening as I could see Leeds kicking-off again with Hernandez tapping the ball back to O'Kane. Eunan moved it left to Berardi and he in turn knocked it a few yards further forward to Stuart Dallas who set off down the wing. He stopped, turned back onto his right foot in front of the East Stand and whipped the ball in towards the near post, five yards from goal. Chris Wood met it on the volley with his left foot and into the net it went! Unbelievable! We'd just seen two goals scored inside 60 seconds and there were at least 45 minutes still left in the game... plenty of time for Leeds to get the three goals we now needed. The half-time whistle blew and Lynn informed us the score at Fulham was still 1 – 1. We might be down but we were by no means out although the way the defences were playing it could yet end 7 – 6 or something daft like that.

During the break, Mrs W and I popped along to have a chat with my old school pal Rob and his son Pete and they were as dazed by the first half shenanigans as we were. Rob does a bit of cricket umpiring in the summer months and I joked we might see a cricket score at Elland Road the way things were going!

Folk were still settling into their places as Leeds kicked-off again and immediately pressed forward with Luke Ayling setting up Hernandez for a shot that struck the side netting. It was enough to get the crowd on their toes and the noise began to rise all around the ground with impassioned shouts of *"Come on Leeds"* mixed in with the regular Leeds anthems that were belting out. Then Leeds won a corner, over to our left and little Pablo went over to take it. Kyle Bartley came steaming in for a header but Ryan Bennett got to it first to knock it out for a second corner. This was now sustained Leeds pressure and the noise went up another few decibels as Pablo stood with his right hand up in the air. Mrs W nudged me and pointed to the tiny figure of Alex Pritchard who was stood only a matter of ten yards or so from us as he guarded the back post. *"Blimey, he's small"* Mrs W exclaimed. *"Yeah, let's hope Bartley can nod it over his head"* I shouted, trying to make myself heard over the din that was going on all around us. The ball floated across and Pontus Jansson this time rose to head the ball at goal; not towards the space above

Pritchard's head but right down at his feet. The soundtrack to the action at that moment was a deafening *"Leeds, Leeds, Leeds"* and the ground almost seemed to shake with each guttural *"Leeds"*. Perhaps it was that which put Pritchard off as he struggled to get his feet untangled allowing the ball to bobble off his thighs. He swung a leg to try to knock the ball further away but missed it completely while Kyle Bartley was alert enough to get his boot in there to somehow knock it over the line. I wondered if the effort would be disallowed as there was a bit of a melee going on with Pritchard, Bartley and the Norwich keeper John Ruddy all wrestling with each other, but no, the ref was happy. 2 – 3 and almost the entire second half left to play. Jo had her mobile in her hand showing the Championship scores and that Fulham - Brentford game was still 1 – 1. We could do this!

The atmosphere around Elland Road was now as good as I could remember; memories of that Bristol game came flooding back. Garry Monk mentioned it in his programme notes, saying someone told him recently how *"... you the supporters never stopped believing, you booed every Bristol touch and made it so intimidating that they caved in and Leeds came back to win the game 2 – 1"*. He challenged the Leeds fans *"to create that exact atmosphere this afternoon. The odds may be against us, but I ask you to believe and crank up the noise."*

Well, we were certainly rising to his challenge. Once again we needed two goals against a side in yellow and green and in one way this was less of a daunting task as that day in 2010; back then we only had ten men after Max Gradel was sent off.

We were now booing every Norwich touch and then roaring our own lads on when we won the ball back. *"Attack, Attack, Attack-Attack-Attack!"* we chanted, imploring them to drive towards us. Shots rained in on that Ruddy goal just yards away from me but the ruddy Norwich defenders were throwing themselves in front of them as if their lives depended on it. Roofe, Hernandez and O'Kane all had shots blocked in the space of a couple of minutes and as each struck Norwich flesh we'd hold our heads with our hands and moan *"Arghhhhhhhhhh no I don't believe it"* like thirty thousand Victor Meldrews. Every now and again Norwich would race up the other end but Rob Green was doing his part too and was proving his worth yet again. Doukara came on just after the hour mark to replace Dallas and then we groaned as Pontus picked up that 15th yellow card of the season although it didn't seem that important now. Unless Leeds could get another two goals it would be of no importance at all other than Pontus missing the last game, at Wigan next Sunday and a couple at the start of next season. Were we to find those two goals though we'd be without him at Wigan and the two play-off semi-finals. *"He'll be available again for the Wembley though"* Mike joked from the row behind.

Leeds were really going for it now and Ayling was sacrificed for Pedraza with Leeds going three at the back. It was a sort of 3 – 4 – 3 with Roofe, Wood and Hernandez all playing up front and Pedraza and Douk out wide. The clock on the big screen at the far end of the ground was showing 77:00 as Gaetano Berardi barrelled forward onto a pass from Doukara, on the edge of the Norwich area over to our left. Graham Dorrans lent on him and down went our man right on the line of the box. Berardi jumped up to try and grab the ball but Dorrans already had it to prevent a quick free-kick and a bit of handbags took place. The ref eventually calmed it all down but both men were booked while Hernandez placed the ball on the grass. The noise was still incredible, we knew we still had a chance of the play-offs as that Fulham game was *still* level. We needed two goals though and this was as good a chance as we'd had. Pablo took two steps and then clipped it perfectly over the right hand end of the wall and it curled and curled and curled almost in slow motion until it rippled the net in the top corner; it was mayhem as we celebrated like only we know how. There were at least 12 minutes of normal time to go plus a sizeable chunk of added time too. We sensed the come-back of all comebacks; something to rival that 4 – 3 we got down at Southampton back in 2005 or when we did the same against Derby here in '97. There was that game at Guiseley in pre-season too, so this group of players had form. We sang *"We're gonna win 4 – 3"* just as we did at Nethermoor. A shiver went down my spine as I recalled those games and I wondered... I just wondered and hoped and prayed. This game was right up there with the most memorable of all time already and it could yet become historic too. It began to look as if the footy gods were behind us for once and we got another sign when Naismith lunged at Vieira. Naismith missed the ball but got plenty of Vieira and the ref was soon holding up a red card. Just after this the added time board was raised; there would be at least six more minutes! Another huge roar greeted that and everyone was jumping on the spot urging the players forward once more. Surely Leeds would get just one more chance. Kentley and I looked at each other and we both mouthed *"One more chance"* as we always do when a game gets to the final few minutes. There is always one more chance...

It came when Pedraza collected a ball wide on the Leeds left. He had to dig it out from under a Norwich boot and then, despite a slight stumble, he curled it nicely in towards the near post where Kyle Bartley was again racing on to it. He got to the ball but steered it wide under pressure and heads were cradled in hands once more. Seconds later we got another 'one more chance' as Bartley flicked on a long deep cross from Hernandez into the path of Chris Wood but the ball struck Woody on the chest and went away to safety. It was not to be; Leeds had given themselves too much to do following that awful 17 minutes, 17 bloody minutes at the end of the first half and valiant as their efforts were, it was not enough. At the final whistle the players mostly slumped down onto their haunches and no doubt, like us, began to wonder just how they'd managed to lose their way since that last international break. On the 18th March, having just comfortably beaten a high flying and soon to be promoted Brighton, Leeds had an 8 point lead over Fulham in 7th spot. Since then, Leeds had picked up only five points from seven games while Fulham, including their all-important point against Brentford today, had collected 16 and against arguably tougher opponents than Leeds faced. There was no denying Leeds had thrown away a glorious opportunity this season and it was hard to escape the conclusion that Fulham had earned their reward.

After the game, Garry Monk refused to be critical of his players but he conceded that the key factor was probably that the young group he'd assembled just weren't ready for this type of pressure. As he pointed out, several had never been in the situation before and some were actually only in their first full season at this level. It had all come a bit too soon but he was confident the experience would stand them in good stead in future campaigns and he was convinced some great foundations had been laid for the future of the club.

At the final whistle, Mrs W and I made a quick exit to try to beat the crowds. Many stopped behind to salute the players on their lap of honour but we knew we'd see them later at the Awards Dinner so we were soon back on the road.

We were heading for the Clayton Hotel where we just had time for a shower and a change of clothes before grabbing a taxi back to the ground. There were lots of folk doing the same and I spotted Lilly in the hotel reception all dressed up and awaiting her taxi; Lilly's been a constant presence in these last seven seasons having been at most games with her Dad, Andy. As I introduced her to Mrs W she reminded me that, years ago, I dubbed her *"Helicopter Girl"* when I first wrote about her twirling her scarf around her head as I bobbed and weaved out of the way. Another lady spoke to me as we waited and I wracked my brain as to who it was. In the end I had to explain how I have this appalling memory for faces and she explained she was @DebsHLUFC , a Twitter contact I'd met a couple of times before. I apologised profusely for not recognising her and then bumped into her again in the huge queue outside the Pavilion. The doors should have opened fifteen minutes earlier but we'd learn later that some twonk forgot to get the pens for the players to use for their autograph session!

It was a good night once it got underway. Mrs W and I were joined on our table by Keith and Gill, Derek and Shirley, Kentley and Lottie, Kev and Nigel and we sunk a few beers and chatted about Leeds all night as the disappointment of the season's outcome eventually wore off. Chris Wood walked away with the Player of the Year Award and the Players' Player of the Year trophy while there were other awards for Rob Green, Souley Doukara (who inevitably got Goal of the Season for his cracker against Forest) and Ronaldo Vieira who was named Young Player of the Season. Andrea Radrizzani presented the main award to Chris Wood and in case Radz was still undecided who his manager was to be next season the fans in the Pavilion gave him lots of pointers with regular chants of *"Garry, Garry Monk"*! It was *the* big question we all wanted answering but there was no clue either from Radrizzani or Monk himself who was also quizzed on his future plans by Bryn Law who hosted the evening.

There was lots of speculation that Radrizzani was going ahead with his buyout of Cellino, with one suggested date being June 1st. We'd already been told this week that Radz had appointed Ivan Bravo to the Leeds Board of Directors and that was seen as more confirmation of him taking full control. Bravo was an interesting appointment; he'd served as Director of Strategy at Real Madrid no less, between 2003 and 2010, before overseeing the growth of the Aspire Academy for Sports Excellence in Qatar into one of the worlds most renowned football development programmes. What it all meant for Garry Monk, no one knew, but *The Sun* published an article the day after the Norwich game claiming they'd been told Monk was to be fired, with Radrizzani likely to appoint a foreign coach in the summer.[1] It was only *The Sun* but a worry none the less.

For now we could only wait and wonder and we still had one more game in any case; a trip to Wigan next Sunday, the final game of the season... well, unless we could overturn that 14 goal advantage Fulham had over us by beating Wigan and seeing the Londoners thumped at Hillsborough. If that happened we might have three more!

One more piece of bad news was revealed to me during the Awards Dinner; Kentley looked up the Worcester City result for me. City had lost 4 – 2 at AFC Fylde and were thus relegated from the National League North Division.

Leeds United 3 Norwich City 3 (Naismith (28), Oliveira (34, 45), **Wood (45+1), Bartley (49), Hernandez (78)**)
34,292 (Norwich 950)

---

[1] *https://www.thesun.co.uk/sport/football/3447258/leeds-united-sack-garry-monk-championship-play-offs-cellino/?CMP=Spklr-_-Editorial-_-TheSunFootball-_-Football-_-FBLink-_-Statement-_-FBPAGE*

When the Stars Almost Aligned

And so we came to what proved to be the final game of the season. We knew it was likely to be the final game as the only way we'd get three more, was if we could beat Wigan and Wednesday could beat Fulham and in the process we could overturn the 13 goal advantage the Cottagers held over us. There were a few optimistic bets being placed that the miracle would happen if some Twitter posts were to be believed. Well, if Leicester could win the Premier League...

I was driving for the final game and having picked up Kentley just after 8:30am we were parking up opposite the Red Robin pub a few minutes before 10am. Over the course of the next hour or so the pub filled up with an assortment of monks, cowboys, smurfs and Oompah Loompahs as the Leeds away contingent had once again thrown themselves into the last day fancy dress tradition with typical enthusiasm.

I worked my way through a very generous All Day Breakfast and a pint of Fosters while Kentley did his best to give me even more calories by heaping all the stuff he doesn't like (and that's plenty!) off his plate onto mine as he is wont to do. I drew the line at the chicken fingers in chilli sauce that he'd ordered but didn't like; Smithy arrived at one point and had a few of those.

As we walked the short distance to the DW Stadium, the sun was beating down and it all felt like a typical final day scenario... with the one important difference that for the last five seasons we have had bugger all riding on the last game, having regularly seen our seasons end just after Christmas. OK, it was unlikely we'd overturn that goal difference but mathematically *it could* happen if the stars all aligned for once. As we took our places high up in the stand, right above the goal at the north end of the DW, Kentley and I were both surprised at how few Latics fans had bothered to turn up for their final game in the Championship for at least a season; their relegation back to League One having been confirmed last weekend while Leeds were stumbling against Norwich. Looking around the other three sides of the DW there seemed to be very few Wigan fans in the ground and huge empty spaces everywhere. By contrast, Leeds had sold out their allocation of 3,200 tickets and our end was packed. During the first half we would eventually realise there were also a good many Leeds fans sat in the Wigan section over to our right and we annoyed the locals with a chant of *"We're Leeds United, we sit where we want"* to great applause from our fans in that area.

Chatting with Phil B just before kick-off, he told us that he'd heard Charlie Taylor had refused to play today and sure enough, when I checked off the players now lining up for the hand-shakes, young master Taylor was nowhere to be seen. The assumption had to be that he'd decided he didn't want to risk an injury with an impending transfer probably in the offing. We'd have to wait until after the game to get chapter and verse on it though.

Green
Coyle Bartley (Capt) Ayling Berardi
Vieira O'Kane
Dallas Hernandez Roofe
Wood

Subs: Peacock-Farrell, Denton, Phillips, Sacko, Doukara, Antonsson, Pedraza.

We knew of course that Pontus Jansson was suspended after he collected that 15th yellow card last week and we assumed Liam Bridcutt was still not one hundred per cent recovered from his latest Achilles injury. We'd also be told by Garry Monk after the game that Liam Cooper had picked up an ankle injury in training so there were very few options left for the back line. Hence we had a return to the match-day squad of Tyler Denton, who we'd not seen since the Sutton debacle.

The midfield and forward six remained as against Norwich, whilst Wigan had our old friend Steven Warnock in their back four. My conversation with Phil B was brought to an abrupt halt by the familiar stench of a flare that had been lit somewhere not far away to our left and we had to try not to inhale the rancid fumes for a few minutes as the game kicked off.

Leeds were straight into the attack and for a few minutes Wigan looked a very poor side as Leeds moved the ball quickly and with purpose to a backing track of *"Fourteen-nil, who gives a f***, we're Leeds United and we're going up"* and then, with not quite so much tongue in cheeks, *"Sign Garry Monk"* as we again tried to influence Mr Radrizzani. It was a bright start; Roofe had a shot blocked away for our first corner and Hernandez shot high and wide. Leeds were wearing all yellow for the first time since the opening game of the season (as far as I could remember), it being rumoured that Garry Monk didn't like the all yellow ensemble. Not surprising really after that QPR result last August. Quite how they decide on the kit I'd love to know as I could see no reason why we couldn't have worn the white shorts as we'd done in similar situations against sides in blue. Perhaps it's just at the kit man's whim. Six minutes passed with Wigan hardly having a touch and then, inexplicably, they scored.

Wigan had the ball in their inside right channel about ten yards inside their own half and suddenly it was stabbed through to Michael Jacobs. He collected it facing his own goal but quickly turned, took two paces and then prodded the ball through a Pontus Jansson shaped hole in our back line. Ryan Tunnicliffe ran onto it, went round the outside of Rob Green, and then, as Lewie Coyle went sliding past in his attempt to block the first dummied shot, Tunnicliffe stroked the ball home from a tight angle into the unguarded net.

There was much shaking of heads at first in the North Stand but then, as we reasoned that it probably wouldn't matter anyway we broke into a revised chant of *"Fifteen – one, who gives a f***, we're Leeds United and we're going up"* and that sort of set the tone for the rest of the game. We'd all had a good day out and we weren't about to let the odd Wigan goal spoil it!

There was just a bit of a worry that Wigan could really mess the day up by scoring a few more and that lasted for much of the rest of the first half as Rob Green was called into action far more that the Wigan stopper at the far end. Green even had to take a yellow card for the team as he raced out of his area to prevent a quick Wigan throw-in by knocking the ball out of Tunnicliffe's hands. We loved that and gave him a rousing *"Greeneh, Greeneh, Greeneh"* chant and then *"England's number one"* to which Green responded by holding up both hands with one finger pointing skywards. He was enjoying himself and his new found love-in with the Leeds fans. Kyle Bartley got his name in the book too for a clumsy challenge as Leeds just about saw out the first half with no more damage. Just before the break Berardi had a shot followed by the inevitable *"If Berardi scores we're on the pitch"* and he'd get a raucous *"Shooooooooot"* every time he touched the ball thereafter. Half-time; 1 – 0 Wigan.

The information from Hillsborough was that Wednesday were drawing 1 – 1 with Fulham but worse was the news filtering through that Wednesday were down to ten men following a red card for Marco Matias. It was of academic interest only of course if we couldn't even beat the Latics.

Leeds were out a good three or four minutes ahead of the home side after the break and whatever Monk had whispered in their shell-likes seemed to have done the trick as we finally took control of the game. Quite why we rarely started games with the same intensity we usually displayed in the second half, was probably as much of a mystery to Monk as it was to the rest of us but finally his players were standing up to be counted. Eunan O'Kane in particular started to dominate the midfield and with only five minutes of the new half ticked off he was driving into the penalty area just below us. Ryan Tunnicliffe was with him as he went and then as O'Kane felt Tunnicliffe lean on him, Eunan did the decent thing and collapsed in a heap. It was a soft penalty and Kentley and I gave each other a knowing look before we joined in the cheering now going on all around. The Leeds fans really were getting demob happy now and we were all shouting *"Berardi, Berardi, Berardi"* as loud as we could, trying to get Chris Wood to hand over the ball to our favourite non-scoring full-back. Sensibly, Wood ignored our plea and placed the ball himself. As he'd done with every spot kick this season, he despatched it cleanly, this time to the keeper's left while Gilks dived away to his right. It was not lost on us that Wood had thus reached thirty goals for the season and joined a pretty exclusive club of only five other Leeds strikers to achieve that. The great John Charles, a bloke called Tom Jennings who did it in the 1920s, Peter Lorimer, Lee Chapman and Jermaine Beckford were the only players on that particular list. Who'd have thought it eh? Chris Wood, thirty goals in a season. He had transformed himself from the wayward shooting, penalty missing player of last season into an accomplished finisher and had obviously worked very hard to achieve the turnaround. I was happy for him, despite having been amongst his greatest critics last season and in the first few games of this campaign; may he score many more next term. He'd also end the season with the Championship golden boot with 27 league goals.

Leeds were now looking much better and we were roaring them on in the hope of at least ending the season on a winning note. It would mean nothing in terms of a play-off place as Fulham had now taken the lead up at Hillsborough but it would have sent us home happy. Kemar Roofe looked most likely to grab a winner as he crashed a volley against the bar and then had a free header well saved by Gilks but there was now a nagging doubt about Roofe; for all his effort, he doesn't quite seem able to cut it at Championship level, least not yet. He's on a long contract and, like Wood, cost us a rumoured three million quid so we could only hope that his second season would be better just as we've seen with Woody. Kentley wasn't convinced and had christened him *"League One Roofe"* but I saw him smack the ball in the net for Oxford and to me it doesn't matter what league you're in, you can either hit the ball or you can't. Time will tell.

Leeds continued to press right to the final whistle but it wasn't to be our day, as it hadn't proved to be our season; those footballing stars just wouldn't quite align. Monk went all out attack towards the end with Sacko, Phillips and Pedraza replacing Dallas, Vieira and Hernandez but as with Roofe, Sacko and Pedraza always seem just short of the quality we need at this level. The game ended 1 – 1 and the Leeds players and staff came across at the final whistle and all received genuine and rapturous applause and appreciation. The biggest cheers were reserved for Garry Monk who clapped us and gave us the thumbs up as we chanted *"Sign Garry Monk"* once more; there was nothing more we could do, we'd made it plain what we wanted, now it was down to Radrizzani.

In the car on the way home we listened as Adam Pope interviewed Monk who first of all explained that Charlie Taylor had indeed refused to play.

"There's no sugar-coating this - Charlie refused to play the game. I think he's been terribly advised...I think he's been poorly advised all season. To refuse to play the game, for me as a manager and for the club, that's unacceptable. I've got a lot of time for Charlie, as we all have at the club.

"He's not very experienced in these situations, and you need proper guidance, and people around you who can help you do things right. He'll learn from this but, as a manager and a club, you cannot have a player refusing to play. The club will have a strong stance on this, I'm sure." [1]

Asked about his own future, Monk reiterated that he would be seeking to establish what plans the club had and whether those plans aligned with his own. He gave the impression that as long as they did, we'd be seeing him again next season. We could but only hope.

When the dust settled, Blackburn joined Wigan and Rotherham to complete the relegated trio while Newcastle pipped Brighton to the title. The four sides to contest the play-offs would be Reading, Wednesday, Huddersfield and Fulham. The Terriers beat both Wednesday and Reading in penalty shoot-outs to secure their Premier League place.

Wigan 1 **Leeds United 1** (Tunnicliffe (6), **Wood (50 pen)**)
15,280 (**Leeds 4,720**)

---

[1] *http://www.bbc.co.uk/sport/football/39760470*

Pos		Played	GD	Points
1	Newcastle United	46	45	94
2	Brighton H A	46	34	93
3	Reading	46	4	85
4	Sheffield W	46	15	81
5	Huddersfield T	46	-2	81
6	Fulham	46	28	80
7	Leeds United	46	14	75
8	Norwich City	46	16	70
9	Derby County	46	4	67
10	Brentford	46	10	64
11	Preston N E	46	1	62
12	Cardiff City	46	-1	62
13	Aston Villa	46	-1	62
14	Barnsley	46	-3	58
15	Wolverhampton W	46	-4	58
16	Ipswich T	46	-10	55
17	Bristol City	46	-6	54
18	Queens Park Rangers	46	-14	53
19	Birmingham City	46	-19	53
20	Burton Albion	46	-14	52
21	Nottingham Forest	46	-10	51
22	Blackburn Rovers	46	-12	51
23	Wigan Athletic	46	-17	42
24	Rotherham United	46	-58	23

The Final Championship Table 2016/17

And so the season ended with Leeds 7th, just as it did back in 2010/11 under Simon Grayson. Back then we had a squad that looked like it only needed a few more quality players to catapult it on to bigger and better things. Instead, we used academy graduates and signings like Paul Rachubka and Michael Brown to replace Kasper Schmeichel and Bradley Johnson. We all know that a policy of relying on loanees and academy graduates doesn't work and we paid the price in these last five seasons; mired in mid-table as a succession of like-minded owners with little or no money tried in vain to find a manager who could perform miracles. This time around we have to do better than bringing in Darren O'Dea.

The stars almost aligned. Monk may not have been Cellino's first choice but he proved to be exactly what we needed. His astute assessment quickly established that defence was where Leeds were lacking and by bringing in Green, Ayling, Bartley, and Jansson and teaming them up with Berardi or Taylor he created a solid, powerful rear guard that became the envy of most in the Championship. That side of Grayson's six years ago conceded 70 goals; this campaign we conceded 47 and only Brighton, Newcastle and Wednesday let in fewer. Sadly, this season we only scored 61, whereas Grayson's crew hit 81! Grayson needed cash spent on his defence whereas it could be argued Monk needed some spent at the other end of the pitch. That still needs to happen this summer if we are not once again going to waste the opportunity we now have.

With Cellino becoming ever more remote as Radrizzani moved in, Monk was allowed to get on with the job, something his predecessors never enjoyed and that too is a prerequisite for future success. So what went wrong?

For whatever reason, the winter transfer window didn't produce the quality we needed to cover Bartley and Jansson, give us more creativity and provide that added punch up front. Instead we brought in two more loanee wingers, players no better than we already had and in testing them out Monk may well have unwittingly confused himself and his players such that we lost track of our best combinations. We battled right through the campaign with very little quality cover for our best XI, many of whom were young and inexperienced and hence perhaps why we looked so jaded in those final eight games.

We were so close, that's the real disappointment; going into the final eight games Leeds had an eight point advantage over Fulham in 7th and I was confident we had the easier run-in. Sadly, that lack of cover, that lack of those three or four more quality players, and the inexperience of our young squad let us down badly just when it mattered most. The stars almost aligned perfectly, but not quite. As I write these last few words, news has come though that Garry Monk has resigned having failed to be convinced by Radrizzani that he'd get the support he needed to push on next season. Once again we set out on a new season with a new manager. Let's hope whoever it is gets the resources needed to ensure next season is *the one*.

Lightning Source UK Ltd.
Milton Keynes UK
UKHW022002060120
356462UK00015B/3328/P

9 781787 231092

An Anthology of Mine

·19· ·23·

Res. John Whistler.

Henry Brocken meets Annabel Lee

E. A. Poe. * Annabel Lee

It was many & many a year ago,
In a Kingdom by the sea,
That a maiden there lived whom you may know
By the name of Annabel Lee;
And this maiden she lived with no other thought
Than to love & be loved by me.

I was a child & she was a child,
In this Kingdom by the sea:
But we loved with a love that was more than love—
I & my Annabel Lee;
With a love that the winged Seraphs of Heaven
Coveted her & me.

And this was the reason that, long ago,
In this Kingdom by the sea,
A wind blew out of a cloud chilling
My beautiful Annabel Lee;
So that her high born Kinsmen came

And bore her away from me,
And shut her up in a sepulchre
In this Kingdom by the sea.

The angels, not half so happy in Heaven,
Went envying her & me —
Yes! — That was the reason (as all men know,
In this Kingdom by the sea)
That the wind came out of the cloud by night,
Chilling & killing my Annabel Lee.

But our love it was stronger by far than the love
Of those who were older than we —
Of many far wiser than we —
And neither the angels in Heaven above,
Nor the demons down under the sea,
Can ever dissever my soul from the soul
Of the beautiful Annabel Lee:

For the moon never beams without bringing me dreams

f the beautiful Annabel Lee;
ud the stars never rise but I see the bright eyes
Of the beautiful Annabel Lee;
ud so, all the night tide, I lie down by the side
f my darling, my darling, my life & my bride,
u her sepulchre there by the sea
u her tomb by the side of the sea.

N.D.Fuller.

Wanderlust

Stay me not, ah! stay me not
For the salt winds calling me,
And the Wanderlust is blazing strong —
I must say good bye to thee.
For the sands are shining cool & white
And the ship stands out to sea!

Stay me not, for the ~~winds~~ spray flies high,
And the huge waves, mad with glee,
Fiend ridden, by whirlwind spirits of night
Are calling, shrill voiced to me,
nd the Stars are wreathed in a golden mist,

[And the ship stands
out to sea!

E. A. Poe.   ULALUME.

The skies they were ashen & sober;
The leaves they were withered & sere —
The leaves they were withering & sere;
It was night in the lonesome October
Of my most immemorial year;
It was hard by the dim lake of Auber,   *
In the misty mid region of Weir —
It was down by the dark tarn of Auber,
In the ghoul-haunted woodland of Weir.

Here once, through an alley Titanic,
Of cypress, I roamed with my Soul —
Of cypress, with Psyche, my Soul.
These were the days when my heart was volcanic
As the scoriac rivers that roll —
As the lavas that restlessly roll
Their sulphorous currents down Yaanek,
In the realms of the boreal pole

Our talk had been serious & sober,
But our thoughts they were palsied & sere —
Our memories were treacherous & sere —
For we knew not the month was October,
And we marked not the night of the year —
(Ah, night of all nights in the year!)
We noted not the dim lake of Auber —
(Though once we had journeyed down here) —
Remembered not the dark tarn of Auber,
Nor the ghoul-haunted woodland of Weir.

And now, as the night was senescent
And star dials pointed to morn —
As the star dials hinted of morn —
At the end of our path a liquescent
And nebulous lustre was born,
Out of which a miraculous crescent
Arose with a duplicate horn —
Astarte's bediamonded crescent
Distinct with its' duplicate horn.

And I said — "She is warmer than Dian:
She rolls through an ether of sighs —
She revels in an ether of sighs:
She has seen that the tears are not dry on
These cheeks, where the worm never dies,
And has come past the stars of the Lion
To point us the path to the skies —
To the Leathen peace of the skies —
Come up, in despite of the Lion,
To shine on us with her bright eyes —
Come up through the lair of the Lion
With love in her luminous eyes."

But Psyche, uplifting her finger,
Said "— Sadly this star I mistrust —
Her pallor I strangely mistrust:
Oh, hasten — Oh, let us not linger!
Oh, fly! — let us fly! — for we must."
In terror she spoke, letting sink her
Wings till they trailed in the dust —

In agony sobbed, letting sink her
Plumes 'till they trailed in the dust —
Till they sorrowfully trailed in the dust —

I replied — " This is nothing but dreaming :
Let us on by this tremulous light !
Let us bathe in this crystaline light !
It's sibyllic splendour is beaming
With hope & in beauty to night : —
See ! — It flickers up the sky through the night !
Ah ! we safely may trust to it's gleaming,
And be sure it will lead us aright —
We safely may trust to a gleaming
That cannot but guide us aright :"

Thus I pacified Psyche & kissed her,
And tempted her out of her gloom —
And conquered her scruples & gloom ;
And we passed to the end of a vista,
But were stopped by the door of a tomb —

By the door of a legended tomb
And I said — "What is written, sweet sister,
On the door of this legended tomb?"
She replied — "Ulalume — Ulalume —
Tis the vault of thy lost Ulalume!"

Then my heart it grew ashen & sober
As the leaves that were crispéd & sere —
As the leaves that were withering & sere;
And I cried — "It was surely October
Of this very night of last year
That I journeyed — I journeyed down here —
That I brought a dread burden down here!
On this night of all nights of the year!
Ah, what demon has tempted me here?
Well I know, now, this dank tarn of Auber
This ghoul-haunted woodland of Weir."

To Autumn

John Keats.

Season of mists & mellow fruitfulness,
Close bosom-friend of the maturing sun;
Conspiring with him how to load & bless
With fruit the vines that round the thatch-eves run;
To bend with apples the mossed cottage trees,
And fill all fruit with ripeness to the core;
To swell the gourd, & plump the hazel shells
With a sweet kernel; to set budding more,
And still more, later flowers for the bees,
Until they think warm days will never cease,
For Summer has o'erbrimmed their clammy cells.

Who hath not seen thee oft amid thy store?
Sometimes whoever seeks abroad may find
Thee sitting careless on a granary floor,
Thy hair soft lifted by the winnowing wind;
Or on a half reaped furrow sound asleep,
Drowsed with the fume of poppies, while thy hook
Spares the next swath & all its twinèd flowers:

And sometimes like a gleaner thou dost keep
Steady thy laden head across a brook;
Or by a cider-press, with patient look,
Thou watchest the last oozings hours by hours.

Where are the songs of Spring? Ay, where are they?
Think not of them, thou hast thy music too—
While barred clouds bloom the soft-dying day,
And touch the stubble-plains with rosy hue;
Then in a wailful choir the small gnats mourn
Among the river shallows, borne aloft
Or sinking as the light wind lives or dies;
And full grown lambs loud bleat from hilly bourn
Hedge-crickets sing; and now with treble soft
The redbreast whistles from a garden croft;
And gathering swallows twitter in the skies

Thomas Gray.   *Selections from **Elegy** written in a church-yard*

The Curfew tolls the knell of parting day,
The lowing herd wind slowly o'er the lea,
The plowman homeward plods his weary way,
And leaves the world to darkness & to me.

Now fades the glimmering landscape on the sight,
And all the air a solemn stillness holds,
Save where the beetle wheels his droning flight,
And drowsy tinklings lull the distant folds:

Save that from yonder ivy-mantled tow'r
The moping owl does to the moon complain
Of such as, wand'ring near her secret bow'r,
Molest her ancient solitary reign.

Beneath those rugged elms, that yew-tree's shade,
Where heaves the turf in many a mould'ring heap,
Each in his narrow cell for ever laid,

The rude Forefathers of the hamlet sleep.

The breezy call of incense-breathing Morn,
The swallow twitt'ring from the straw-built shed,
The cock's shrill clarion, or the echoing horn,
No more shall rouse them from their lowly bed.

Let not ambition mock their useful & toil,
Their homely joys, & destiny obscure;
Nor grandeur hear with a disdainful smile
The short & simple annals of the poor. —

The boast of heraldry, the pomp of pow'r,
And all that beauty, all that wealth e'er gave,
Awaits alike th' inevitable hour.
The paths of glory lead but to the grave.

Full many a gem of purest ray serene,
The dark unfathomed caves of ocean bear:
Full many a flower is born to blush unseen,
& waste its sweetness on the desert air.

Far from the madding crowd's ignoble strife,
Their sober wishes never learned to stray;
Along the cool sequester'd vale of life.
They kept the noiseless tenor of their way.

— "Oft have we seen him at the peep of dawn
Brushing with hasty steps the dews away
To meet the sun upon the upland lawn.

There scatter'd oft, the earliest of the Year,
By hands unseen are showers of Violets found;
The redbreast loves to build & warble there,
And little footsteps lightly print the ground.

17 60
Large was his bounty, & his soul sincere,
Heav'n did a recompense as largely send:
He gave to Misry all he had, — a tear,
He gained from Heaven ('twas all he wish'd)
        — a friend

Ben Jonson.

My mind to me a Kingdom is

My mind to me a Kingdom is;
Such perfect joy therin I find
As far exceeds all earthly bliss
That God or Nature hath assigned.
Tho' much I want that most would have,
Yet still my mind forbids to crave.

Content I live, this is my stay;
I seek no more than may suffice;
I press to bear no haughty sway;
Look what I lack, my mind supplies.
Lo! thus I triumph like a King,
Content with what my mind doth bring.

Some have too much, yet still they crave,
I little have yet seek no more:
They are but poor, though much they have
And I am rich with little store.
They poor, I rich; they beg, I give;
They lack, I lend; they pine, I live.

The Listeners

W. De La Mare.

'Is there anybody there?' said the Traveller,
Knocking on the moonlit door;
And his horse in the silence champed the grasses
Of the forest's ferny floor:
And a bird flew up out of the turret,
Above the Travellers head:
And he smote upon the door a second time;
'Is there anybody there?' he said.
But no one descended to the Traveller;
No head from the leaf-fringed sill
Leaned over and looked into his grey eyes,
Where he stood perplexed & still.
But only a host of phantom listeners
That dwelt in the lone house then
Stood listening in the quiet of the moonlight
To that voice from the world of men:
Stood thronging the faint moonbeams on the dark stair,
That goes down to the empty hall,
Hearkening in an air stirred & shaken

By the lonely Travellers call.
And he felt in his heart their strangeness,
Their stillness answering his cry,
While his horse moved, cropping the dark turf,
'Neath the starred and leafy sky;
For he suddenly smote on the door, even
Louder, and lifted his head:—
'Tell them I came, & no one answered,
That I kept my word', he said.
Never the least stir made the listeners,
Though every word he spake
Fell echoing through the shadowiness of the still house
From the one man left awake:
Ay, they heard his foot upon the stirrup,
And the sound of iron on stone,
* And how the silence surged softly backward,
When the plunging hoofs were gone.

Herrick.

Upon Julia's Voice

So smooth, so sweet, so silv'ry is thy voice
As, could they hear, the damned would make
  no noise,
But listen to thee, walking in thy chamber,
Melting melodious words to lutes of amber. ~,~,

Khayyám.

Selections from the Rubáiyát

Awake! for Morning in the Bowl of Night
Has flung the stone that puts the stars to flight:
And Lo! the Hunter of the East has caught
The Sultán's Turret in a Noose of Light.

Irám indeed is gone with all its Rose,
And Jamshyd's Sev'n-ringed Cup where no one knows:
But still the Vine her ancient Ruby yields,
And still a garden by the Water blows,

*Think, in this battered Caravanserai
Whose Doorways are alternate Night & Day,
How Sultán after Sultán with his pomp
Abode his Hour or two, and went his way ~.

*I sometimes think that never blows so red
The Rose as where some buried Caesar bled;
That every Hyacinth the garden wears
Dropt in its lap from some once lovely Head.

Into this Universe, and why not Knowing,
Nor whence, like water willy-nilly flowing:
And out of it, as Wind along the waste,
I Know not wither, willy nilly blowing.

~For in the Market place, one Dusk of day,
I watched the Potter thumping his wet Clay:
And with its all obliterated tongue
It murmured — "Gently Brother, gently, pray!"

One moment in Annihilation's waste,
One moment, of the Well of Life to taste —
The Stars are setting & the Caravan
Starts for the Dawn of Nothing — Oh, make haste!

'Tis all a Chequer-board of Nights and Days
Where Destiny with Men for pieces plays:
Hither & thither moves, & mates, and slays,
And one by one back in the Closet lays.

For in & out, above, about, below,
'Tis nothing but a Magic shadow-show,
Played in a Box whose candle is the Sun,
Round which we phantom figures come & go —

E. A. Poe

To One in Paradise

Thou wast that all to me, love
 For which my soul did pine —
A green isle in the sea, love,
A fountain & a shrine,
All wreathed with fairy fruits & flowers,
& all the flowers were mine ~

Ah, dream too bright to last!
Ah, starry Hope! that didst arise
But to be overcast!
A voice from out the Future cries
"On! On!" — but o'er the Past
(Dim gulf!) my spirit hovering lies,
 Mute, motionless, aghast!

For, alas! alas! with me
The light of life is o'er!
"No more — no more – no more —"
(Such language holds the solemn sea

To the sands upon the shore)
Shall bloom the thunder-blasted tree,
Or the stricken eagle soar!

& all my days are trances
& all my nightly dreams
Are where thy dark eye glances,
& where thy footstep gleams —
In what ethereal dances!
By what eternal streams!

Herrick.   <u>The Night-piece to Julia</u>

Her eyes the glow-worm lend thee,
The shooting stars attend thee;
And the elves also,
Whose little eyes glow
Like the sparks of fire, attend thee.

No will-o'-the-wisp mislight thee,
Nor snake or slow-worm bite thee.

But on, on thy way,
Not making a stay,
Since ghost there's none to affright thee.

Let not the dark thee cumber;
What though the moon does slumber?
The stars of the night
Will lend thee their light,
Like tapers clear without number.

Then Julia, let me woo thee,
Thus, thus to come unto me;
And, when I shall meet
Thy silv'ry feet,
My soul I'll pour into thee.

*La Belle Dame sans merci

J. Keats.

O what can ail thee, Knight-at-arms,
Alone & palely loitering?
The sedge has withered from the Lake
And no birds sing.

*What's the matter
Kid?*

O what can ail the knight-at-arms!
So haggard & so woe-begone?
The squirrel's granary is full
And the harvest's done.

I see a lily on thy brow
With anguish moist & fever dew,
And on thy cheeks a fading rose
Fast withereth too.

I met a Lady in the meads,
Full beautiful — a faery's child,
Her hair was long, her foot was   light
And her eyes were wild.

I made a garland for her head,
And bracelets too, and fragrant zone;
She look'd at me as she did love,
And made sweet moan.

I set her on my pacing steed,
And nothing else saw all day long,
For sidelong would she bend, and sing
A faery's song.

She found me roots of relish sweet,
And honey wild, and manna dew,
And sure in language strange she said—
"I love thee true."

She took me to her elfin grot,
And there she wept, and sighed full sore,
And there I shut her wild wild eyes
With kisses four.

I saw pale Kings & princes too,
Pale warriors, death-pale were they all;
They cried—"La belle Dame sans Merci
Hath thee in thrall!"

I saw their starved lips in the gloam,
With horrid warning gaped wide,
And I awoke & found me here,
On the cold hill's side.

And this is why I sojourn here,
Alone and palely loitering,
Though the sedge is withered from the lake
And no birds sing—

· LOVE-IN-A-MIST ·

Norman Ross — A. Trinket —

Dear, you gave me love-in-a-mist
The night you gave your heart —
In a garden veiled with amethyst,
Dear you gave me love-in-a-mist.
And with those very lips I kissed
You framed that question: "Shall
  we part?"
Dear you gave me love in a mist
The night you gave me your
    heart.

P.B.Shelley.

The waning Moon.

And like a dying lady, lean & pale,
Who totters forth, wrapt in a gauzy veil,
Out of her chamber, led by the insane
And feeble wanderings of her fading brain,
The Moon arose upon the murky earth,
A white and shapeless mass ~

la Mare.

The Stranger

Half hidden in a graveyard,
In the blackness of a yew,
Where never living creature stirs,
Nor sunbeam pierces through,

Is a tombstone green & crooked,
Its faded legend gone,
And but one rain-worn cherub's head
To sing of the unknown

There, when the dusk is falling,
Silence broods so deep
It seems that every wind that breathes
Blows from the fields of sleep —

Day breaks in heedless beauty,
Kindling each drop of dew,
But unforsaking shadow dwells
Beneath this lonely yew.

But, all else lost and faded,
Only this listening head
Keeps with a strange unanswering smile
It's secret with the dead —

J. Keats **To a Nightingale** *

My heart aches, and a drowsy numbness pains
My sence, as though of hemlock I had drunk,
Or emptied some dull opiate to the drains
One minute past, & Lethe-wards had sunk:
'Tis not through envy of thy happyness,—
That thou, light-winged Dryad of the trees,
In some melodious plot
Of beechen green, and shadows numberless,
Singest of summer in full-throated ease.

O, for a draught of vintage! that hath been
Cool'd a long age in the deep-delved earth,
Tasting of Flora and the country green,
Dance & Provençal song, and sunburnt mirth

O for a beaker full of the warm South,
Full of the true, the blushful Hippocrene,
With beaded bubbles winking at the brim,
And purple-stained mouth;
That I might drink & leave the world unseen,
And with thee fade away into the forest dim:

Fade far away, dissolve, and quite forget
What thou among the leaves hast never known,
The weariness, the fever, & the fret
Here, where men sit & hear each other groan;
When palsy shakes a few, sad, last grey hairs,
Where youth grows pale, & spectre-thin, & dies;
Where but to think is to be full of sorrow
And leaden-eyed despairs,
Where Beauty cannot keep her lustrous eyes,
Or new Love pine at them beyond tomorrow.

Away! Away! for I will fly to thee,
Not charioted by Bacchus and his pards,

But on the viewless wings of Poesy,
Though the dull brain perplexes & retards :
Already with thee !   Tender is the night,
And haply the Queen-Moon is on her throne,
Cluster'd round by all her starry fays,
But here there is no light,
Save what from Heaven is with the breezes blown
Through verdurous glooms & winding mossy ways

I cannot see what flowers are at my feet,
Nor what soft incense hangs upon the boughs,
But in embalmed darkness, guess each sweet
Wherewith the seasonable month endows
The grass, the thicket, & the fruit tree wild ;
White hawthorn, and the pastoral eglantine ;
Fast fading violets cover'd up in leaves ;
And mid-May's eldest child,
The coming musk-rose, full of dewy wine,
The murmorous haunt of flies on summer eves.

Darkling I listen; and, for many a time
I have been half in love with easeful Death,
Call'd him soft names in many a mused rhyme,
To take into the air my quiet breath;
Now more than ever seems it rich to die,
To cease upon the midnight with no pain,
While thou art pouring forth thy soul abroad
In such an ecstacy!
Still wouldst thou sing, & I have ears in vain —
To thy high requiem become a sod

Thou wast not born for death, immortal Bird!
No hungry generations tread thee down;
The voice I hear this passing night, was heard
In ancient days by emperor & clown:
Perhaps the self-same song that found a path
Through the sad heart of Ruth, when, sick for home,
She stood in tears amid the alien corn;
The same that oft-times hath
Charmed magic casements, opening on the foam
Of perilous seas, in faery lands forlorn -

Forlorn! the very word is like a bell
To toll me back from thee to my sole self!
Adieu! the fancy cannot cheat so well
As she is famed to do, deceiving elf.
Adieu! Adieu! thy plaintive anthem fades
Past the near meadows, over the still stream,
Up the hill-side; and now 'tis buried deep
In the next valley-glades:
Was it a vision, or a waking-dream?
Fled is that music:— Do I wake or sleep?

Silence

There is a silence where hath been no sound,
There is a silence where no sound may be,
In the cold grave — under the deep deep sea,
Or in wide desert where no life is found,
Which hath been mute, and still must sleep profound;
No voice is hush'd — no life treads silently,
But clouds & cloudy shadows wander free,
That never spoke, over the idle ground:
But in green ruins, in the desolate walls
Of antique palaces, where Man hath been,
Though the dun fox, or wild hyena, calls,
And owls, that flit continually between,
Shriek to the echo, and the low winds moan,
There the true Silence is, self-concious and alone.

A. Tennyson   **Tears, idle tears.** (from the Princess)

Tears, idle tears, I know not what they mean,
Tears from the depth of some divine despair
Rise in the heart, and gather to the eyes,
In looking on the happy Autumn fields,
And thinking of the days that are no more.

Ah, sad and strange as in dark summer dawns
The earliest pipe of half-awaken'd birds
To dying ears, when unto dying eyes
The casement slowly grows a glimmering square;
So sad, so strange the days that are no more.

Dear as remember'd kisses after death,
And sweet as those by hopeless fancy feign'd
On lips that are for others; deep as love,
Deep as first love, and wild with all regret;
O Death in Life, the days that are no more.

Ode to the West Wind (Selections.)

B. Shelley.

O wild West Wind, thou breath of Autumn's being,
Thou, from whose unseen presence the leaves dead
Are driven, like ghosts from an enchanter fleeing,
Yellow, & black, and pale, and hectic red,
Pestilence-stricken multitudes: O thou
Who chariotest to their dark wintry bed
The wingéd seeds, where they lie cold & low,
Each like a corpse within it's grave, until
Thine azure sister of the Spring shall blow
Her clarion o'er the dreaming earth, & fill
(Driving sweet buds like flocks to feed in air)
With living hues and odours plain and hill:
Wild Spirit, which art moving everywhere;
Destroyer & Preserver; Hear, oh, hear!

Thou who didst waken from his summer-dreams,
The blue Mediterranean, where he lay,
Lulled by the coil of his crystalline streams,
Beside a pumice isle in Baiae's bay,

And saw in sleep old palaces and towers
Quivering within the wave's intenser day,
All overgrown with azure moss and flowers
So sweet, the sense faints picturing them! Thou
For whose path the Atlantic's level powers
Cleave themselves into chasms, while far below
The sea-blooms and the oozy woods which wear
The sapless foliage of the ocean, know
Thy voice, and suddenly grow grey with fear,
And tremble & despoil themselves: oh hear!

Make me thy lyre, ev'n as the forest is:
What if my leaves are falling like its own!
The tumult of thy mighty harmonies
Will take from both a deep autumnal tone,
Sweet though in sadness.   Be thou, Spirit fierce,
My spirit! be thou me, impetuous one!
Drive my dead thoughts over the universe
Like withered leaves to quicken a new birth!
And, by the incantation of this verse,

Scatter, as from an unextinguished hearth
Ashes and sparks, my words among mankind!
Be through my lips to unawakened earth
The trumpet of a prophecy! O, Wind,
If Winter comes, can Spring be far behind?

V. De la Mare ~   ## Arabia.

Far are the shades of Arabia,
Where the Princes ride at noon,
Mid the verdurous vales & thickets,
Under the ghost of the moon;
& so dark is that vaulted purple
Flowers in the forest rise
& toss into blossom 'gainst the phantom stars
Pale in the noonday skies.

Sweet is the music of Arabia
In my mind, when out of dreams
I still in the thin clear mirk of dawn
Descry her gliding streams;
Hear her strange lutes on the green banks

Ring loud with the grief & delight
Of the dim-silked, dark-haired Musicians
In the brooding silence of night.

They haunt me — her lutes & her forests;
No beauty on Earth I see
But shadowed with that dream recalls
Her Corliness to me:
Still eyes look coldly upon me:
Cold voices whisper & say —
He is crazed with the spell of far Arabia,
They have stolen his wits away!

J. Keats.

On the Sea.

It keeps eternal whisperings around
Desolate shores, and with its mighty swell
Gluts twice ten thousand caverns, till the spell
Of Hecate leaves them their old shadowy sound.
Often 'tis in such gentle temper found,
That scarcely will the very smallest shell
Be moved for days from where it sometime fell,
When last the winds of Heaven were unbound.
Oh ye! who have your eye-balls vex'd and tired,
Feast them upon the wilderness of the sea;
Oh ye! whose ears are dinn'd with uproar rude,
Sit ye near some old cavern's mouth & brood
Until ye start, as if the sea-nymphs quired.

W. De la Mare

Peacock Pie

Who said "Peacock Pie"?
The Old King to the sparrow.
Who said "Crops are ripe"?
Rust to the Harrow.
Who said "Where sleeps she now?
Where rests she now her head
Bathed in Eve's Loveliness?"
          That's what I said

Who said; "Aye, mum's the word"
Sexton to Willow.
Who said; "Green dusk for dreams
Moss for a pillow."
Who said;   "All Time's Delight
Hath she for narrow bed,
Life's troubled bubble broken —   "
          That's what I said

Jn. Drinkwater.

The Witch-Ball

Never, oh, never came
Witch in this garden,
We would not pardon
Would we, dear, anyone
Who should say things were done
Such as in hell they name
Here in our garden?
Never was poison-root
In this Hesperides.
Girdled by gentle trees;
Mould that our lilies made
Mothered ~~en~~ no nightshade;
Never passed Endor's foot
Over so smooth a green
Lawn as is laid between
Borders that virtue
Only can print,
Of pansies and mint,
With no herb to hurt you

Here where the thrush & jay,
Robin & linnet,
Find through the longest day
Songs for each minute,
No path or plantation
Ever has heard
Vext incantation
With song of the bird;
Never a muttered spell
Learnt in the writ of hell,
Psalter obscene,
On warlock or witch's lip
Whispered in stewardship
Curst & unclean.
The day & the night
Are holy, all hours,
With heaven alight
Again in the flowers;
All blossoms, by day
Flashing back to the sun

Many beams to repay
The succour of one;
All blossoms, when sweet
Stars of even have birth,
Lying orbed at our feet,
Pale planets of earth,
And, chaste beyond whisper
Of sorcerer's rune,
Moon-virgin when Hesper
Is lost in the moon.
Go comrade, go lover,
Go, pass through the portal,
Laugh & rest, till your mortal
Date falls as it must
To the gospel of dusk,
And the dark wing shall cover
The sun from our portal.
Till then laugh & rest,
While the garden shall keep
All charms that are best

For fortune & sleep;
Clean rites to deliver
Roof-timber & Stair
And hearthstone for ever
From plaigues of the air.
No witch may come nearer
Than pass down the Cane,
A fugitive peerer,
An impotent bane;
No kirtle of devil
May dip from the night,
Our lintel with evil
To brush in its flight.
Here melody lives,
The spirit burns purely,
And what the year gives
We harvest securely.
Still shall the blue witch-ball
Hang from the parlour-beam
Catching the garden-gleam

Globed from the window-pane,
Marking our steps again
Is in the room they fall;
A fair little world of dream,
Still it shall hang by day,
Still it shall hang by night,
Just for the eyes' delight,
Just as a story told,
Just as a fear of old,
Gathered away;
And never shall haunted breath
Breath cloud in the glass
The little enchanted
Long alleys of grass,
And birds of sweet lustres,
And gathering bees,
And blossoms in clusters,
And orcharded trees,
All mirrored in flame
From our acre of light

[Where witch never came
From fogs of the night ~

The End. ⁓

Prayers, Charms & Witch recipes

Prayer for a night-bound Traveller

Let not the dark me cumber
E'en though the moon does slumber
O, Stars of the night
Pray lend me your light
Like tapers clear, without number.—

A Witch Recipe (for what?)

Round about the cauldron go;
In the poisoned entrails throw.
Toad that under cold stone
Days & nights has thirty one
Swelter'd venom sleeping got,
Boil thou first i'the charmed pot.
Fillet of a fenny snake,
In the cauldron boil & bake;
Eye of newt & toe of frog,

Wool of bat, & tongue of dog,
Adders' fork & blind-worm's sting,
Lizard's leg & owlet's wing,
For a charm of powerful trouble,
Like a hell-broth boil & bubble).
Scale of dragon, tooth of woolf,
Witches' mummy, maw & gulf
Of the ravined salt-sea shark,
Root of hemlock digg'd i' the dark,
Liver of blaspheming Jew,
Gall of goat & slips of yew
Silver'd in the moon's eclipse,
Nose of Turk & Tartar's lips,
Finger of birth strangled babe
Ditch-deliver'd by a drab,
Make the gruel thick & slab:
Add thereto a tigers chaudron
For the ingredients of your cauldron;
B. Cool it with a baboon's blood,
Then the charm is firm & *good* ~

(A hroved Recipe.)

Sir H. Wotton.

Lord of Himself

How happy is he born or taught,
Who serveth not another's will;
Whose armour is his honest thought,
And simple truth his highest skill;

Whose passions not his masters are;
Whose soul is still prepared for death —
Not tied unto the world with care
Of prince's ear or vulgar breath;

Who hath his ear from rumours freed;
Whose conscience is his strong retreat;
Whose state can neither flatterers feed,
Nor ruin make oppressors great;

Who envies none whom chance doth raise
Or vice; who never understood
How deepest wounds are given with praise,
Nor rules of state but rules of good;

Who God doth late & early pray
More of his grace than gifts to lend,
And entertains the harmless day
With a well-chosen book or friend—

This man is free from servile bands
Of hope to rise or fear to fall.
Lord of himself, though not of lands,
And, having nothing, yet hath all ~

R.W.D.Fuller

I see the sun above the hill
And the stars across the sea,
As I have seen them many a time
In the days that used to be.

The same sea under the golden hill,
And the same world under the sea,
And I can remember the old dream still
Of the boy that was not I.

And the world I love, and the sea and the sky,
And the long grey, windy street,
And the woods that bend as the wind goes by
Have been trodden by other feet.

And men that are dead have heard the cry
Of the sea-birds circling low
O'er the wintry waves. Dead men that lie
Where strange seas ebb and flow
Have loved the world the same as I
Ten thousand years ago!

De la Mare.   ## Noon & night-flower

Not any flower that blows
But shining watch doth keep;
Every swift changing chequered hour it knows
Now to break forth in beauty; now to sleep.

This for the roving bee
Keeps open house, and this
Stainless & clear is, that in darkness she
May lure the moth to where her nectar is.

Lovely beyond the rest
Are these of all delight :—
The tiny Pimpernel: that noon loves best,
The primrose palely burning through the night.

One n'eath days burning sky
With ruby decks her place,
The other when Eve's chariot glideth by
Lifts her dim torch to light that dreaming face —

Emily Dickinson. ## Sunset.

Where ships of purple gently toss
On seas of daffodil,
Fantastic sailors mingle,
And then — the wharf is still.

A sloop of amber slips away
Upon an ether sea,
And wrecks in peace a purple tar
The son of ecstasy.

P.B. Shelley. ## Ozymandias.

I met a traveller from an antique land
Who said: Two vast and trunkless legs of stone
Stand in the desert. Near them, on the sand,
Half sunk, a shattered visage lies, whose frown,
And wrinkled lip, and sneer of cold command,
Tell that its sculptor well those passions read
Which yet survive, stamped on these lifeless things,
The hand that mocked them & the heart that fed:

And on the pedestal these words appear :
"My name is Ozymandias, King of Kings :
Look on my works, ye Mighty, and despair!"
Nothing beside remains.   Round the decay
Of that colossal wreck, boundless and bare
The lone and level sands stretch far away

For Annie.

Poe.

1.

Thank Heaven! the crisis—
The danger is past,
And the lingering illness
Is over at last—
And the fever called "living"
Is conquered at last.

2.

Sadly, I know
I am shorn of my strength,
And no muscle I move
As I lie at full length.—
But no matter—I feel
I am better at length.

3.

And I rest so composedly
Now, in my bed,
That any beholder
Might fancy me dead—
Might start at beholding me
Thinking me dead.

4.

The moaning and groaning
The sighing and sobbing
Are quieted now,
With that horrible throbbing
At heart—ah, that horrible
Horrible throbbing!

5.

The sickness — the nausea —
The pitiless pain —
Have ceased with the fever
That maddened my brain —
With the fever called "Living"
That burned in my brain.

6.

And Oh! of all tortures
That torture the worst
Has abated — the terrible
Torture of Thirst
For the Naphthaline river
Of passion accurst —
I have drunk of a water
That quenches all thirst —
Of a water that flows,
With a lullaby sound,
From a spring but a very few
Feet underground —
From a cavern not very far
Down under ground.

7.

And Ah! let it never
Be foolishly said
That my room it is gloomy
And narrow my bed;
For man never slept
In a different bed —
And to sleep, you must slumber
In just such a bed.

8.

My tantalised spirit
Here blandly reposes,
Forgetting, or never
Regretting its roses —
Its old agitations
Of myrtles & roses:

9.

For now, while so quietly
Lying, it fancies
A holier odour
About it, of pansies —

A rosemary odour,
Commingled with pansies—
With rue & the beautiful
Puritan pansies.

10.

And so it lies happily
Bathing in many
A dream of the truth
And the beauty of Annie—
Drowned in a bath
Of the tresses of Annie.

11.

She tenderly kissed me,
She fondly caressed,
And then I fell gently
To sleep on her breast—
Deeply to sleep
From the heaven of her breast

12.

When the light was extinguished
She covered me warm
And she prayed to the Angels
To keep me from harm—
To the queen of the Angels
To shield me from harm

13.

And I lie so composedly,
Now, in my bed
(Knowing her love),
That you fancy me dead—
And I rest so contentedly,
Now in my bed
(With her love at my breast),
That you fancy me dead—
That you shudder to look at me
Thinking me dead—

14

But my heart it is brighter
Than all of the many

Stars in the sky,
For it sparkles with Annie—
It glows with the light
Of the love of my Annie—
With the thought of the light
Of the eyes of my Annie.

V. DelaMare.

Alone

1.

A very old woman
Lives in yon house—
The squeak of the cricket,
The stir of the mouse,
Are all she knows of the Earth & us.

2.

Once she was young,
Would dance & play,
Like many another
Young popinjay;
And run to her mother
At dusk of day.

3.

And colours bright
She delighted in;
The fiddle to hear
And to lift her chin,
And to sing as small
As a twittering wren

4.

But age apace
Comes at last to all;
And a lone house filled
With the cricket's call;
& the scampering mouse
In the hollow wall.

END

Edith Sitwell.   Spring.

When Spring begins, the maids in flocks
Walk in soft fields, & their sheepskin locks

Fall shadowless, soft as music, round
Their jonquil eyelids, and reach the ground,

Where the small fruit-buds begin to harden
Into sweet tunes in the palace garden

They peck at the fruit-buds' hairy herds
With their lips like the gentle bills of birds.

But King Midas heard the swan-bosomed sky
Say "All is surface and so must die."

And he said "It is spring; I will have a feast
To woo eternity; for my least

Palace is like a berg of ice:
          And the spring winds for birds of paradise

With the leaping goat-footed waterfalls cold
Shall be served for me on a dish of gold

By a maiden fair as an almond tree:
With hair like the waterfall's goat locks; she

Has lips like that jangling harsh pink rain,
The flower-bells that spirt on the trees again."

In Midas' garden the simple flowers
Laugh, and the tulips are bright as the showers,

For Spring is here; the auriculas
And the Emily coloured primulas

Bob in their pinafores on the grass
As they watch the gardener's daughter pass.

Then King Midas said "At last I feel
Eternity conquered beneath my wheel.

Like the glittering snakes of Paradise —
And you are my Eve!"— but the maiden flies

Like the leaping goat-footed waterfalls
Singing their cold folorn madrigals.

A. Poe.

Dreamland.

By a route obscure & lonely,
Haunted by ill angels only,
Where an Eidolon, named Night,
On a black throne reigns upright,
I have reached these lands but newly
From an ultimate dim Thule —
From a wild weird clime, that lieth, sublime
Out of Space — out of Time.

Bottomless vales & boundless floods,
And chasms, & caves, & Titan woods,
With forms that no man can discover
For the dews that drip all over;
Mountains toppling evermore
Into seas without a shore;
Seas that restlessly aspire,
Surging, unto skies of fire;
Lakes that endlessly outspread
Their lone waters — lone & chilly
With the snows of the lolling lily

By the lakes that thus outspread
Their lone waters, lone & dead, —
Their sad waters, sad & chilly
With the snows of the lolling lily
By the grey woods — by the swamp
Where the toad & the newt encamp
By the dismal tarns & pools
Where dwell the Ghouls, ——

By each spot the most unholy—
In each nook most melancholy,—
There the traveller meets aghast
Sheeted memories of the Past —
Shrouded forms that start & sigh
As they pass the wanderer by—
White robed forms of friends long given,
In agony, to the Earth — & Heaven.

For the heart whose woes are legion
'Tis a peaceful, soothing region—
For the spirit that walks in shadow
'Tis —ah, 'tis an Eldorado!
But the traveller, travelling through it,
May not — dare not openly view it;
Never its misteries are exposed
To the weak human eye unclosed;
So wills its King, who hath forbid
The uplifting of the fringed lid;
And thus the sad soul that here passes

Beholds it but through darkened glasses.

By a route obscure & lonely,
Haunted by ill angels only,
Where an Eidolon, named Night,
On a black throne reigns upright,
I have wandered home but newly
From this ultimate dim Thule. . ~ . ~ . ~ . ❀

Drinkwater

Moonlit Apples

At the top of the house the apples are laid in rows
And the skylight lets the moonlight in, & those
Apples are deep-sea apples of green.   There goes
A cloud on the moon in the autumn night.

A mouse in the wainscot scratches, & scratches, & then
There is no sound at the top of the house of men
Or mice; and the cloud is blown, & the moon again
Dapples the apples with deep-sea light.

They are lying in rows there, under the gloomy beams
On the sagging floor; they gather the silver streams
Out of the moon, those moonlit apples of dreams,
And quiet is the steep stair under.

In the corridors under there is nothing but sleep.
And stiller than ever on orchard boughs they keep
Tryst with the moon, and deep is the silence, deep
In Moon-washed apples of wonder.

A. Marvell   The Garden (Selections.)

Fair Quiet, have I found thee here,
And Innocence, thy sister dear?
  Mistaken long, I sought you then
In busy companies of men.
Your sacred plants, if here below,
  Only among the plants will grow;
  Society is all but rude
  To this delicious solitude

What wondrous life is this I lead!
Ripe apples drop about my head;
The luscious clusters of the vine
Upon my mouth do crush their wine;
The nectarine & curious peach
Into my hands themselves do reach;
Stumbling on melons, as I pass,
Ensnared with flowers, I fall on grass.

Meanwhile the mind, from pleasure less,
Withdraws into its' happiness;
The mind, that ocean where each kind
Does straight its' own resemblance find;
Yet it creates, transcending these,
Far other worlds, & other seas,
Annihilating all that's made
To a green thought in a green shade.

Here at the fountains' sliding foot,
Or at some fruit trees' mossy root,
Casting the bodys' vest aside,
My soul into the boughs does glide:
There, like a bird, it sits & sings,
Then whets & combs its' silver wings,
And, till prepared for longer flight,
Weaves in its' plumes the various light.

Such was that happy garden-state,
While man there walked without a mate:

After a place so pure & sweet,
What other help could yet be meet!
But 'twas beyond a mortal's share
To wander solitary there:
Two paradises 'twere in one,
To live in paradise alone.

How well the skilful gardener drew
Of flowers and herbs this dial new;
Where from above, the milder sun
Does through a fragrant zodiac run,
And, as it works, the industrious bee
Computes its time as well as we!
How could such sweet and wholesome hours
Be reckoned but with herbs and flowers?

This is the personal anthology of a young artist who had recently discovered poetry. When my brother Rex began to make it he was eighteen and already the star pupil of the Slade. It is strange to think that today he would not even get in – nor into any recognized art school: he would not have done well enough in ordinary school subjects to qualify. This is not to say that he was idle at Haileybury (except in class); for he was industrious enough on his own, turning out endless drawings, mostly funny or grotesque, but sometimes romantic, as he began to discover with a friend the rapture of poetry, from then on the greatest of the arts in his opinion. The word rapture is no exaggeration. He planned his own anthology, not primarily in order to do decorations, though of course he would, but to have his favourite poems, and only those, at hand in a convenient form. Therefore he bought a fat manuscript book with a limp cover, and with faint lines to keep his handwriting straight – handwriting that was still upright in his boyhood manner. There was no calligraphic model or purpose.

Choice and sequence are revealing. First we have *Annabel Lee*, Poe's poem about childish lovers by the sea, and one that had special significance for Rex; for which reason I introduce as a frontispiece a separate and more careful drawing of this period, dated 1924. Henry Brocken – the narrator in de la Mare's novel of that title – meets various characters in literature; and here, with the lost girl on the shore, he is given a distinct likeness to the self-identifying artist. Rex made several such drawings for that favourite novel, none intended for publication. Keats, Gray, Hood, Tennyson and Shelley follow, in no definable order, and de la Mare himself, with more poems than anyone else – intermixed with one or two slighter poets that had caught perhaps only a temporary liking; for nothing was put in because it 'ought' to be in.

The romantic taste that formed this book, seeing sixteenth- and seventeenth-century poets as romantics too, and the book itself were my own introduction to poetry at the age of eleven and twelve; so if I overvalue the decorations, as he afterwards claimed, it is not merely from affection, as recalling the sound of his crooked-lipped whistle and the tap of his toe, the smell of his inks and the ticking of his active nib; they hold for me still, or some of them, a lively and spontaneous response to great poetry.

Almost all is serious illustration here, no page intentionally comic except the title page, though some were presently seen by Rex to have been made so by accident: hence the comment added to his 'knight-at-arms' – 'What's the matter, kid?' No page is in the style he would very soon be known by, except the last one, for *The Garden*, and this may have been embellished a little later on. Rather, several styles are being tried. Within two or three years, changing fast, he outgrew his anthology, but never the poems, and many more besides. It was a pocket *Golden Treasury* he bought in June 1944, when a troop commander in the Guards Armoured Division, to take with him to France – where he was killed during his first hour in action.

Laurence Whistler

ACKNOWLEDGEMENTS

Permission to use copyright material is gratefully acknowledged to the following:

The literary trustees of Walter de la Mare and the Society of Authors as their representative for Walter de la Mare's 'Peacock Pie', 'The Listener', 'The Stranger', 'Arabia', 'Noon and Night Flower' and 'Alone', from *The Complete Poems* of Walter de la Mare;

The Belknap Press of Harvard University Press, The President and Fellows of Harvard College, and the Trustees of Amherst College for Emily Dickinson's 'Sunset', from *The Poems of Emily Dickinson*;

Mrs Joyce Lombardini for Ronald Fuller's 'Wanderlust' and 'Lines';

Macmillan Limited and David Higham Associates for Edith Sitwell's 'Spring', from *Collected Poems*.

While every effort has been made to secure permission, it has in one case – the poem by Norman Roe – proved impossible to trace the author or his executor. We apologize for our apparent negligence.

First published in Great Britain 1981
by Hamish Hamilton Limited
Garden House, 57-59 Long Acre,
London WC2E 9JZ

An Anthology of mine
1. English poetry
I. Whistler, Rex
821'. 008   PR1175

ISBN 0 241 10667 2

Produced by Rock Lambert
17 Albemarle Street, London W1

Reproduced by Martin Bragg Associates
Chalfont St Peter
Printed in Great Britain by Tabro Litho
St Ives, Cambridgeshire